Behind the Scenes!!

Behind the Scenes!!

05

STORY AND ART BY **BISCO HATORI**

Behind the Scenes !!

05

CONTENTS

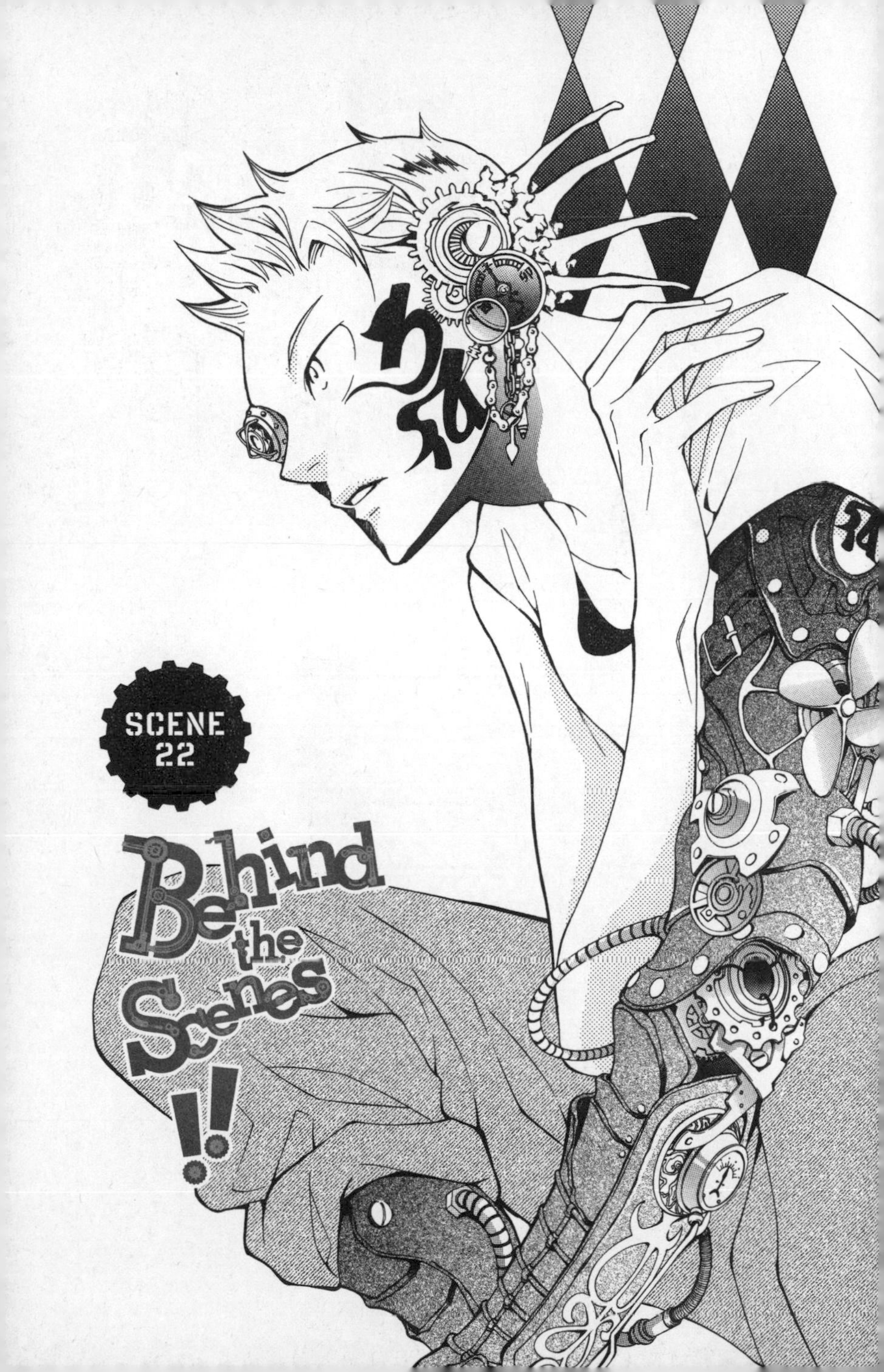
SCENE
22
Behind the Scenes!!

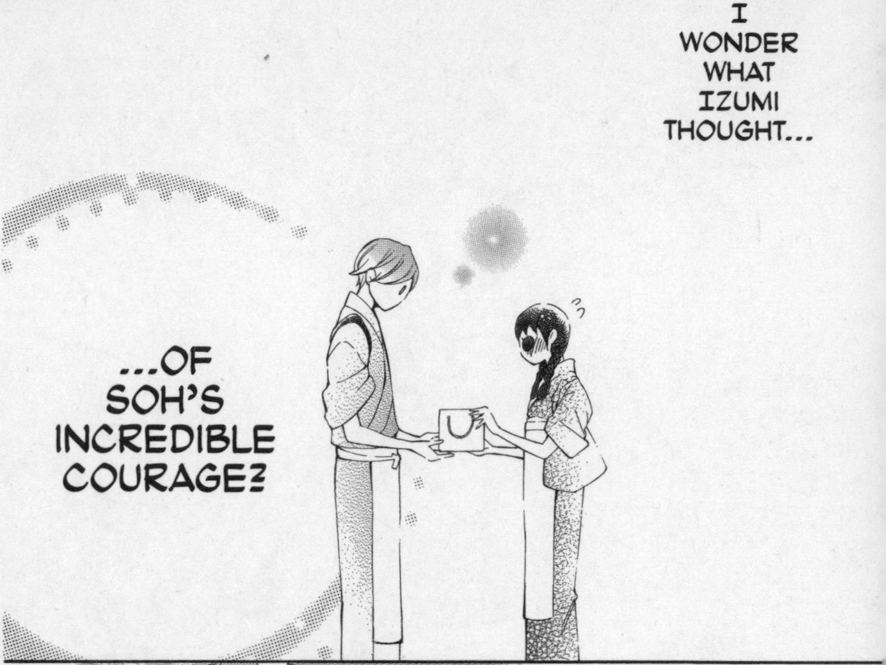
I WONDER WHAT IZUMI THOUGHT...
...OF SOH'S INCREDIBLE COURAGE?

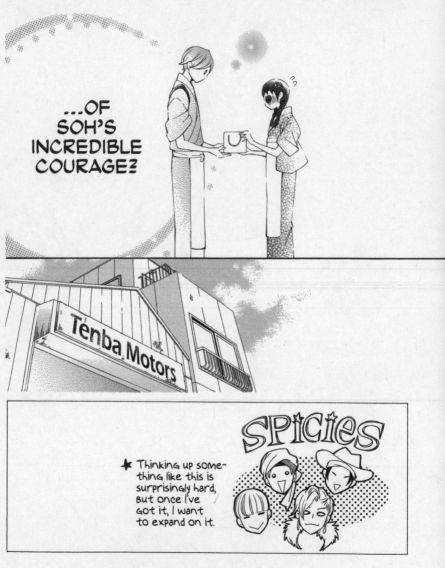

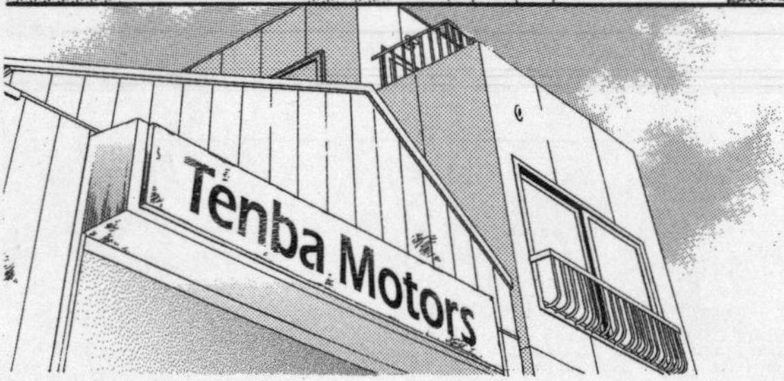
Tenba Motors

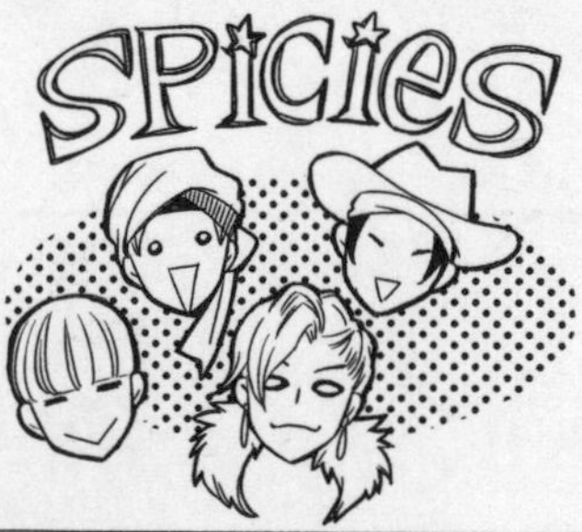
SPICIES

★ Thinking up something like this is surprisingly hard, but once I've got it, I want to expand on it.

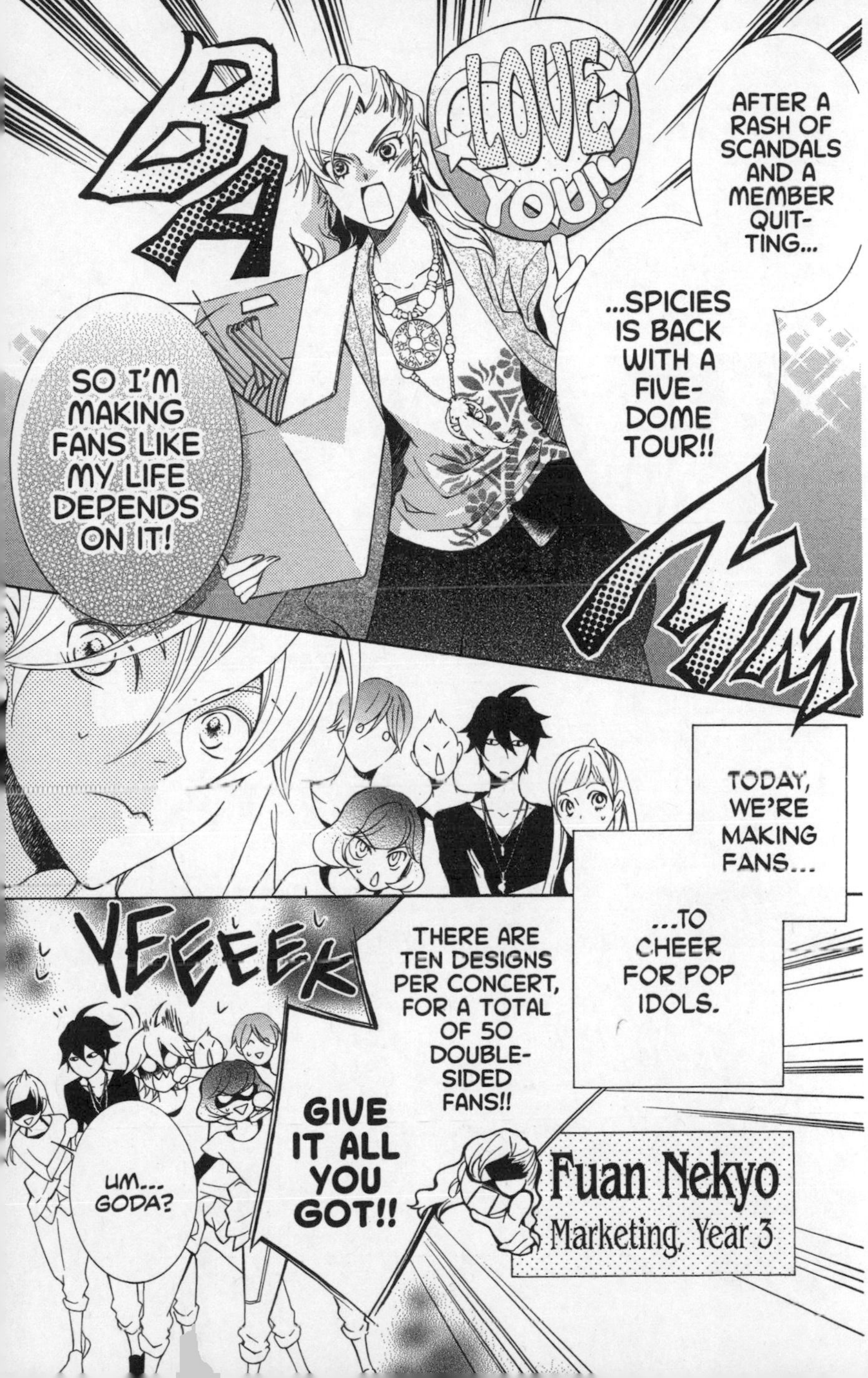
BA
LOVE YOU!
AFTER A RASH OF SCANDALS AND A MEMBER QUIT-TING...
...SPICIES IS BACK WITH A FIVE-DOME TOUR!!
SO I'M MAKING FANS LIKE MY LIFE DEPENDS ON IT!
MM
TODAY, WE'RE MAKING FANS...
...TO CHEER FOR POP IDOLS.
Fuan Nekyo
Marketing, Year 3
THERE ARE TEN DESIGNS PER CONCERT, FOR A TOTAL OF 50 DOUBLE-SIDED FANS!!
GIVE IT ALL YOU GOT!!
YEEEEK
UM... GODA?

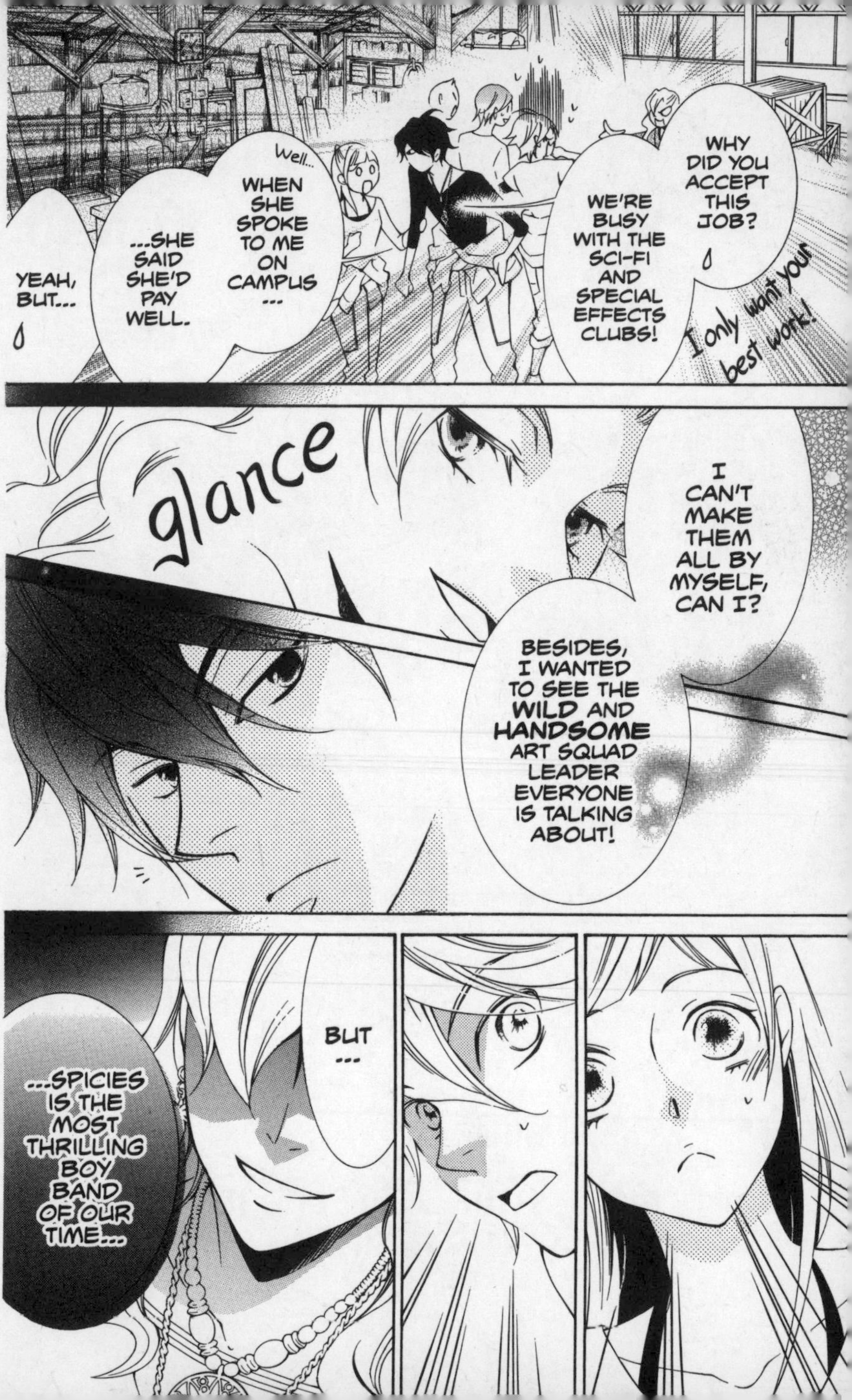
WHY DID YOU ACCEPT THIS JOB?
I only want your best work!
WE'RE BUSY WITH THE SCI-FI AND SPECIAL EFFECTS CLUBS!
Well...
WHEN SHE SPOKE TO ME ON CAMPUS...
...SHE SAID SHE'D PAY WELL.
YEAH, BUT...
I CAN'T MAKE THEM ALL BY MYSELF, CAN I?
glance
BESIDES, I WANTED TO SEE THE WILD AND HANDSOME ART SQUAD LEADER EVERYONE IS TALKING ABOUT!
BUT...
...SPICIES IS THE MOST THRILLING BOY BAND OF OUR TIME...

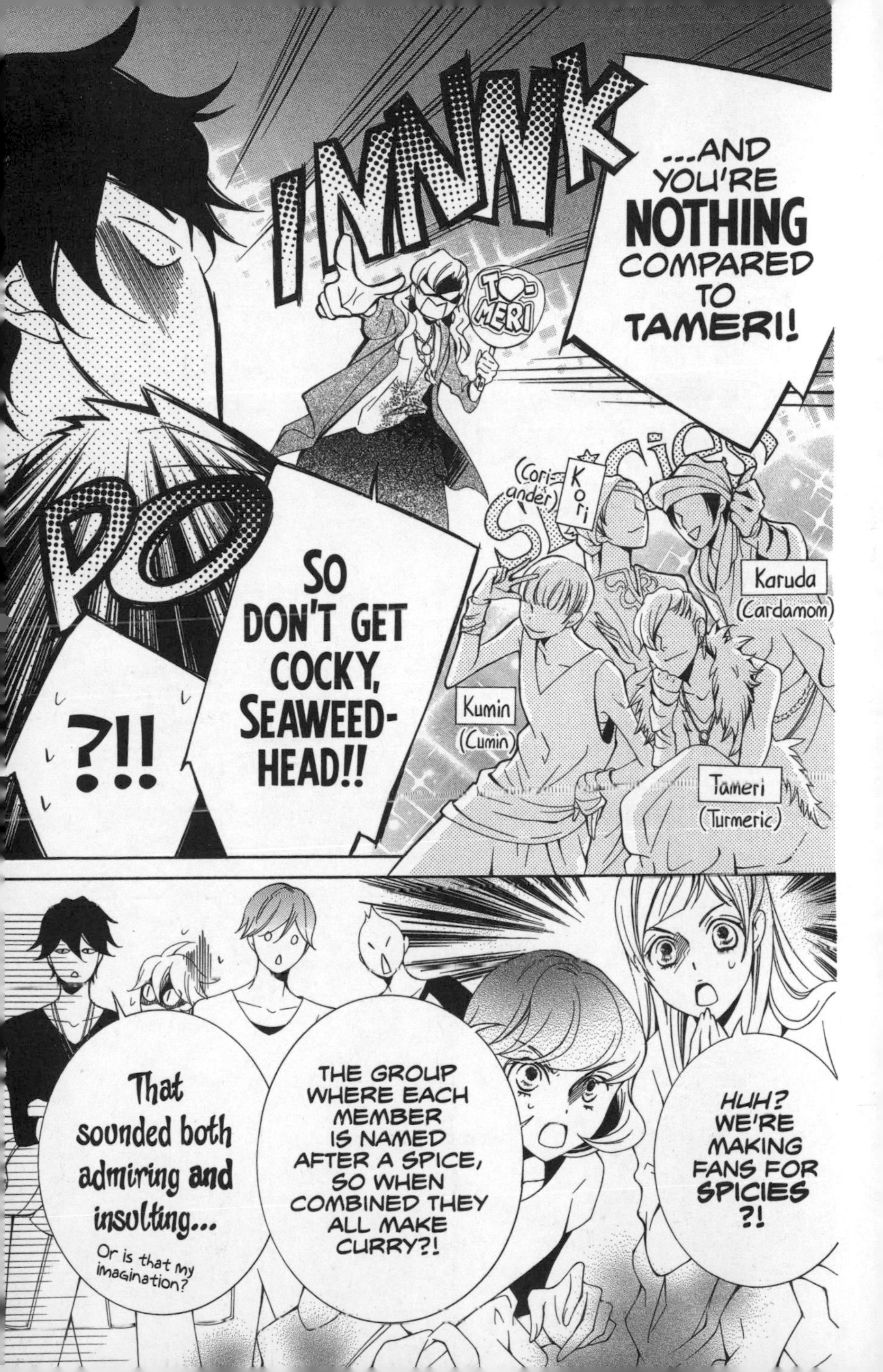

...AND YOU'RE NOTHING COMPARED TO TAMERI!
IMNWK
Kori
(Coriander)
Karuda
(Cardamom)
Tameri
(Turmeric)
Kumin
(Cumin)
SO DON'T GET COCKY, SEAWEED-HEAD!!
DO
?!!
HUH? WE'RE MAKING FANS FOR SPICIES?!
THE GROUP WHERE EACH MEMBER IS NAMED AFTER A SPICE, SO WHEN COMBINED THEY ALL MAKE CURRY?!
That sounded both admiring and insulting...
Or is that my imagination?

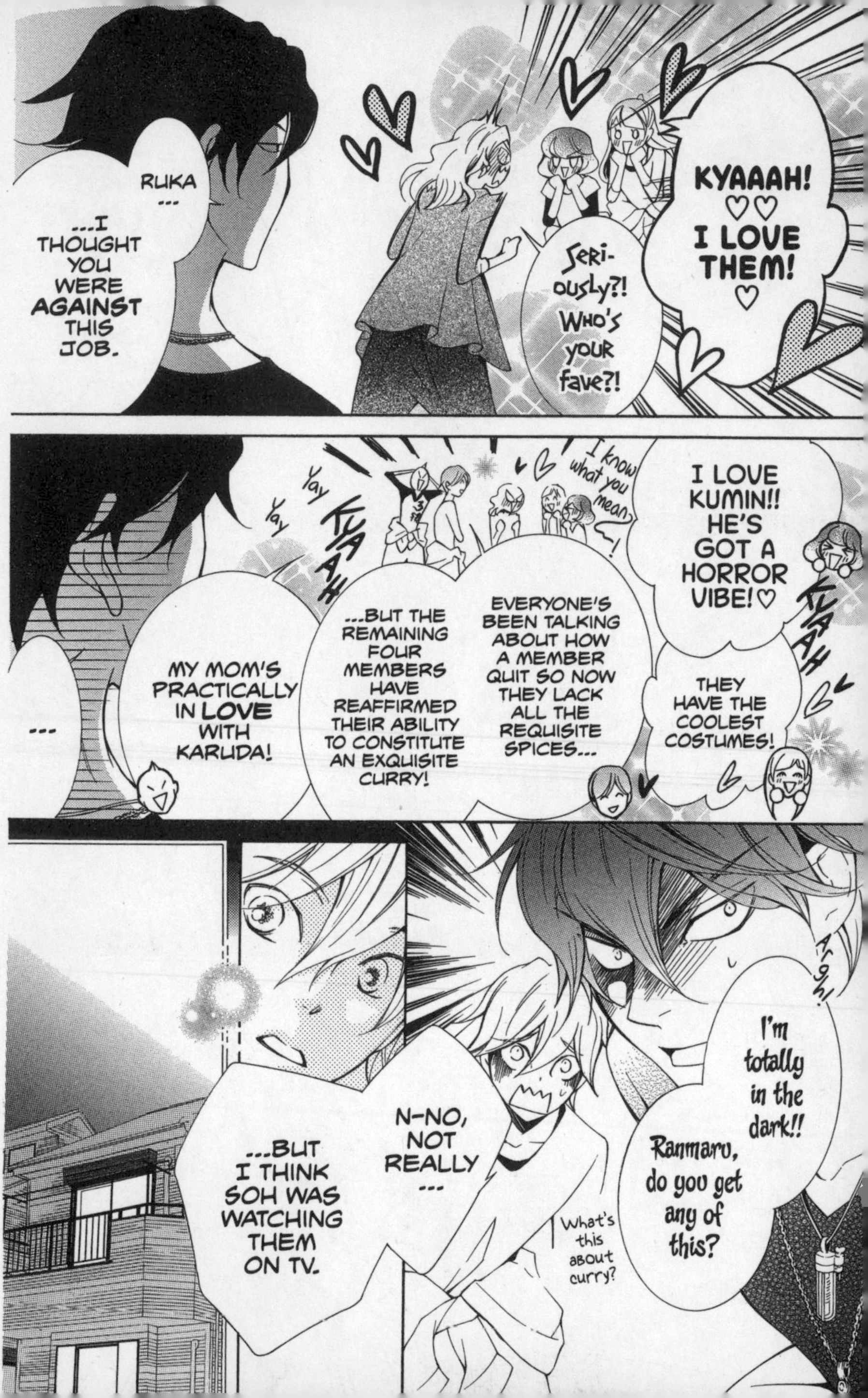
KYAAAH! ♡♡ I LOVE THEM! ♡
Seri-ously?! Who's your fave?!
RUKA...
...I THOUGHT YOU WERE AGAINST THIS JOB.
I LOVE KUMIN!! HE'S GOT A HORROR VIBE! ♡
KYAAAH
THEY HAVE THE COOLEST COSTUMES!
I know what you mean~!
EVERYONE'S BEEN TALKING ABOUT HOW A MEMBER QUIT SO NOW THEY LACK ALL THE REQUISITE SPICES...
...BUT THE REMAINING FOUR MEMBERS HAVE REAFFIRMED THEIR ABILITY TO CONSTITUTE AN EXQUISITE CURRY!
KYAAAH
Yay Yay
MY MOM'S PRACTICALLY IN LOVE WITH KARUDA!
...
Argh!
I'm totally in the dark!!
Ranmaru, do you get any of this?
What's this about curry?
N-NO, NOT REALLY...
...BUT I THINK SOH WAS WATCHING THEM ON TV.

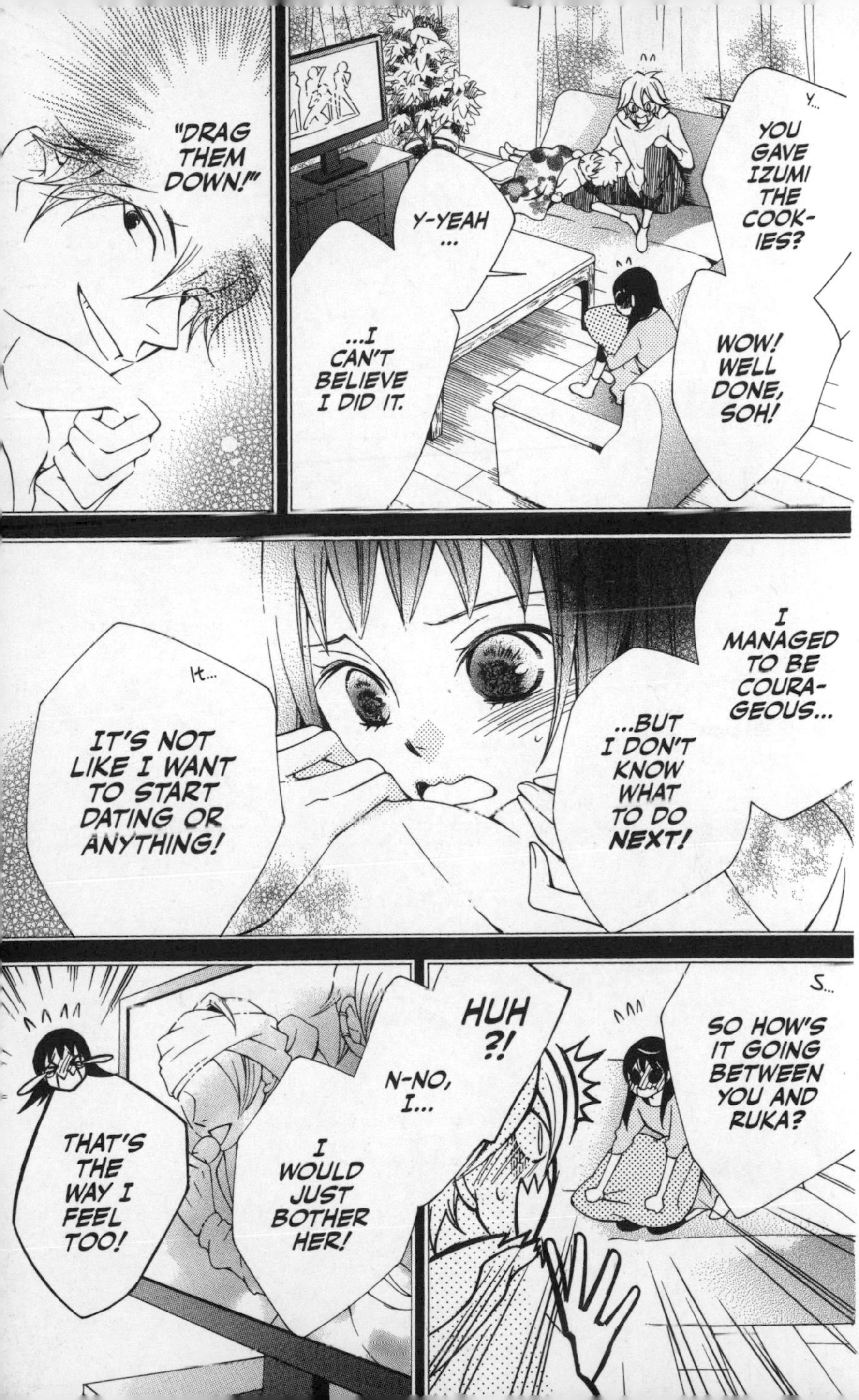
Y...
YOU GAVE IZUMI THE COOK-IES?
WOW! WELL DONE, SOH!
Y-YEAH ...
...I CAN'T BELIEVE I DID IT.
"DRAG THEM DOWN!"
I MANAGED TO BE COURA-GEOUS...
...BUT I DON'T KNOW WHAT TO DO NEXT!
It...
IT'S NOT LIKE I WANT TO START DATING OR ANYTHING!
S...
SO HOW'S IT GOING BETWEEN YOU AND RUKA?
HUH ?!
N-NO, I...
I WOULD JUST BOTHER HER!
THAT'S THE WAY I FEEL TOO!

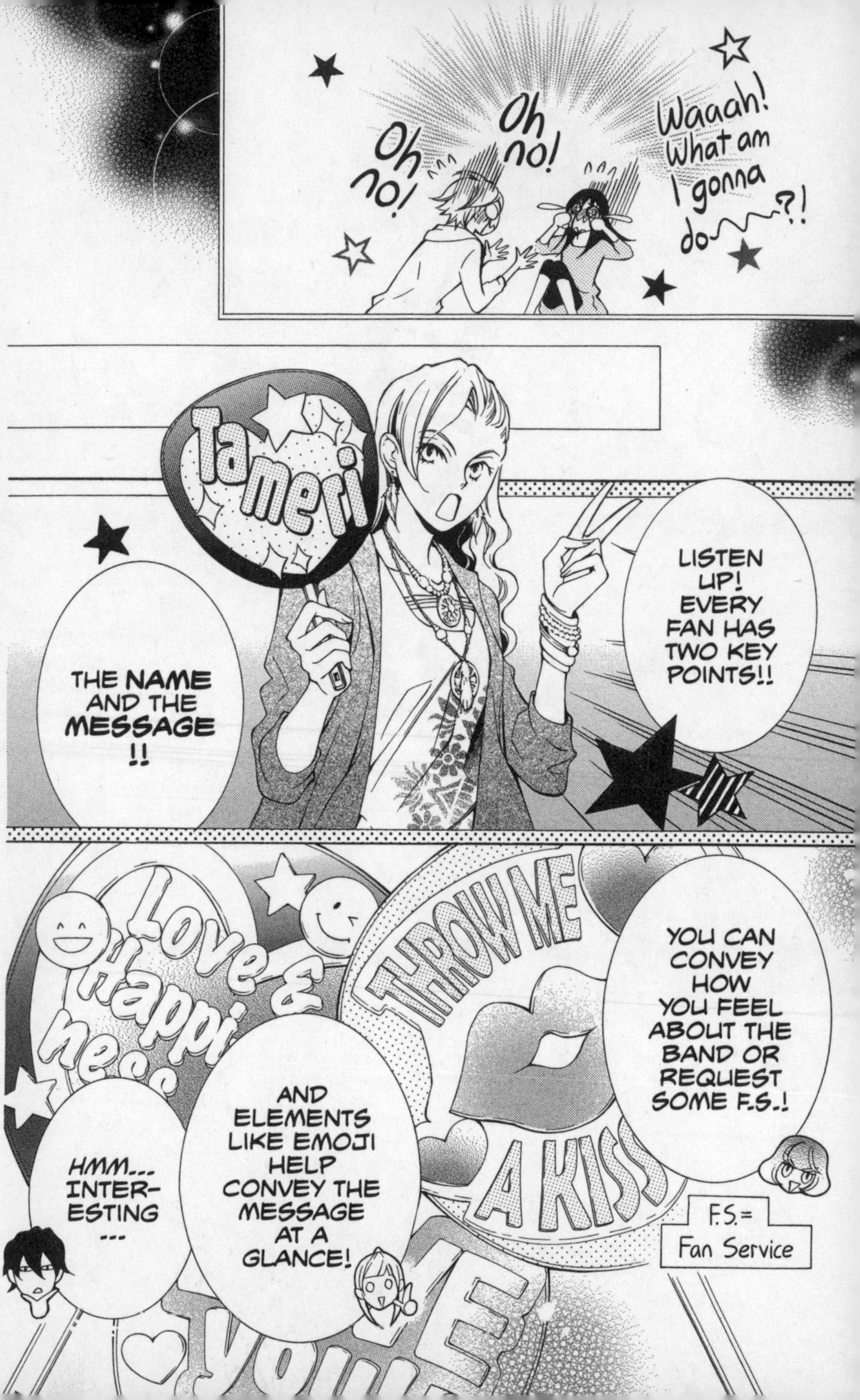
Waaah! What am I gonna do~~?!
Oh no!
Oh no!
LISTEN UP! EVERY FAN HAS TWO KEY POINTS!!
Tameri
THE NAME AND THE MESSAGE !!
YOU CAN CONVEY HOW YOU FEEL ABOUT THE BAND OR REQUEST SOME F.S.!
THROW ME A KISS
F.S. = Fan Service
AND ELEMENTS LIKE EMOJI HELP CONVEY THE MESSAGE AT A GLANCE!
Love &
HMM... INTER-ESTING ...

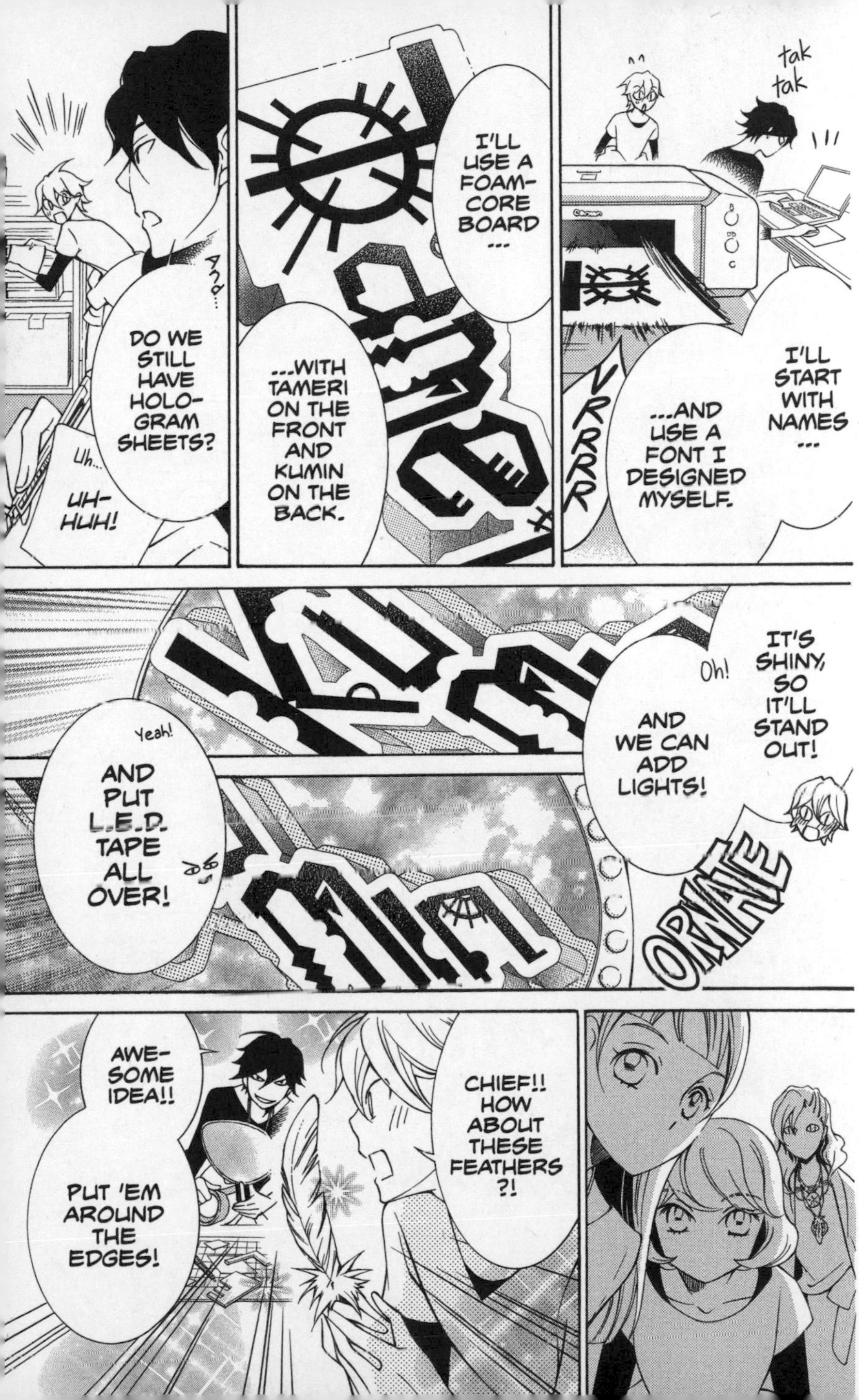
tak tak
I'LL START WITH NAMES ...
...AND USE A FONT I DESIGNED MYSELF.
VRRRR
I'LL USE A FOAM-CORE BOARD ...
...WITH TAMERI ON THE FRONT AND KUMIN ON THE BACK.
And...
DO WE STILL HAVE HOLOGRAM SHEETS?
Uh...
UH-HUH!
IT'S SHINY, SO IT'LL STAND OUT!
Oh!
AND WE CAN ADD LIGHTS!
ORNATE
Yeah!
AND PUT L.E.D. TAPE ALL OVER!
CHIEF!! HOW ABOUT THESE FEATHERS?!
AWESOME IDEA!!
PUT 'EM AROUND THE EDGES!

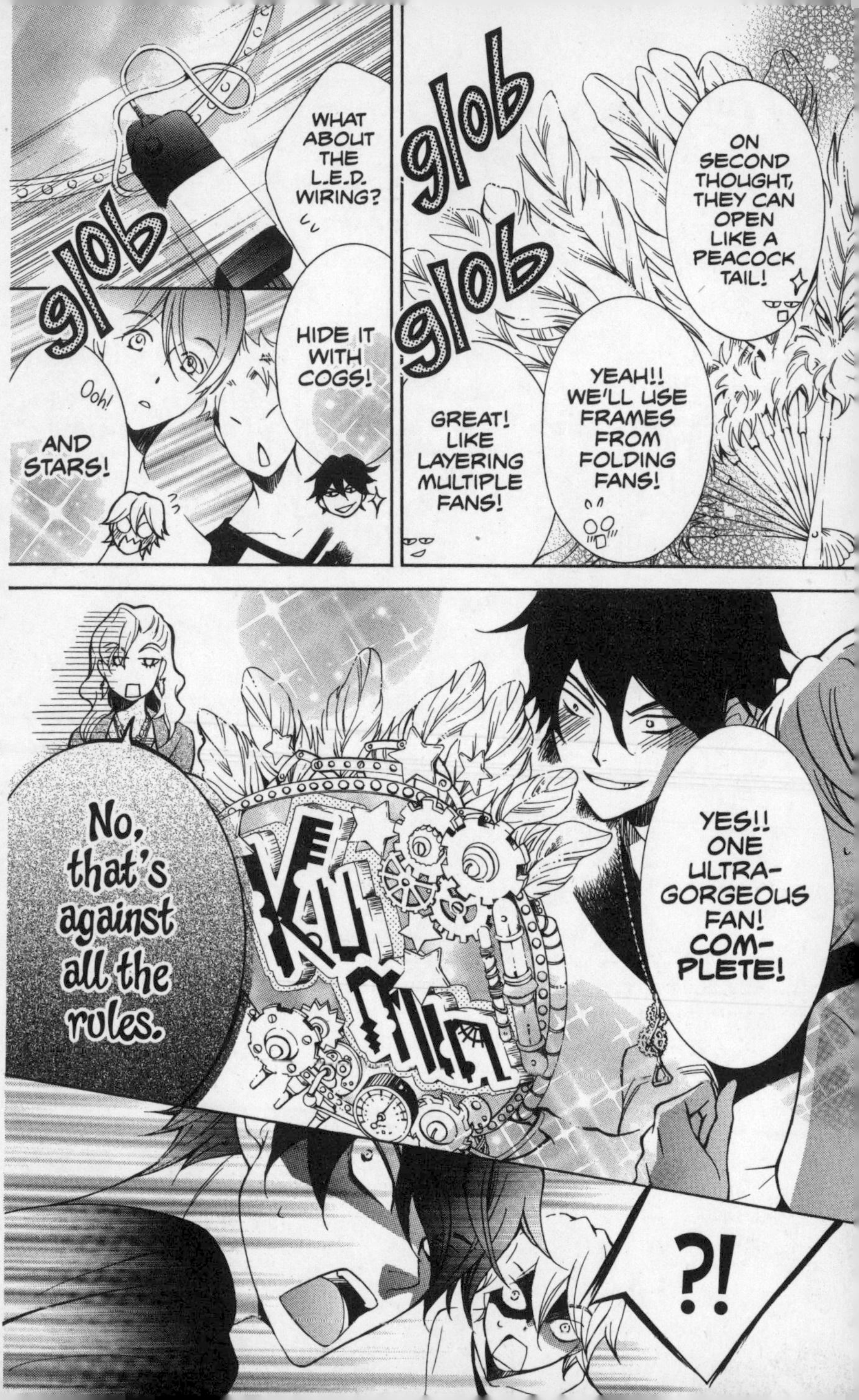
ON SECOND THOUGHT, THEY CAN OPEN LIKE A PEACOCK TAIL!
glob glob
YEAH!! WE'LL USE FRAMES FROM FOLDING FANS!
GREAT! LIKE LAYERING MULTIPLE FANS!
WHAT ABOUT THE L.E.D. WIRING?
glob
HIDE IT WITH COGS!
Ooh!
AND STARS!
YES!! ONE ULTRA-GORGEOUS FAN! COM-PLETE!
No, that's against all the rules.
?!

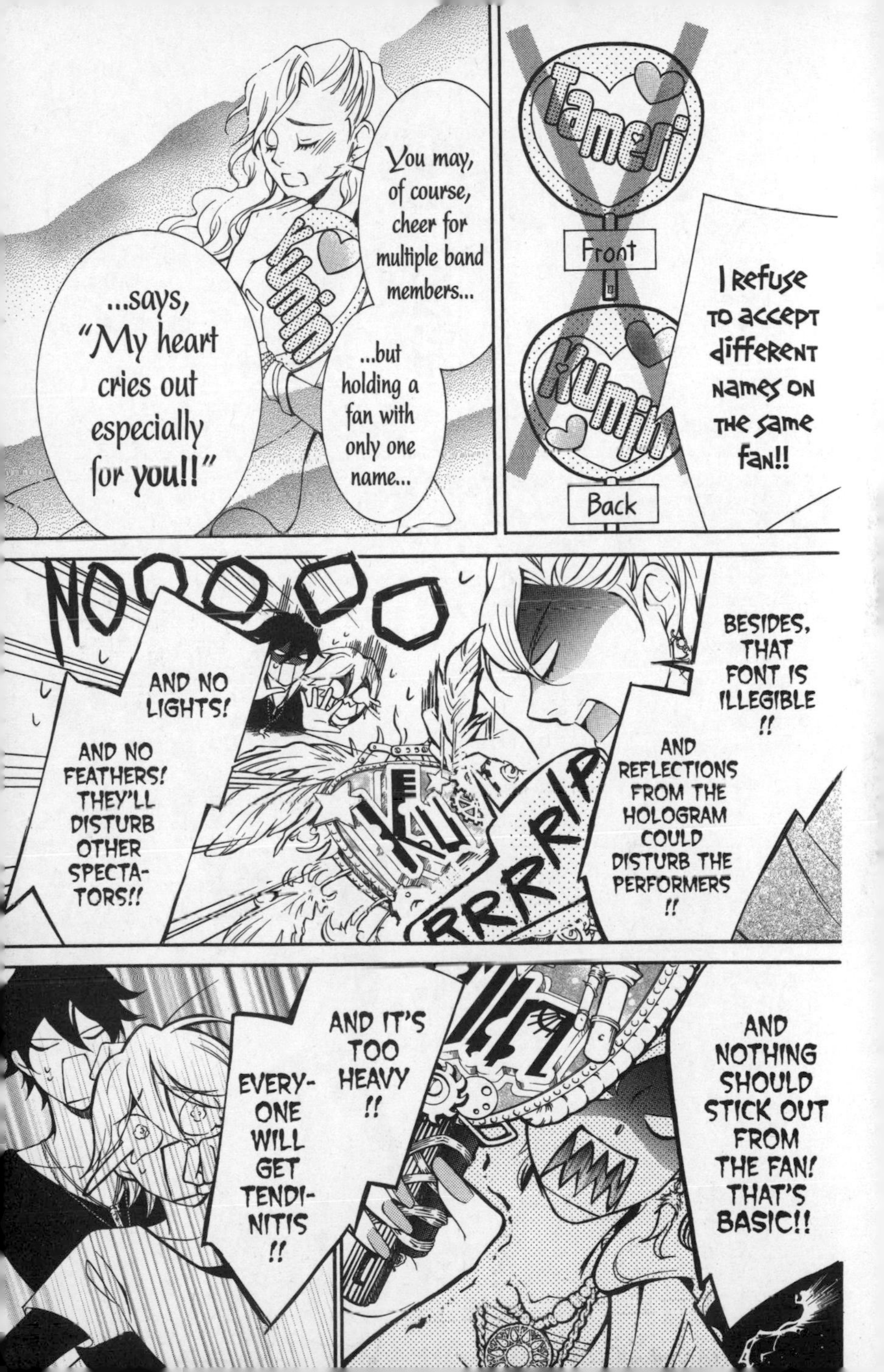
Tameri
Front
Kumin
Back
I refuse to accept different names on the same fan!!
You may, of course, cheer for multiple band members...
...but holding a fan with only one name...
...says, "My heart cries out especially for you!!"
BESIDES, THAT FONT IS ILLEGIBLE!!
AND REFLECTIONS FROM THE HOLOGRAM COULD DISTURB THE PERFORMERS!!
RRRRIP
NOOOOO
AND NO LIGHTS!
AND NO FEATHERS! THEY'LL DISTURB OTHER SPECTATORS!!
AND NOTHING SHOULD STICK OUT FROM THE FAN! THAT'S BASIC!!
AND IT'S TOO HEAVY!!
EVERYONE WILL GET TENDINITIS!!

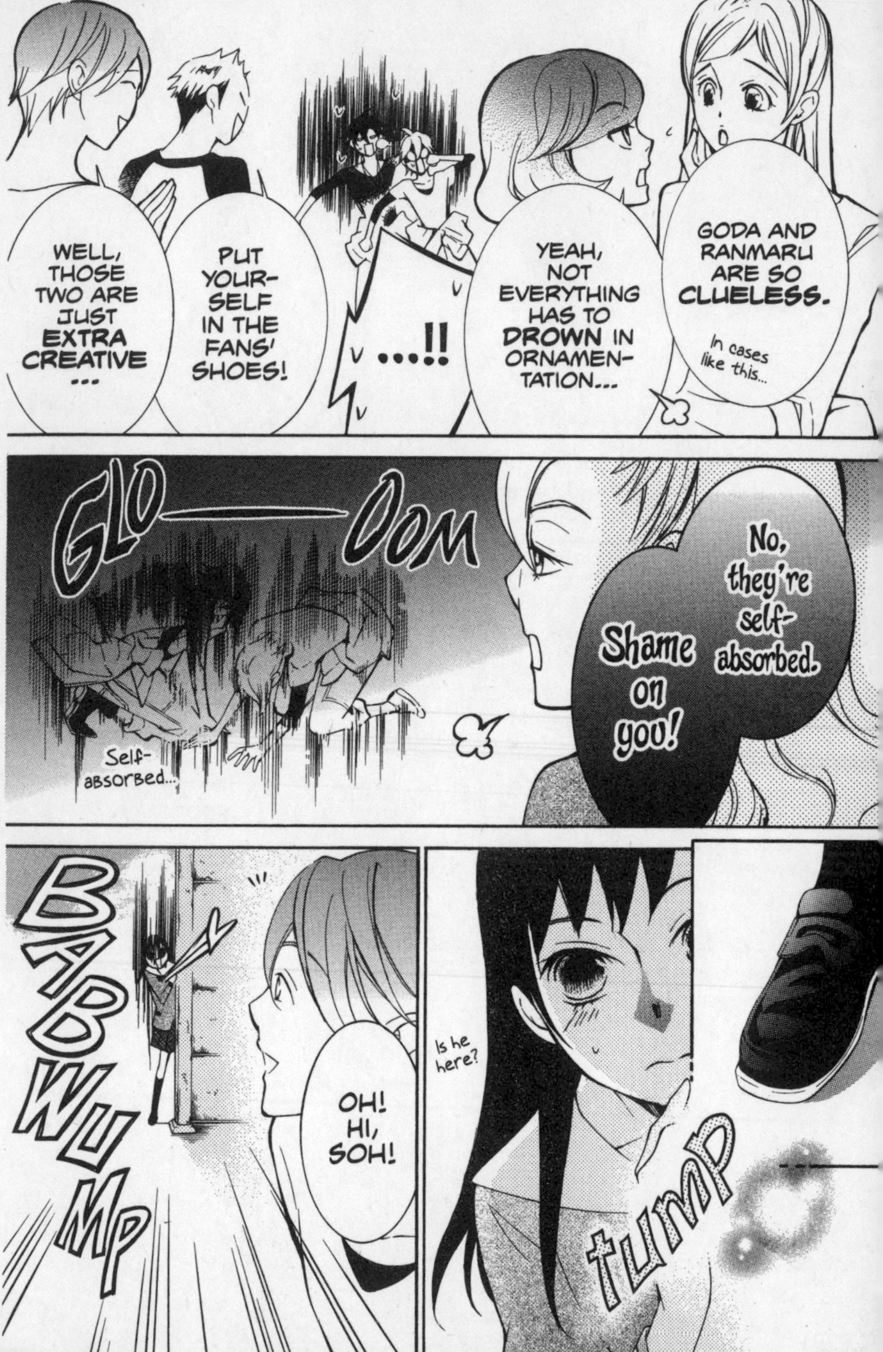
GODA AND RANMARU ARE SO CLUELESS.
In cases like this...
YEAH, NOT EVERYTHING HAS TO DROWN IN ORNAMENTATION...
...!!
PUT YOURSELF IN THE FANS' SHOES!
WELL, THOSE TWO ARE JUST EXTRA CREATIVE...
No, they're self-absorbed.
Shame on you!
GLO—OOM
Self-absorbed...
tump
Is he here?
OH! HI, SOH!
BABWUMP

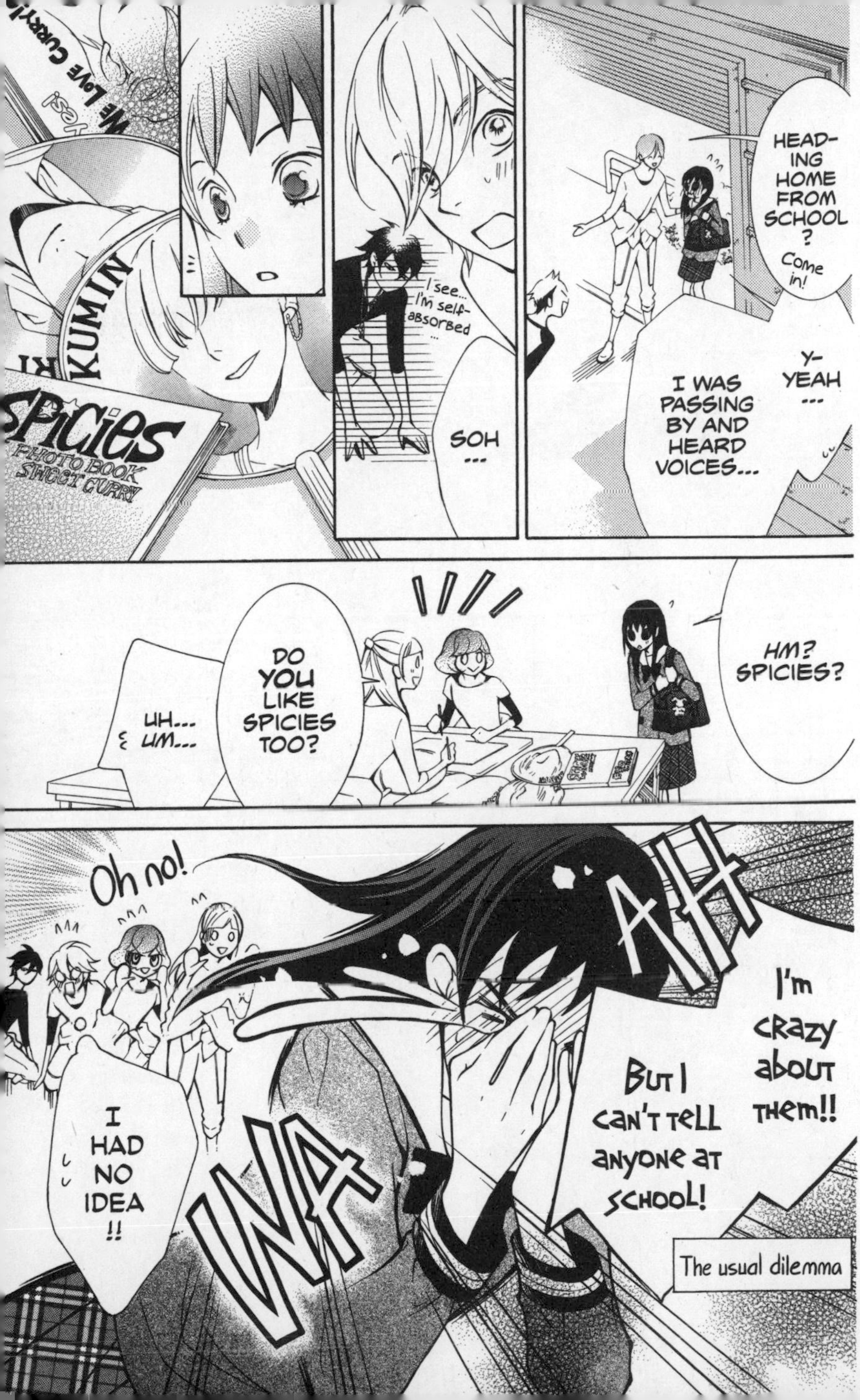
HEADING HOME FROM SCHOOL? Come in!
Y-YEAH...
I WAS PASSING BY AND HEARD VOICES...
I see... I'm self-absorbed...
SOH...
KUMIN
SPICIES PHOTO BOOK SWEET CURRY
HM? SPICIES?
DO YOU LIKE SPICIES TOO?
UH... UM...
AH
I'm crazy about them!!
But I can't tell anyone at school!
The usual dilemma
WA
Oh no!
I HAD NO IDEA!!

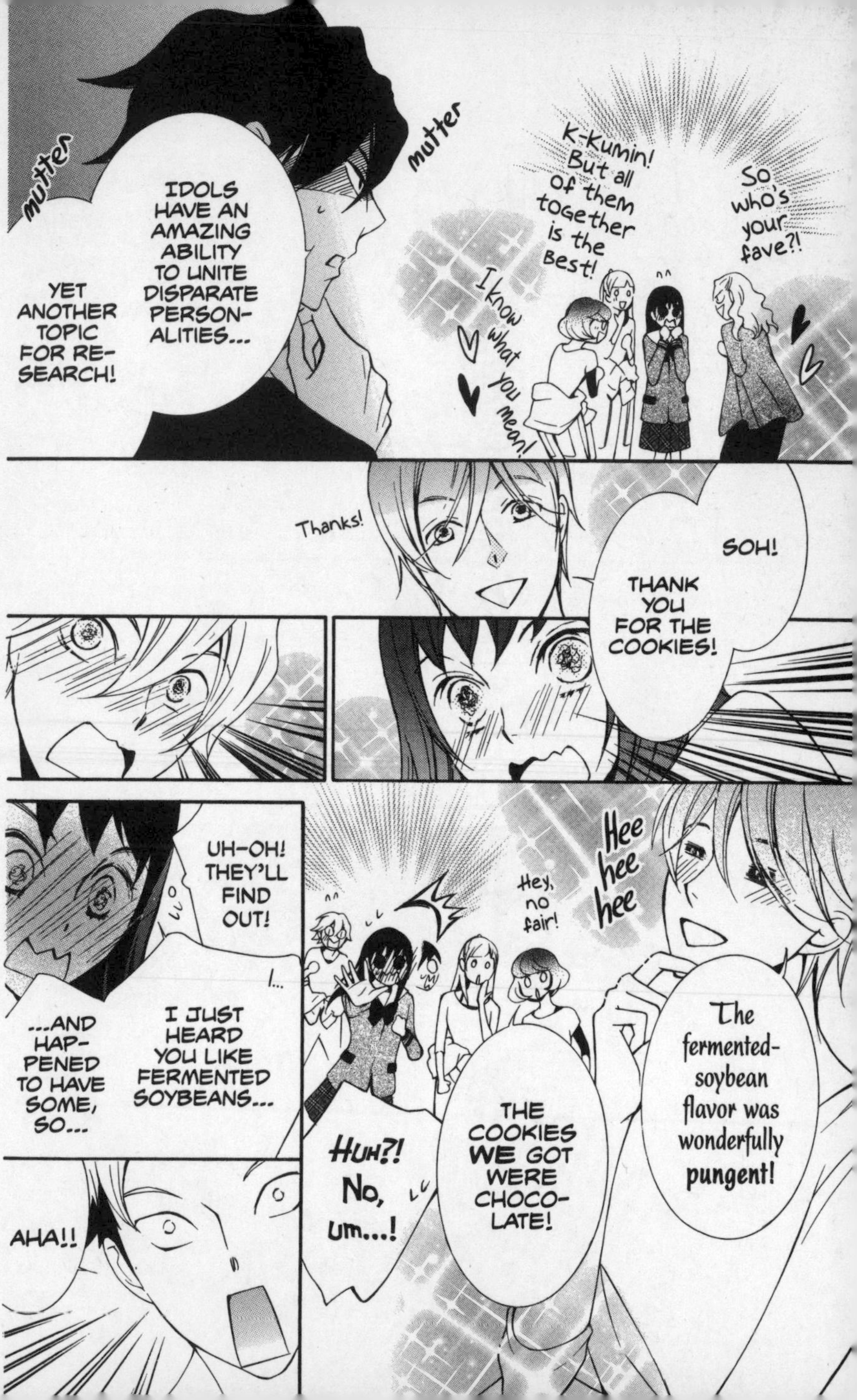
So who's your fave?!
K-Kumin! But all of them together is the Best!
I know what you mean!
mutter
IDOLS HAVE AN AMAZING ABILITY TO UNITE DISPARATE PERSON-ALITIES...
YET ANOTHER TOPIC FOR RE-SEARCH!
mutter
SOH!
THANK YOU FOR THE COOKIES!
Thanks!
The fermented-soybean flavor was wonderfully pungent!
Hee hee hee
Hey, no fair!
THE COOKIES WE GOT WERE CHOCO-LATE!
HUH?! No, um...!
UH-OH! THEY'LL FIND OUT!
I...
I JUST HEARD YOU LIKE FERMENTED SOYBEANS...
...AND HAP-PENED TO HAVE SOME, SO...
AHA!!

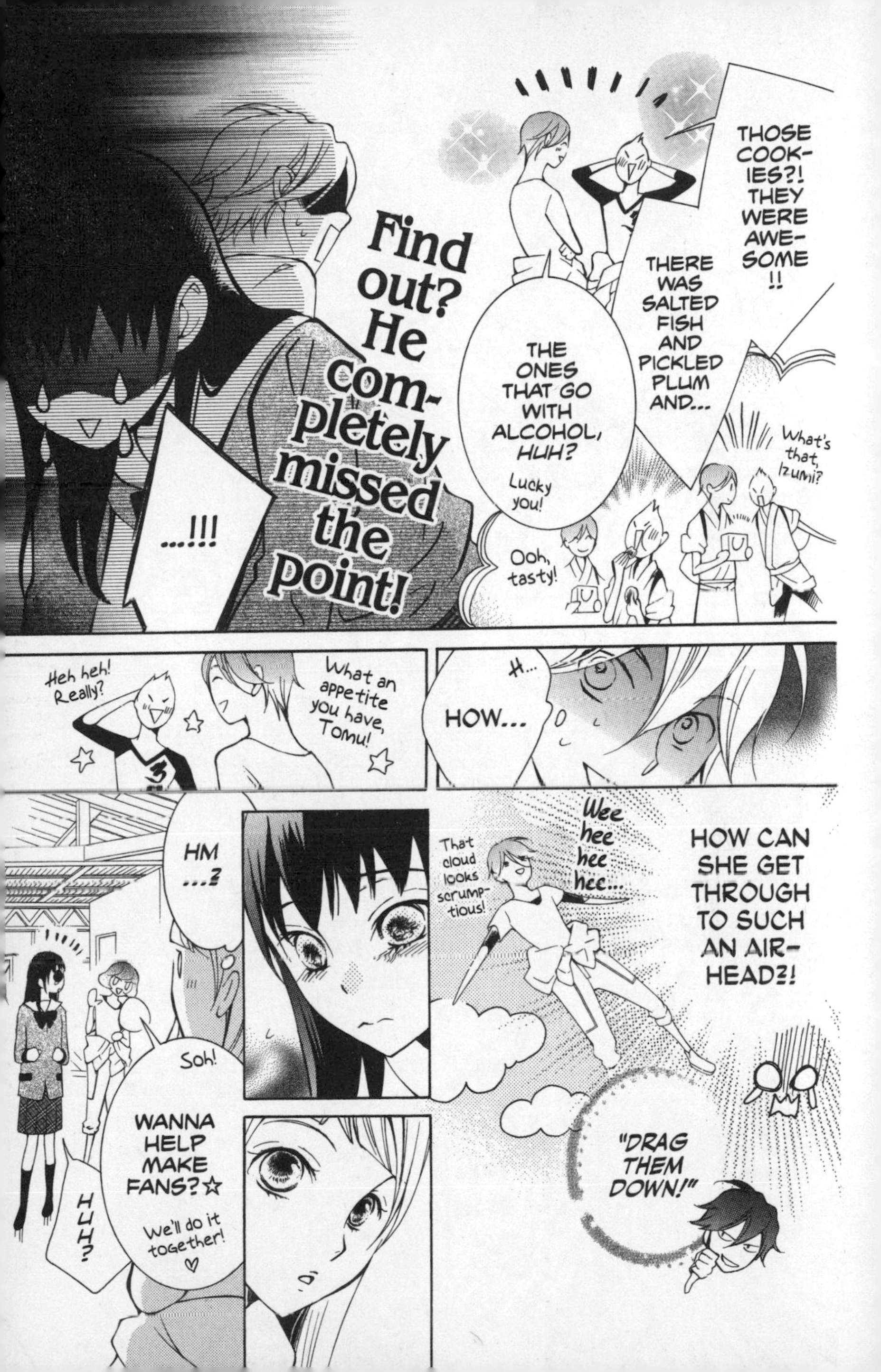
THOSE COOKIES?! THEY WERE AWESOME!!
THERE WAS SALTED FISH AND PICKLED PLUM AND...
THE ONES THAT GO WITH ALCOHOL, HUH?
Lucky you!
What's that, Izumi?
Ooh, tasty!
Find out? He completely missed the point!
...!!!
H...
HOW...
What an appetite you have, Tomu!
Heh heh! Really?
HOW CAN SHE GET THROUGH TO SUCH AN AIR-HEAD?!
Wee hee hee hee...
That cloud looks scrumptious!
"DRAG THEM DOWN!"
HM ...?
Soh!
WANNA HELP MAKE FANS?☆
We'll do it together! ♡
HUH?

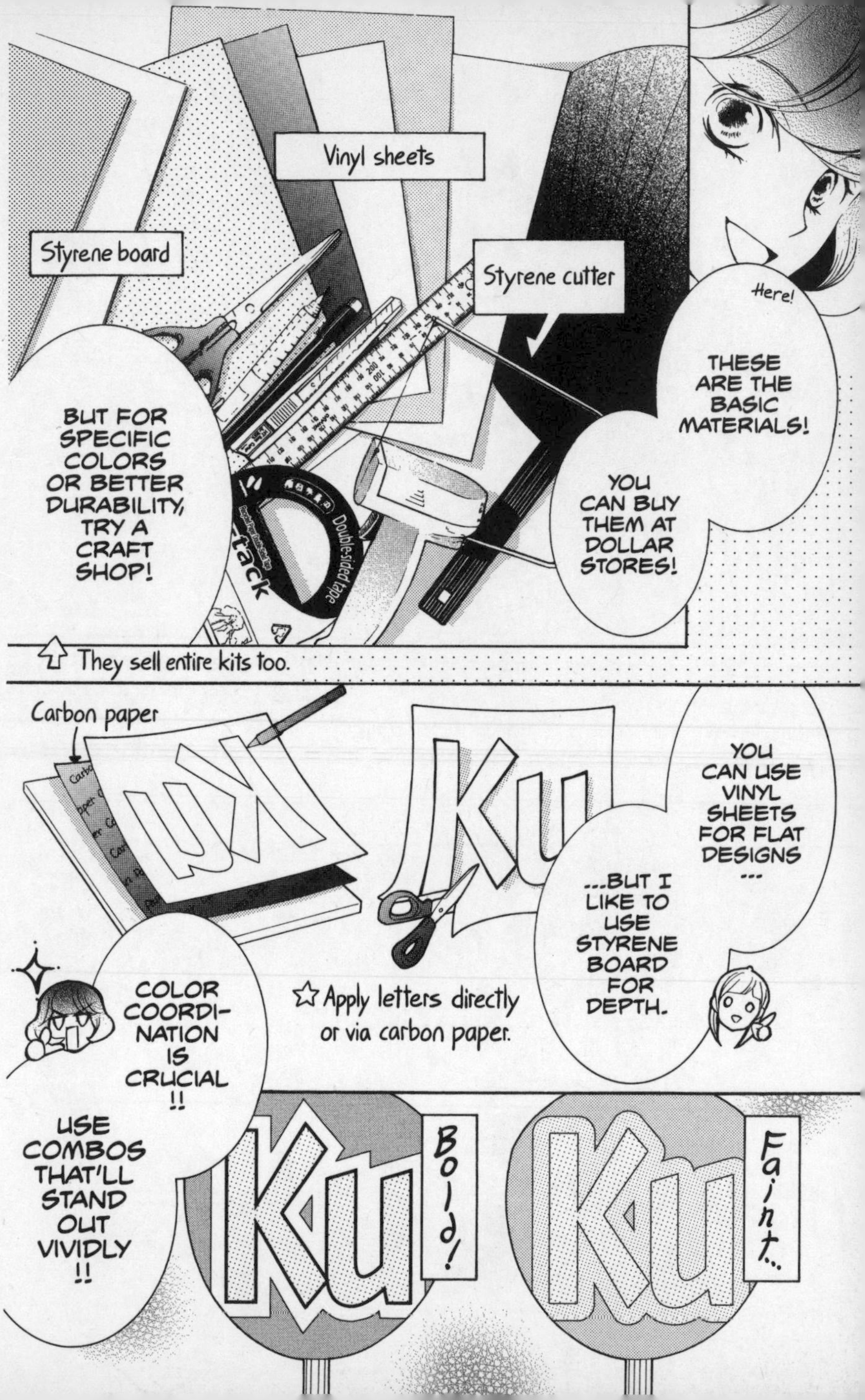
Here!
THESE ARE THE BASIC MATERIALS!
YOU CAN BUY THEM AT DOLLAR STORES!
Styrene cutter
Vinyl sheets
Styrene board
BUT FOR SPECIFIC COLORS OR BETTER DURABILITY, TRY A CRAFT SHOP!
Double-sided tape
They sell entire kits too.
YOU CAN USE VINYL SHEETS FOR FLAT DESIGNS...
...BUT I LIKE TO USE STYRENE BOARD FOR DEPTH.
Ku
Apply letters directly or via carbon paper.
Carbon paper
COLOR COORDINATION IS CRUCIAL!!
Faint...
Ku
Bold!
Ku
USE COMBOS THAT'LL STAND OUT VIVIDLY!!

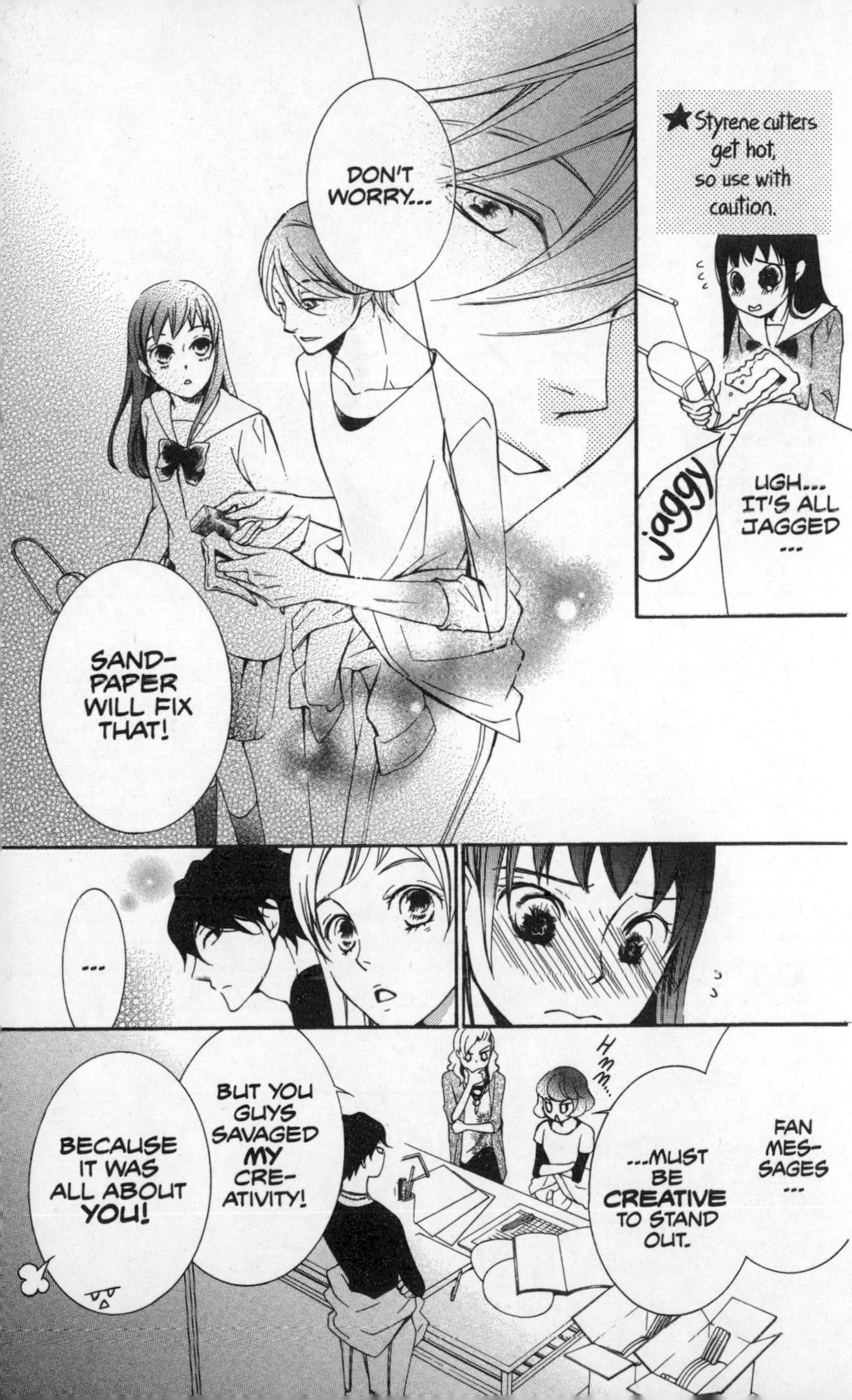
★Styrene cutters get hot, so use with caution.
UGH... IT'S ALL JAGGED ...
jaggy
DON'T WORRY...
SAND-PAPER WILL FIX THAT!
...
FAN MES-SAGES ...
...MUST BE CREATIVE TO STAND OUT.
HMM...
BUT YOU GUYS SAVAGED MY CRE-ATIVITY!
BECAUSE IT WAS ALL ABOUT YOU!

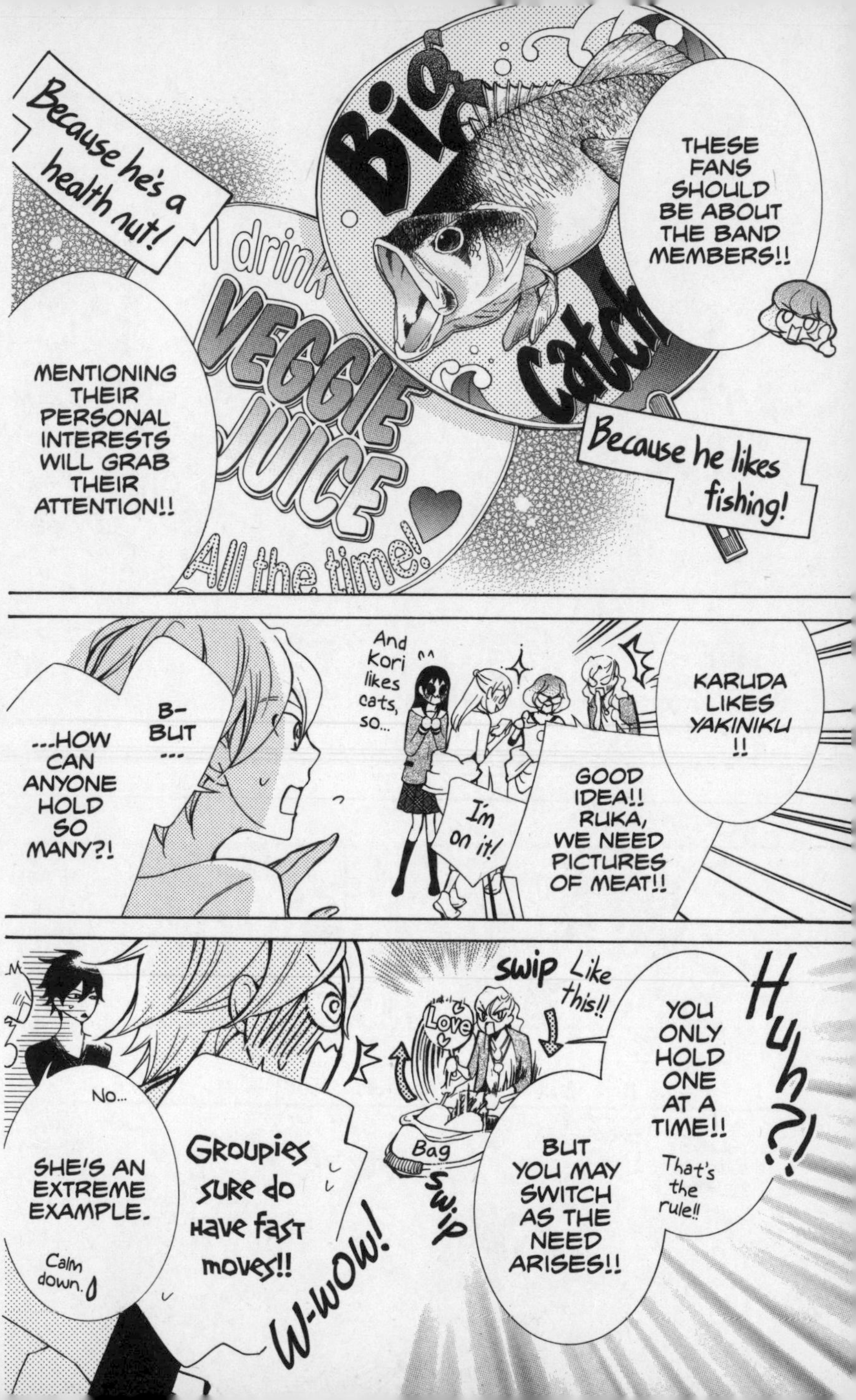
THESE FANS SHOULD BE ABOUT THE BAND MEMBERS!!
Big Catch
Because he likes fishing!
I drink VEGGIE JUICE All the time!
Because he's a health nut!
MENTIONING THEIR PERSONAL INTERESTS WILL GRAB THEIR ATTENTION!!
KARUDA LIKES YAKINIKU!!
GOOD IDEA!! RUKA, WE NEED PICTURES OF MEAT!!
I'm on it!
And Kori likes cats, so...
B-BUT...
...HOW CAN ANYONE HOLD SO MANY?!
Huh?!
YOU ONLY HOLD ONE AT A TIME!!
That's the rule!!
Like this!!
swip
Love
Bag
swip
BUT YOU MAY SWITCH AS THE NEED ARISES!!
W-WOW!
Groupies sure do have fast moves!!
No...
SHE'S AN EXTREME EXAMPLE.
Calm down.

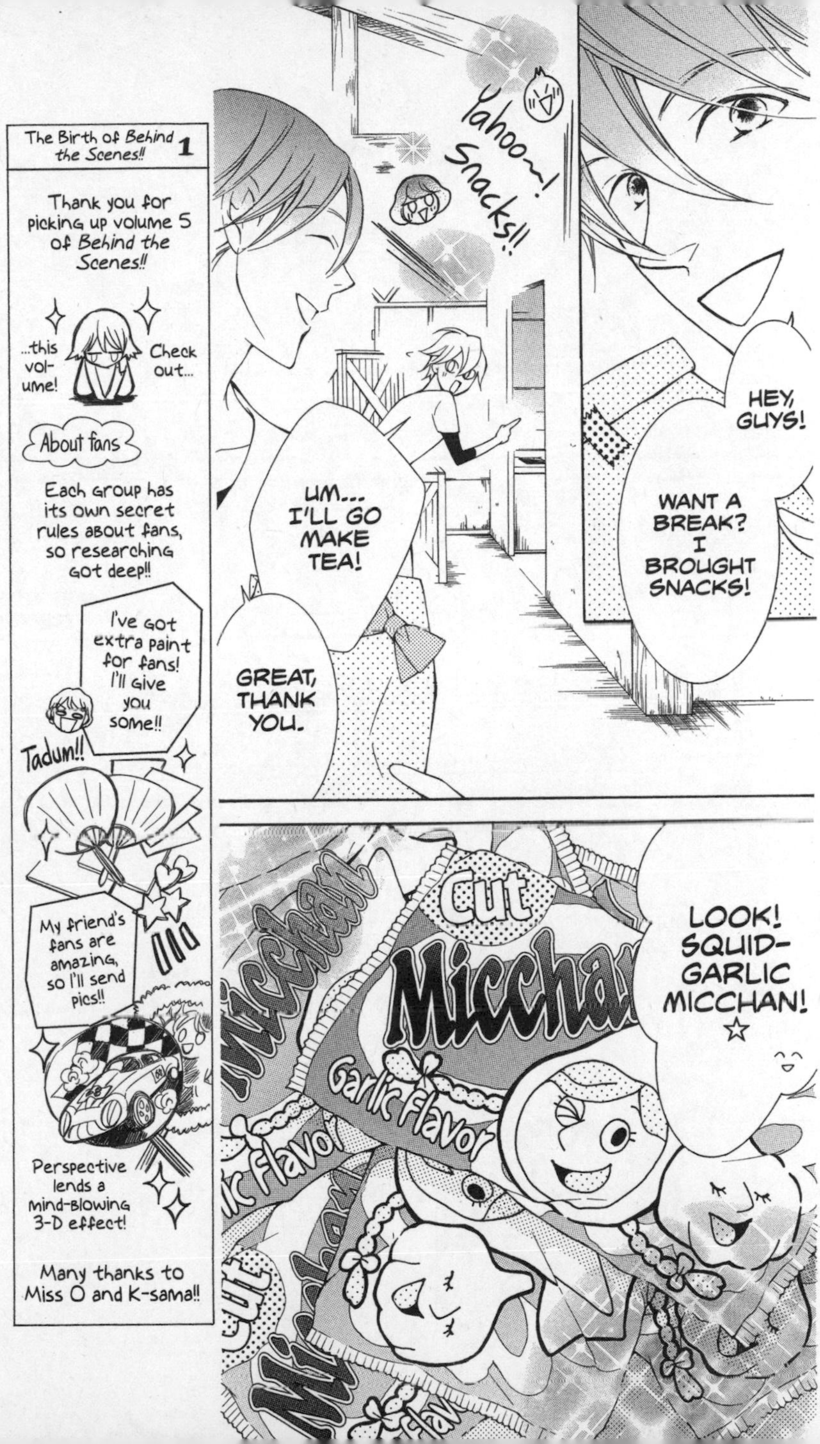
HEY, GUYS!
WANT A BREAK? I BROUGHT SNACKS!
Yahoo~! Snacks!!
UM... I'LL GO MAKE TEA!
GREAT, THANK YOU.
LOOK! SQUID-GARLIC MICCHAN! ☆
Cut
Micchan
Garlic Flavor

The Birth of *Behind the Scenes!!* 1

Thank you for picking up volume 5 of *Behind the Scenes!!*

...this volume! Check out...

About fans

Each group has its own secret rules about fans, so researching got deep!!

I've got extra paint for fans! I'll give you some!!

Tadum!!

My friend's fans are amazing, so I'll send pics!!

Perspective lends a mind-blowing 3-D effect!

Many thanks to Miss O and K-sama!!

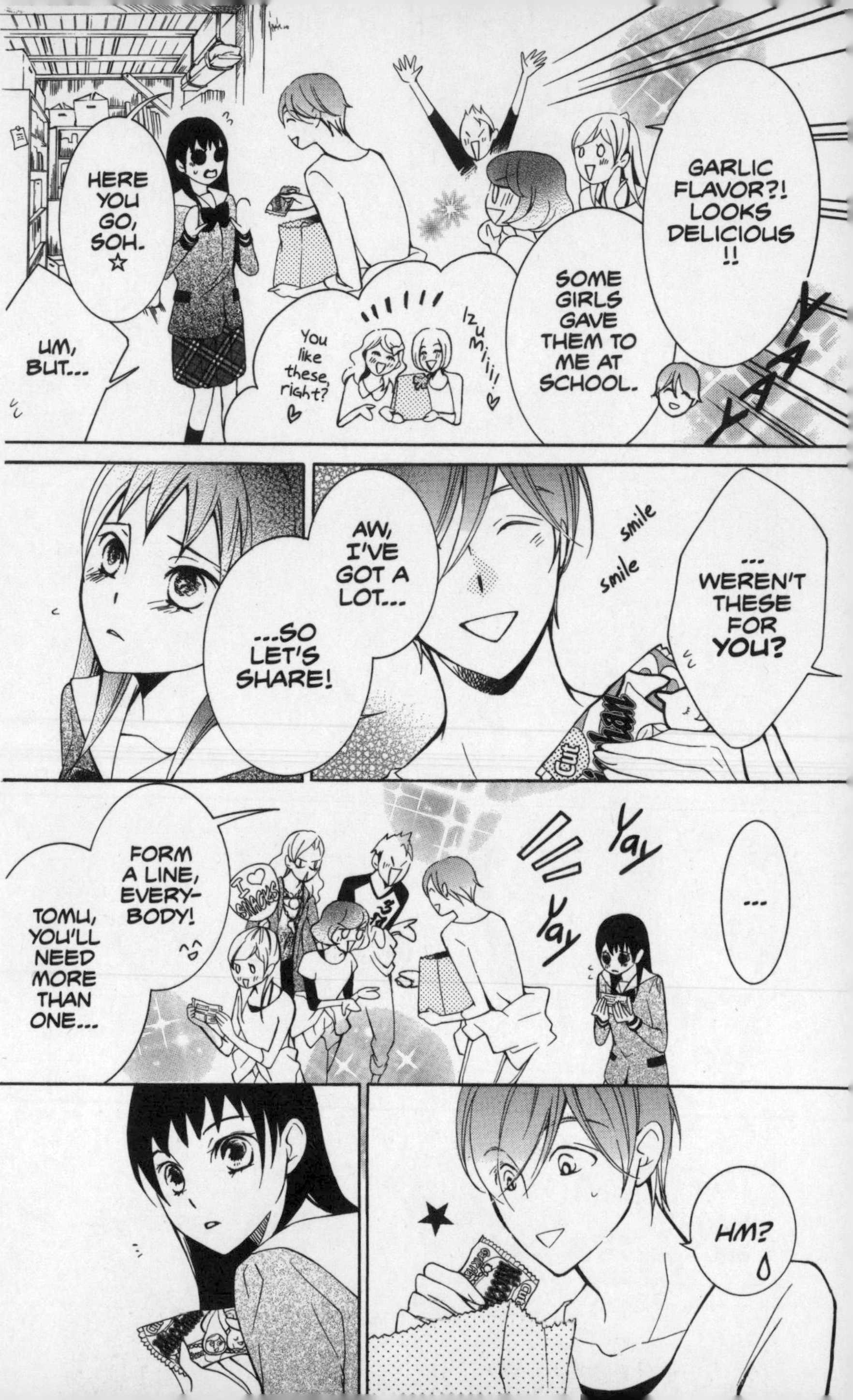
GARLIC FLAVOR?! LOOKS DELICIOUS !!
YAAY
SOME GIRLS GAVE THEM TO ME AT SCHOOL.
IZUMIiii!
You like these, right?
HERE YOU GO, SOH. ☆
UM, BUT...
smile smile
...WEREN'T THESE FOR YOU?
AW, I'VE GOT A LOT...
...SO LET'S SHARE!
...
Yay Yay
FORM A LINE, EVERYBODY!
I ♡ SNACKS
TOMU, YOU'LL NEED MORE THAN ONE...
HM?

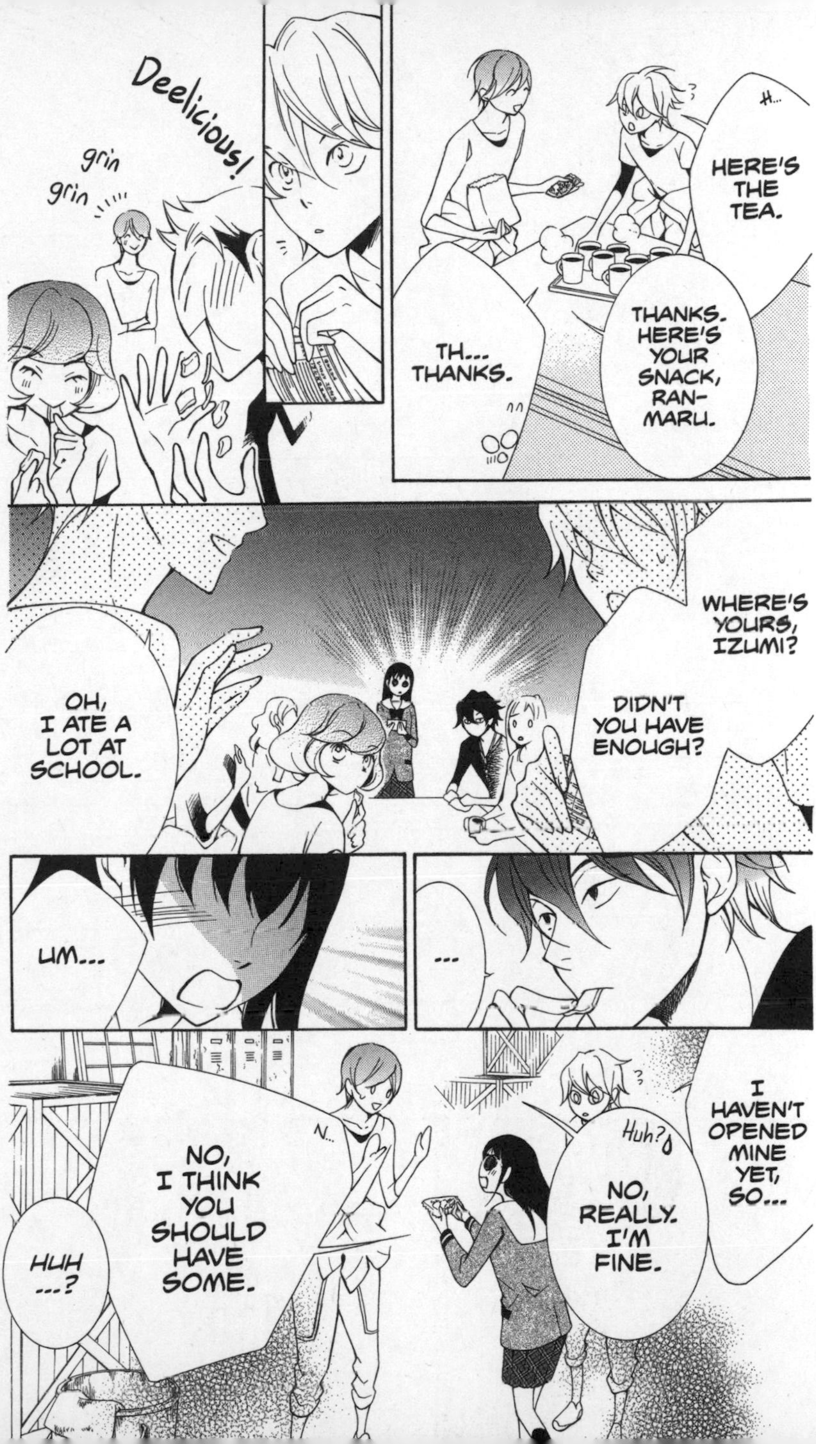
H...
HERE'S THE TEA.
THANKS. HERE'S YOUR SNACK, RAN-MARU.
TH... THANKS.
Deelicious!
grin grin
WHERE'S YOURS, IZUMI?
DIDN'T YOU HAVE ENOUGH?
OH, I ATE A LOT AT SCHOOL.
...
UM...
I HAVEN'T OPENED MINE YET, SO...
Huh?
NO, REALLY. I'M FINE.
N...
NO, I THINK YOU SHOULD HAVE SOME.
HUH ...?

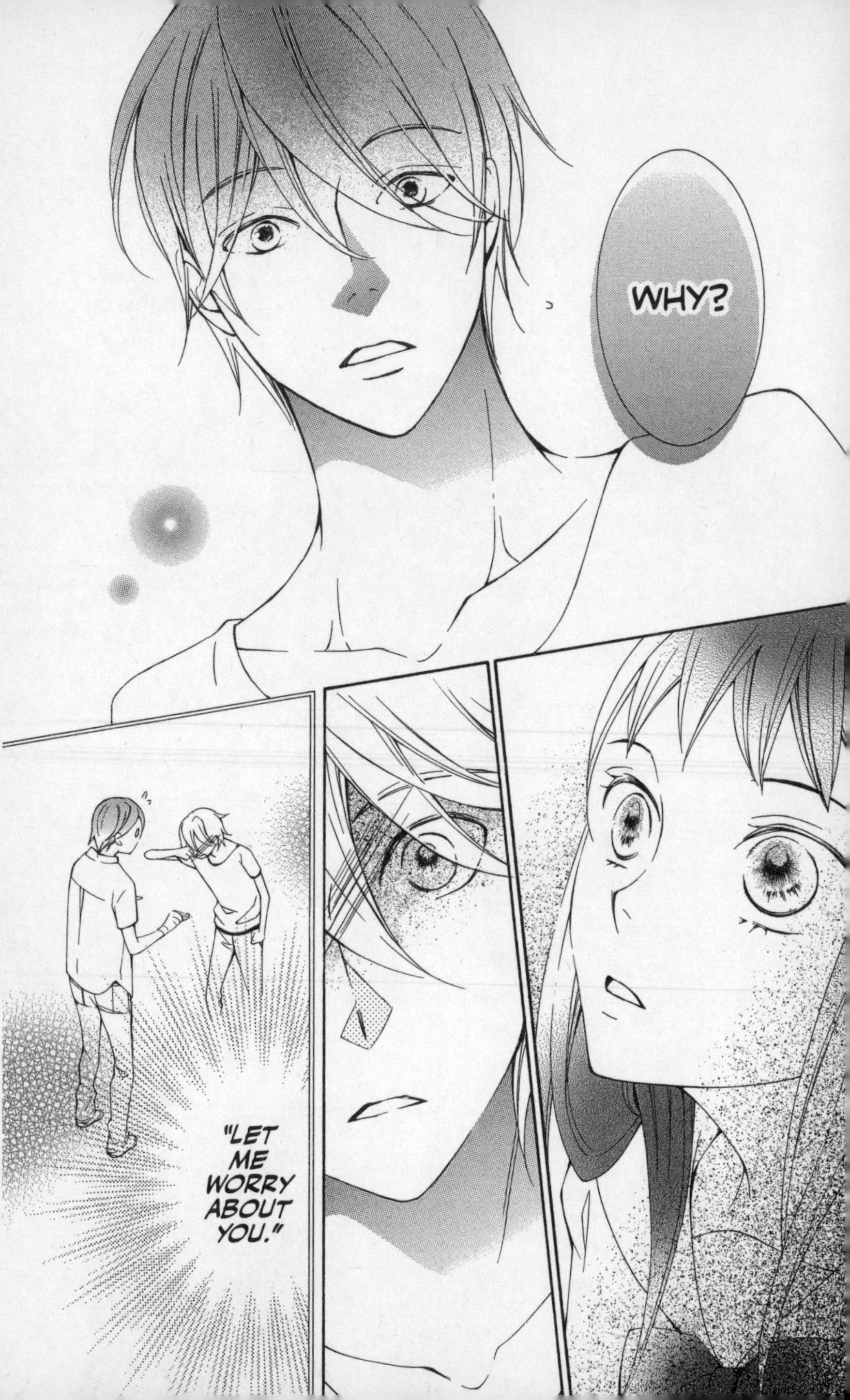
WHY?
"LET ME WORRY ABOUT YOU."

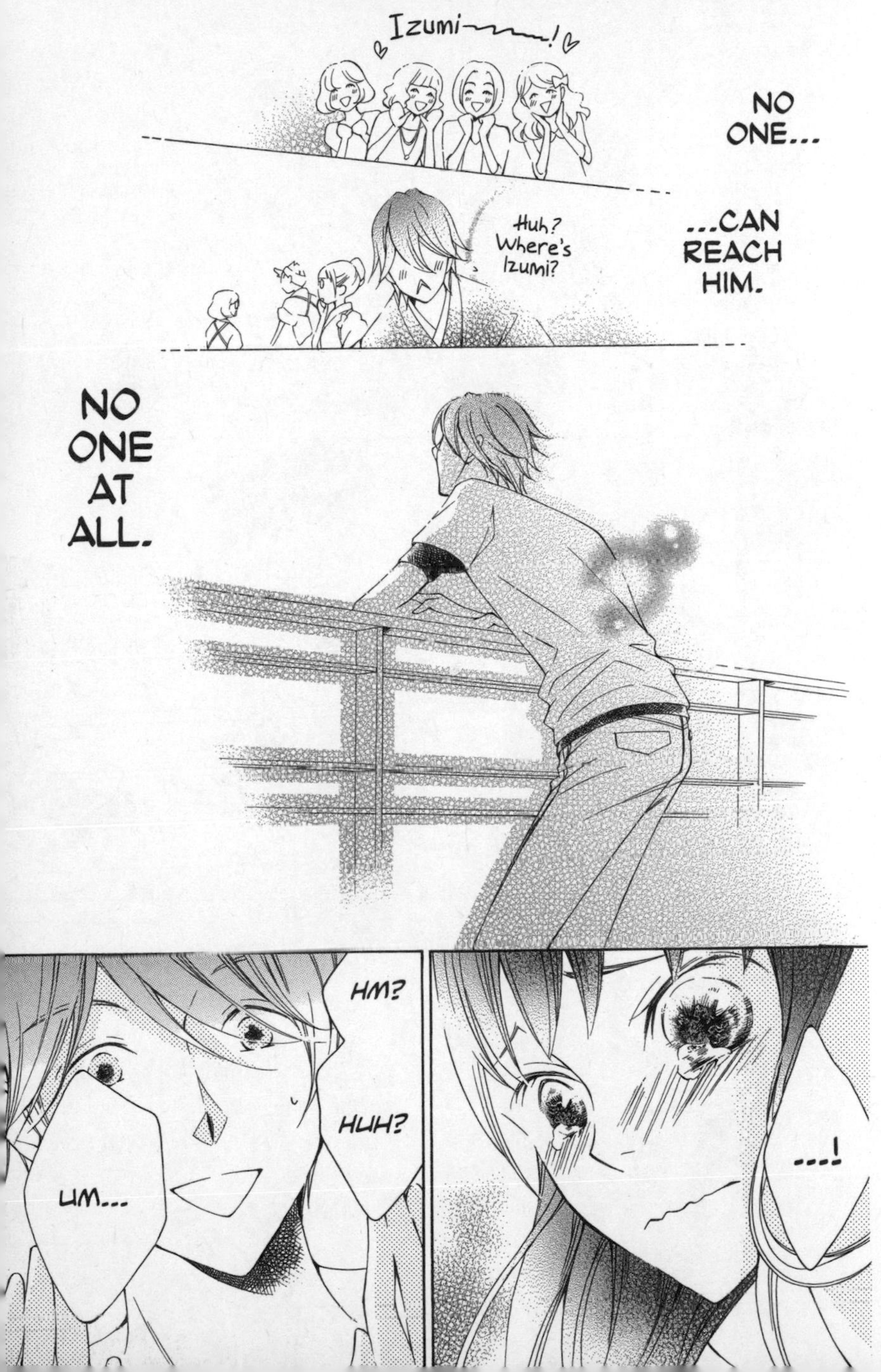
NO ONE...
Izumi~~!
...CAN REACH HIM.
Huh? Where's Izumi?
NO ONE AT ALL.
...!
HM?
HUH?
UM...

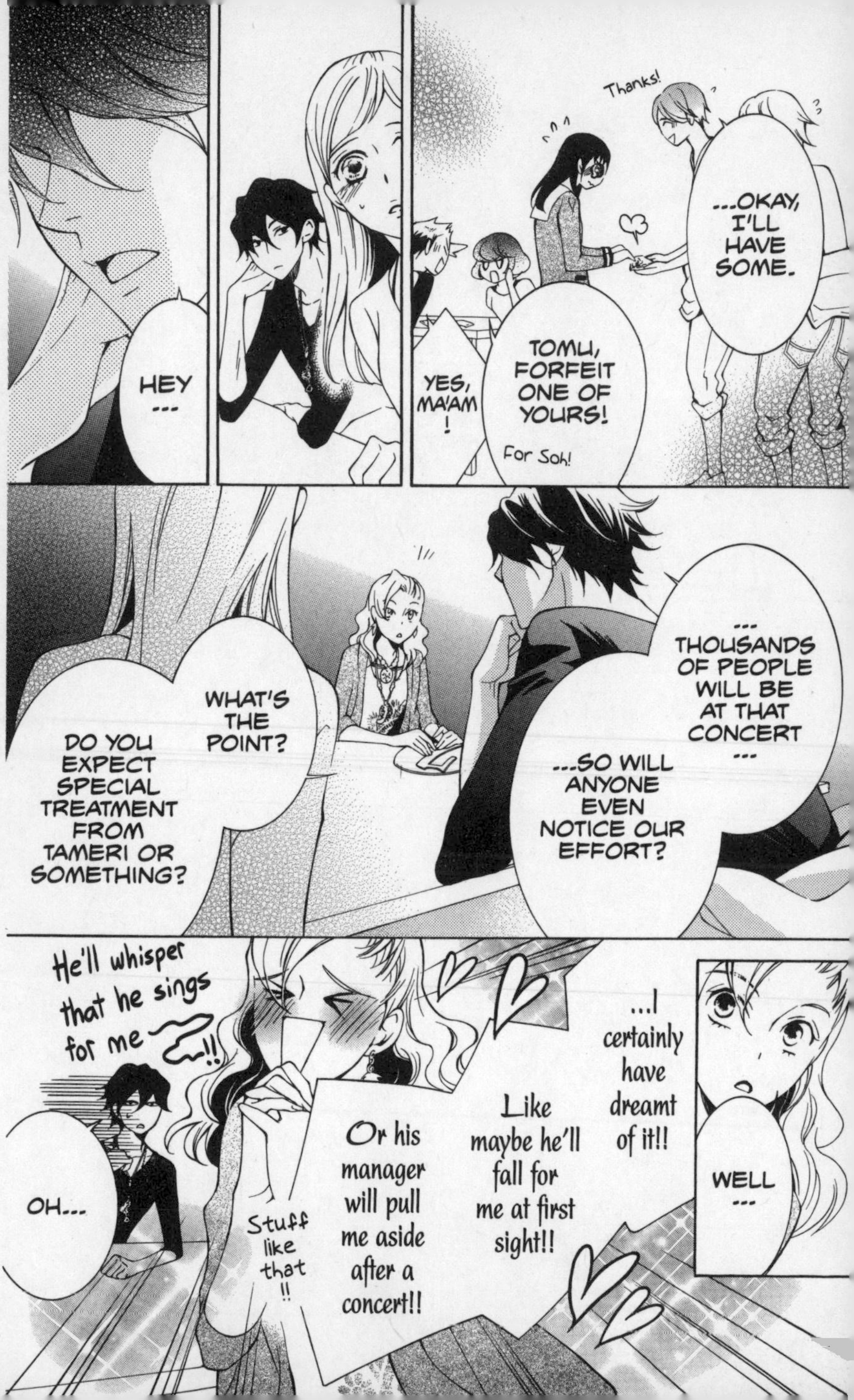
Thanks!
...OKAY, I'LL HAVE SOME.
TOMU, FORFEIT ONE OF YOURS!
For Soh!
YES, MA'AM!
HEY...
...THOUSANDS OF PEOPLE WILL BE AT THAT CONCERT...
...SO WILL ANYONE EVEN NOTICE OUR EFFORT?
WHAT'S THE POINT?
DO YOU EXPECT SPECIAL TREATMENT FROM TAMERI OR SOMETHING?
WELL...
...I certainly have dreamt of it!!
Like maybe he'll fall for me at first sight!!
Or his manager will pull me aside after a concert!!
Stuff like that!!
He'll whisper that he sings for me~!!
OH...

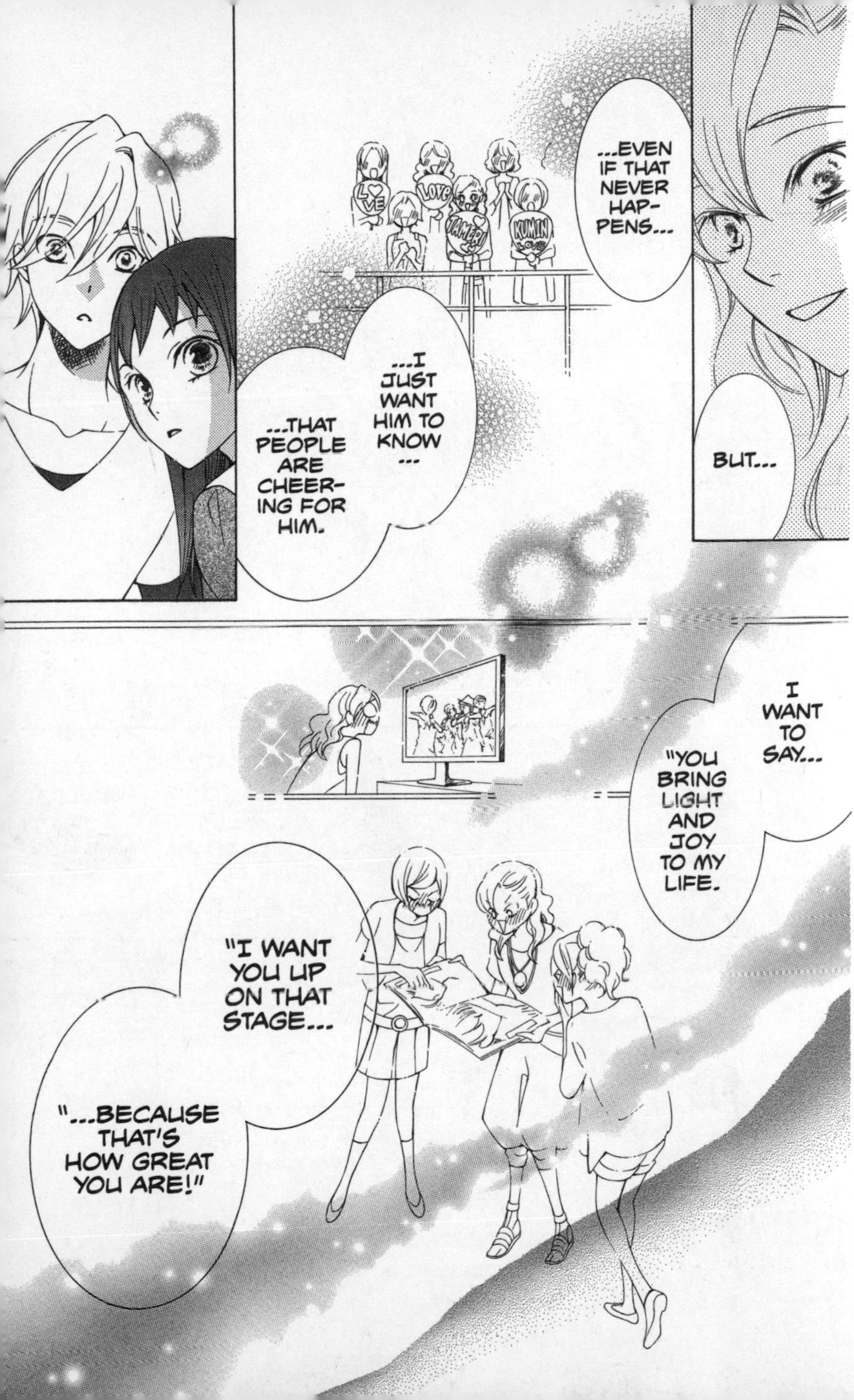
...EVEN IF THAT NEVER HAP-PENS...
BUT...
...I JUST WANT HIM TO KNOW...
...THAT PEOPLE ARE CHEERING FOR HIM.
I WANT TO SAY...
"YOU BRING LIGHT AND JOY TO MY LIFE.
"I WANT YOU UP ON THAT STAGE...
"...BECAUSE THAT'S HOW GREAT YOU ARE!"

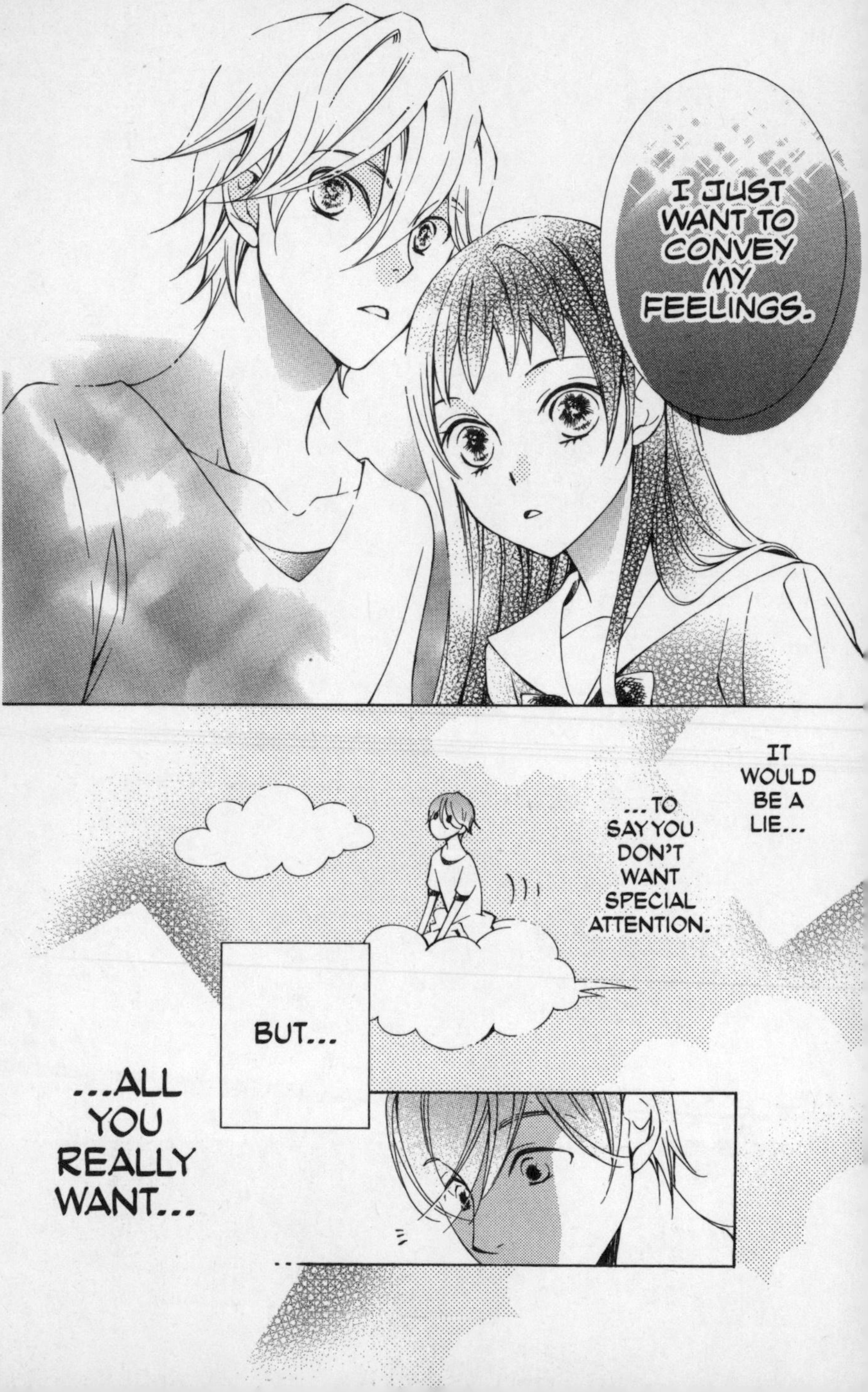
I JUST WANT TO CONVEY MY FEELINGS.
IT WOULD BE A LIE...
...TO SAY YOU DON'T WANT SPECIAL ATTENTION.
BUT...
...ALL YOU REALLY WANT...

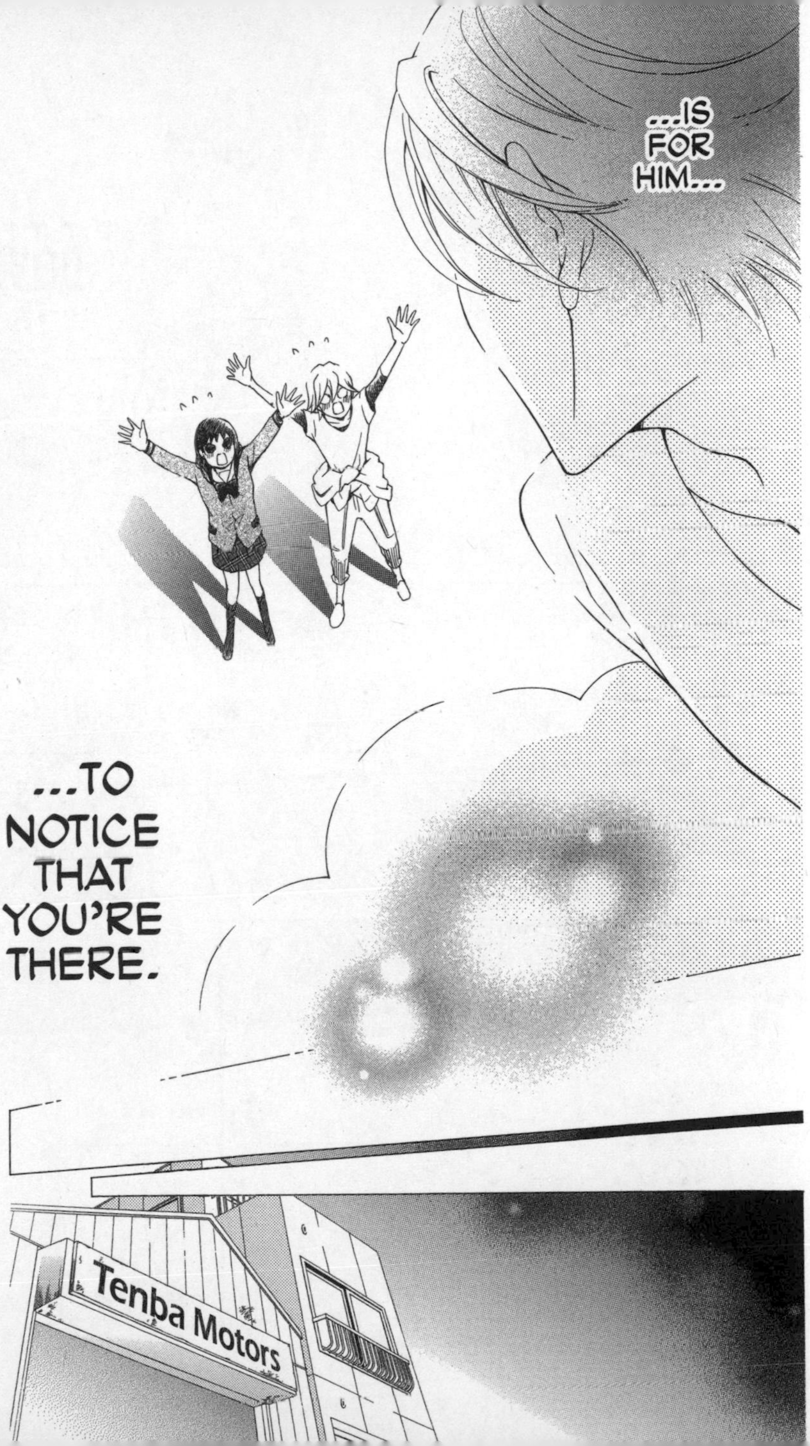
...IS FOR HIM...
...TO NOTICE THAT YOU'RE THERE.
Tenba Motors

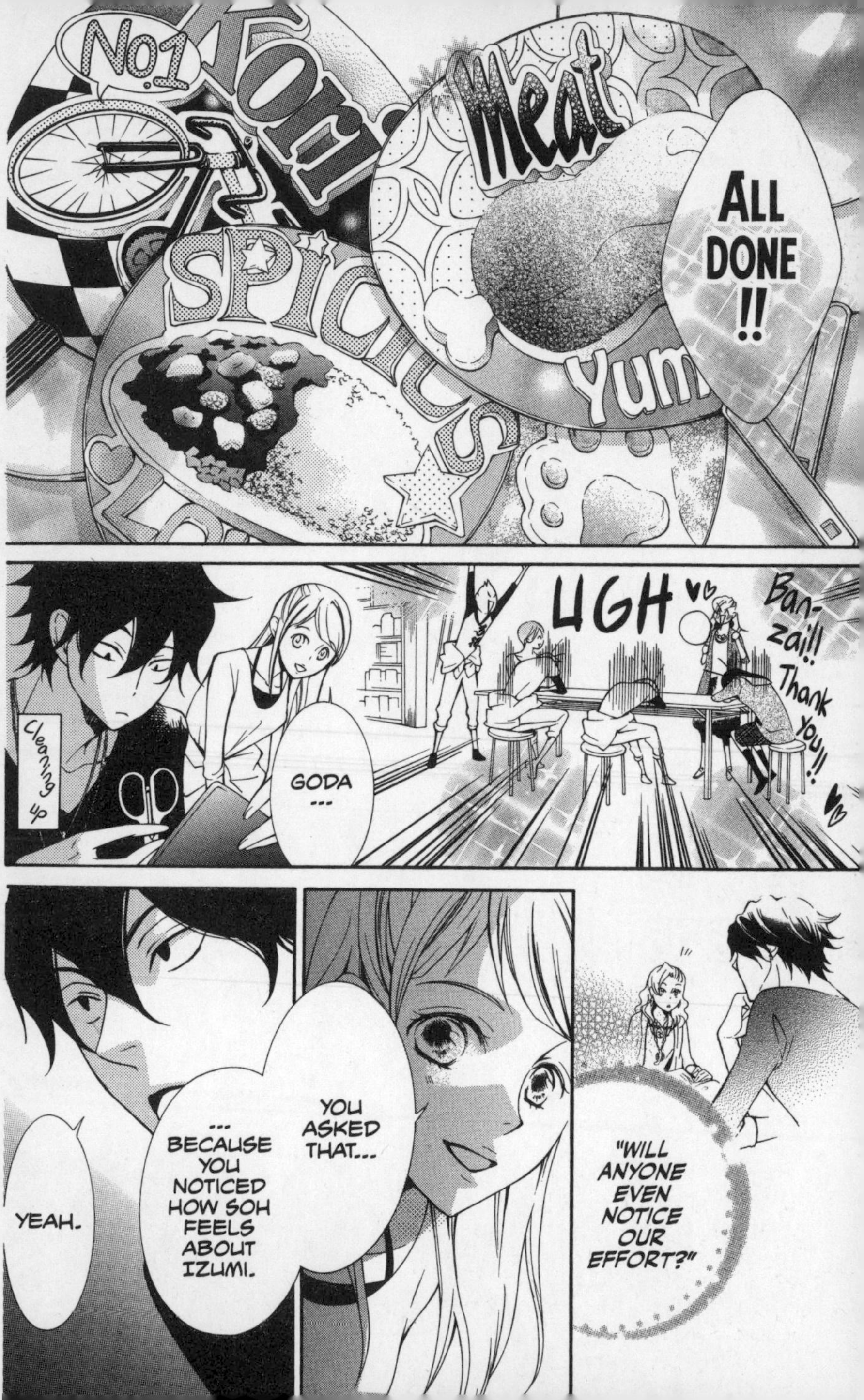
ALL DONE!!
Meat
Yum
No.1
Ban-zai!! Thank you!!
UGH
GODA...
Cleaning up
"WILL ANYONE EVEN NOTICE OUR EFFORT?"
YOU ASKED THAT...
...BECAUSE YOU NOTICED HOW SOH FEELS ABOUT IZUMI.
YEAH.

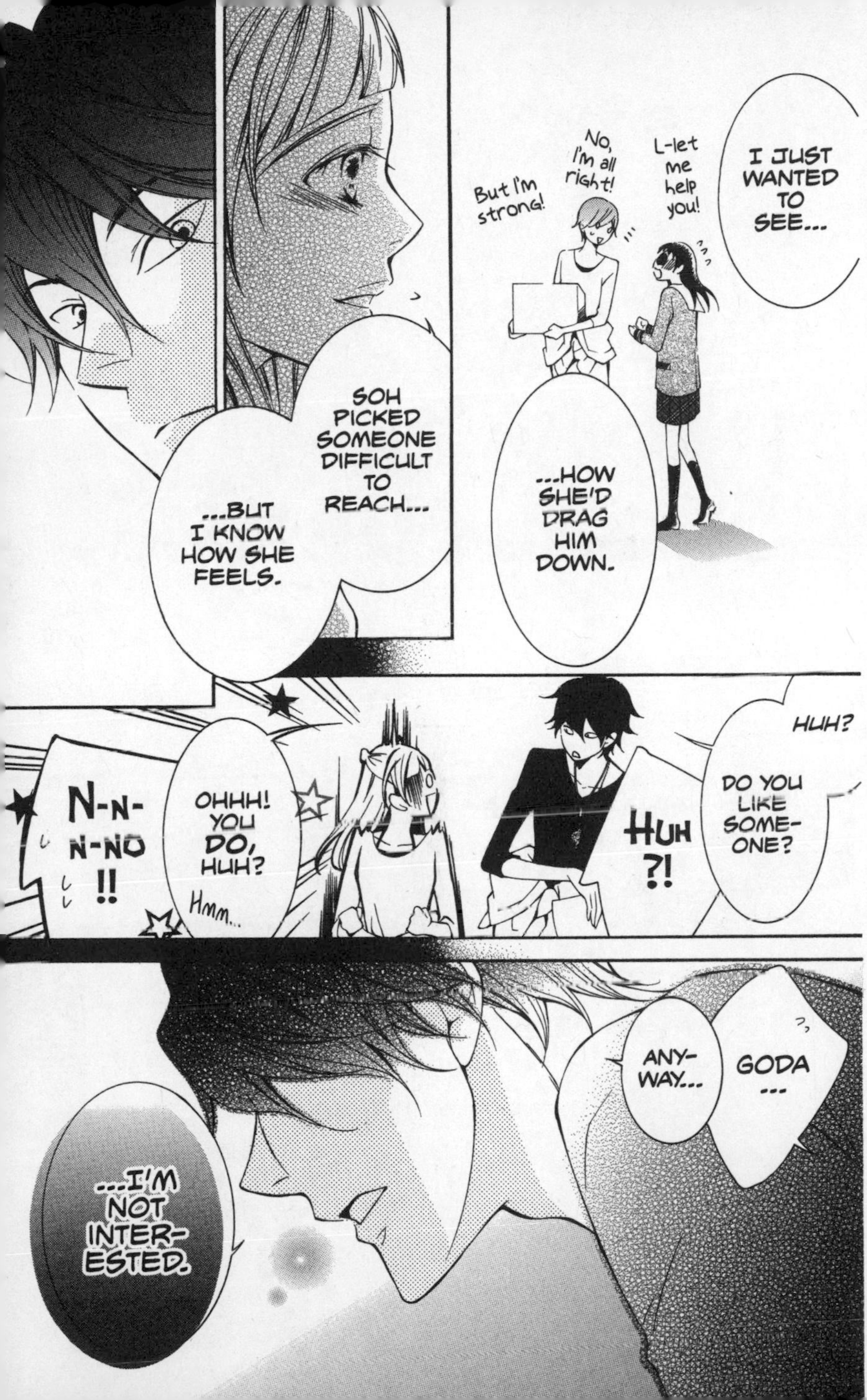
I JUST WANTED TO SEE...
L-let me help you!
No, I'm all right!
But I'm strong!
...HOW SHE'D DRAG HIM DOWN.
SOH PICKED SOMEONE DIFFICULT TO REACH...
...BUT I KNOW HOW SHE FEELS.
HUH?
DO YOU LIKE SOME-ONE?
HUH?!
OHHH! YOU DO, HUH?
Hmm...
N-N-N-NO!!
GODA...
ANY-WAY...
...I'M NOT INTER-ESTED.

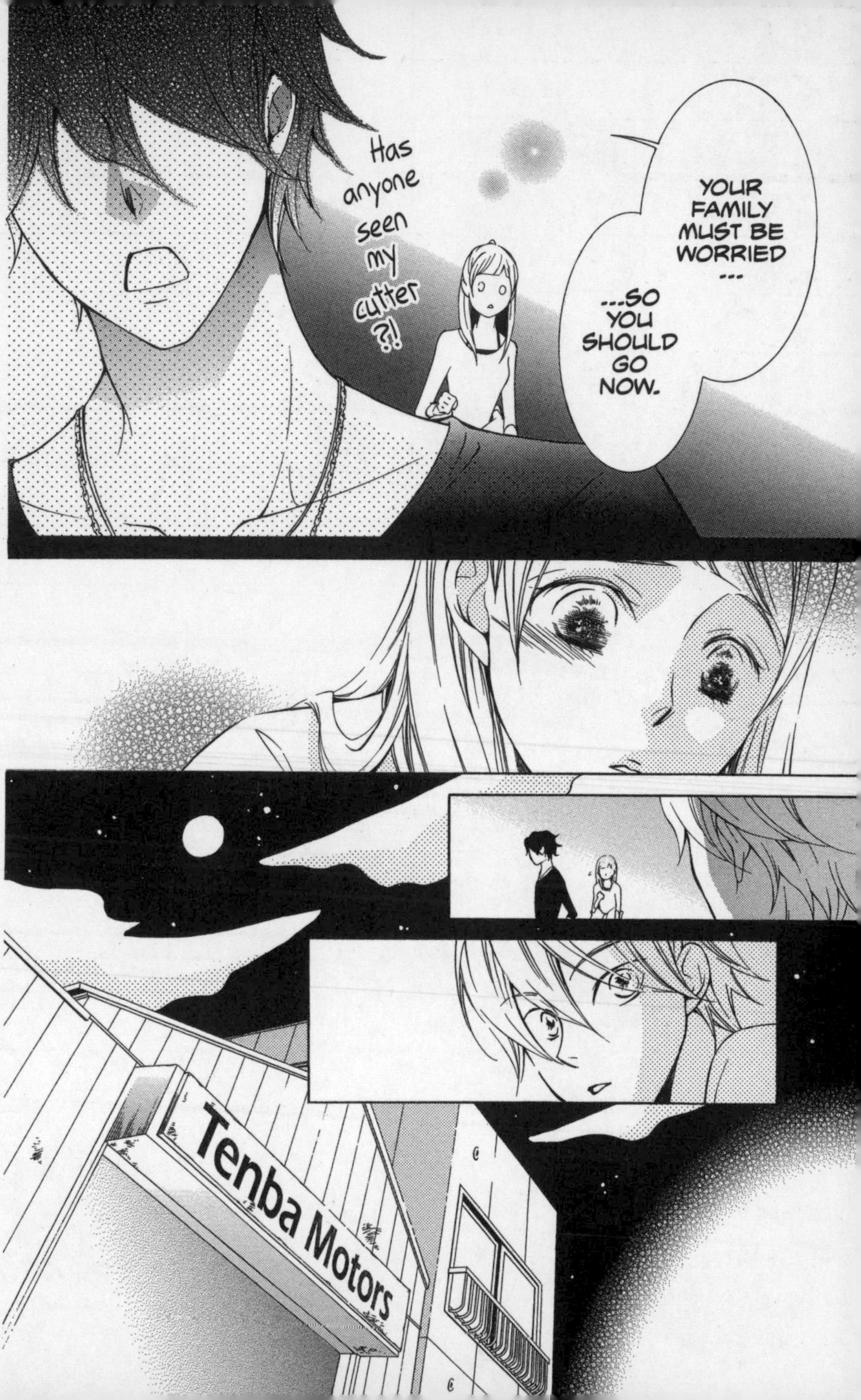
YOUR FAMILY MUST BE WORRIED...
...SO YOU SHOULD GO NOW.
Has anyone seen my cutter?!
Tenba Motors

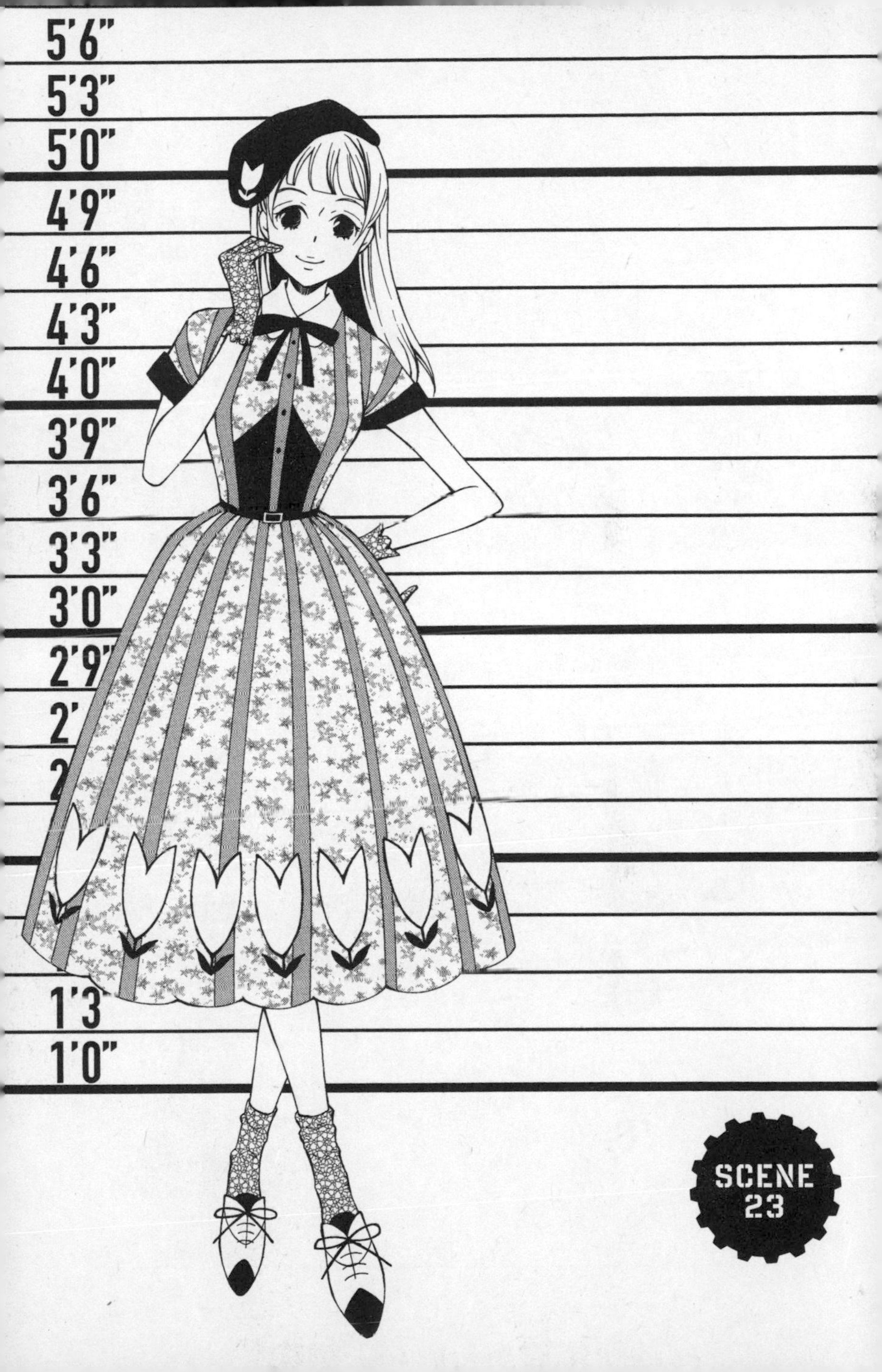
5'6"
5'3"
5'0"
4'9"
4'6"
4'3"
4'0"
3'9"
3'6"
3'3"
3'0"
1'3"
1'0"
SCENE
23

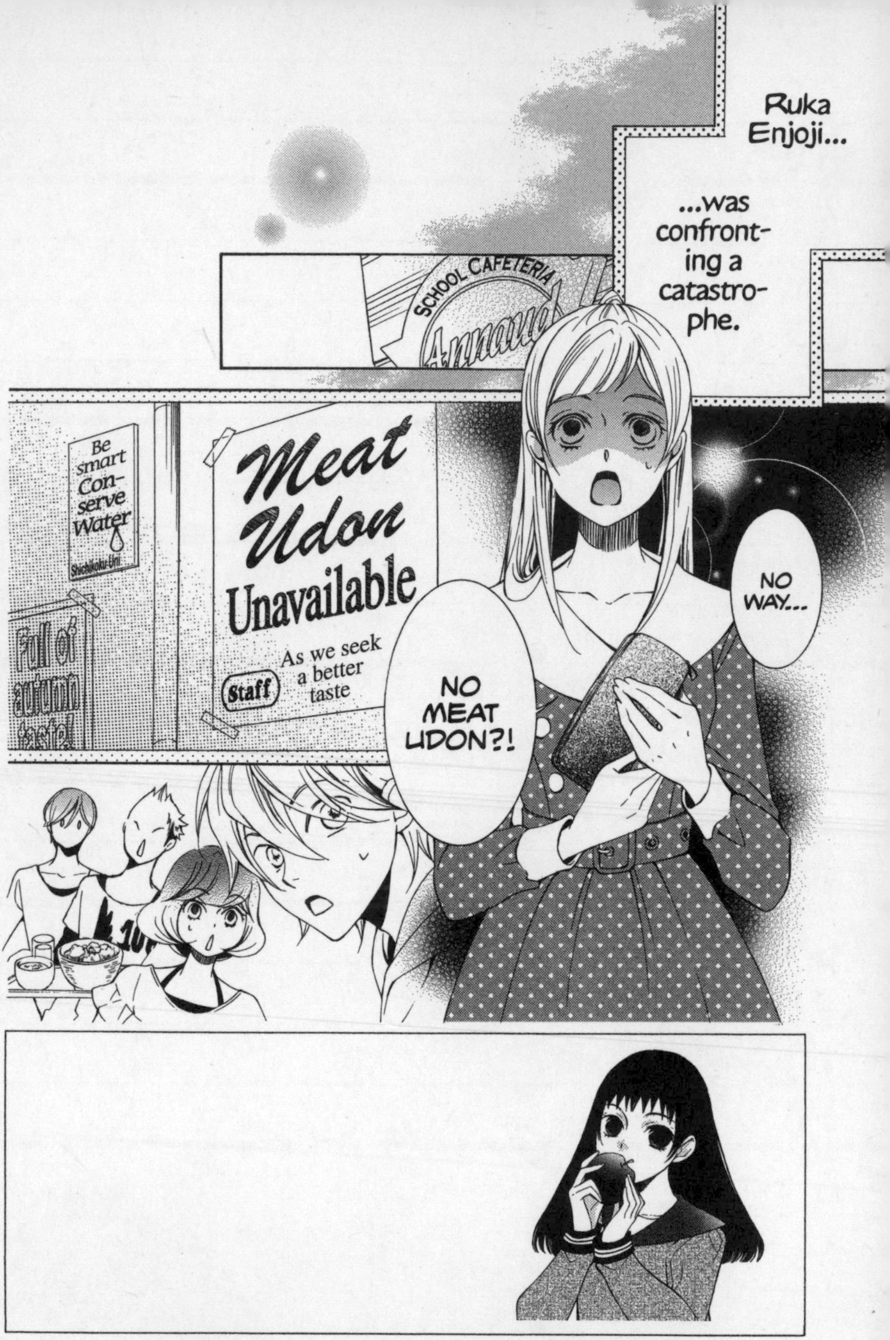
Ruka Enjoji...
...was confronting a catastrophe.
SCHOOL CAFETERIA
Meat Udon Unavailable
As we seek a better taste
Staff
Be smart Conserve Water
Shichikoku-Uni
Full of autumn
NO WAY...
NO MEAT UDON?!

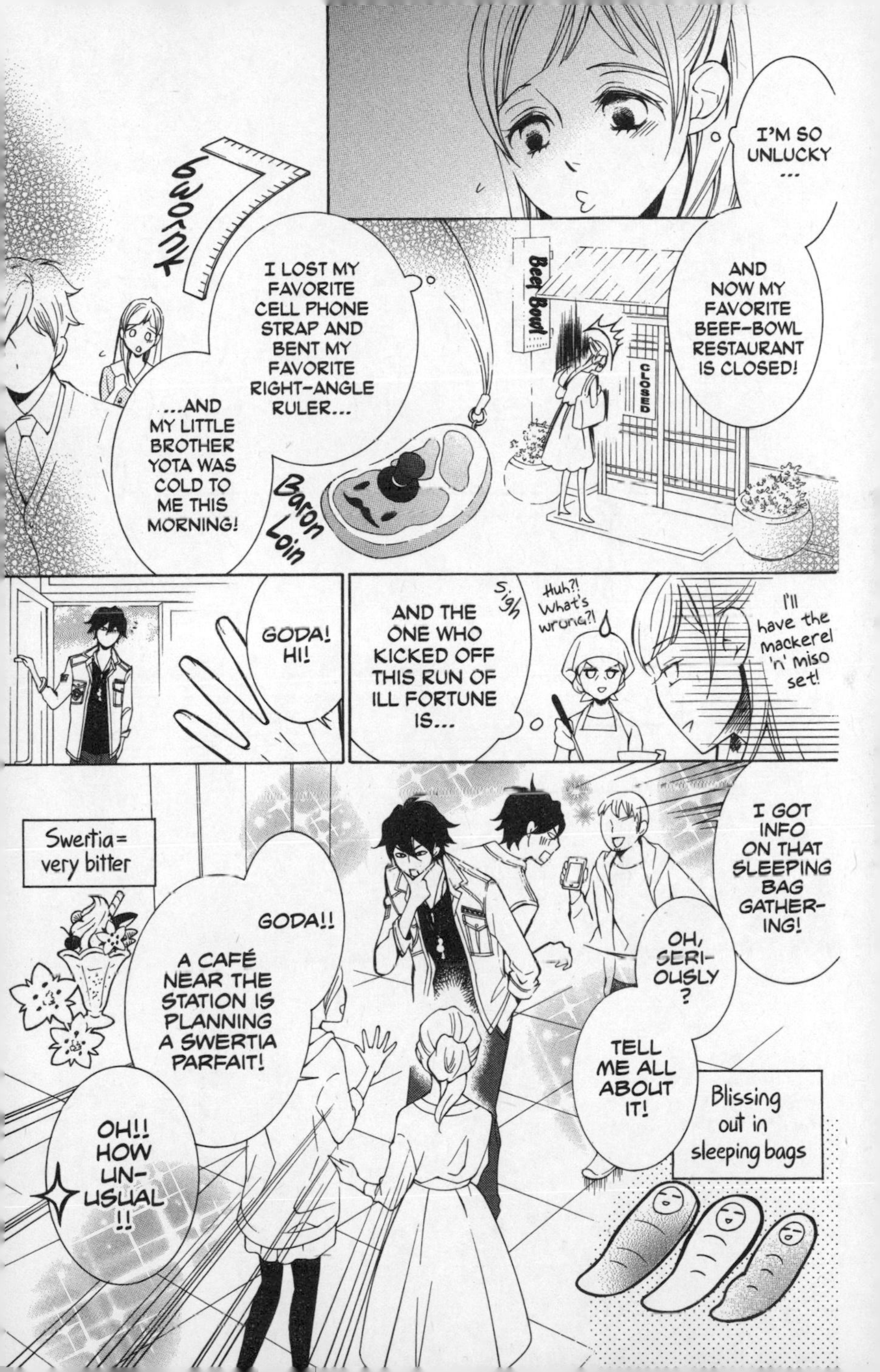
I'M SO UNLUCKY ...
AND NOW MY FAVORITE BEEF-BOWL RESTAURANT IS CLOSED!
Beef Bowl
CLOSED
I LOST MY FAVORITE CELL PHONE STRAP AND BENT MY FAVORITE RIGHT-ANGLE RULER...
...AND MY LITTLE BROTHER YOTA WAS COLD TO ME THIS MORNING!
Baron Loin
I'll have the mackerel 'n' miso set!
Huh?! What's wrong?!
Sigh
AND THE ONE WHO KICKED OFF THIS RUN OF ILL FORTUNE IS...
GODA! HI!
I GOT INFO ON THAT SLEEPING BAG GATHERING!
OH, SERIOUSLY?
TELL ME ALL ABOUT IT!
Blissing out in sleeping bags
GODA!! A CAFÉ NEAR THE STATION IS PLANNING A SWERTIA PARFAIT!
Swertia= very bitter
OH!! HOW UNUSUAL!!

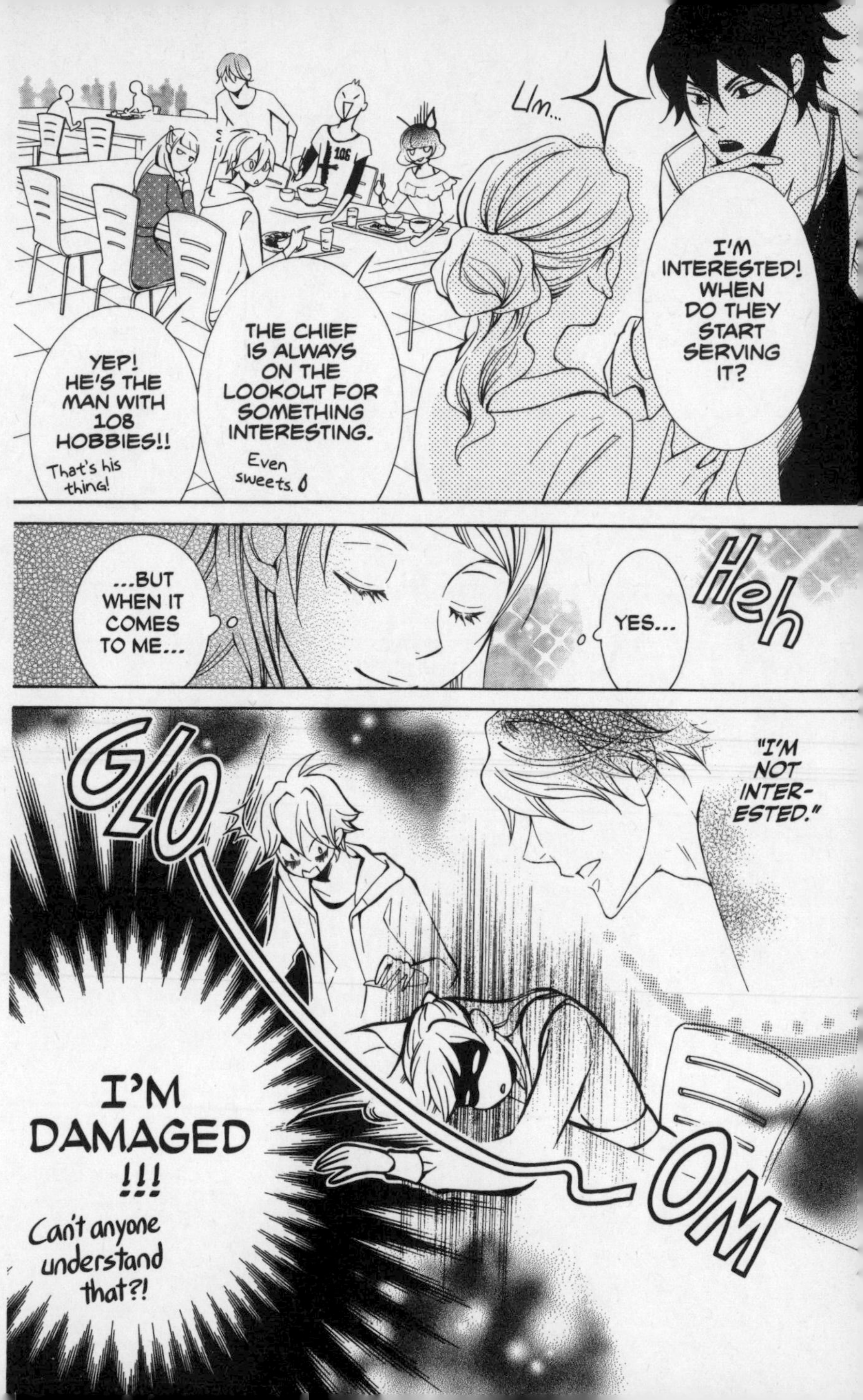
Um...
I'M INTERESTED! WHEN DO THEY START SERVING IT?
THE CHIEF IS ALWAYS ON THE LOOKOUT FOR SOMETHING INTERESTING.
Even sweets.
YEP! HE'S THE MAN WITH 108 HOBBIES!!
That's his thing!
Heh
YES...
...BUT WHEN IT COMES TO ME...
"I'M NOT INTERESTED."
GLOOM
I'M DAMAGED !!!
Can't anyone understand that?!

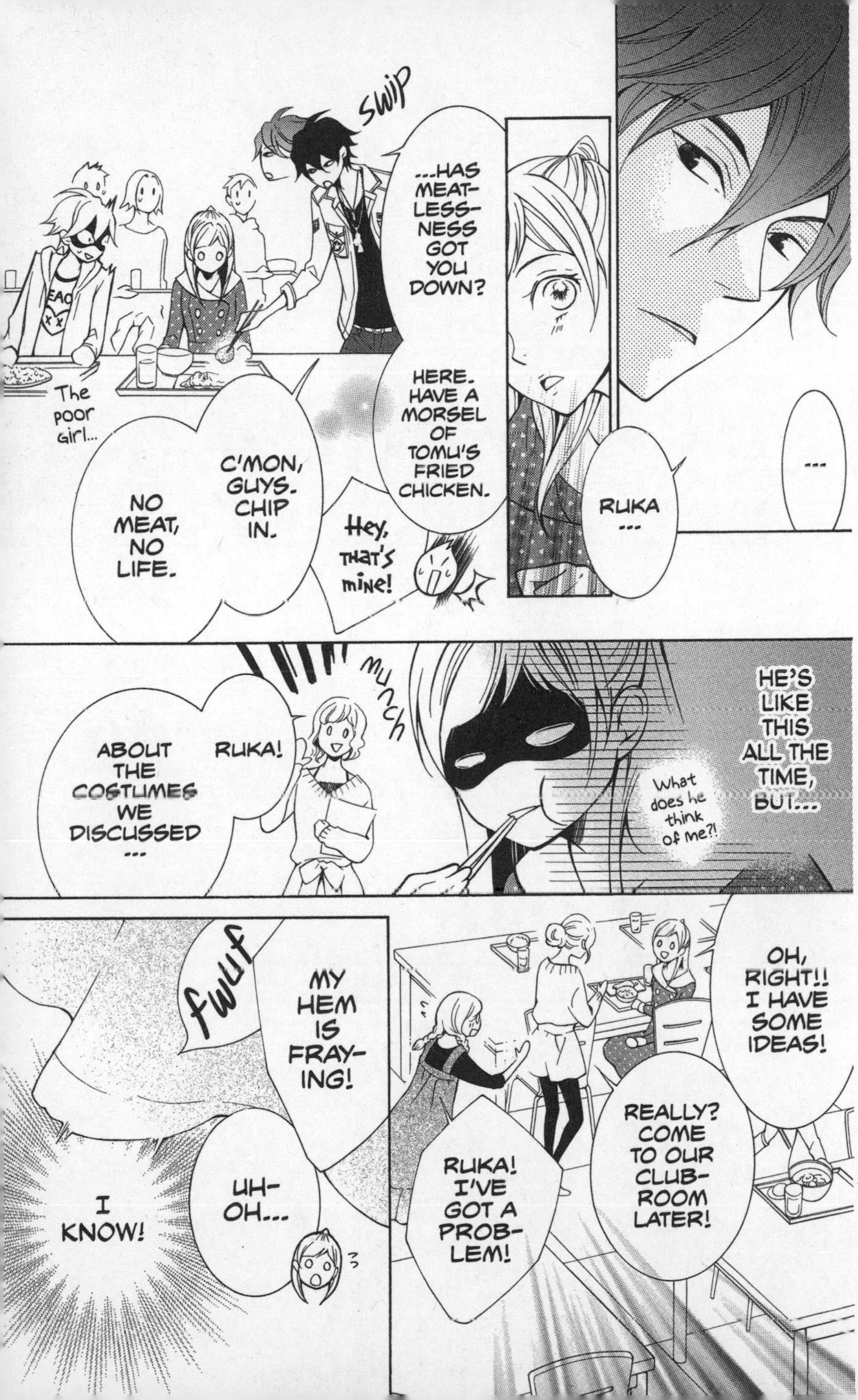
...
RUKA...
...HAS MEATLESSNESS GOT YOU DOWN?
SWIP
HERE. HAVE A MORSEL OF TOMU'S FRIED CHICKEN.
Hey, THAT'S mine!
C'MON, GUYS. CHIP IN.
NO MEAT, NO LIFE.
The poor girl...
HE'S LIKE THIS ALL THE TIME, BUT...
What does he think of me?!
munch
RUKA!
ABOUT THE COSTUMES WE DISCUSSED...
OH, RIGHT!! I HAVE SOME IDEAS!
REALLY? COME TO OUR CLUBROOM LATER!
RUKA! I'VE GOT A PROBLEM!
fwuf
MY HEM IS FRAYING!
UH-OH...
I KNOW!

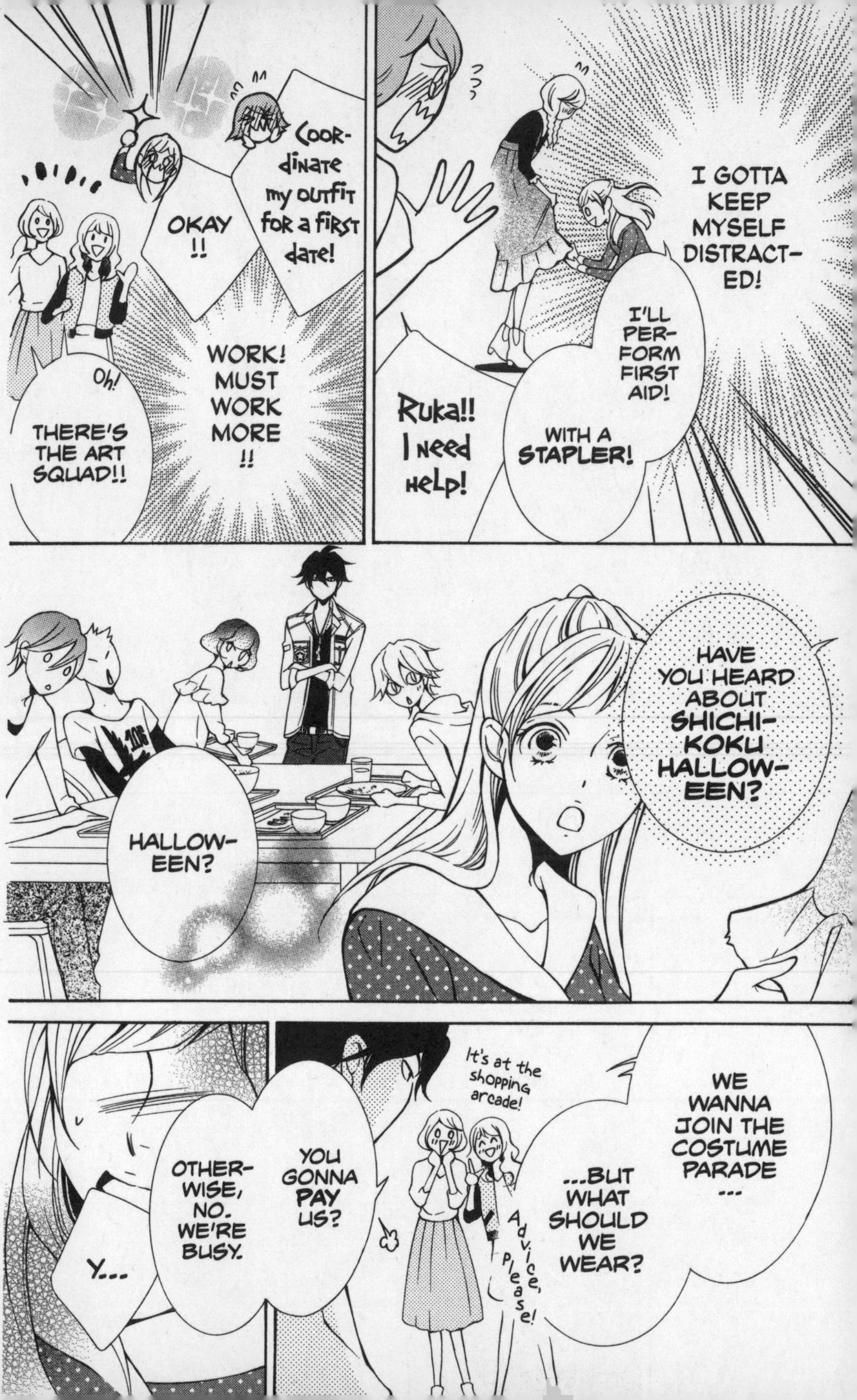

I GOTTA KEEP MYSELF DISTRACTED!
I'LL PERFORM FIRST AID!
WITH A STAPLER!
Ruka!! I need help!
Coordinate my outfit for a first date!
OKAY !!
WORK! MUST WORK MORE !!
Oh! THERE'S THE ART SQUAD!!
HAVE YOU HEARD ABOUT SHICHIKOKU HALLOWEEN?
HALLOWEEN?
WE WANNA JOIN THE COSTUME PARADE ...
...BUT WHAT SHOULD WE WEAR?
It's at the shopping arcade!
Advice, Please!
YOU GONNA PAY US?
OTHERWISE, NO. WE'RE BUSY.
Y...

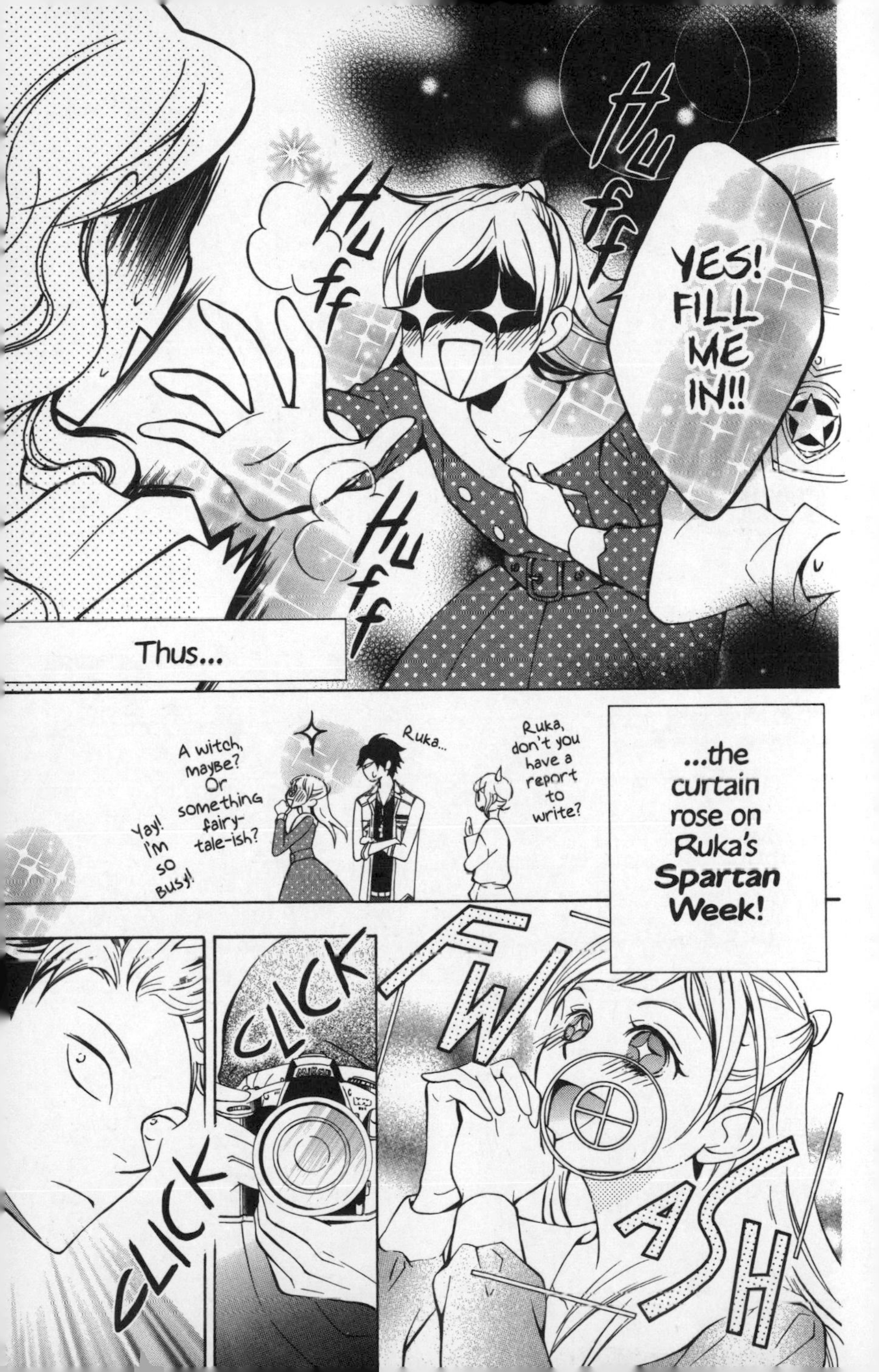
YES! FILL ME IN!!
Huff
Huff
Huff
Thus...
...the curtain rose on Ruka's Spartan Week!
Ruka, don't you have a report to write?
Ruka...
A witch, maybe? Or something fairy-tale-ish?
Yay! I'm so busy!
FWASH
CLICK
CLICK
CLICK

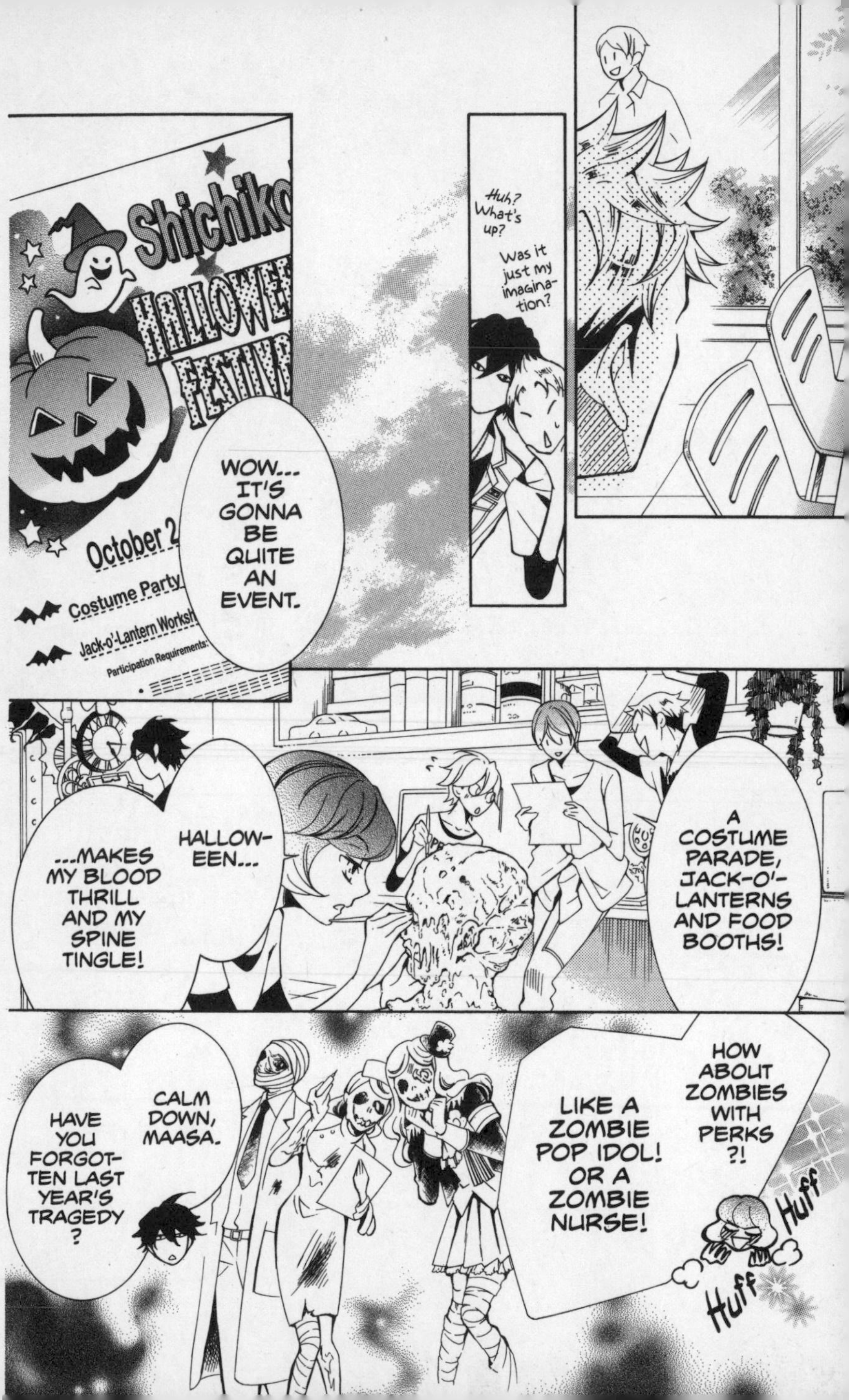
Huh? What's up?
Was it just my imagination?
Shichiko
HALLOWE
FESTIV
October 2
Costume Party
Jack-o'-Lantern Worksh
Participation Requirements:
WOW... IT'S GONNA BE QUITE AN EVENT.
A COSTUME PARADE, JACK-O'-LANTERNS AND FOOD BOOTHS!
HALLOWEEN...
...MAKES MY BLOOD THRILL AND MY SPINE TINGLE!
HOW ABOUT ZOMBIES WITH PERKS?!
LIKE A ZOMBIE POP IDOL! OR A ZOMBIE NURSE!
Huff Huff Huff
CALM DOWN, MAASA.
HAVE YOU FORGOTTEN LAST YEAR'S TRAGEDY?

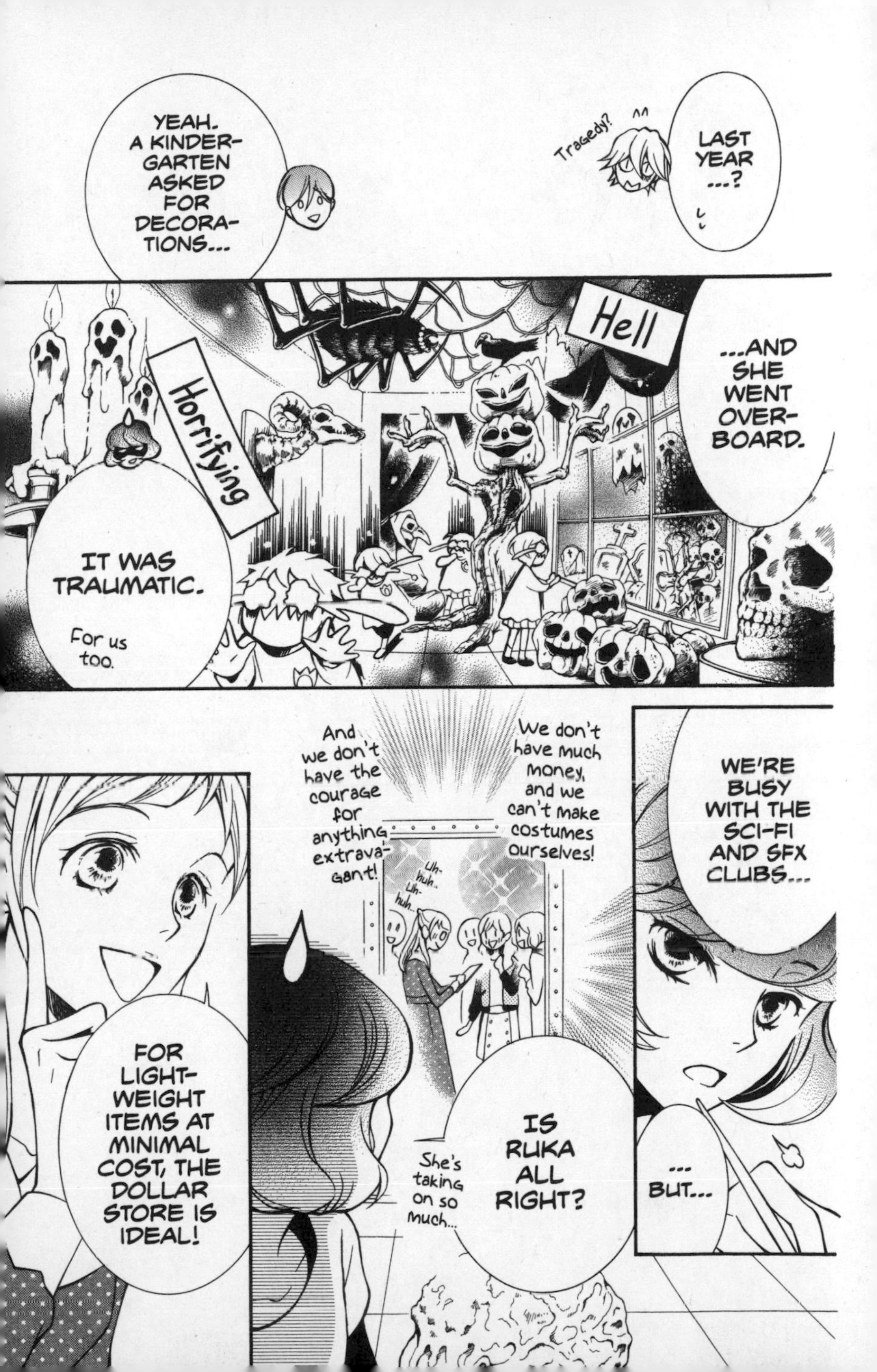
LAST YEAR ...?
Tragedy?
YEAH. A KINDER-GARTEN ASKED FOR DECORA-TIONS...
...AND SHE WENT OVER-BOARD.
Hell
Horrifying
IT WAS TRAUMATIC.
For us too.
WE'RE BUSY WITH THE SCI-FI AND SFX CLUBS...
...BUT...
We don't have much money, and we can't make costumes ourselves!
And we don't have the courage for anything extrava-gant!
Uh-huh. Uh-huh...
IS RUKA ALL RIGHT?
She's taking on so much...
FOR LIGHT-WEIGHT ITEMS AT MINIMAL COST, THE DOLLAR STORE IS IDEAL!

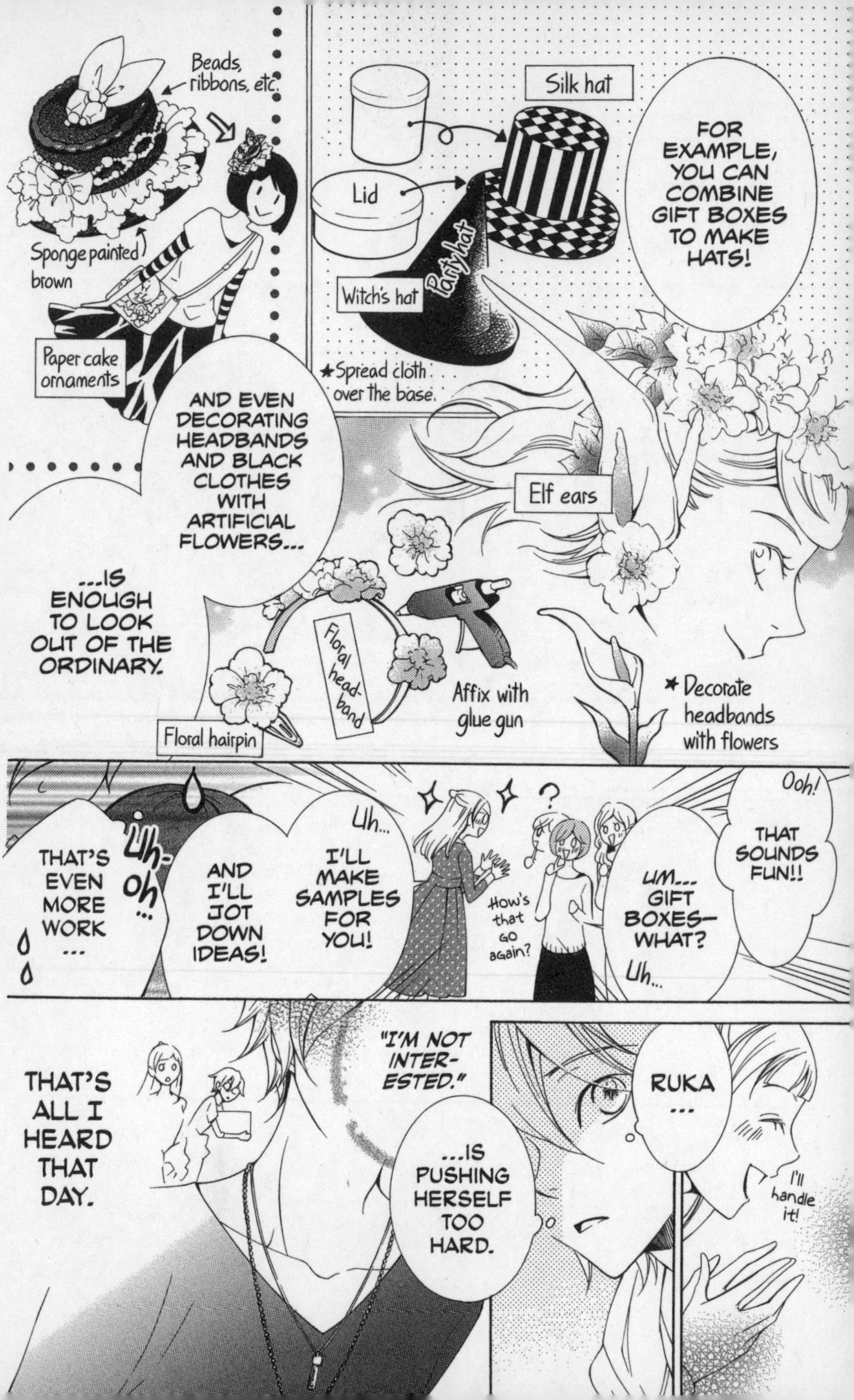
FOR EXAMPLE, YOU CAN COMBINE GIFT BOXES TO MAKE HATS!
Silk hat
Lid
Party hat
Witch's hat
★Spread cloth over the base.
Beads, ribbons, etc.
Sponge painted brown
Paper cake ornaments
AND EVEN DECORATING HEADBANDS AND BLACK CLOTHES WITH ARTIFICIAL FLOWERS...
Elf ears
★Decorate headbands with flowers
Affix with glue gun
Floral headband
Floral hairpin
...IS ENOUGH TO LOOK OUT OF THE ORDINARY.
Ooh!
THAT SOUNDS FUN!!
UM... GIFT BOXES—WHAT?
Uh...
How's that go again?
Uh...
I'LL MAKE SAMPLES FOR YOU!
AND I'LL JOT DOWN IDEAS!
Uh-oh...
THAT'S EVEN MORE WORK...
I'll handle it!
RUKA...
...IS PUSHING HERSELF TOO HARD.
"I'M NOT INTER-ESTED."
THAT'S ALL I HEARD THAT DAY.

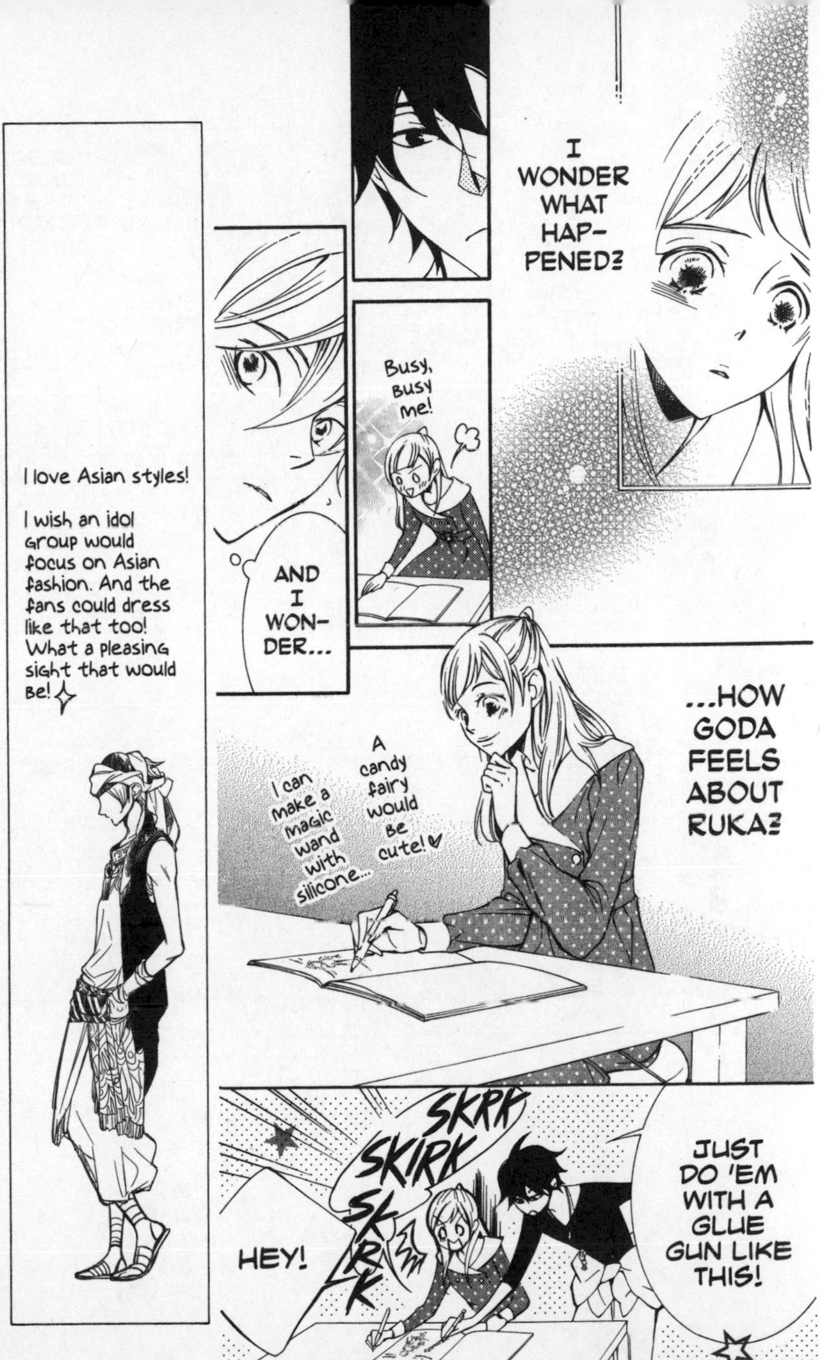
I WONDER WHAT HAP-PENED?
Busy, busy me!
AND I WON-DER...
...HOW GODA FEELS ABOUT RUKA?
A candy fairy would be cute!
I can make a magic wand with silicone...
JUST DO 'EM WITH A GLUE GUN LIKE THIS!
SKRK
SKIRK
SKRK
HEY!
I love Asian styles!
I wish an idol group would focus on Asian fashion. And the fans could dress like that too! What a pleasing sight that would be!

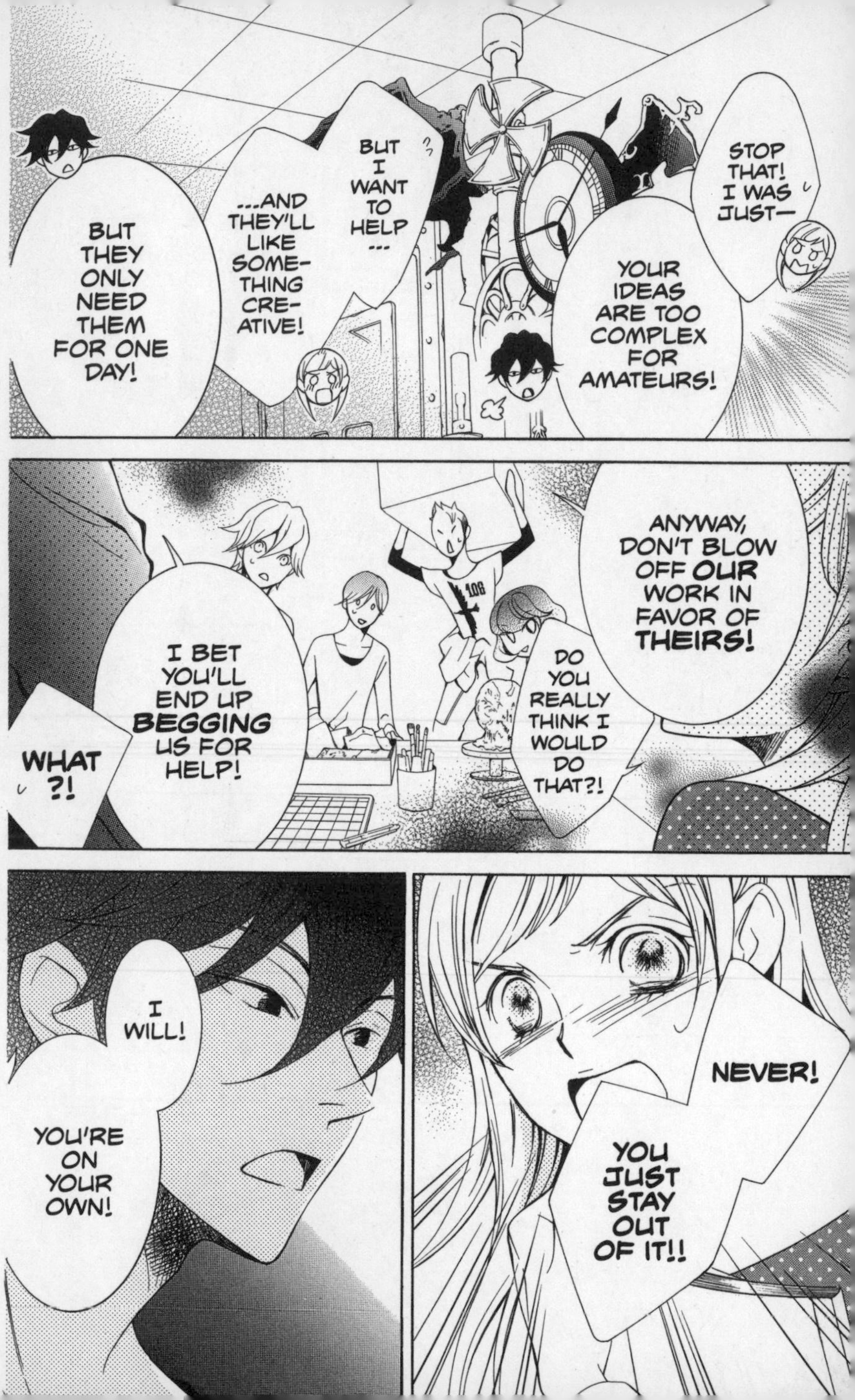
STOP THAT! I WAS JUST—
YOUR IDEAS ARE TOO COMPLEX FOR AMATEURS!
BUT I WANT TO HELP...
...AND THEY'LL LIKE SOMETHING CREATIVE!
BUT THEY ONLY NEED THEM FOR ONE DAY!
ANYWAY, DON'T BLOW OFF **OUR** WORK IN FAVOR OF **THEIRS!**
DO YOU REALLY THINK I WOULD DO THAT?!
I BET YOU'LL END UP **BEGGING** US FOR HELP!
WHAT?!
NEVER!
YOU JUST STAY OUT OF IT!!
I WILL!
YOU'RE ON YOUR OWN!

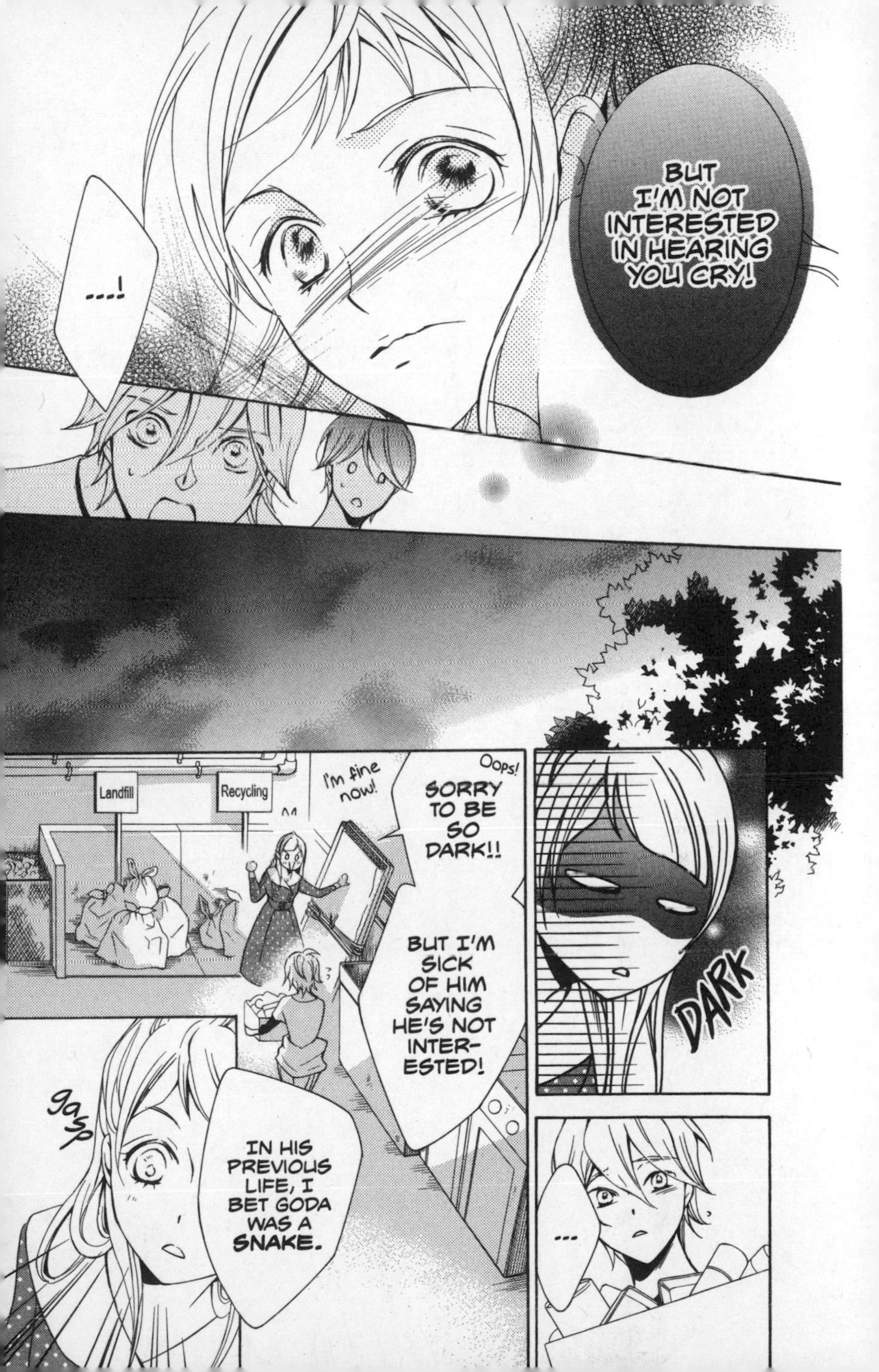
BUT I'M NOT INTERESTED IN HEARING YOU CRY!
...!
DARK
Oops!
SORRY TO BE SO DARK!!
I'm fine now!
BUT I'M SICK OF HIM SAYING HE'S NOT INTER-ESTED!
Recycling
Landfill
...
gasp
IN HIS PREVIOUS LIFE, I BET GODA WAS A SNAKE.

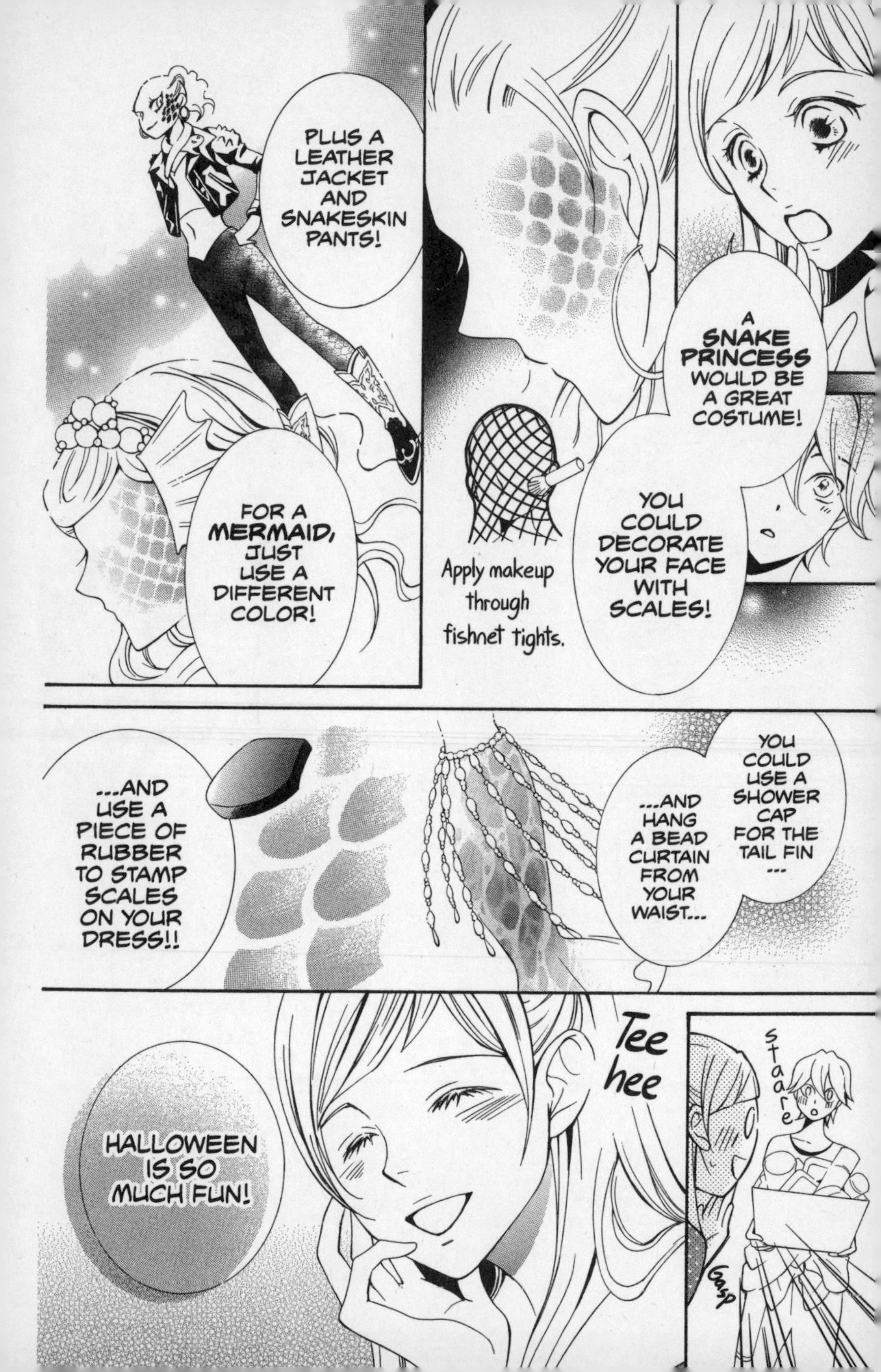
A SNAKE PRINCESS WOULD BE A GREAT COSTUME!
YOU COULD DECORATE YOUR FACE WITH SCALES!
Apply makeup through fishnet tights.
PLUS A LEATHER JACKET AND SNAKESKIN PANTS!
FOR A MERMAID, JUST USE A DIFFERENT COLOR!
YOU COULD USE A SHOWER CAP FOR THE TAIL FIN...
...AND HANG A BEAD CURTAIN FROM YOUR WAIST...
...AND USE A PIECE OF RUBBER TO STAMP SCALES ON YOUR DRESS!!
staare
Gasp
Tee hee
HALLOWEEN IS SO MUCH FUN!

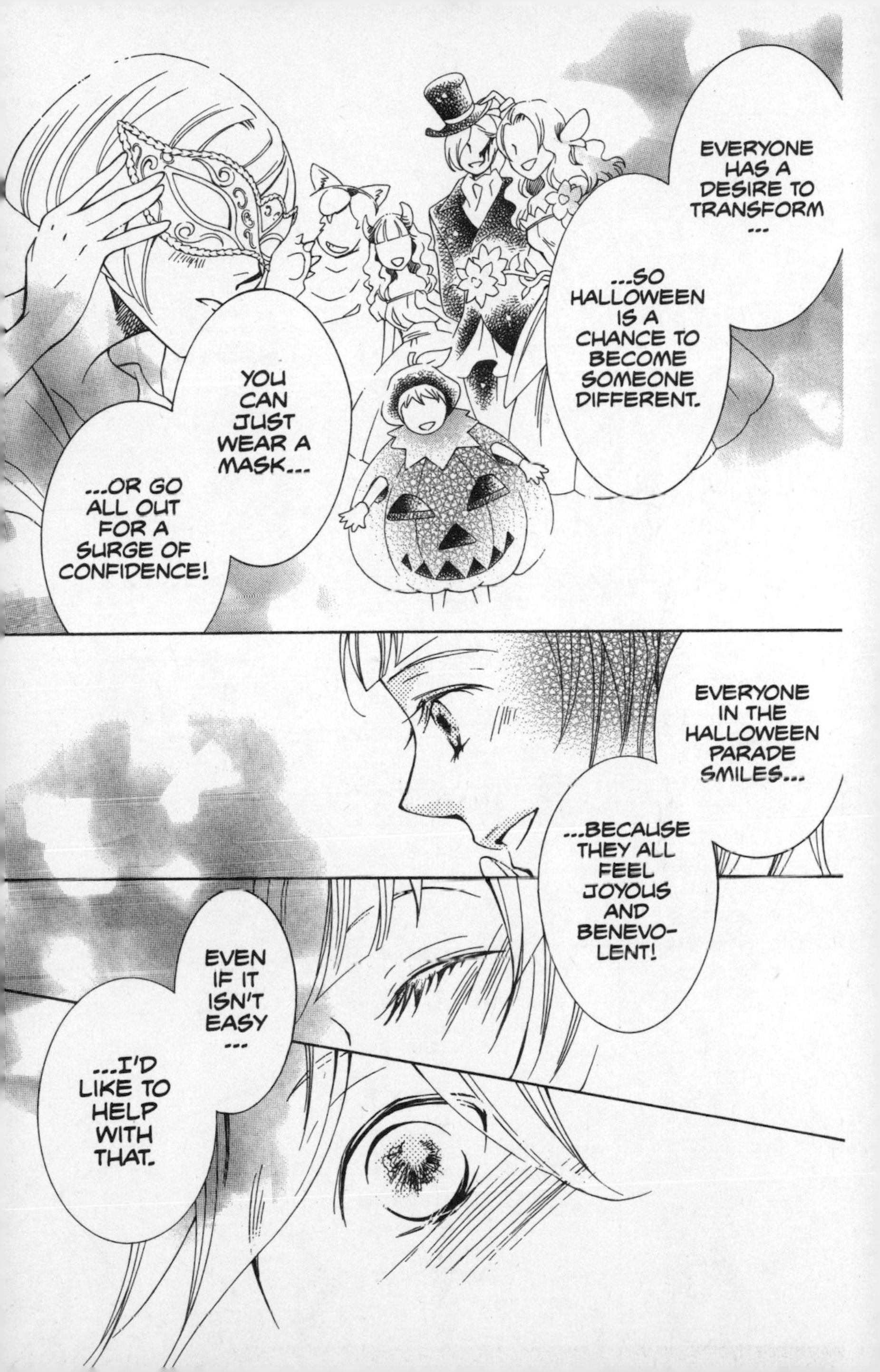
EVERYONE HAS A DESIRE TO TRANSFORM...
...SO HALLOWEEN IS A CHANCE TO BECOME SOMEONE DIFFERENT.
YOU CAN JUST WEAR A MASK...
...OR GO ALL OUT FOR A SURGE OF CONFIDENCE!
EVERYONE IN THE HALLOWEEN PARADE SMILES...
...BECAUSE THEY ALL FEEL JOYOUS AND BENEVO-LENT!
EVEN IF IT ISN'T EASY...
...I'D LIKE TO HELP WITH THAT.

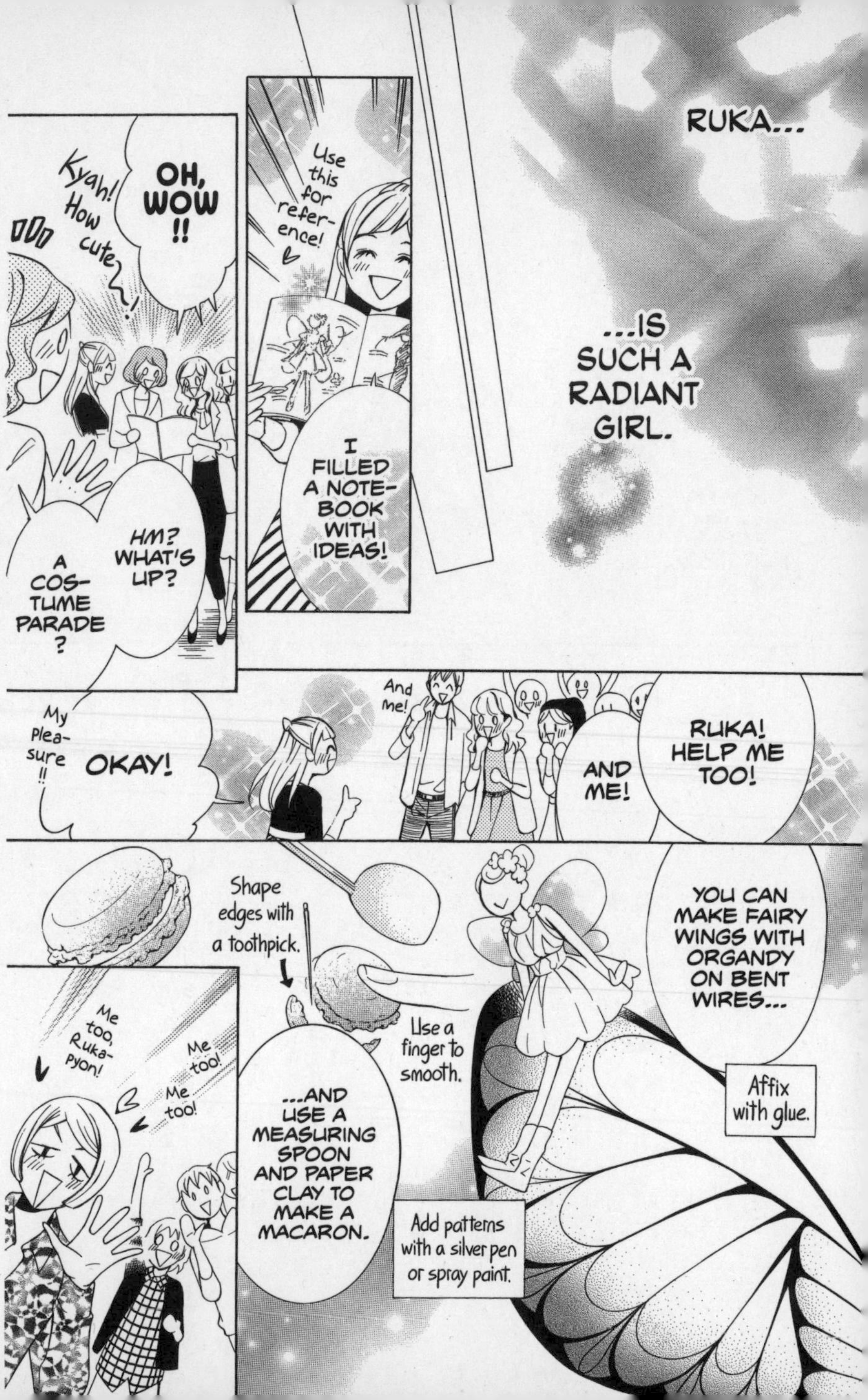
RUKA...
...IS SUCH A RADIANT GIRL.
Use this for reference!
I FILLED A NOTEBOOK WITH IDEAS!
OH, WOW!!
Kyah! How cute~!
HM? WHAT'S UP?
A COSTUME PARADE?
RUKA! HELP ME TOO!
AND ME!
And me!
OKAY!
My pleasure!!
YOU CAN MAKE FAIRY WINGS WITH ORGANDY ON BENT WIRES...
Affix with glue.
Add patterns with a silver pen or spray paint.
Shape edges with a toothpick.
Use a finger to smooth.
...AND USE A MEASURING SPOON AND PAPER CLAY TO MAKE A MACARON.
Me too!
Me too, Ruka-pyon!
Me too!

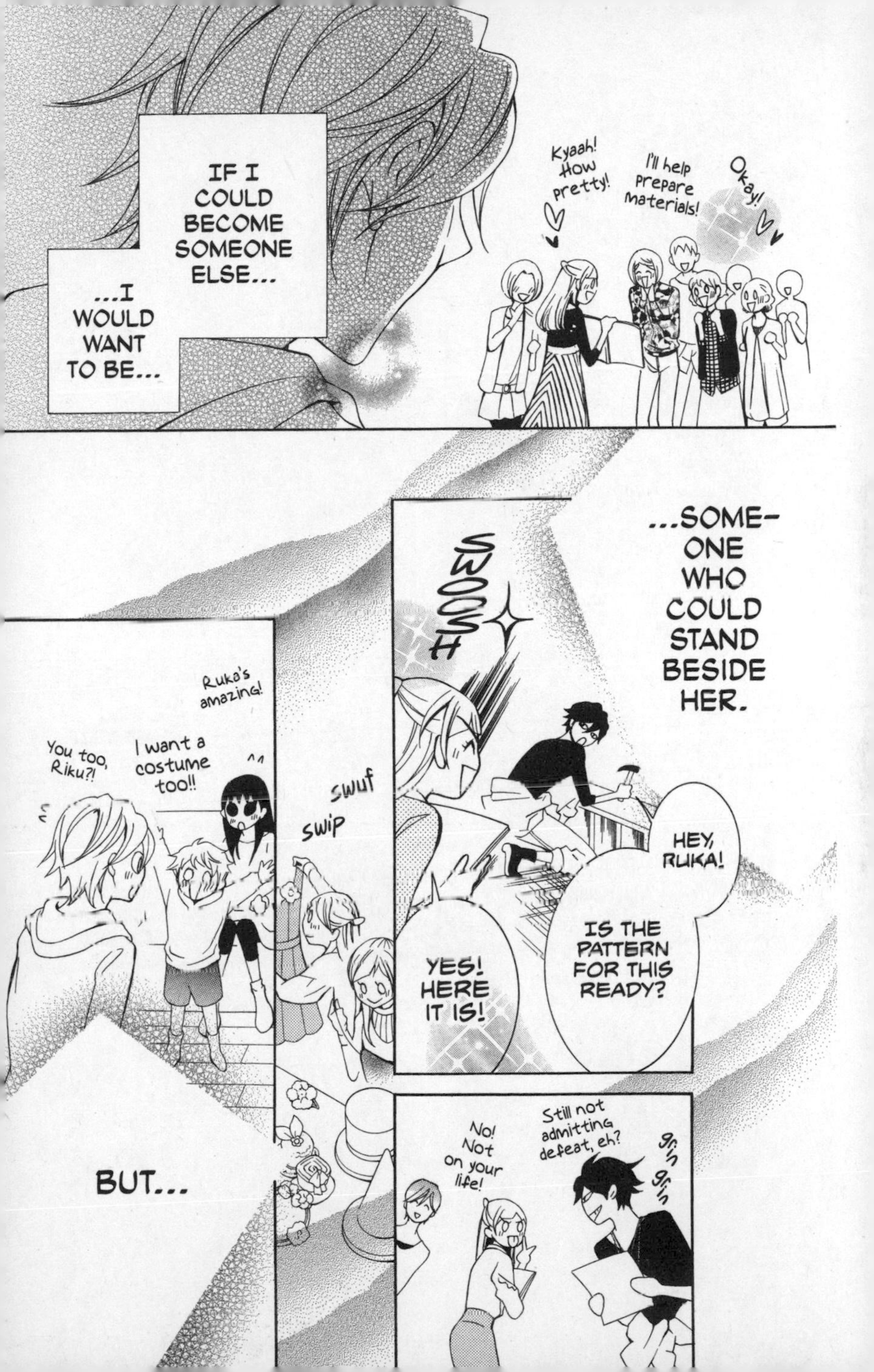
Okay!
I'll help prepare materials!
Kyaah! How pretty!
IF I COULD BECOME SOMEONE ELSE...
...I WOULD WANT TO BE...
...SOME-ONE WHO COULD STAND BESIDE HER.
SWOOSH
HEY, RUKA!
IS THE PATTERN FOR THIS READY?
YES! HERE IT IS!
Ruka's amazing!
swuf
swip
I want a costume too!!
You too, Riku?!
grin grin
Still not admitting defeat, eh?
No! Not on your life!
BUT...

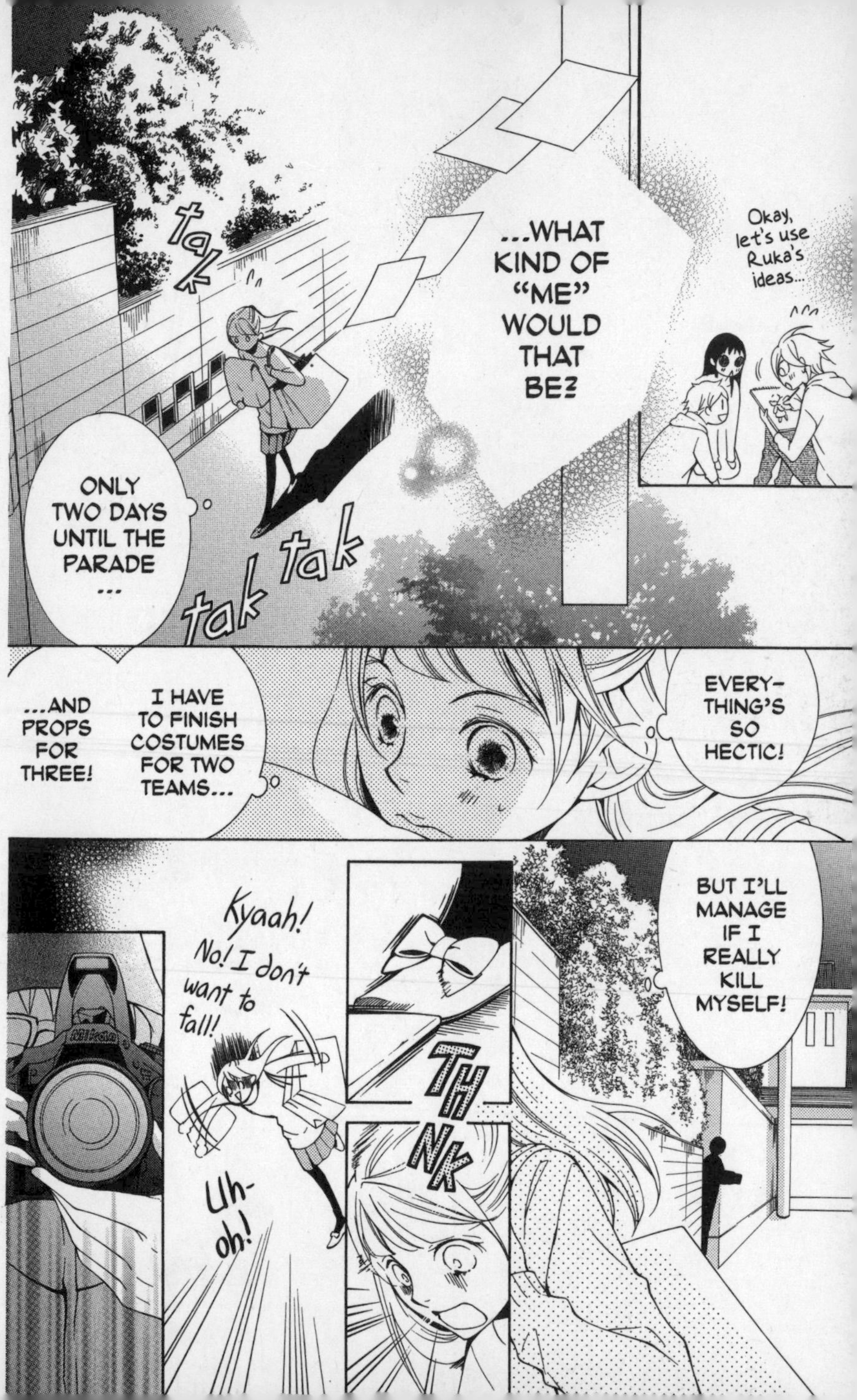
Okay, let's use Ruka's ideas...
...WHAT KIND OF "ME" WOULD THAT BE?
tak
ONLY TWO DAYS UNTIL THE PARADE ...
tak tak
EVERY-THING'S SO HECTIC!
I HAVE TO FINISH COSTUMES FOR TWO TEAMS...
...AND PROPS FOR THREE!
BUT I'LL MANAGE IF I REALLY KILL MYSELF!
THNK
Kyaah! No! I don't want to fall!
Uh-oh!

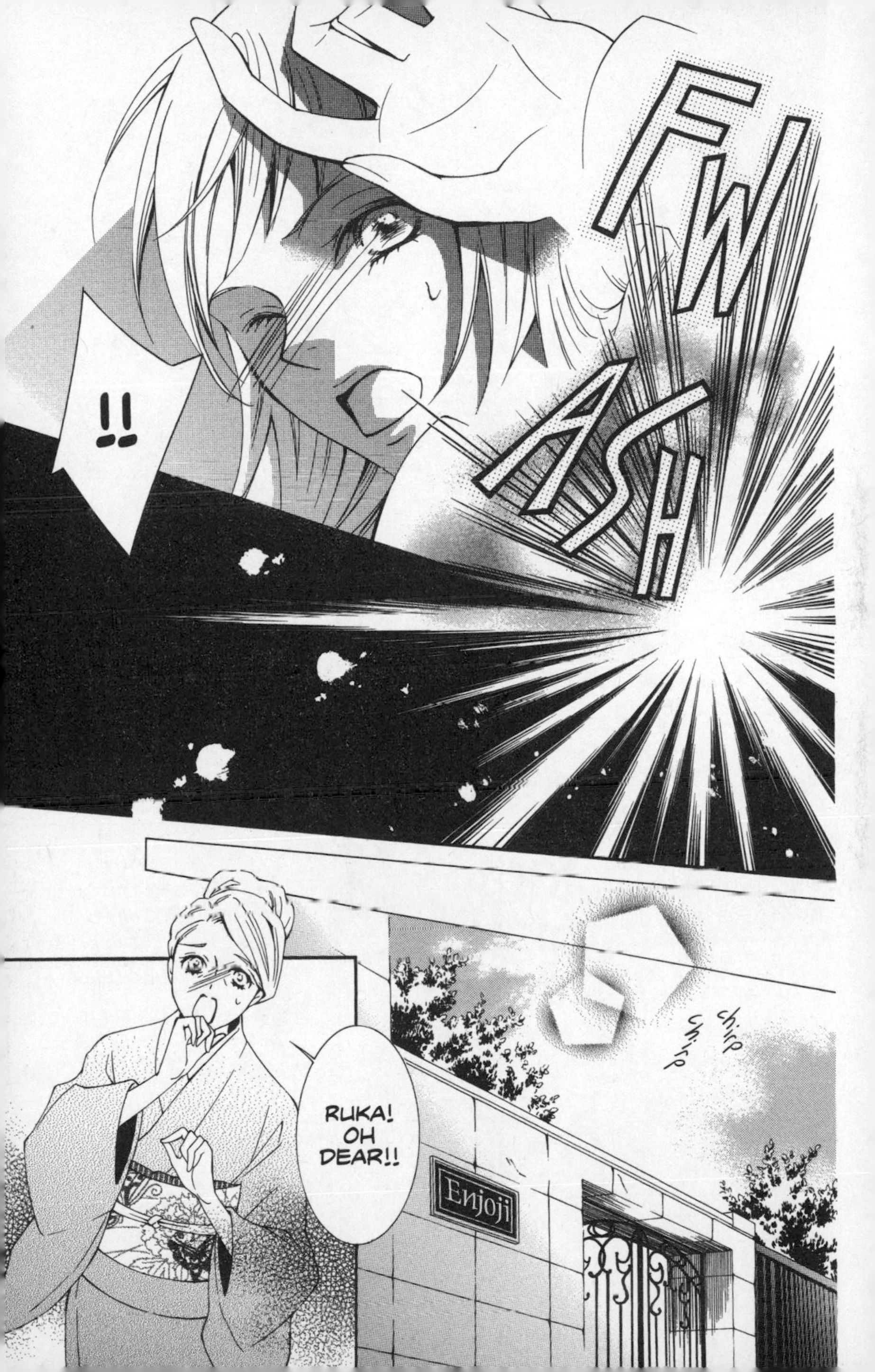
FWASH
!!
chirp chirp
RUKA! OH DEAR!!
Enjoji

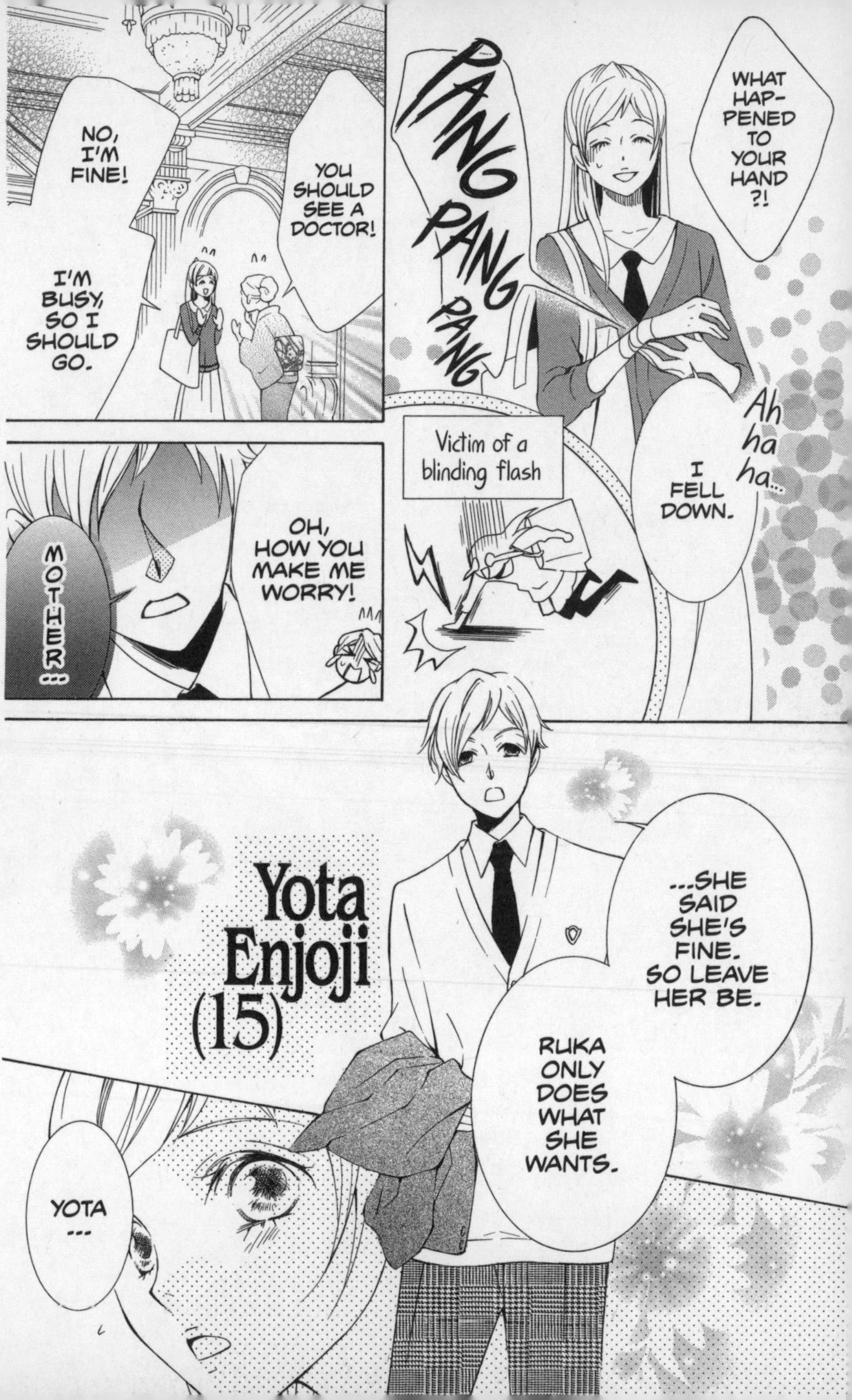
WHAT HAP-PENED TO YOUR HAND?!
PANG PANG PANG
Ah ha ha...
I FELL DOWN.
Victim of a blinding flash
YOU SHOULD SEE A DOCTOR!
NO, I'M FINE!
I'M BUSY, SO I SHOULD GO.
OH, HOW YOU MAKE ME WORRY!
MOTHER...!!
...SHE SAID SHE'S FINE. SO LEAVE HER BE.
RUKA ONLY DOES WHAT SHE WANTS.
Yota Enjoji (15)
YOTA...

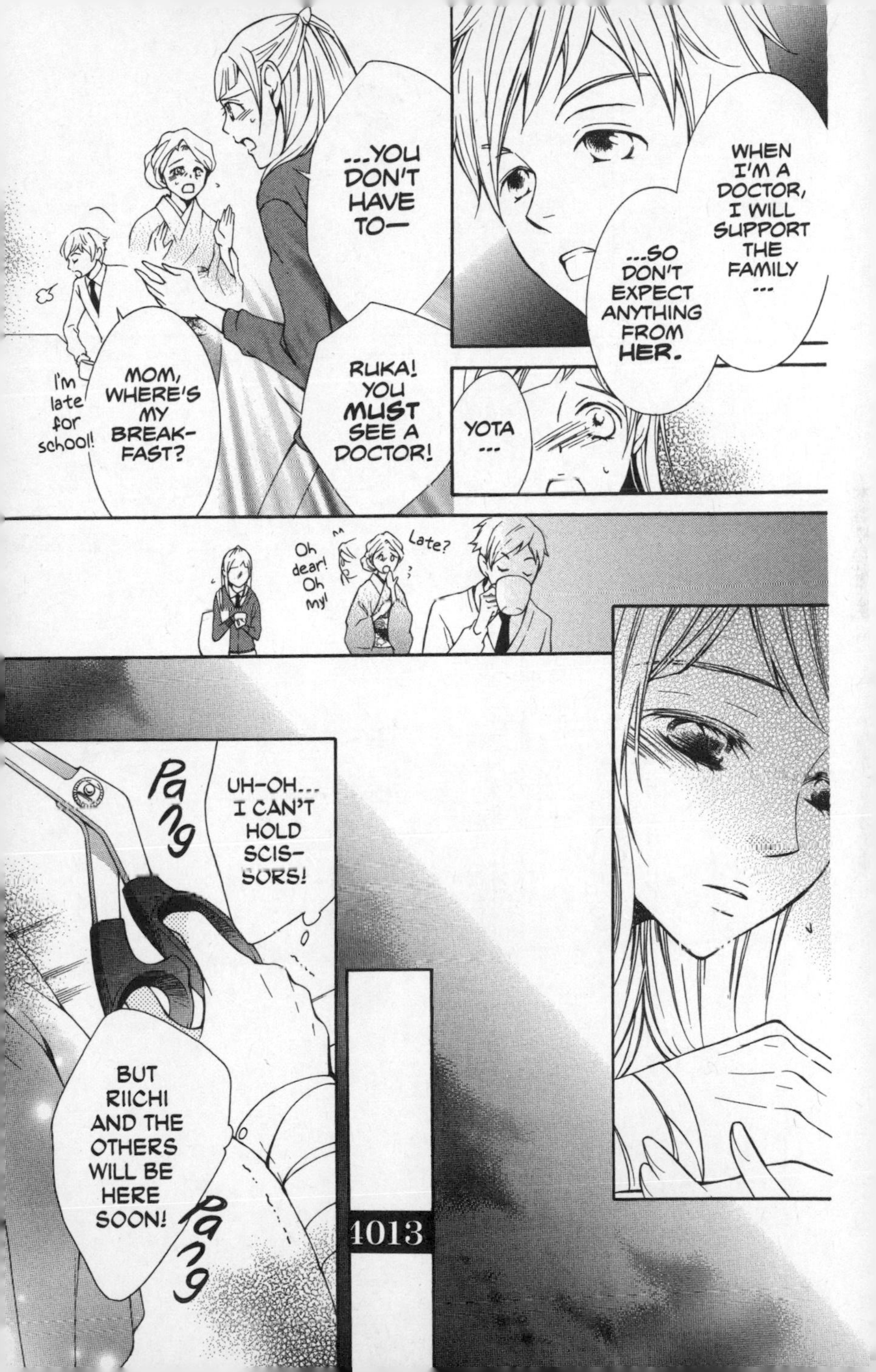
WHEN I'M A DOCTOR, I WILL SUPPORT THE FAMILY...
...SO DON'T EXPECT ANYTHING FROM HER.
YOTA...
...YOU DON'T HAVE TO—
RUKA! YOU MUST SEE A DOCTOR!
MOM, WHERE'S MY BREAK-FAST?
I'm late for school!
Late?
Oh dear! Oh my!
UH-OH... I CAN'T HOLD SCIS-SORS!
Pang
BUT RIICHI AND THE OTHERS WILL BE HERE SOON!
Pang
4013

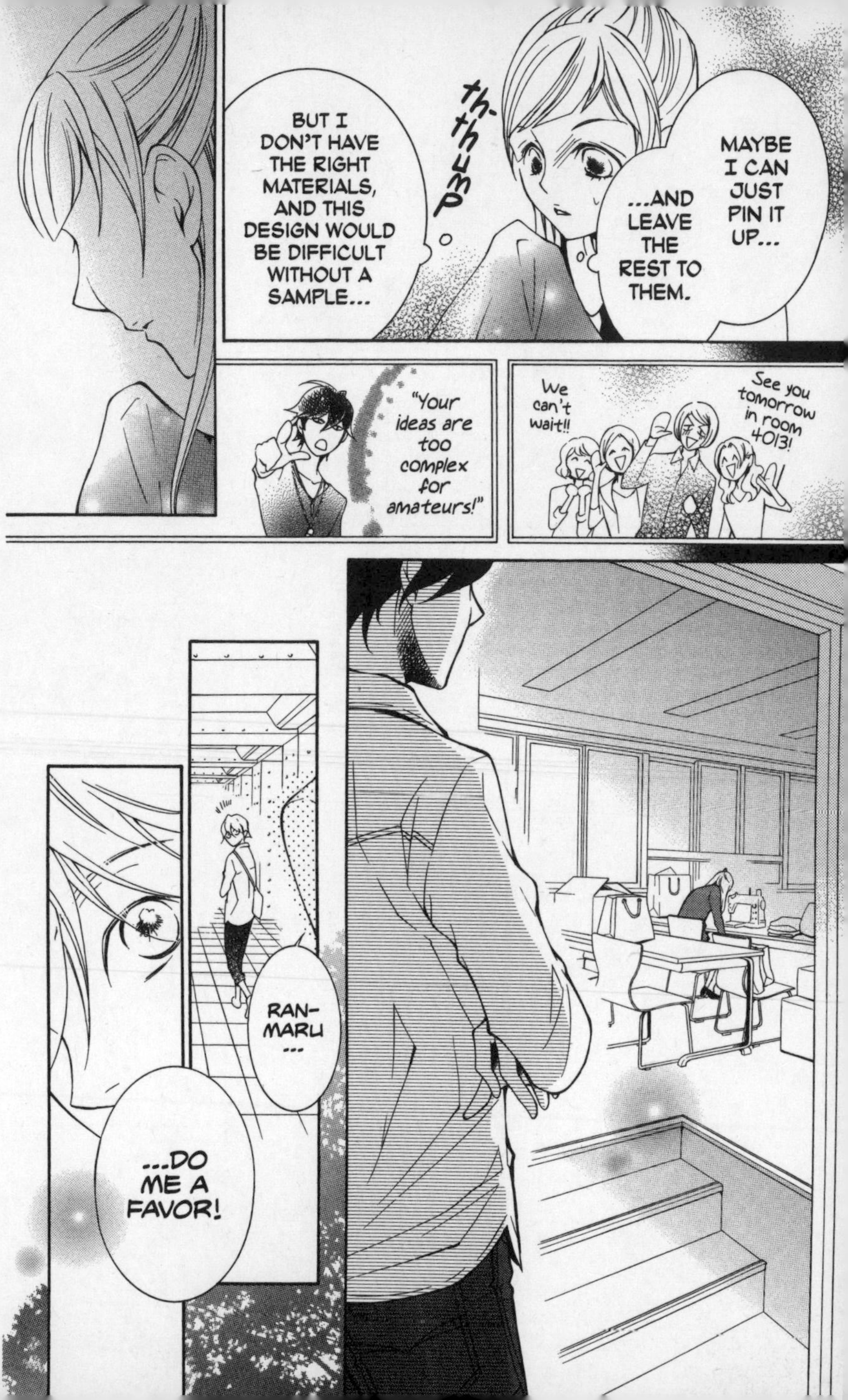
MAYBE I CAN JUST PIN IT UP...
...AND LEAVE THE REST TO THEM.
th-thump
BUT I DON'T HAVE THE RIGHT MATERIALS, AND THIS DESIGN WOULD BE DIFFICULT WITHOUT A SAMPLE...
See you tomorrow in room 4013!
We can't wait!!
"Your ideas are too complex for amateurs!"
RAN-MARU...
...DO ME A FAVOR!

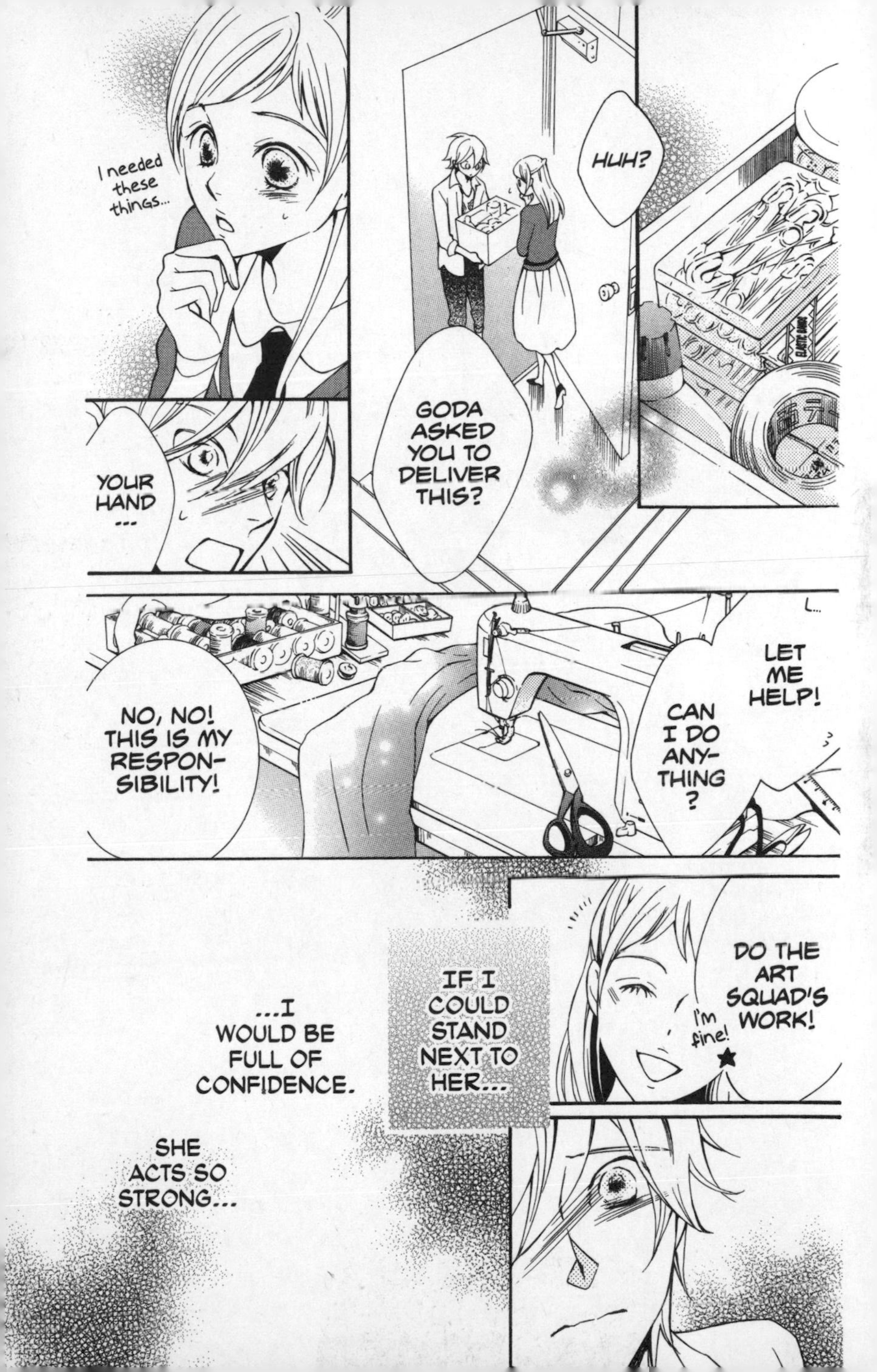
HUH?
GODA ASKED YOU TO DELIVER THIS?
I needed these things...
YOUR HAND ...
L...
LET ME HELP!
CAN I DO ANY-THING?
NO, NO! THIS IS MY RESPON-SIBILITY!
DO THE ART SQUAD'S WORK!
I'm fine!
IF I COULD STAND NEXT TO HER...
...I WOULD BE FULL OF CONFIDENCE.
SHE ACTS SO STRONG...

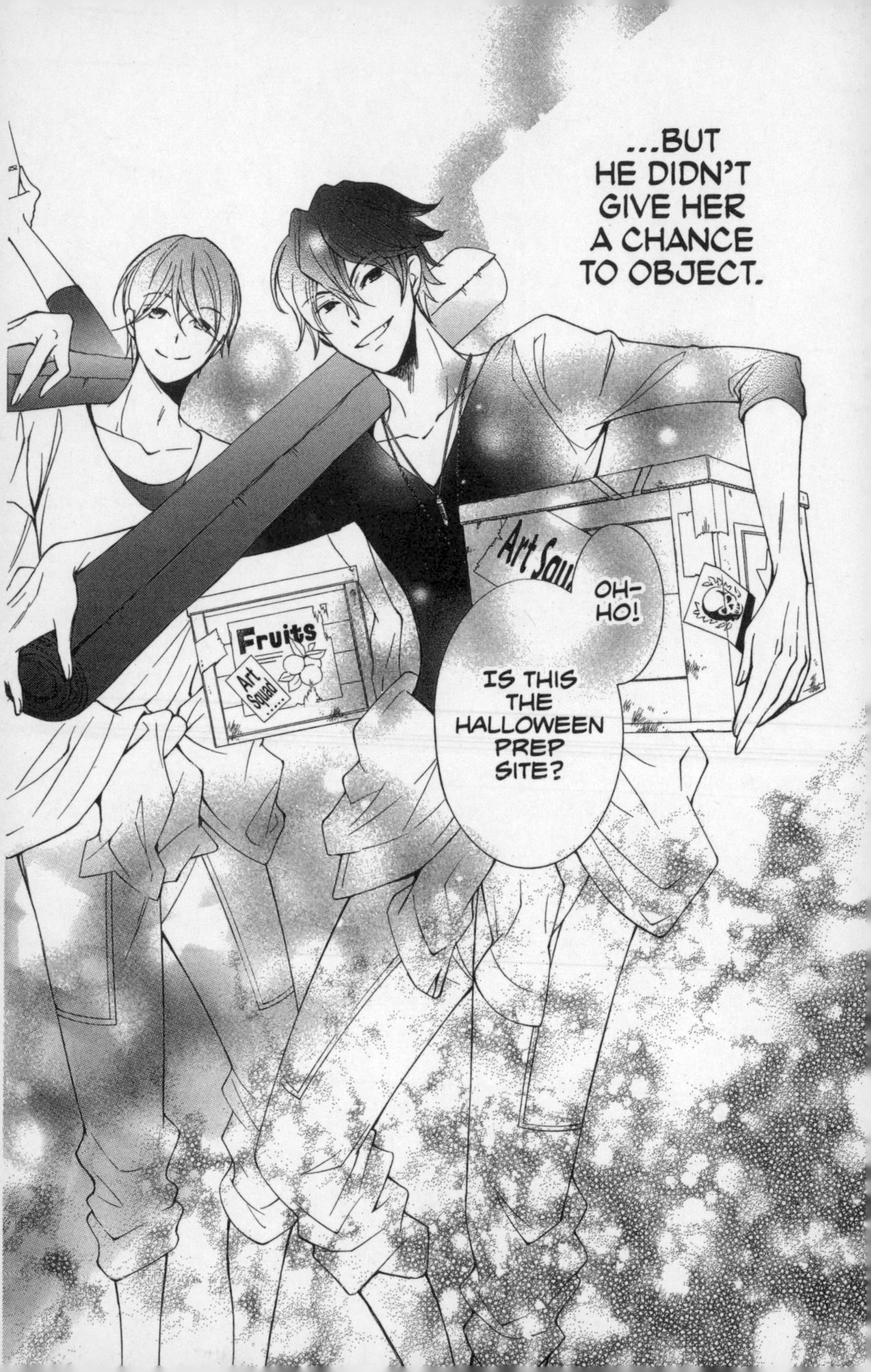
...BUT HE DIDN'T GIVE HER A CHANCE TO OBJECT.
OH-HO!
IS THIS THE HALLOWEEN PREP SITE?
Fruits
Art Squad

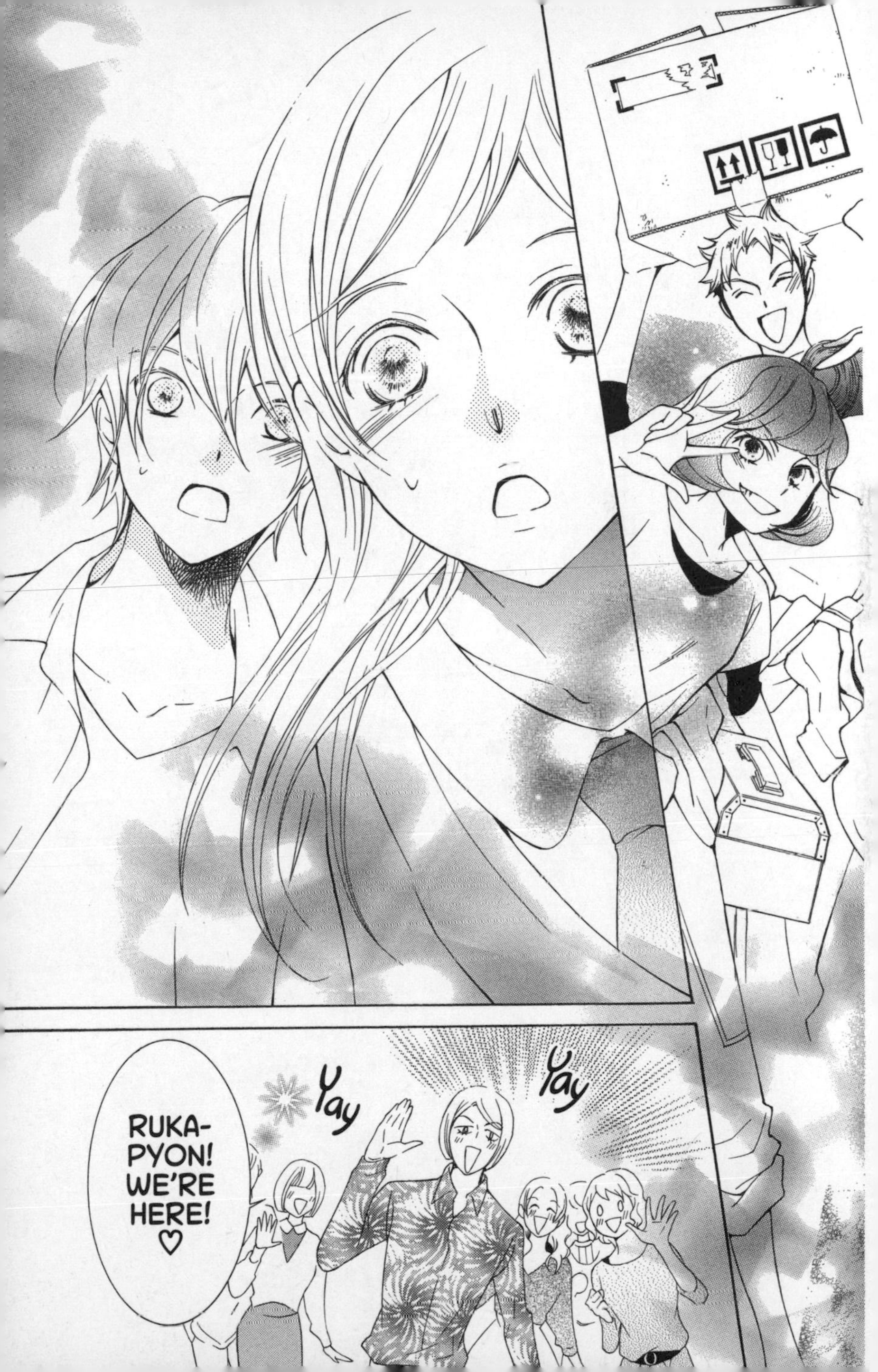
Yay
Yay
RUKA-PYON! WE'RE HERE! ♡

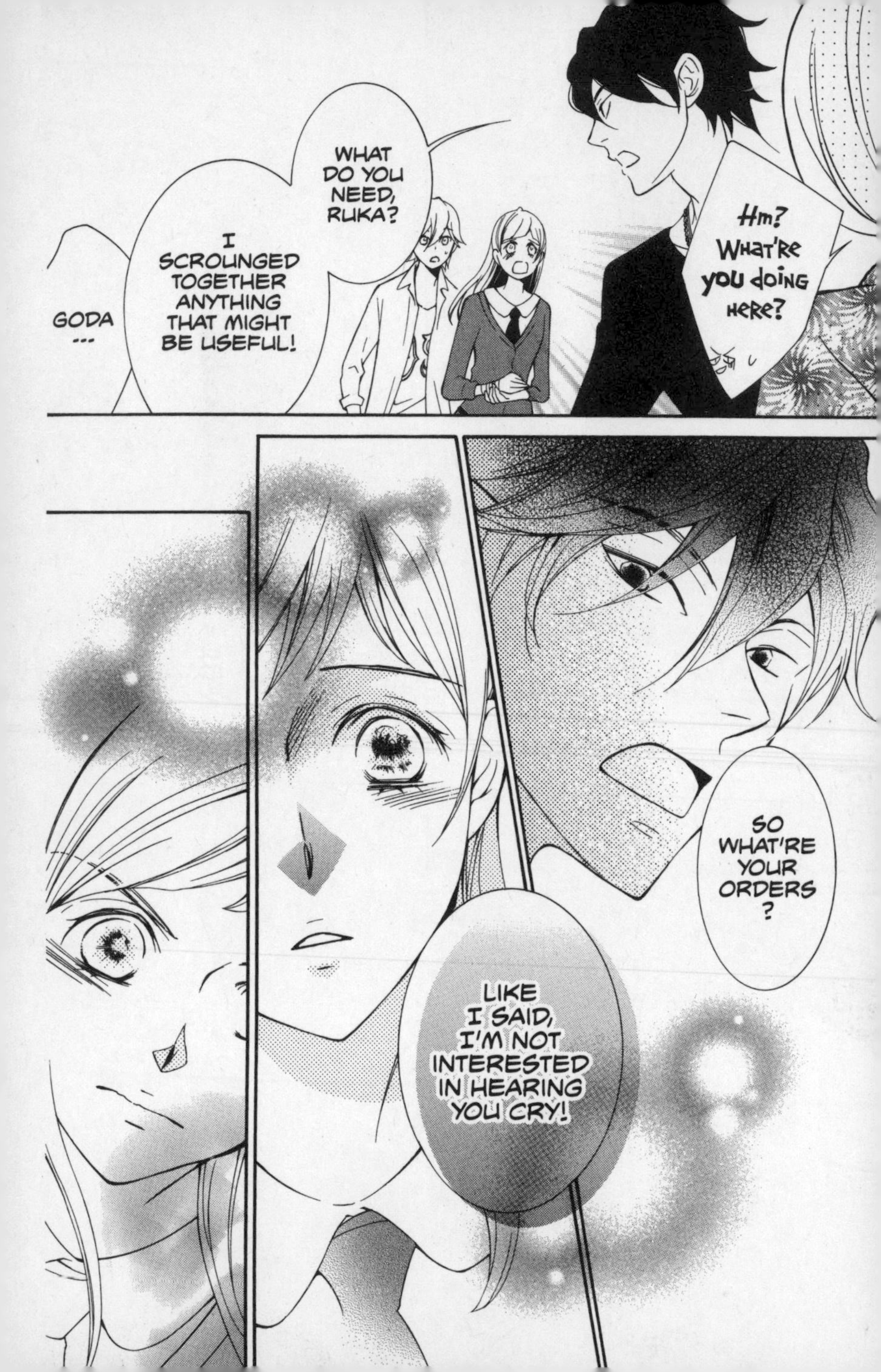
Hm? What're you doing here?
WHAT DO YOU NEED, RUKA?
I SCROUNGED TOGETHER ANYTHING THAT MIGHT BE USEFUL!
GODA...
SO WHAT'RE YOUR ORDERS?
LIKE I SAID, I'M NOT INTERESTED IN HEARING YOU CRY!

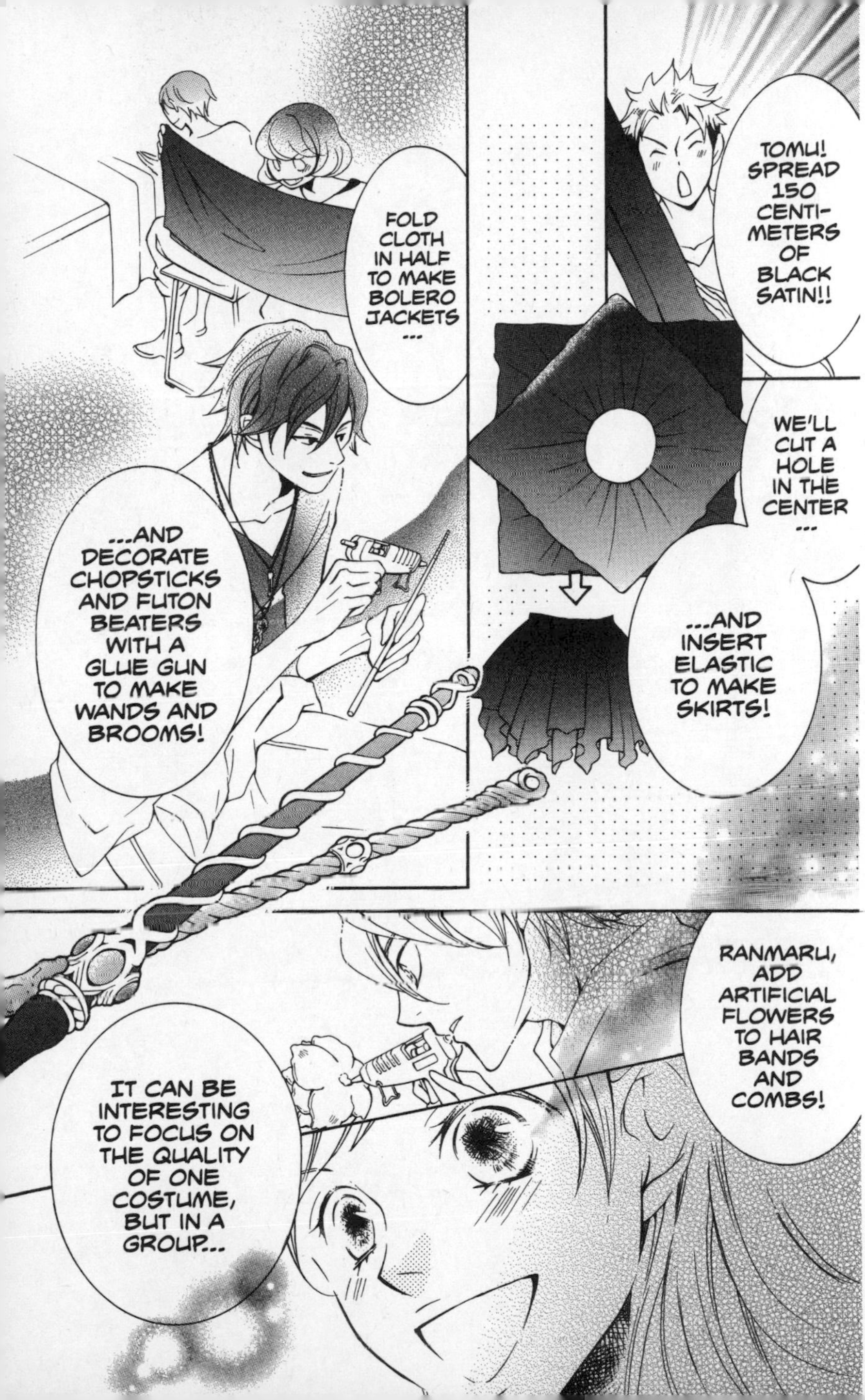
TOMU! SPREAD 150 CENTI-METERS OF BLACK SATIN!!
WE'LL CUT A HOLE IN THE CENTER...
...AND INSERT ELASTIC TO MAKE SKIRTS!
FOLD CLOTH IN HALF TO MAKE BOLERO JACKETS...
...AND DECORATE CHOPSTICKS AND FUTON BEATERS WITH A GLUE GUN TO MAKE WANDS AND BROOMS!
RANMARU, ADD ARTIFICIAL FLOWERS TO HAIR BANDS AND COMBS!
IT CAN BE INTERESTING TO FOCUS ON THE QUALITY OF ONE COSTUME, BUT IN A GROUP...

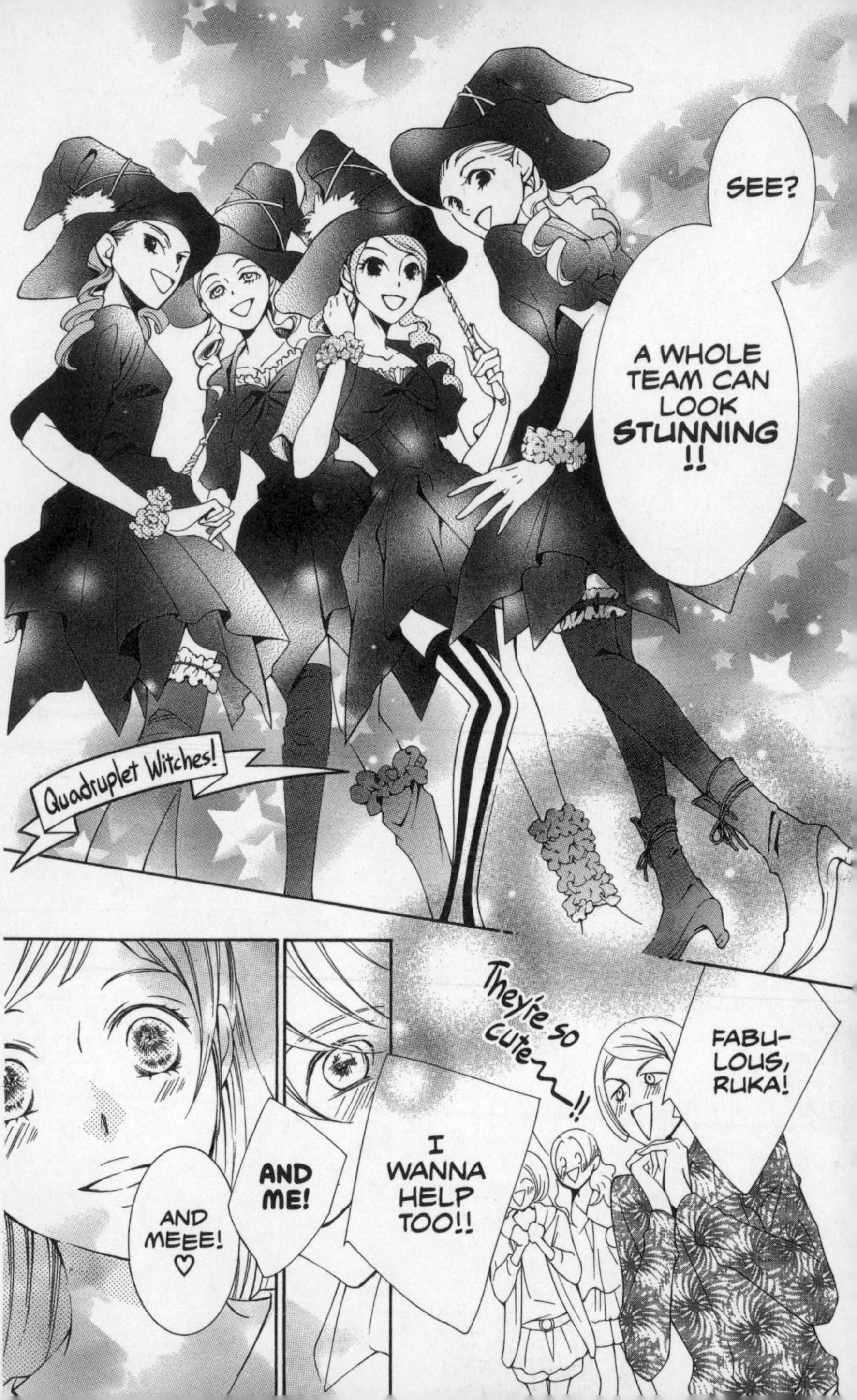
SEE?
A WHOLE TEAM CAN LOOK STUNNING !!
Quadruplet Witches!
FABU-LOUS, RUKA!
They're so cute~!!
I WANNA HELP TOO!!
AND ME!
AND MEEE! ♡

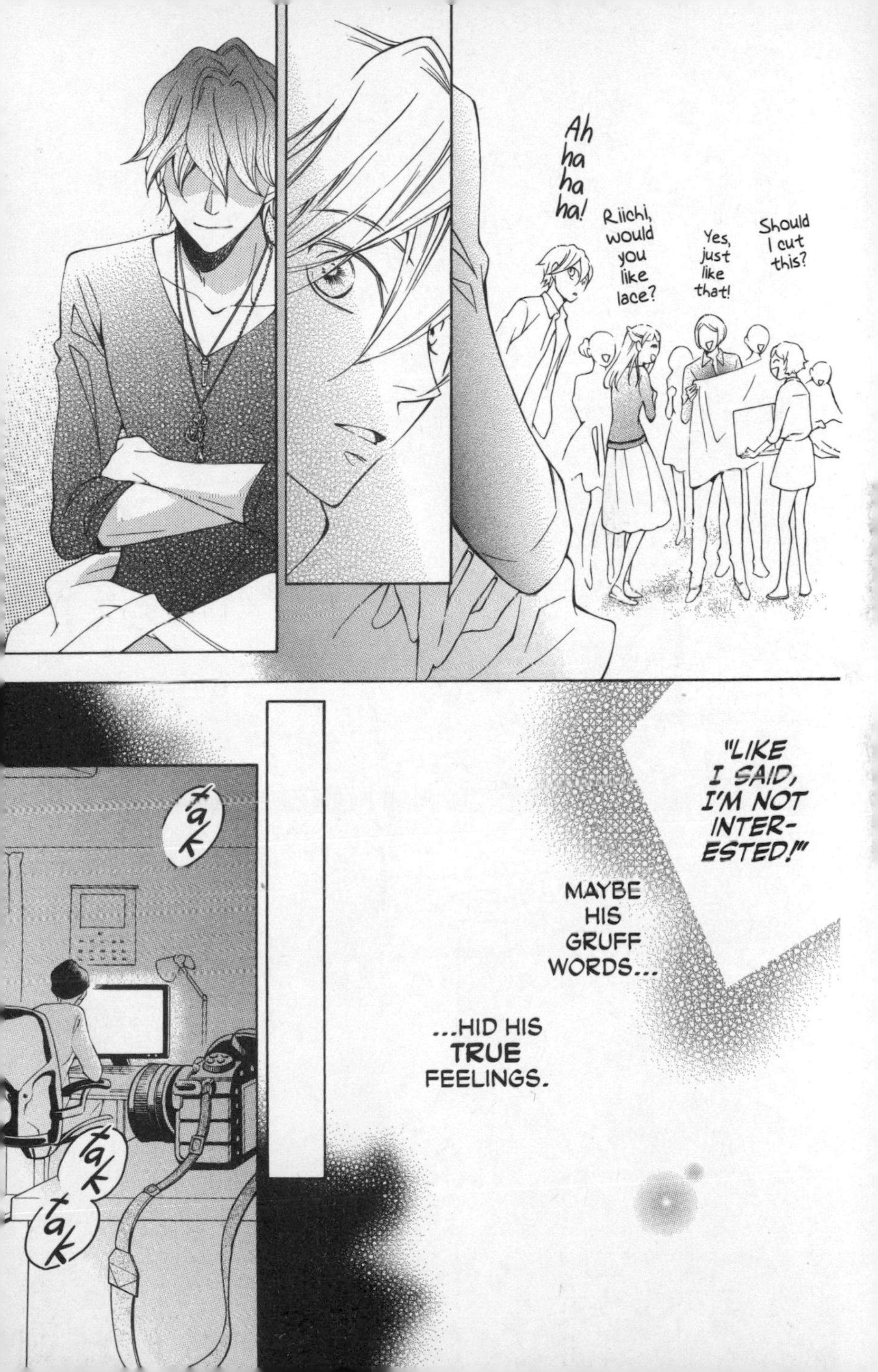
Should I cut this?
Yes, just like that!
Riichi, would you like lace?
Ah ha ha ha!
"LIKE I SAID, I'M NOT INTER-ESTED!"
MAYBE HIS GRUFF WORDS...
...HID HIS TRUE FEELINGS.
tak
tak tak

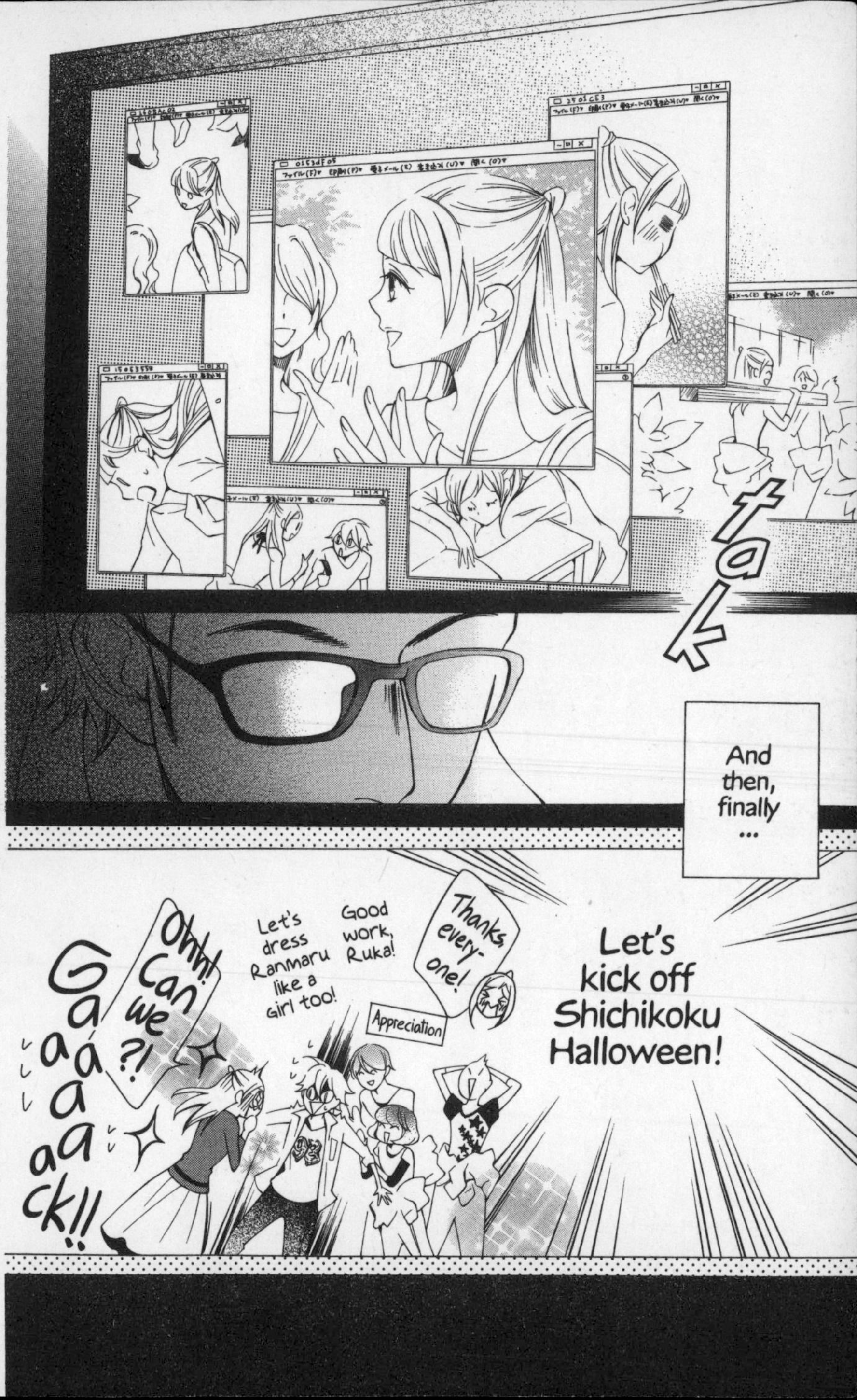
tak
And then, finally ...
Let's kick off Shichikoku Halloween!
Thanks, every-one!
Appreciation
Good work, Ruka!
Let's dress Ranmaru like a girl too!
Ohh! Can we?!
Gaaaaaack!!

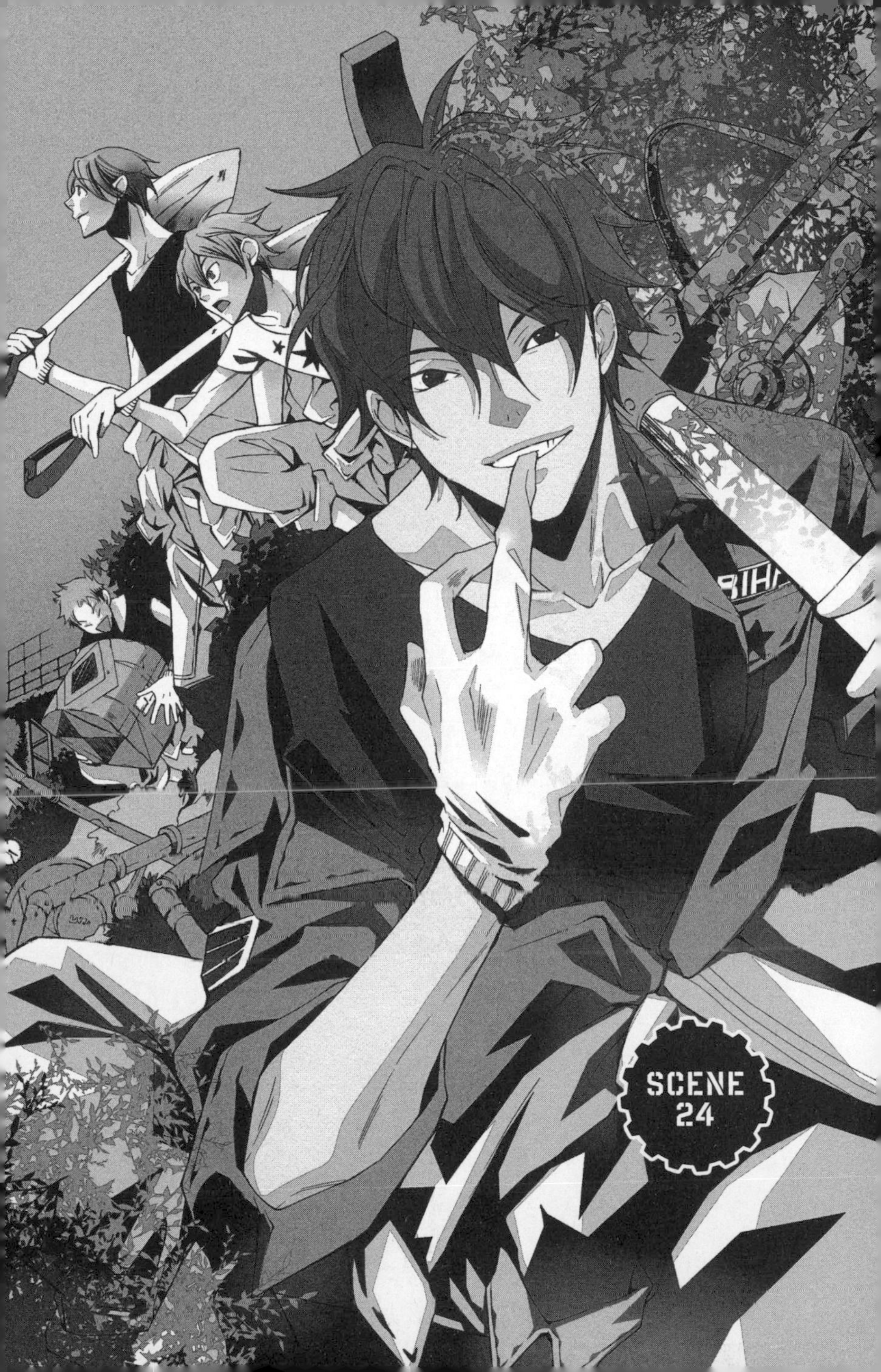
SCENE
24

Behind
the
Scenes
!!

5

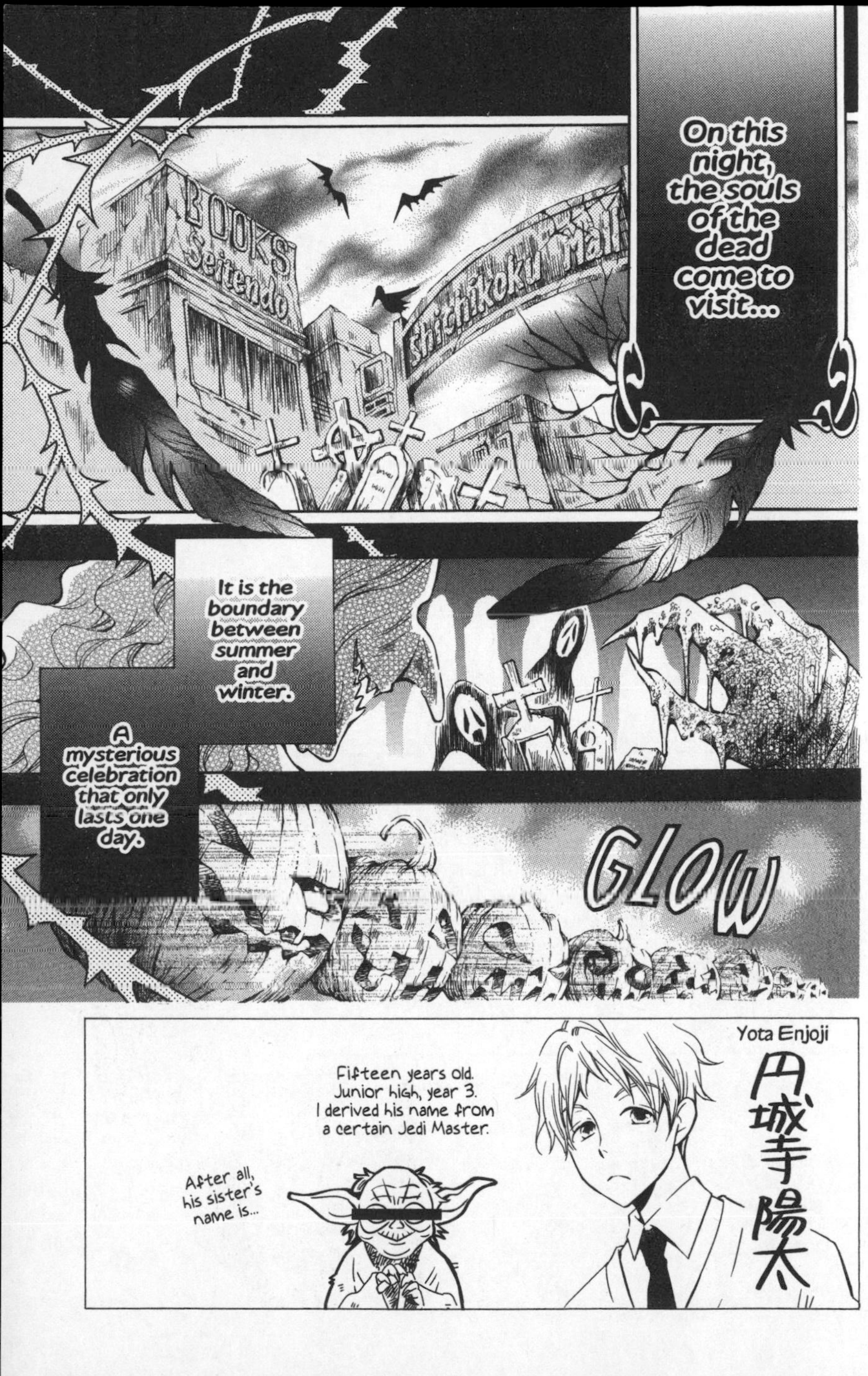
On this night, the souls of the dead come to visit...
Shichikoku Mall
BOOKS Seitendo
It is the boundary between summer and winter.
A mysterious celebration that only lasts one day.
GLOW
Yota Enjoji
円城寺陽太
Fifteen years old. Junior high, year 3. I derived his name from a certain Jedi Master.
After all, his sister's name is...

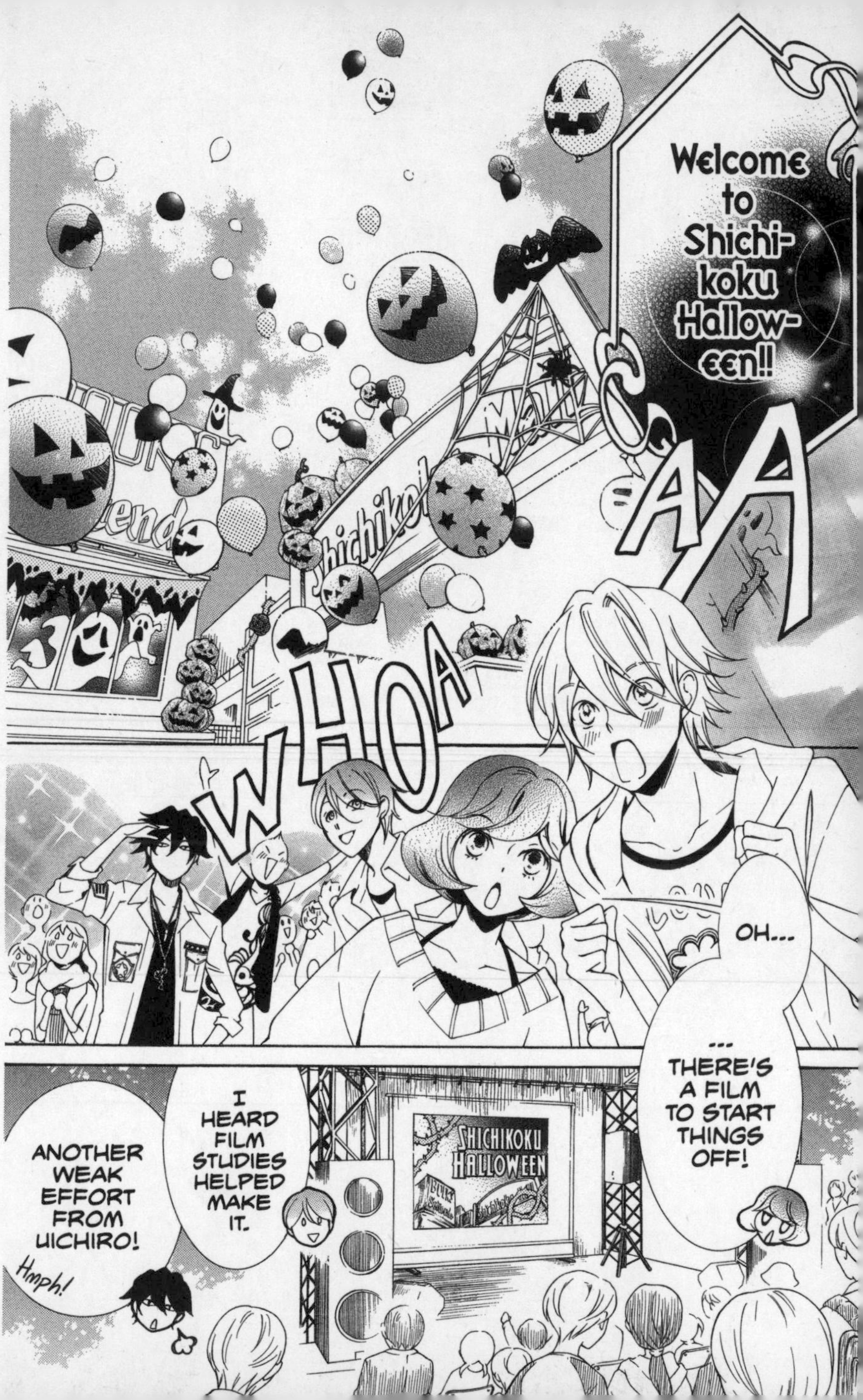
Welcome to Shichikoku Halloween!!
Shichikoku
WHOA
AA
OH...
...THERE'S A FILM TO START THINGS OFF!
SHICHIKOKU HALLOWEEN
I HEARD FILM STUDIES HELPED MAKE IT.
ANOTHER WEAK EFFORT FROM UICHIRO!
Hmph!

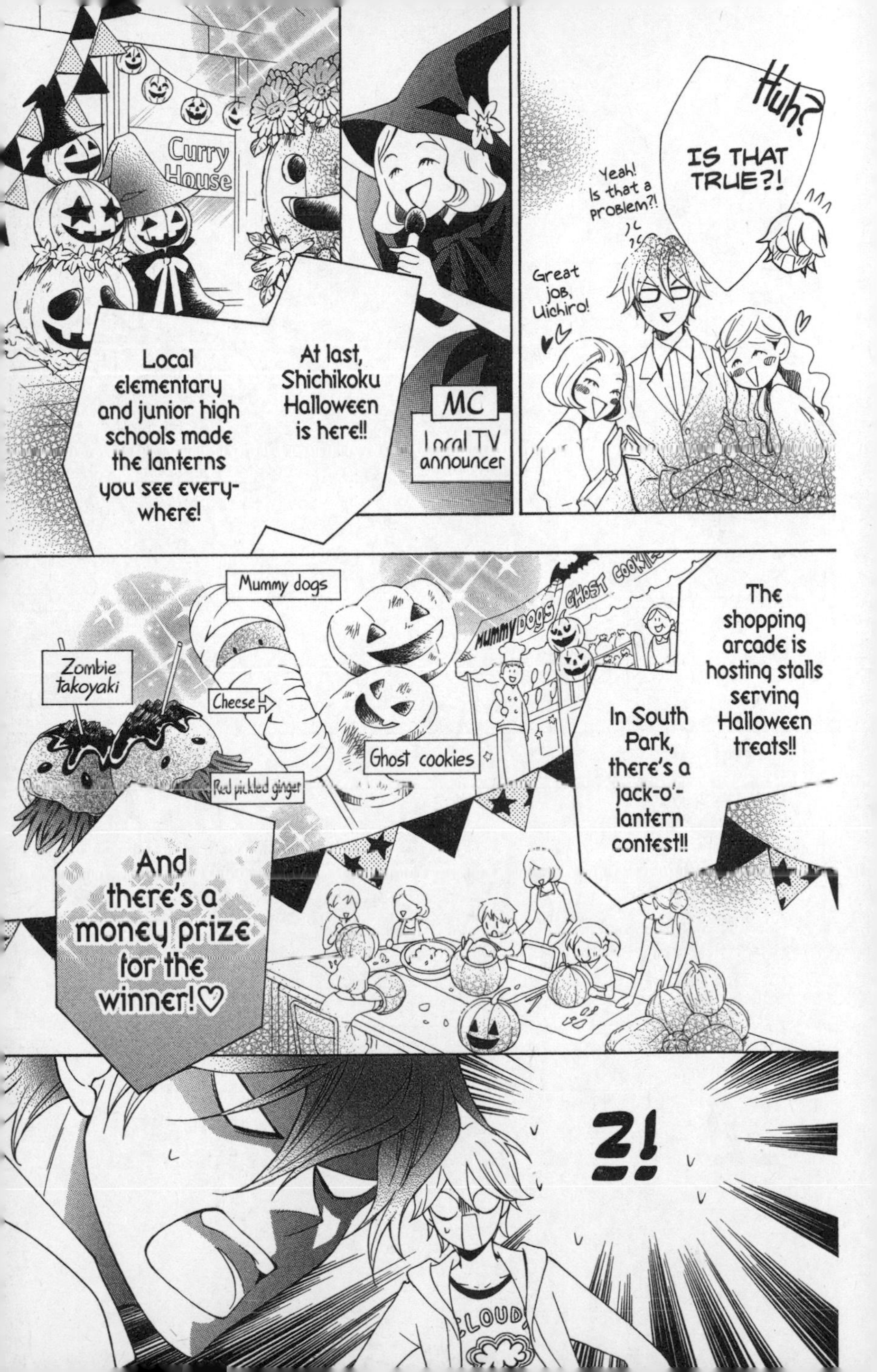
Huh?
IS THAT TRUE?!
Yeah! Is that a problem?!
Great job, Uichiro!
At last, Shichikoku Halloween is here!!
MC
Local TV announcer
Curry House
Local elementary and junior high schools made the lanterns you see every-where!
The shopping arcade is hosting stalls serving Halloween treats!!
MUMMY DOGS / GHOST COOKIES
Mummy dogs
Ghost cookies
Cheese
Zombie takoyaki
Red pickled ginger
In South Park, there's a jack-o'-lantern contest!!
And there's a money prize for the winner!♡
Z!
CLOUD

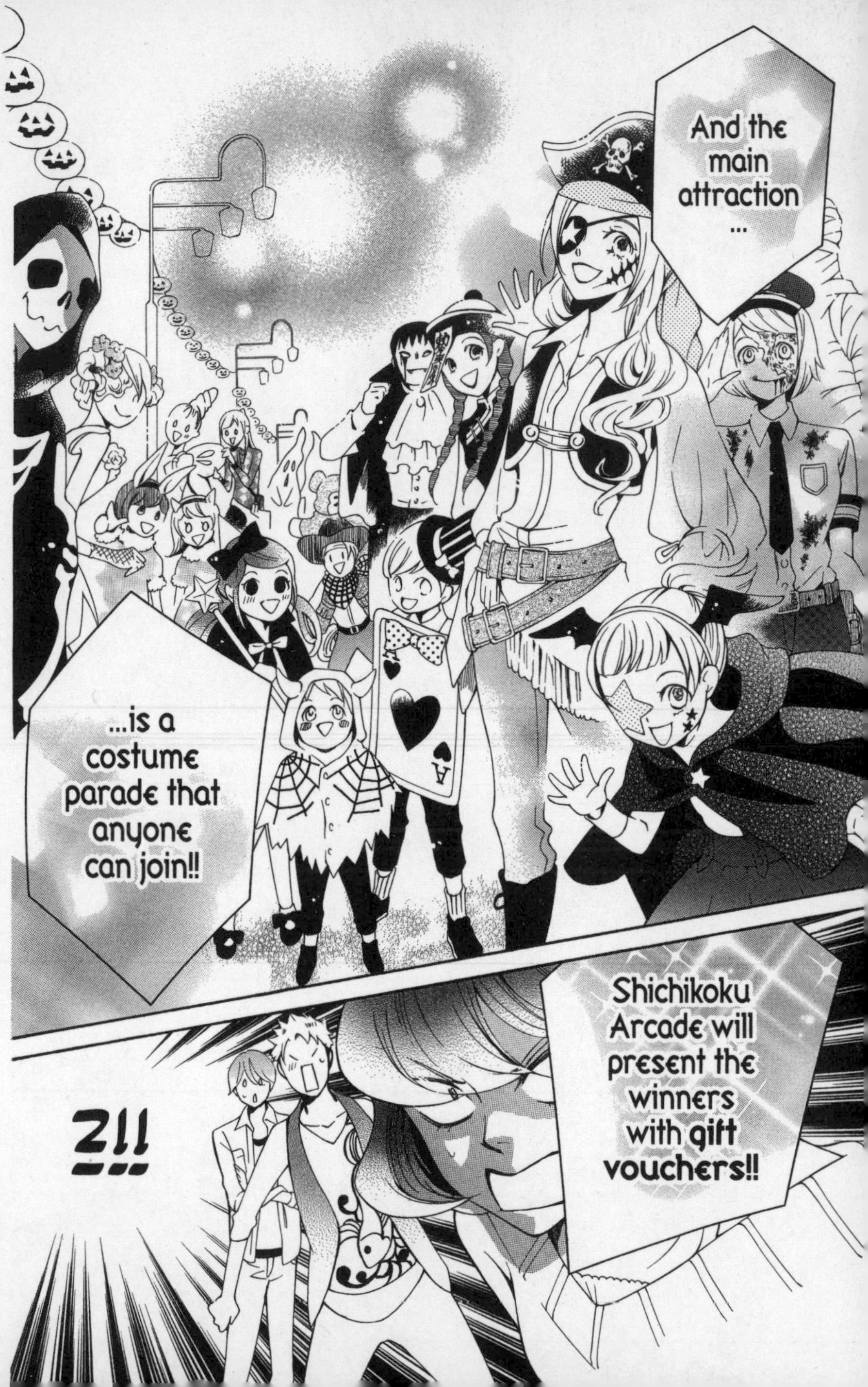
And the main attraction ...
...is a costume parade that anyone can join!!
Shichikoku Arcade will present the winners with gift vouchers!!
?!!

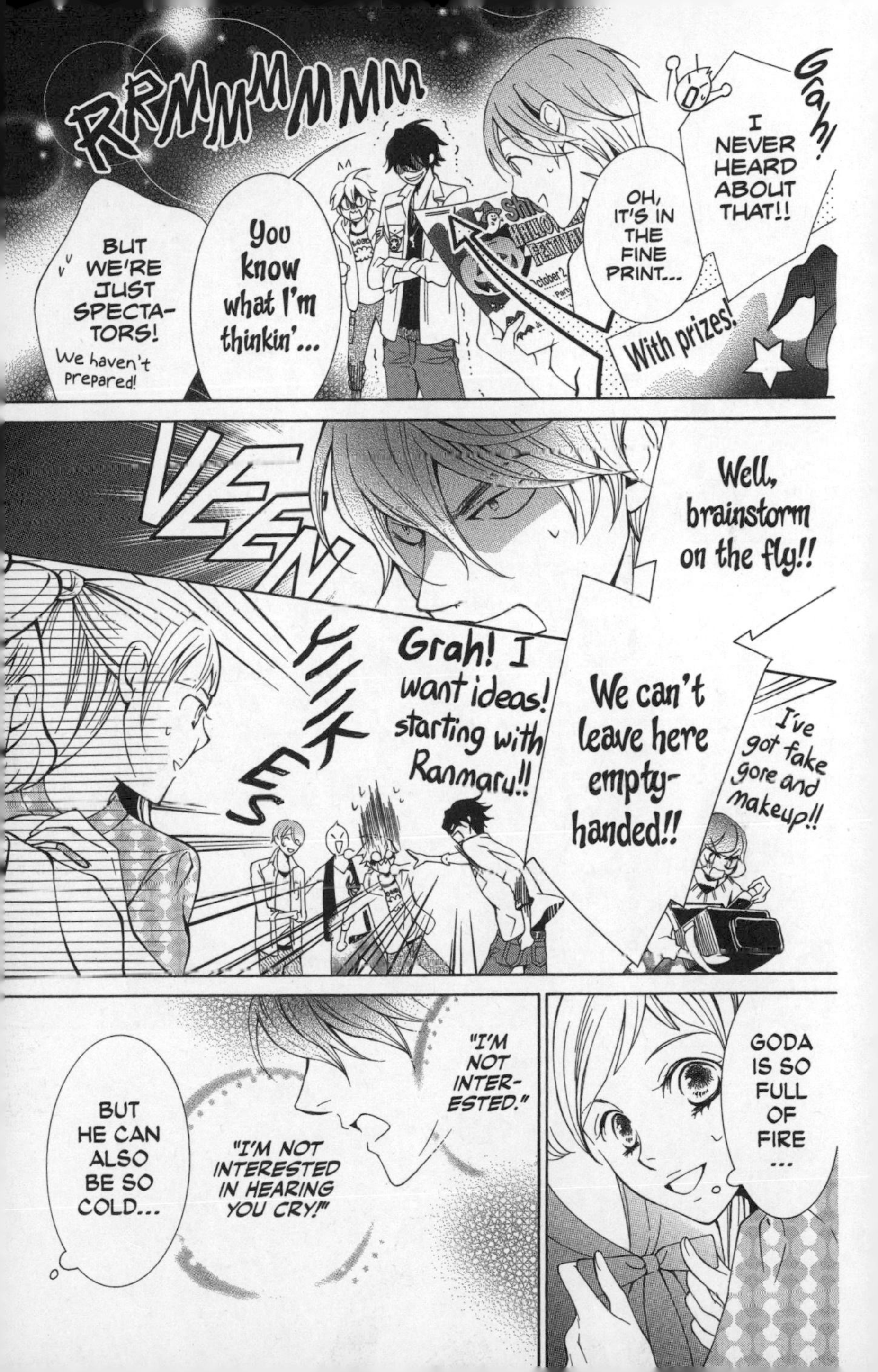

Grah!
I NEVER HEARD ABOUT THAT!!
With prizes!
OH, IT'S IN THE FINE PRINT...
You know what I'm thinkin'...
BUT WE'RE JUST SPECTATORS!
We haven't prepared!
RRMMMMMMM
Well, brainstorm on the fly!!
VEEN
I've got fake gore and makeup!!
We can't leave here empty-handed!!
Grah! I want ideas! starting with Ranmaru!!
YIIIKES
GODA IS SO FULL OF FIRE ...
"I'M NOT INTERESTED."
"I'M NOT INTERESTED IN HEARING YOU CRY!"
BUT HE CAN ALSO BE SO COLD...

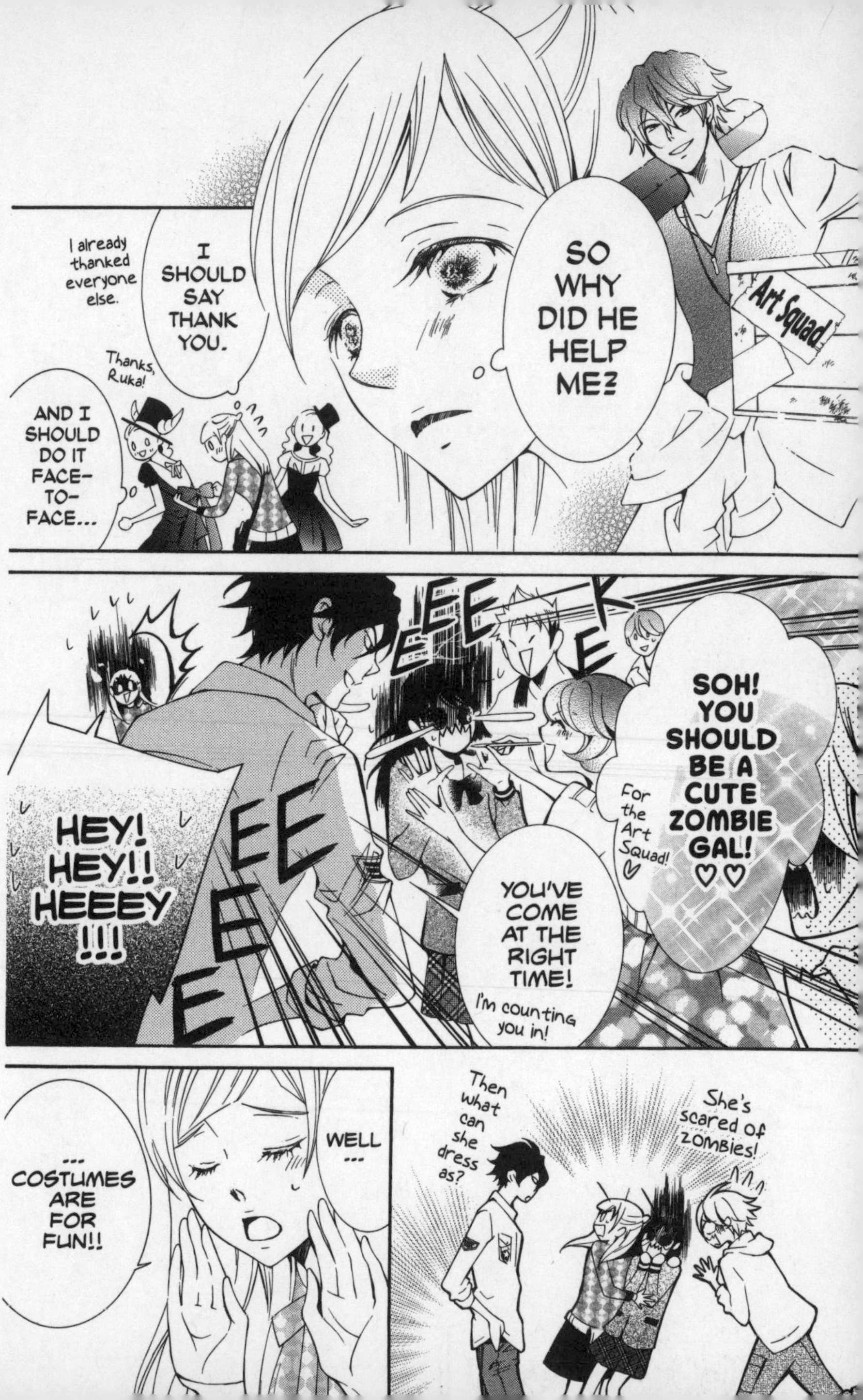
SO WHY DID HE HELP ME?
Art Squad
I SHOULD SAY THANK YOU.
I already thanked everyone else.
Thanks, Ruka!
AND I SHOULD DO IT FACE-TO-FACE...
SOH! YOU SHOULD BE A CUTE ZOMBIE GAL! ♡♡
For the Art Squad! ♡
YOU'VE COME AT THE RIGHT TIME!
I'm counting you in!
EEEEEEK
HEY! HEY!! HEEEY!!!
She's scared of zombies!
Then what can she dress as?
WELL...
...COSTUMES ARE FOR FUN!!

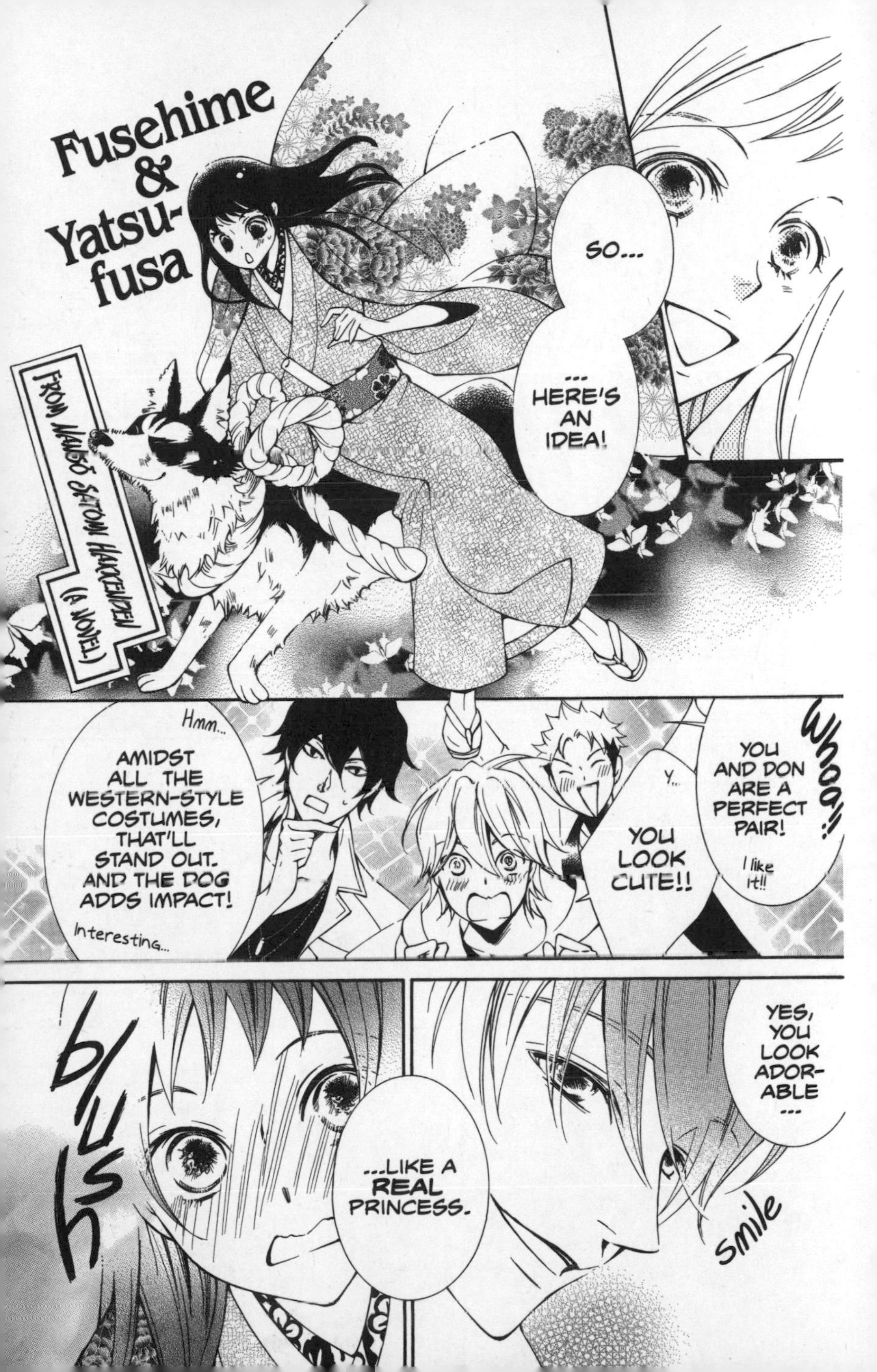
SO...
...HERE'S AN IDEA!
Fusehime & Yatsu-fusa
FROM NANSŌ SATOMI HAKKENDEN (A NOVEL)
Whoa!!
YOU AND DON ARE A PERFECT PAIR!
I like it!!
Y...
YOU LOOK CUTE!!
Hmm...
AMIDST ALL THE WESTERN-STYLE COSTUMES, THAT'LL STAND OUT. AND THE DOG ADDS IMPACT!
Interesting...
YES, YOU LOOK ADOR-ABLE...
smile
...LIKE A REAL PRINCESS.
blush

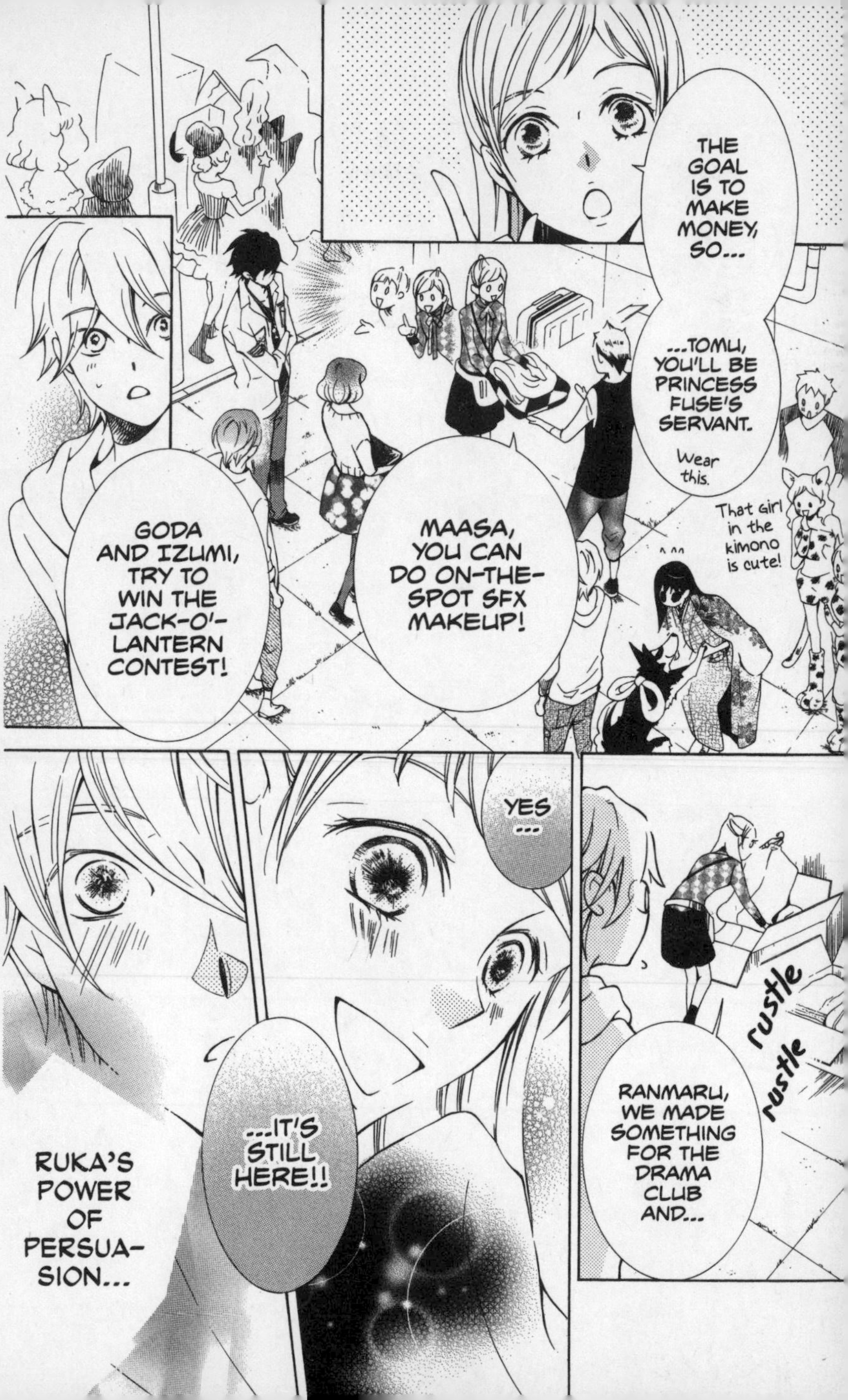

THE GOAL IS TO MAKE MONEY, SO...
...TOMU, YOU'LL BE PRINCESS FUSE'S SERVANT.
Wear this.
That Girl in the kimono is cute!
MAASA, YOU CAN DO ON-THE-SPOT SFX MAKEUP!
GODA AND IZUMI, TRY TO WIN THE JACK-O'-LANTERN CONTEST!
rustle
rustle
RANMARU, WE MADE SOMETHING FOR THE DRAMA CLUB AND...
YES...
...IT'S STILL HERE!!
RUKA'S POWER OF PERSUA-SION...

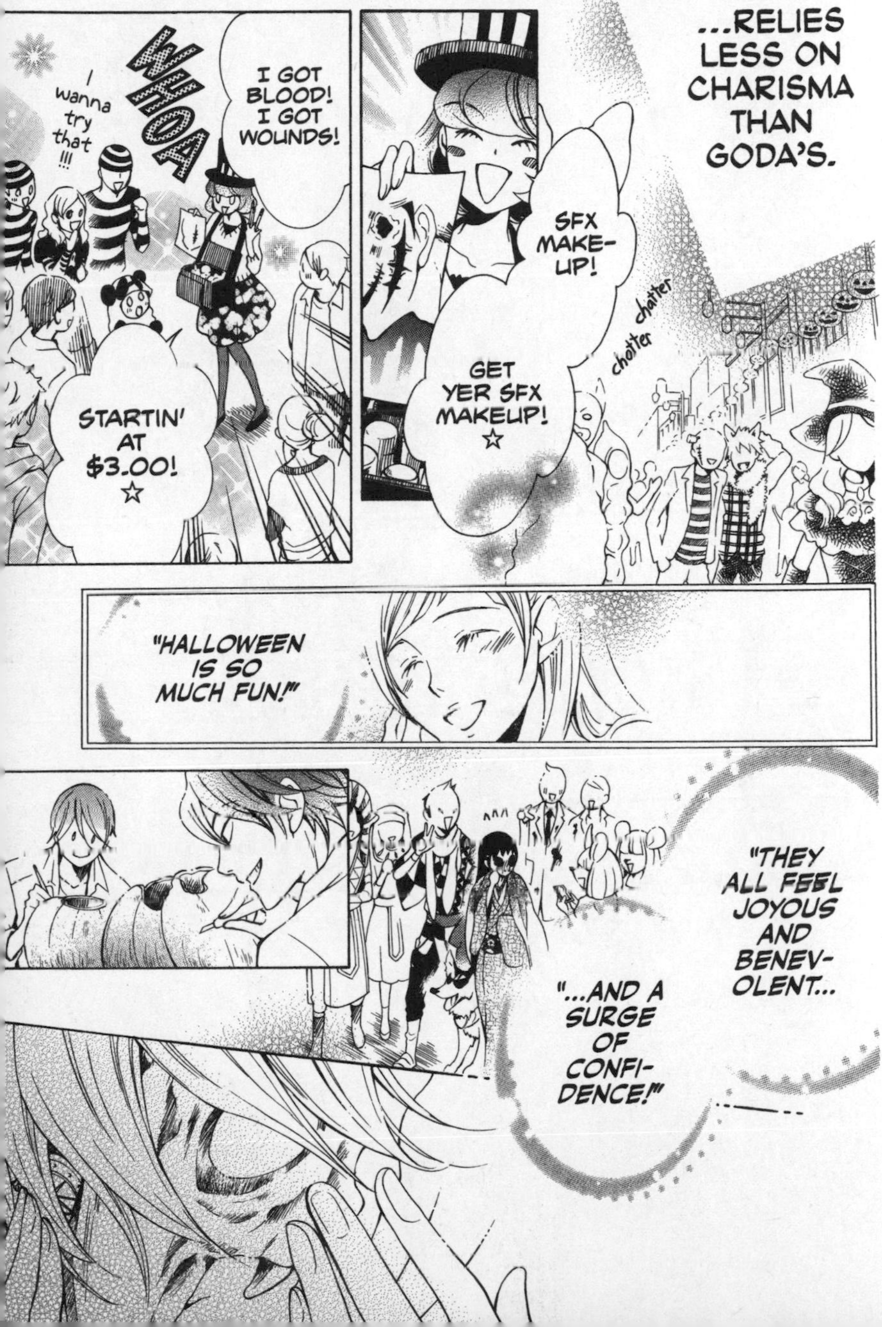
...RELIES LESS ON CHARISMA THAN GODA'S.
chatter chatter
SFX MAKE-UP!
GET YER SFX MAKEUP! ☆
I GOT BLOOD! I GOT WOUNDS!
WHOA
I wanna try that!!!
STARTIN' AT $3.00! ☆
"HALLOWEEN IS SO MUCH FUN!"
"THEY ALL FEEL JOYOUS AND BENEVOLENT...
"...AND A SURGE OF CONFIDENCE!"

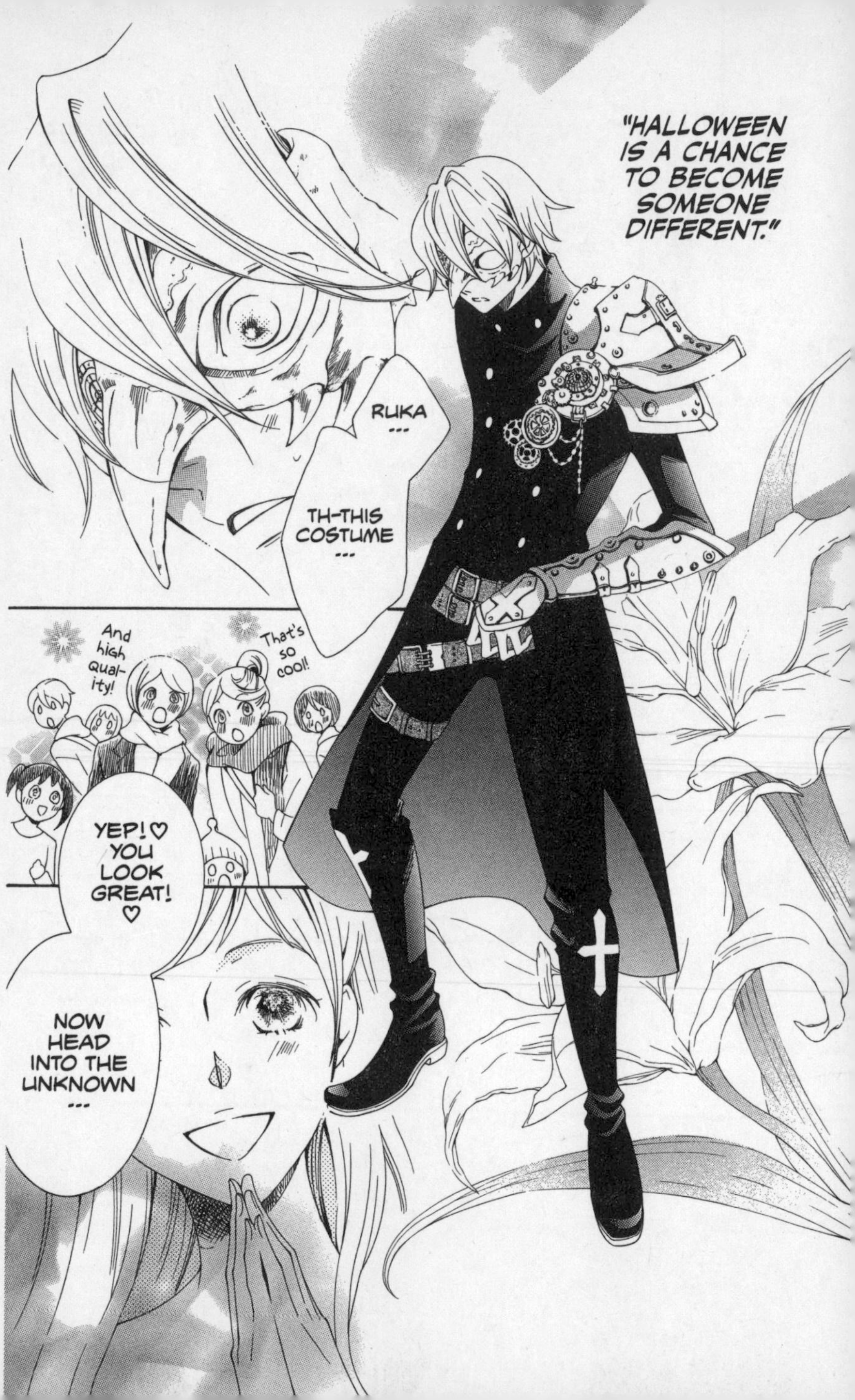
"HALLOWEEN IS A CHANCE TO BECOME SOMEONE DIFFERENT."
RUKA...
TH-THIS COSTUME...
That's so cool!
And high quality!
YEP! ♡ YOU LOOK GREAT! ♡
NOW HEAD INTO THE UNKNOWN...

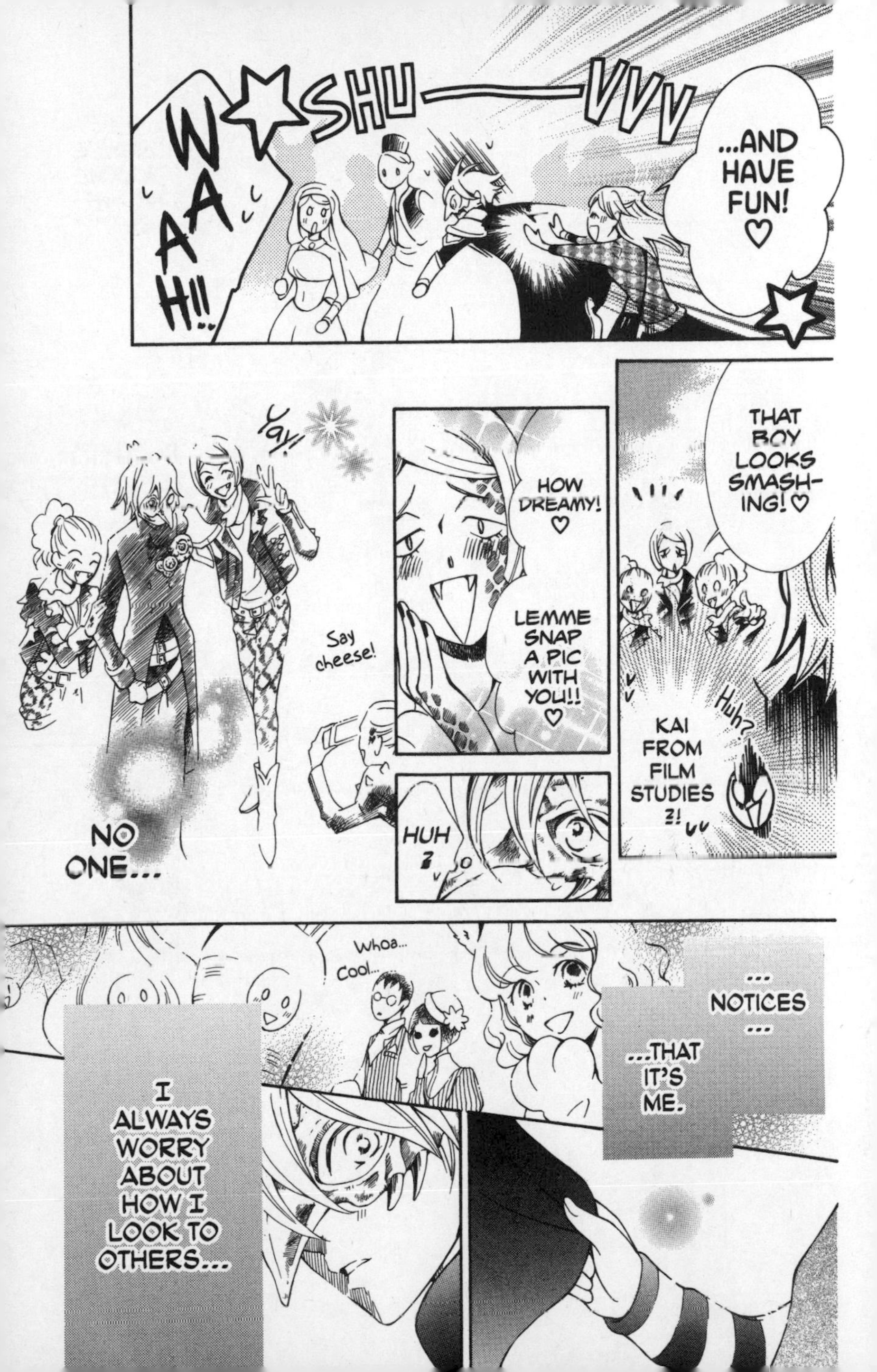
...AND HAVE FUN! ♡
W☆SHU——VVV
WAAH!!
THAT BOY LOOKS SMASHING! ♡
KAI FROM FILM STUDIES?!
Huh?
HOW DREAMY! ♡
LEMME SNAP A PIC WITH YOU!! ♡
HUH?
Yay!
Say cheese!
NO ONE...
...NOTICES...
...THAT IT'S ME.
Whoa...
Cool...
I ALWAYS WORRY ABOUT HOW I LOOK TO OTHERS...

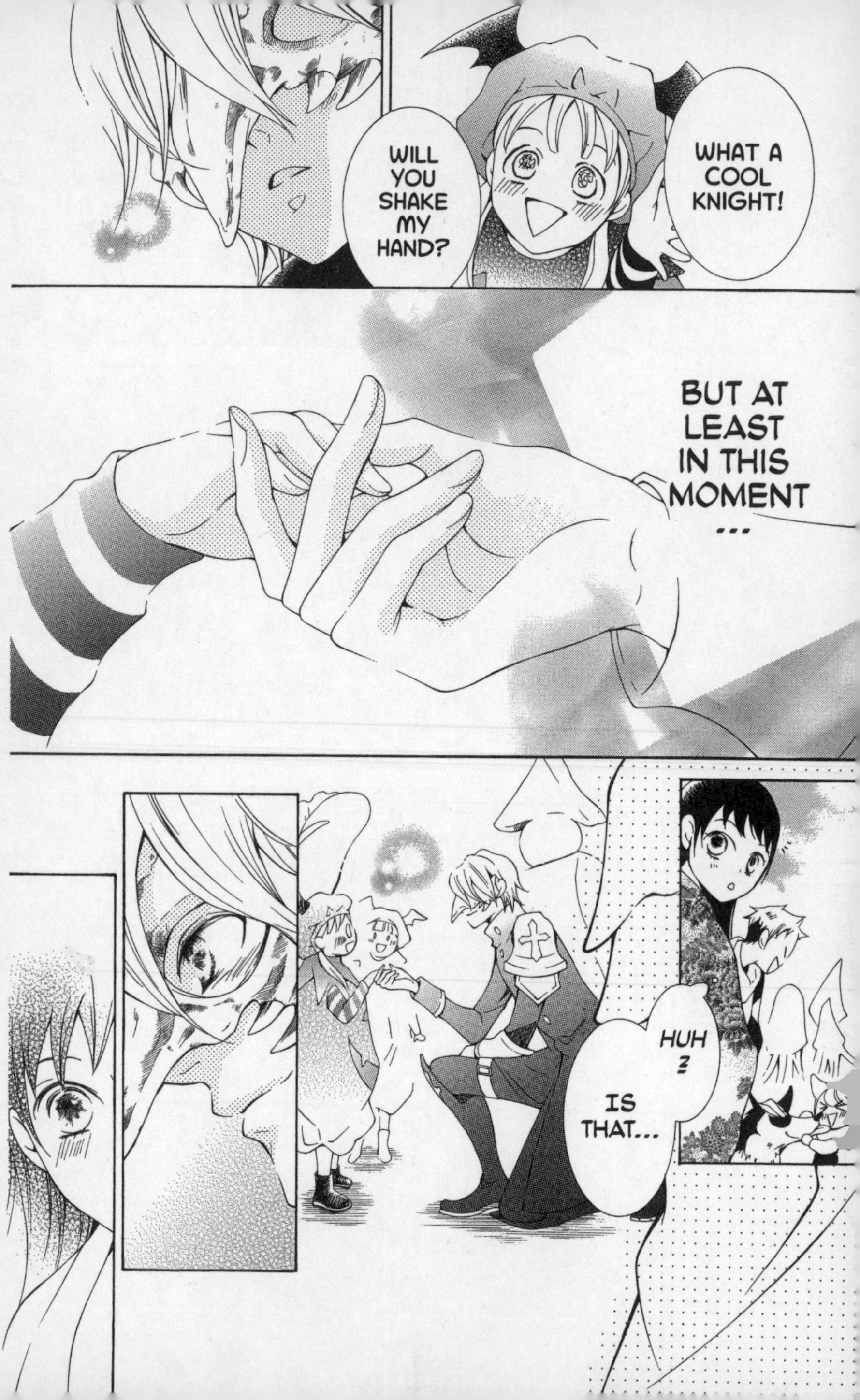
WHAT A COOL KNIGHT!
WILL YOU SHAKE MY HAND?
BUT AT LEAST IN THIS MOMENT...
HUH?
IS THAT...

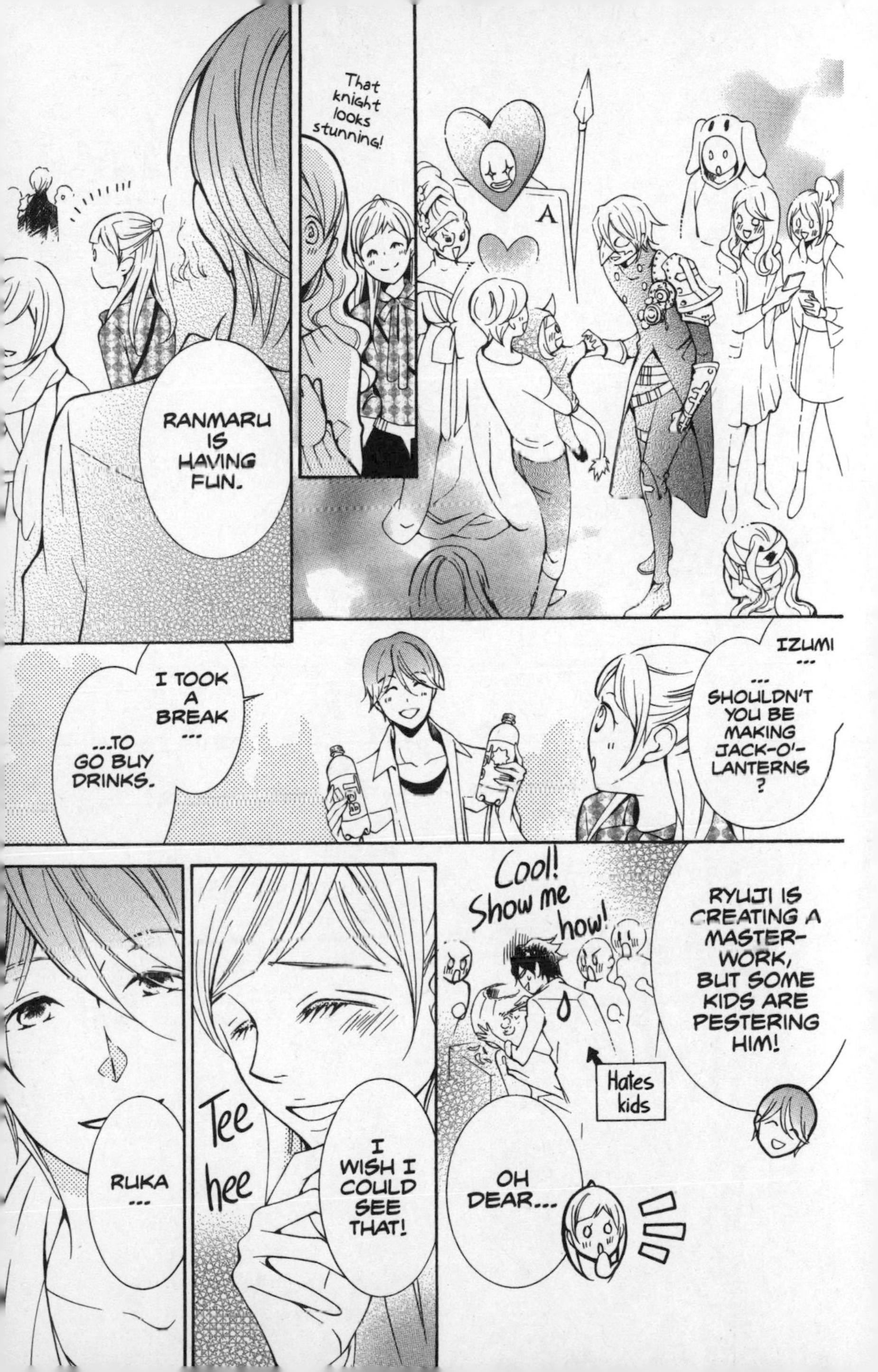

That knight looks stunning!
RANMARU IS HAVING FUN.
IZUMI... ...SHOULDN'T YOU BE MAKING JACK-O'-LANTERNS?
I TOOK A BREAK... ...TO GO BUY DRINKS.
RYUJI IS CREATING A MASTER-WORK, BUT SOME KIDS ARE PESTERING HIM!
Cool! Show me how!
Hates kids
OH DEAR...
I WISH I COULD SEE THAT!
Tee hee
RUKA...

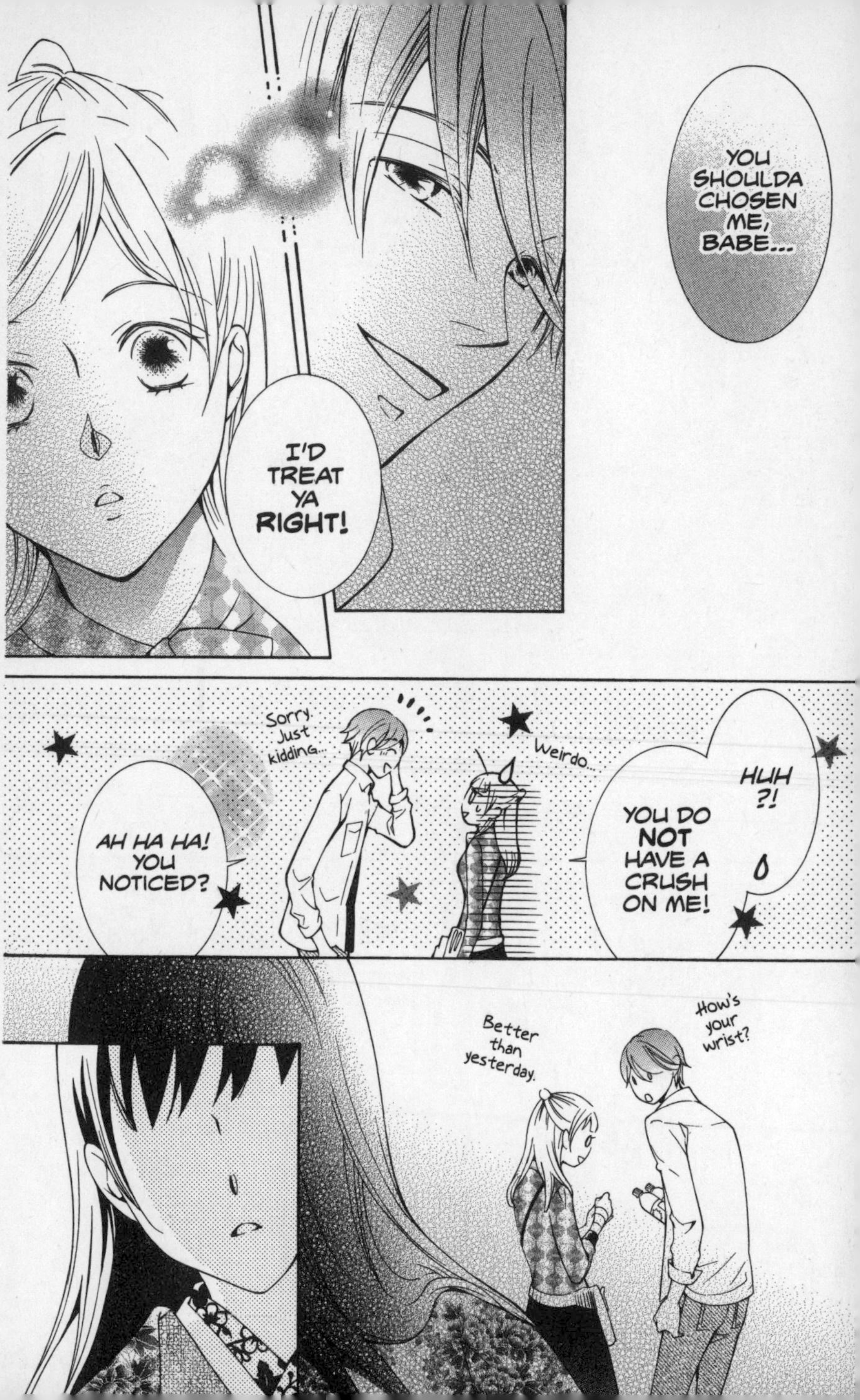
YOU SHOULDA CHOSEN ME, BABE...
I'D TREAT YA RIGHT!
HUH?!
YOU DO NOT HAVE A CRUSH ON ME!
Weirdo...
Sorry. Just kidding...
AH HA HA! YOU NOTICED?
How's your wrist?
Better than yesterday.

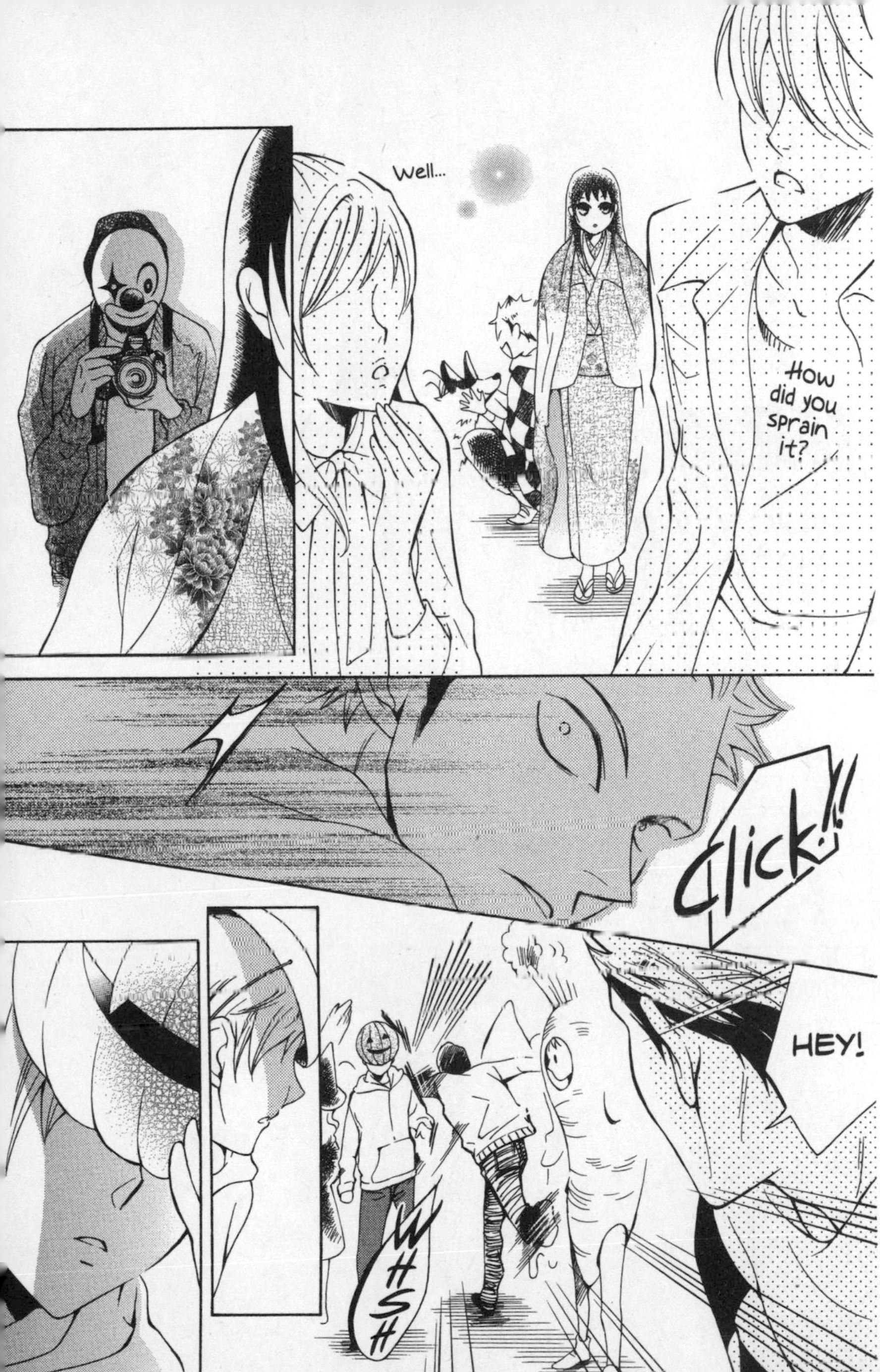
How did you sprain it?
Well...
Click!!
HEY!
WHSH

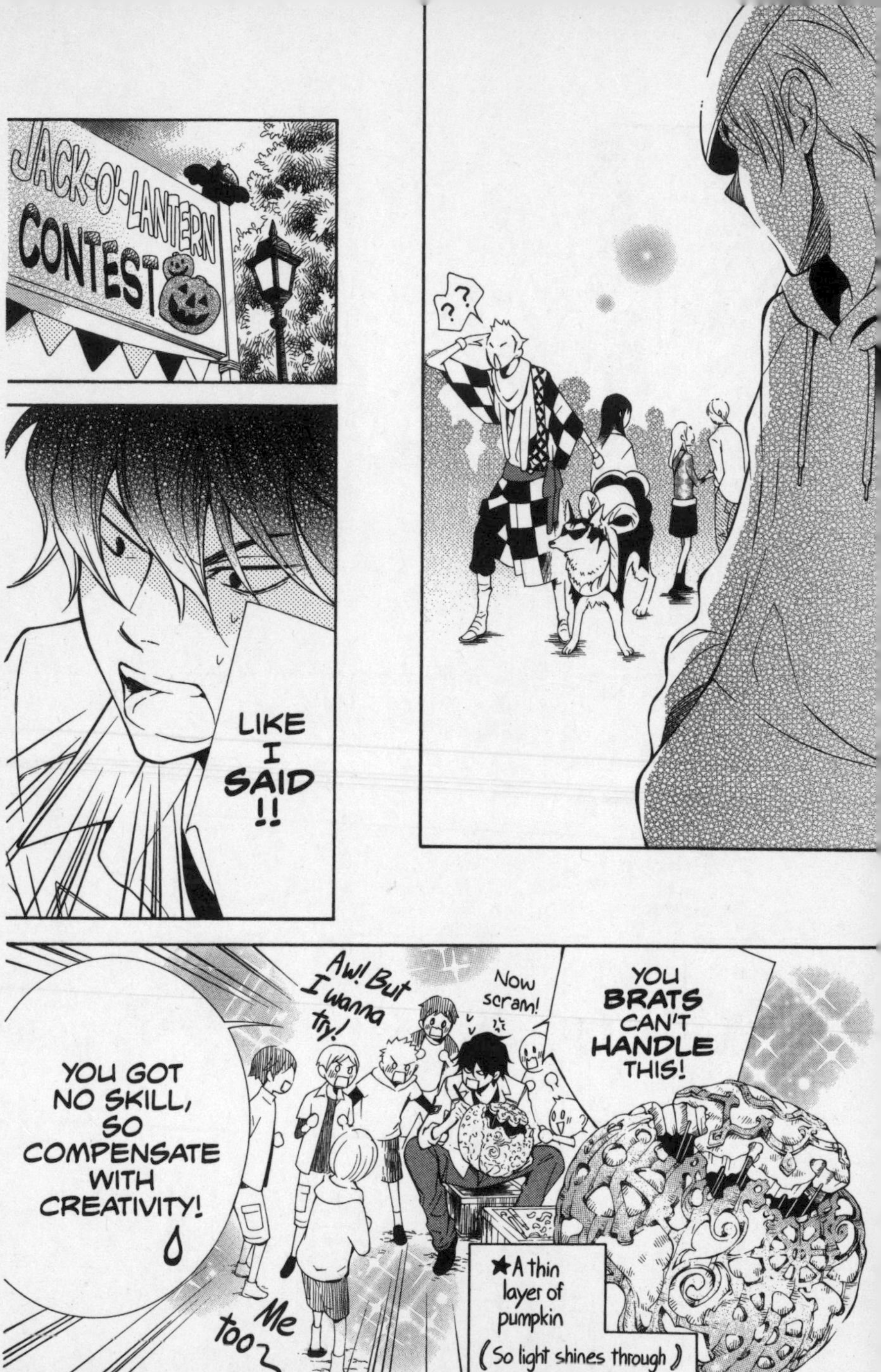
??
JACK-O'-LANTERN CONTEST
LIKE I SAID!!
YOU BRATS CAN'T HANDLE THIS!
Now scram!
Aw! But I wanna try!
YOU GOT NO SKILL, SO COMPENSATE WITH CREATIVITY!
★A thin layer of pumpkin
(So light shines through)
Me too~!

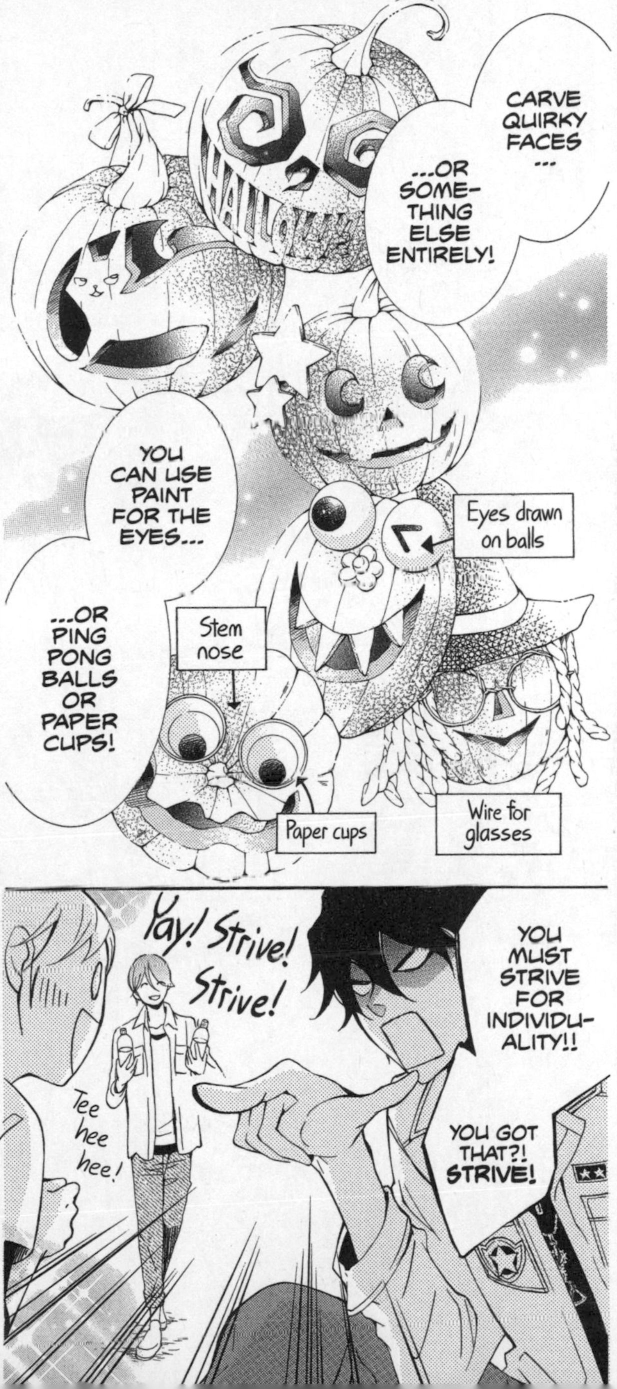
CARVE QUIRKY FACES...
...OR SOME-THING ELSE ENTIRELY!
Eyes drawn on balls
YOU CAN USE PAINT FOR THE EYES...
Stem nose
...OR PING PONG BALLS OR PAPER CUPS!
Wire for glasses
Paper cups
YOU MUST STRIVE FOR INDIVIDU-ALITY!!
YOU GOT THAT?! STRIVE!
Yay! Strive! Strive!
Tee hee hee!

The Birth of *Behind the Scenes!!* 2

Speaking of Halloween...

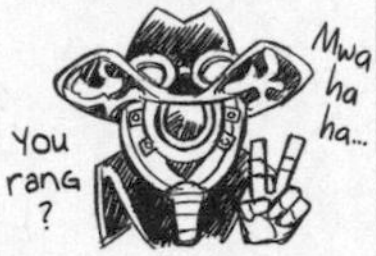
Mwa ha ha...
You rang?

It's Master Rodemu!!

Every year, Master Rodemu participates in Kawasaki Halloween, Japan's largest Halloween event, so I heard all about the love of Halloween from him!

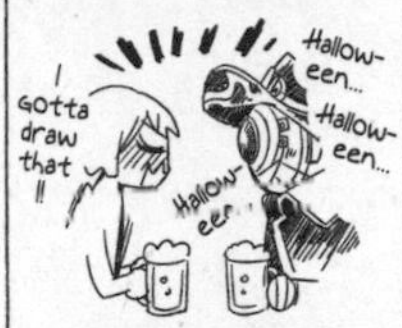
Hallow-een... Hallow-een...
Hallow-eeen
I gotta draw that!!

Master Rodemu went to the dollar store with me...

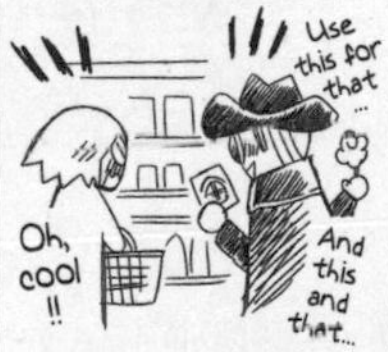
Use this for that...
And this and that...
Oh, cool!!

...and showed me a massive notebook of ideas.

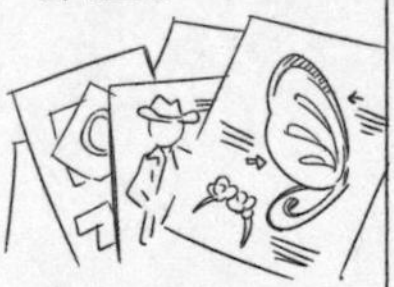

Too bad I didn't use even half of them... But thanks so much, Rodemu-san!!

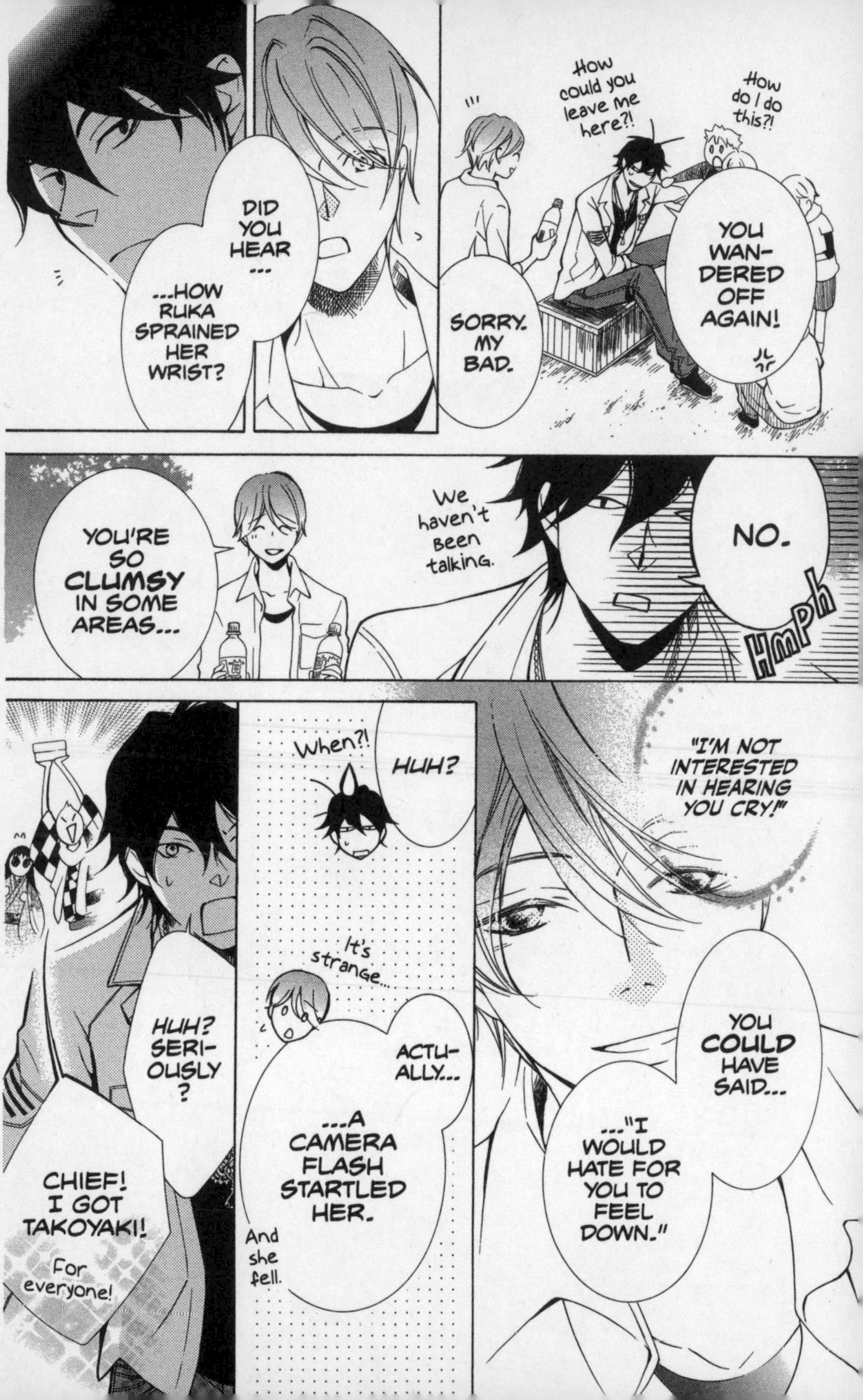
How could you leave me here?!
How do I do this?!
YOU WAN-DERED OFF AGAIN!
SORRY. MY BAD.
DID YOU HEAR ---
...HOW RUKA SPRAINED HER WRIST?
NO.
Hmph
We haven't been talking.
YOU'RE SO CLUMSY IN SOME AREAS...
"I'M NOT INTERESTED IN HEARING YOU CRY!"
YOU COULD HAVE SAID...
..."I WOULD HATE FOR YOU TO FEEL DOWN."
HUH?
When?!
It's strange...
ACTU-ALLY...
...A CAMERA FLASH STARTLED HER.
And she fell.
HUH? SERI-OUSLY?
CHIEF! I GOT TAKOYAKI!
For everyone!

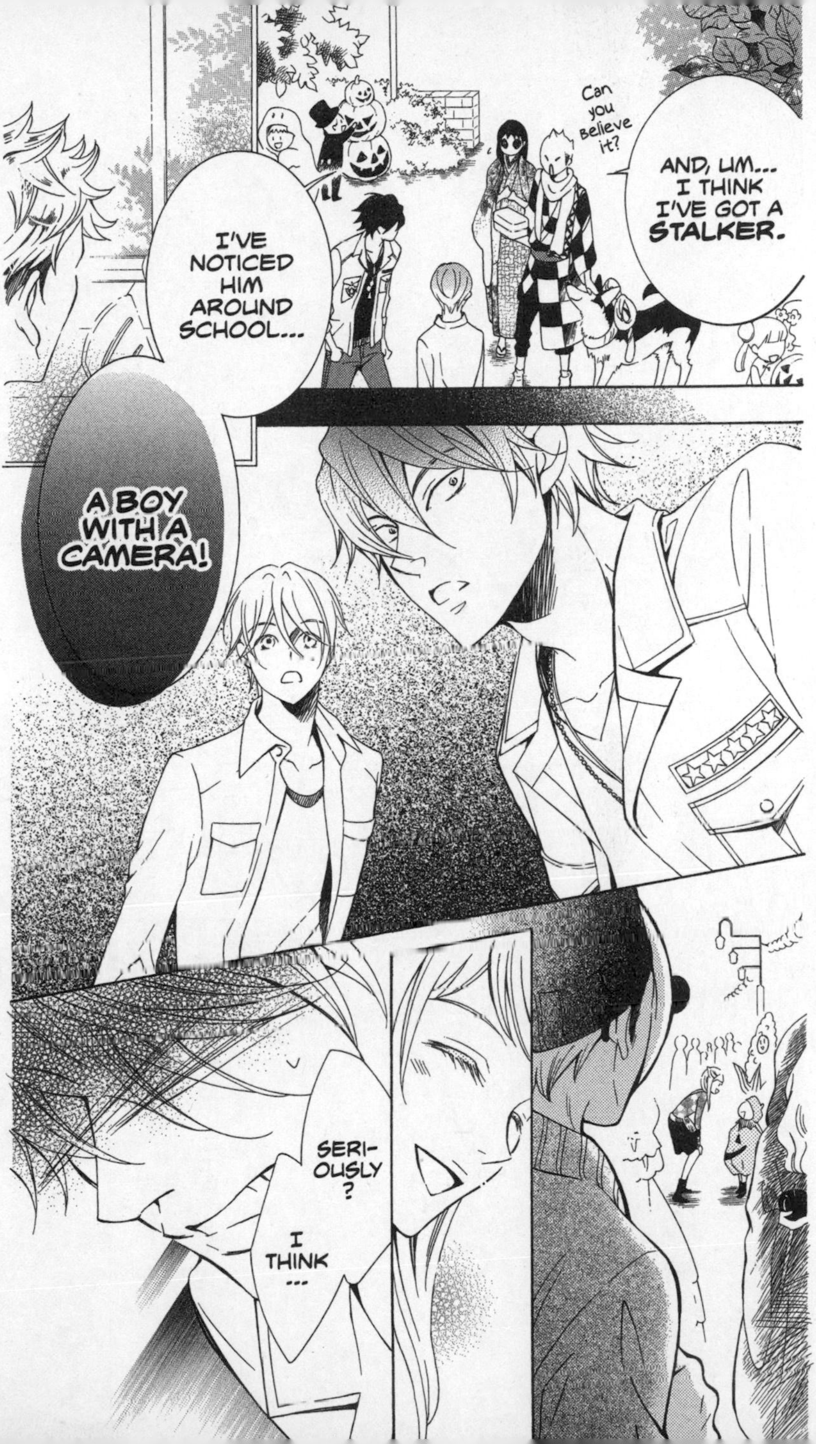
AND, UM... I THINK I'VE GOT A STALKER.
Can you believe it?
I'VE NOTICED HIM AROUND SCHOOL...
A BOY WITH A CAMERA!
SERI-OUSLY?
I THINK...

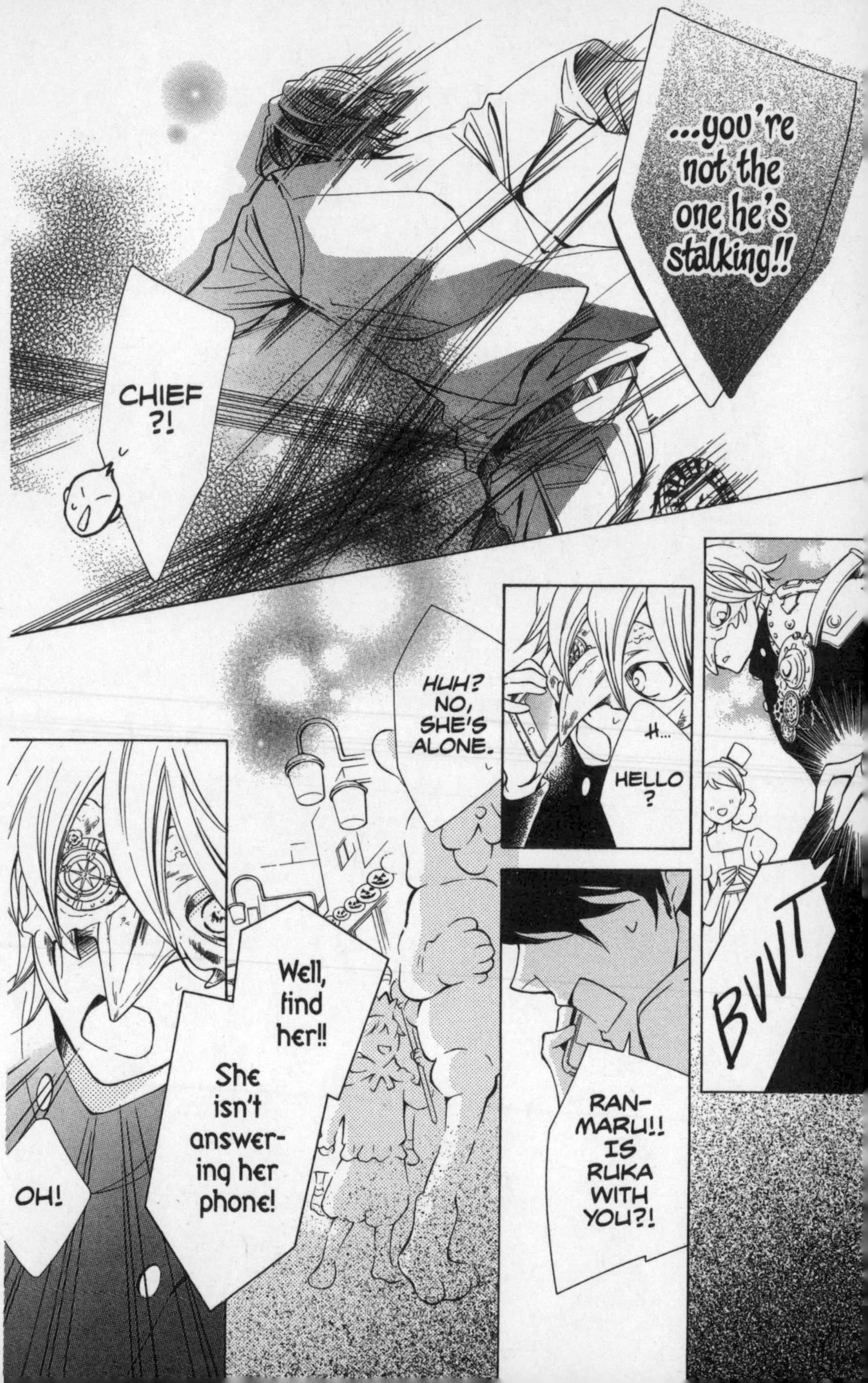
...you're not the one he's stalking!!
CHIEF ?!
BVVT
H... HELLO ?
RAN-MARU!! IS RUKA WITH YOU?!
HUH? NO, SHE'S ALONE.
Well, find her!!
She isn't answering her phone!
OH!

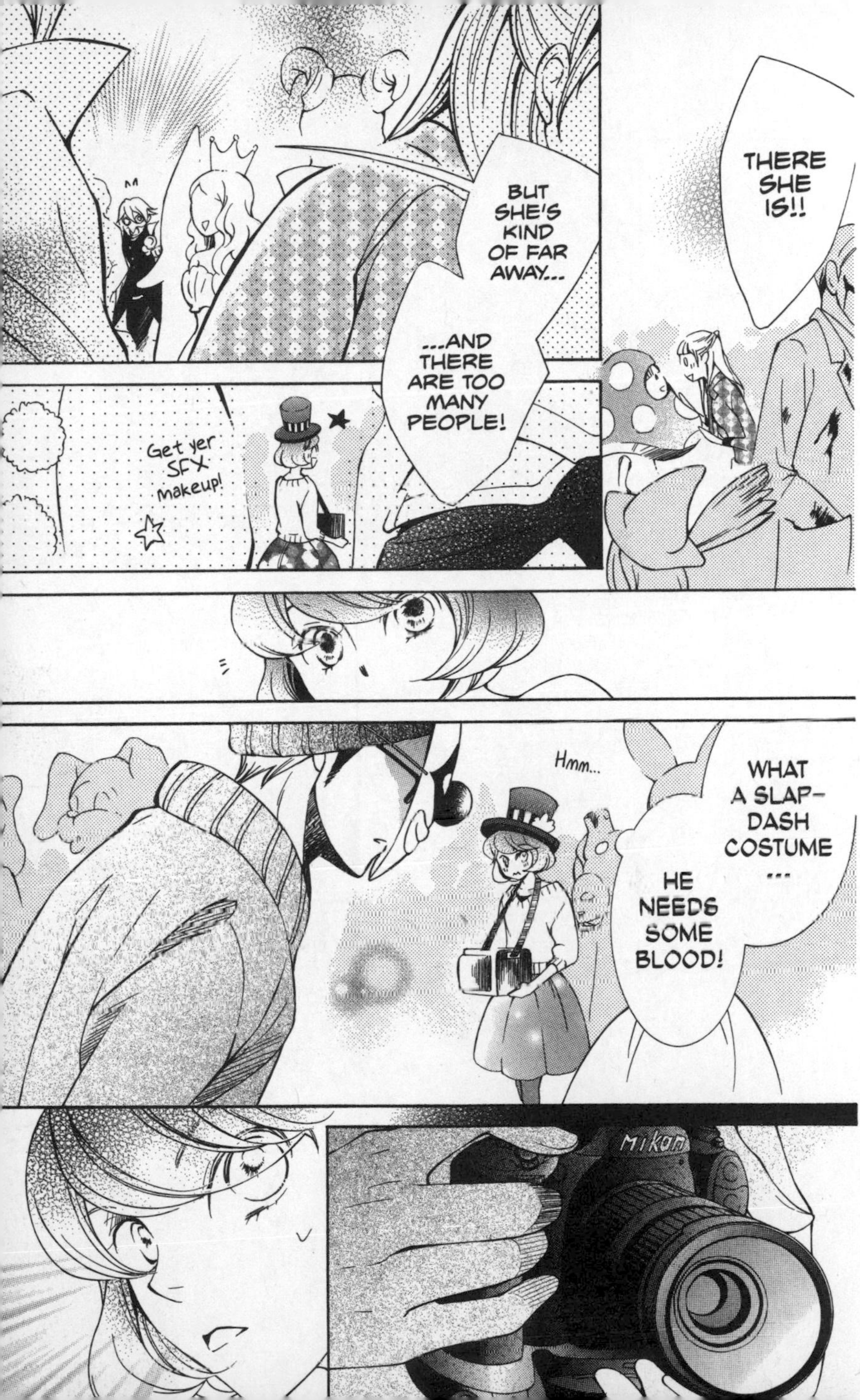
THERE SHE IS!!
BUT SHE'S KIND OF FAR AWAY...
...AND THERE ARE TOO MANY PEOPLE!
Get yer SFX makeup!
WHAT A SLAP-DASH COSTUME...
HE NEEDS SOME BLOOD!
Hmm...
Mikon

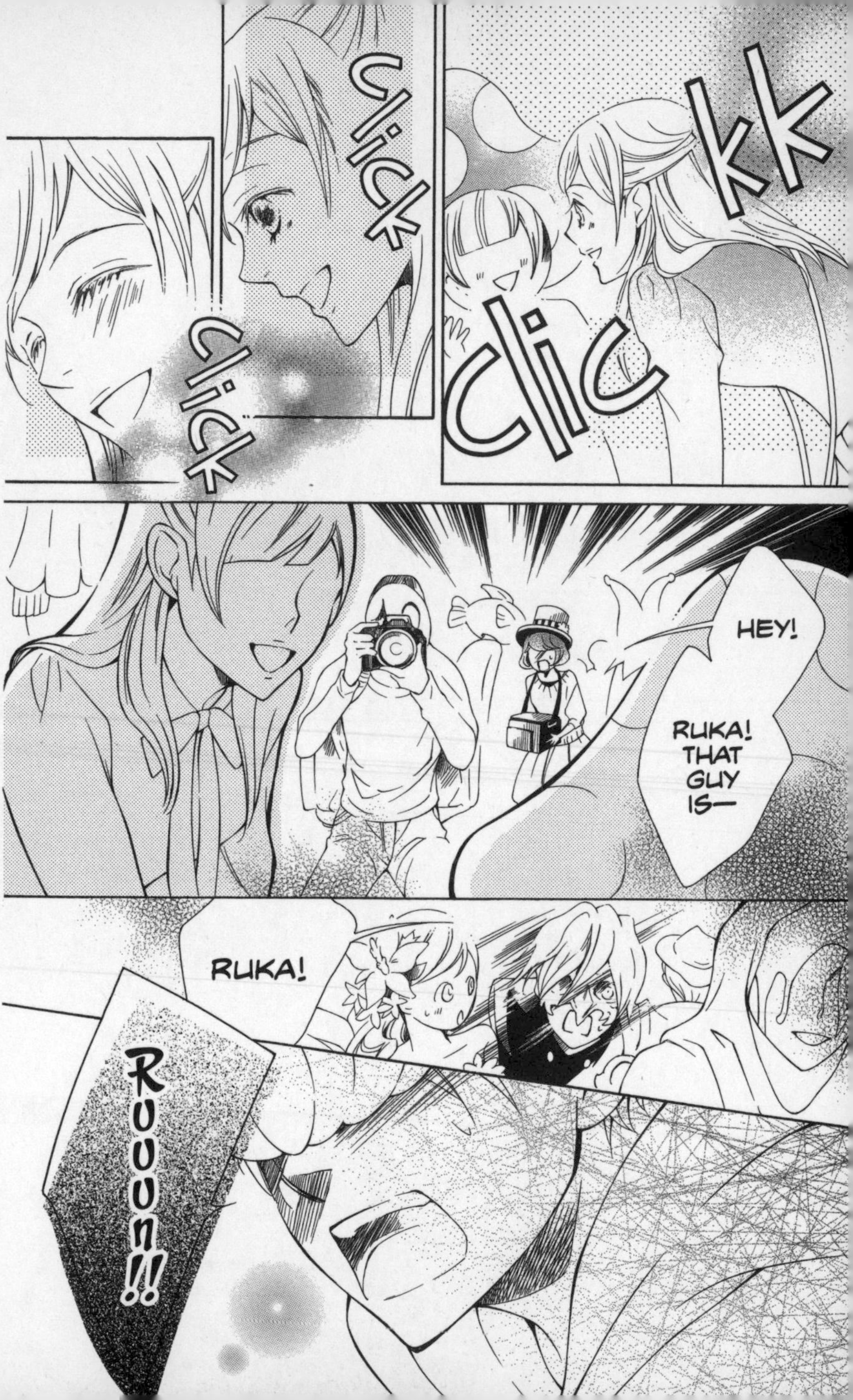
clic kk
click
click
HEY!
RUKA! THAT GUY IS—
RUKA!
RUUUUN!!

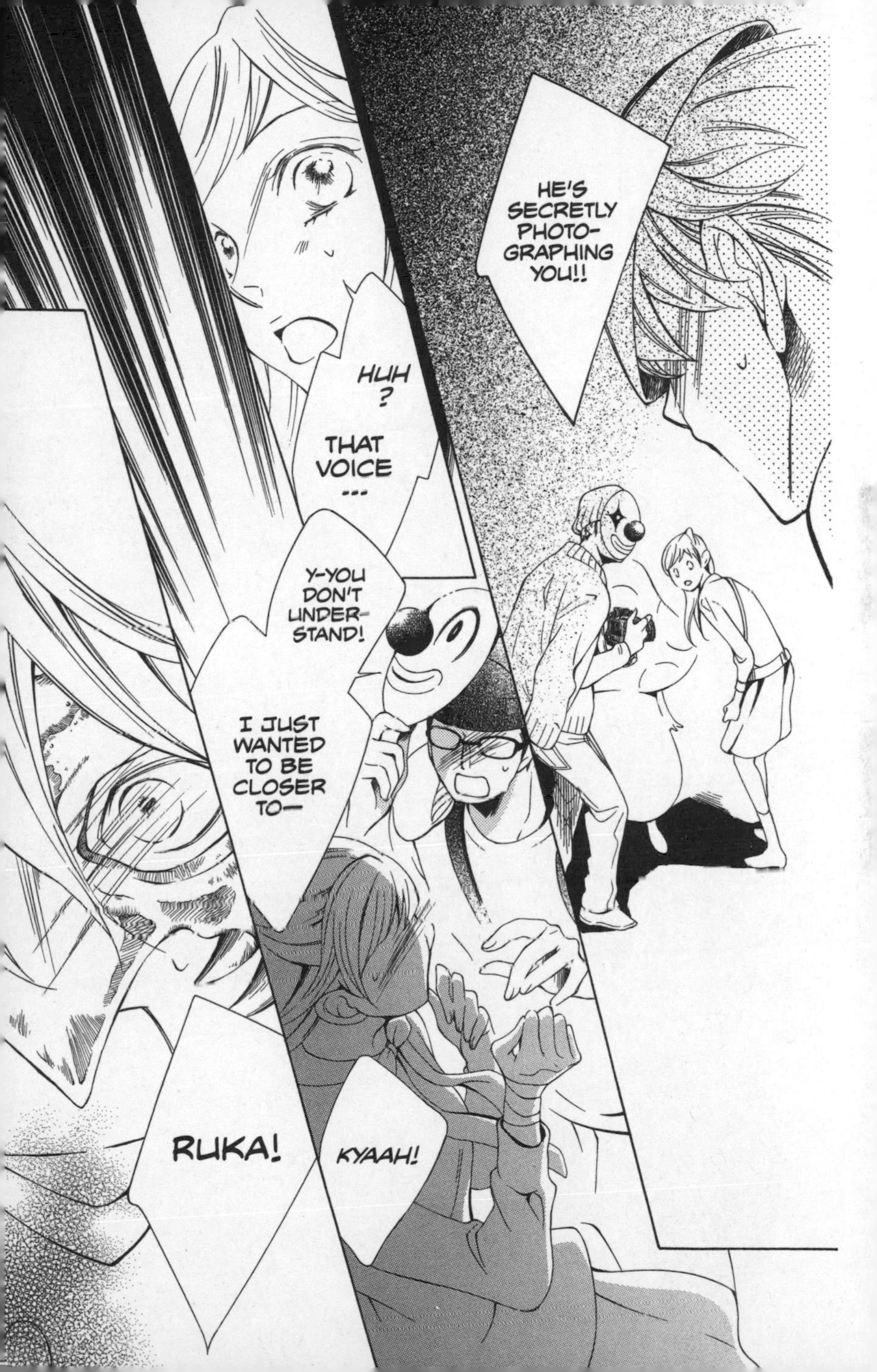
HE'S SECRETLY PHOTO-GRAPHING YOU!!
HUH?
THAT VOICE ---
Y-YOU DON'T UNDER-STAND!
I JUST WANTED TO BE CLOSER TO—
KYAAH!
RUKA!

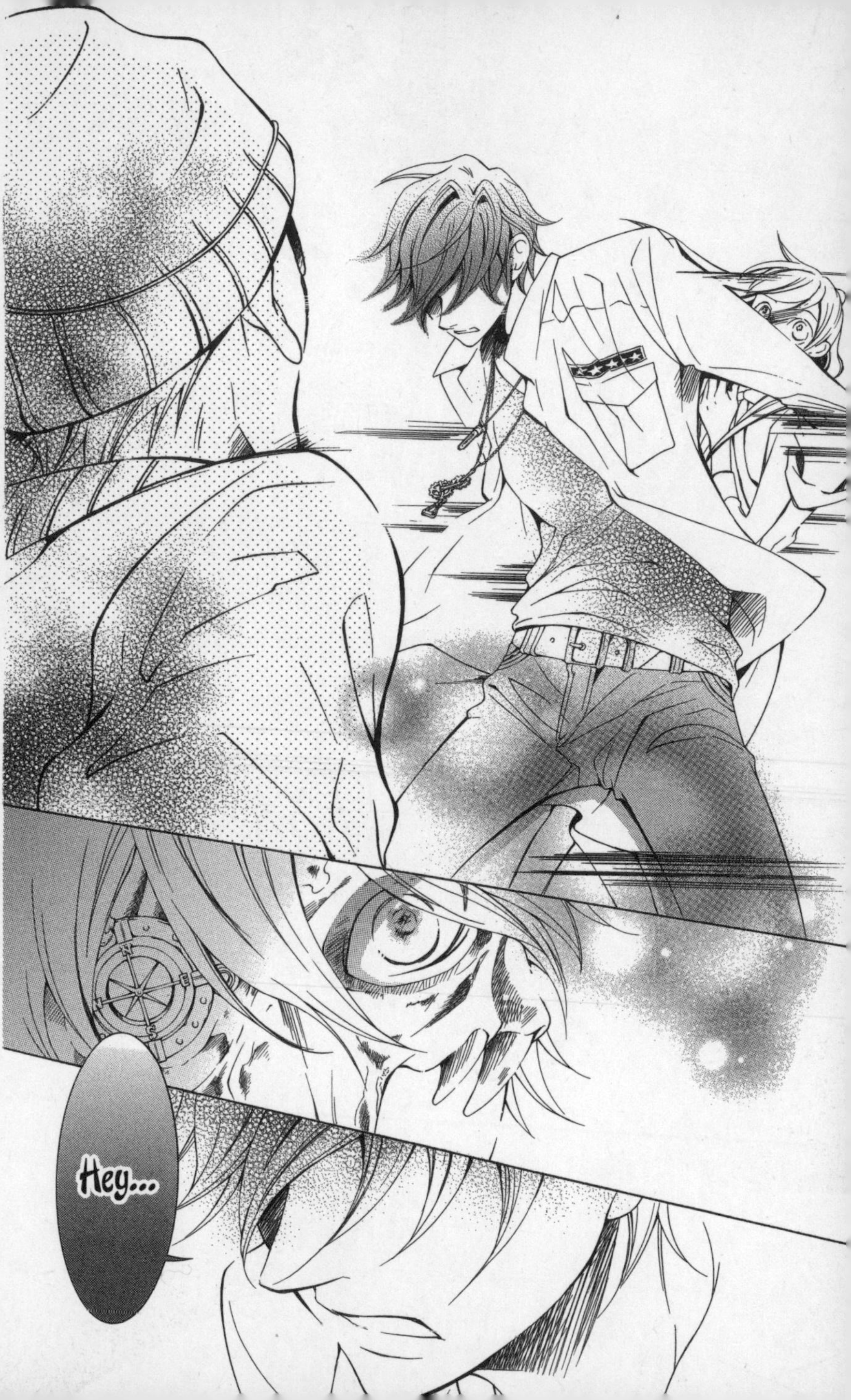
Hey...

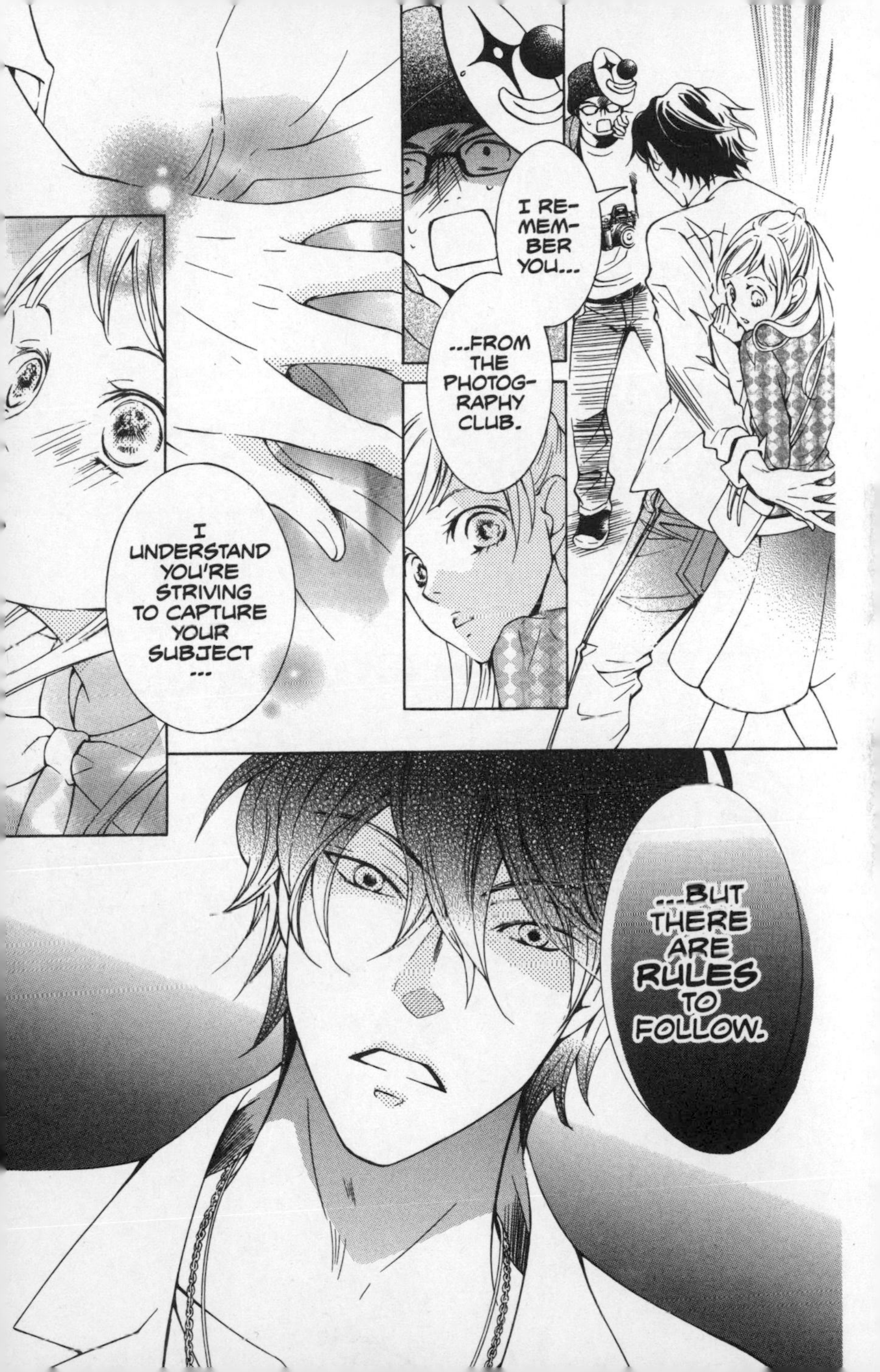
I REMEMBER YOU...
...FROM THE PHOTOGRAPHY CLUB.
I UNDERSTAND YOU'RE STRIVING TO CAPTURE YOUR SUBJECT...
...BUT THERE ARE RULES TO FOLLOW.

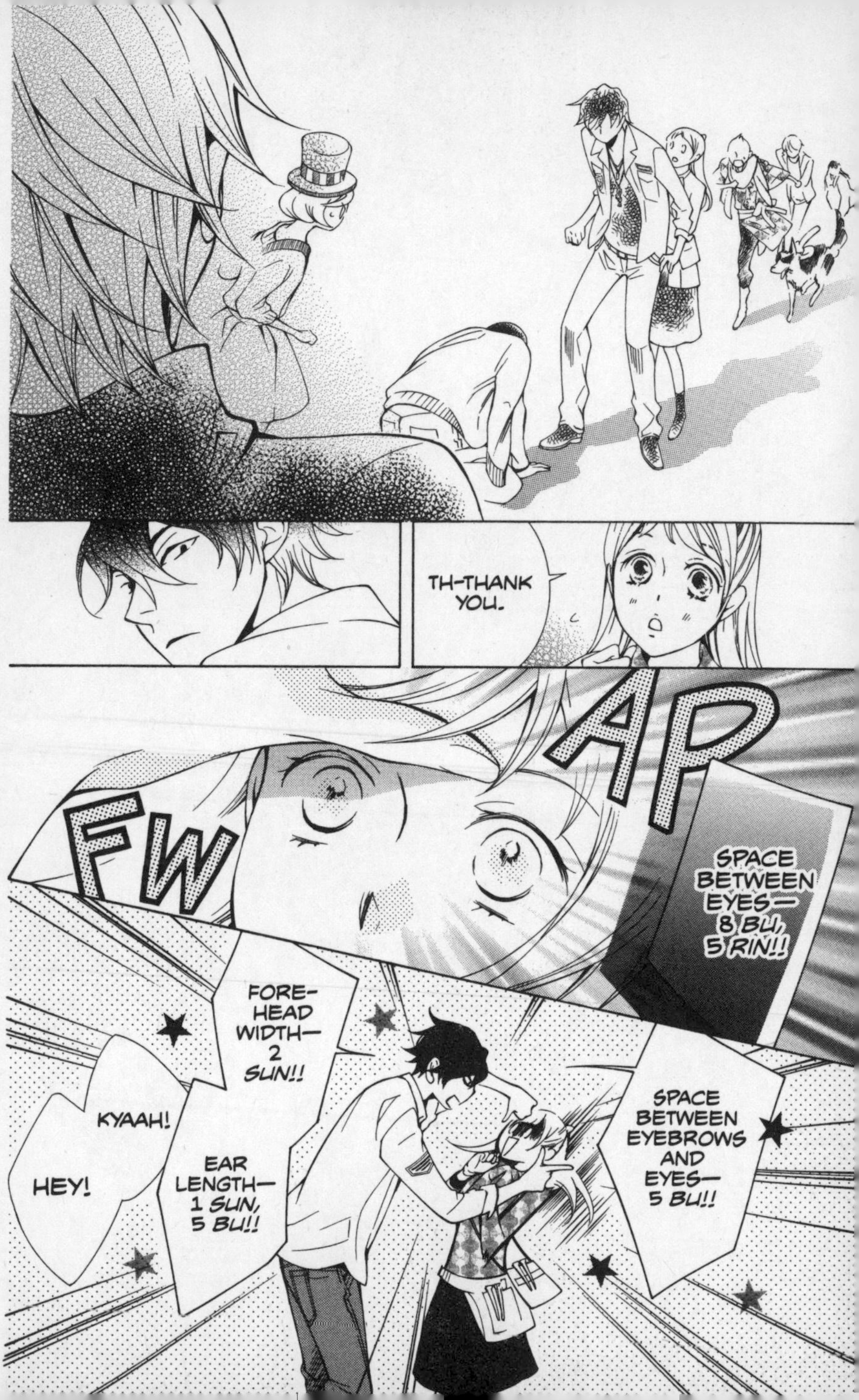
TH-THANK YOU.
FWAP
SPACE BETWEEN EYES— 8 BU, 5 RIN!!
SPACE BETWEEN EYEBROWS AND EYES— 5 BU!!
FOREHEAD WIDTH— 2 SUN!!
EAR LENGTH— 1 SUN, 5 BU!!
KYAAH!
HEY!

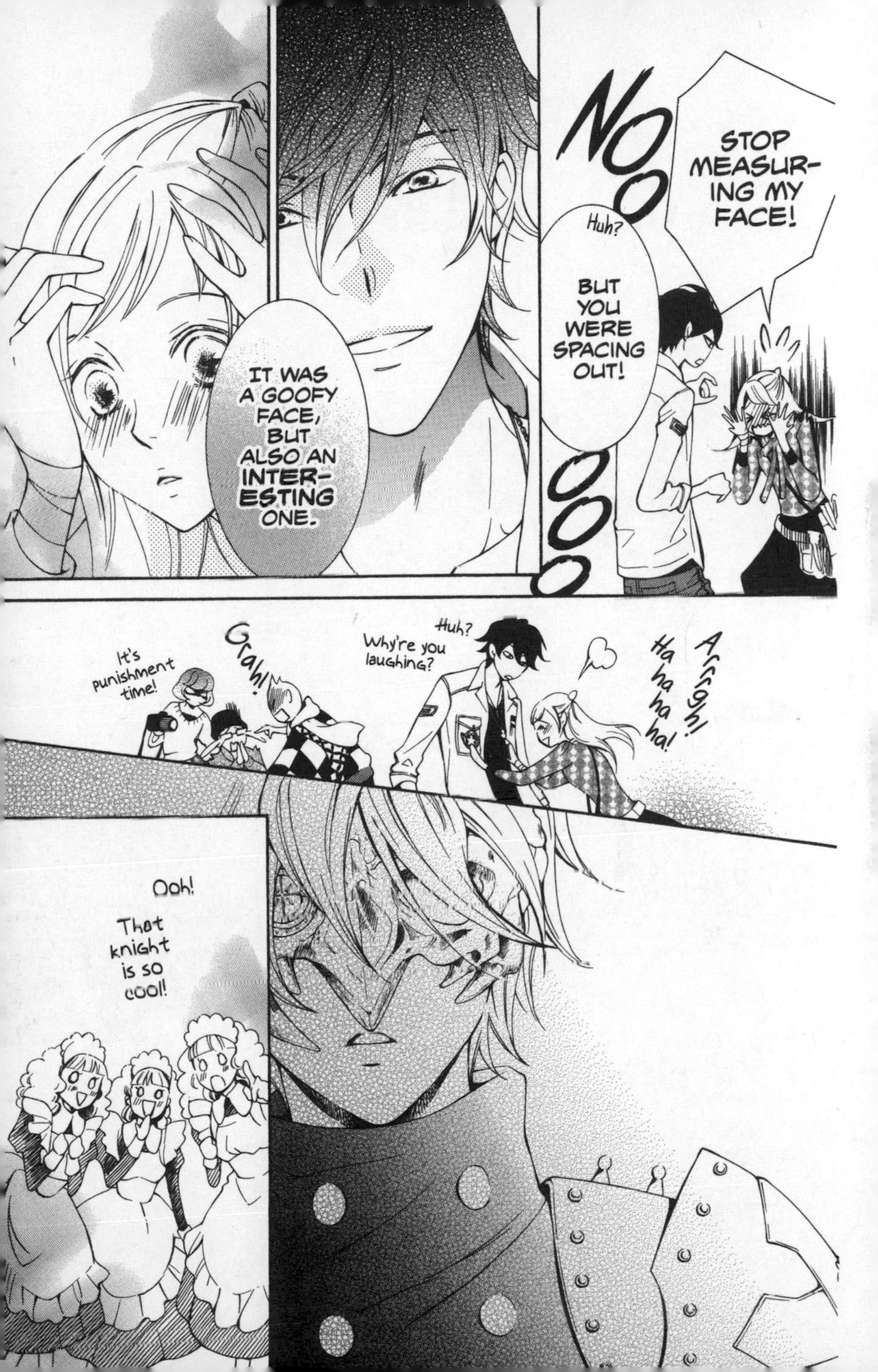
STOP MEASURING MY FACE!
NOOOOOO
Huh?
BUT YOU WERE SPACING OUT!
IT WAS A GOOFY FACE, BUT ALSO AN INTERESTING ONE.
Arrgh!
Ha ha ha ha ha!
Huh?
Why're you laughing?
Grah!
It's punishment time!
Ooh!
That knight is so cool!

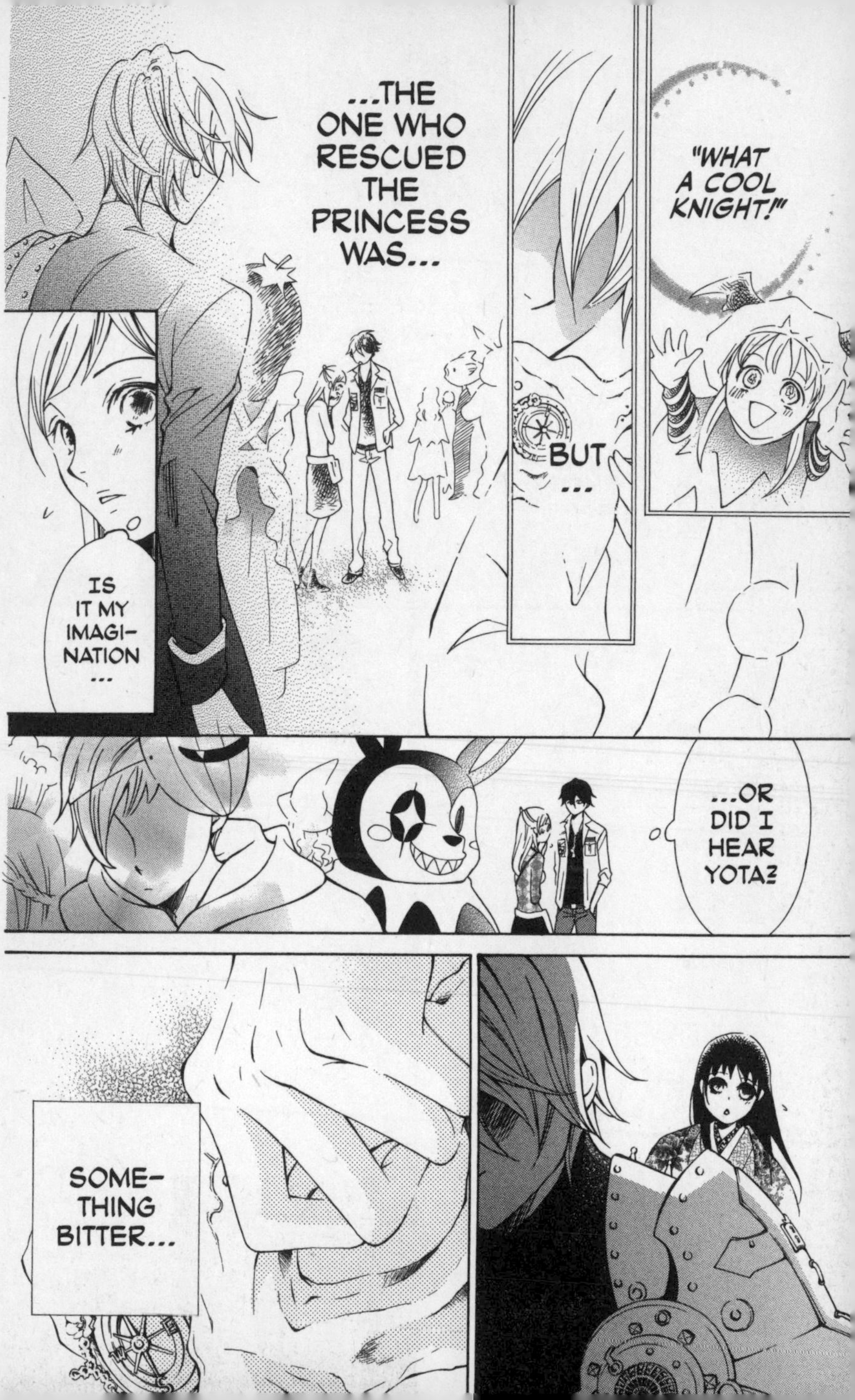
"WHAT A COOL KNIGHT!"
BUT...
...THE ONE WHO RESCUED THE PRINCESS WAS...
IS IT MY IMAGINATION...
...OR DID I HEAR YOTA?
SOMETHING BITTER...

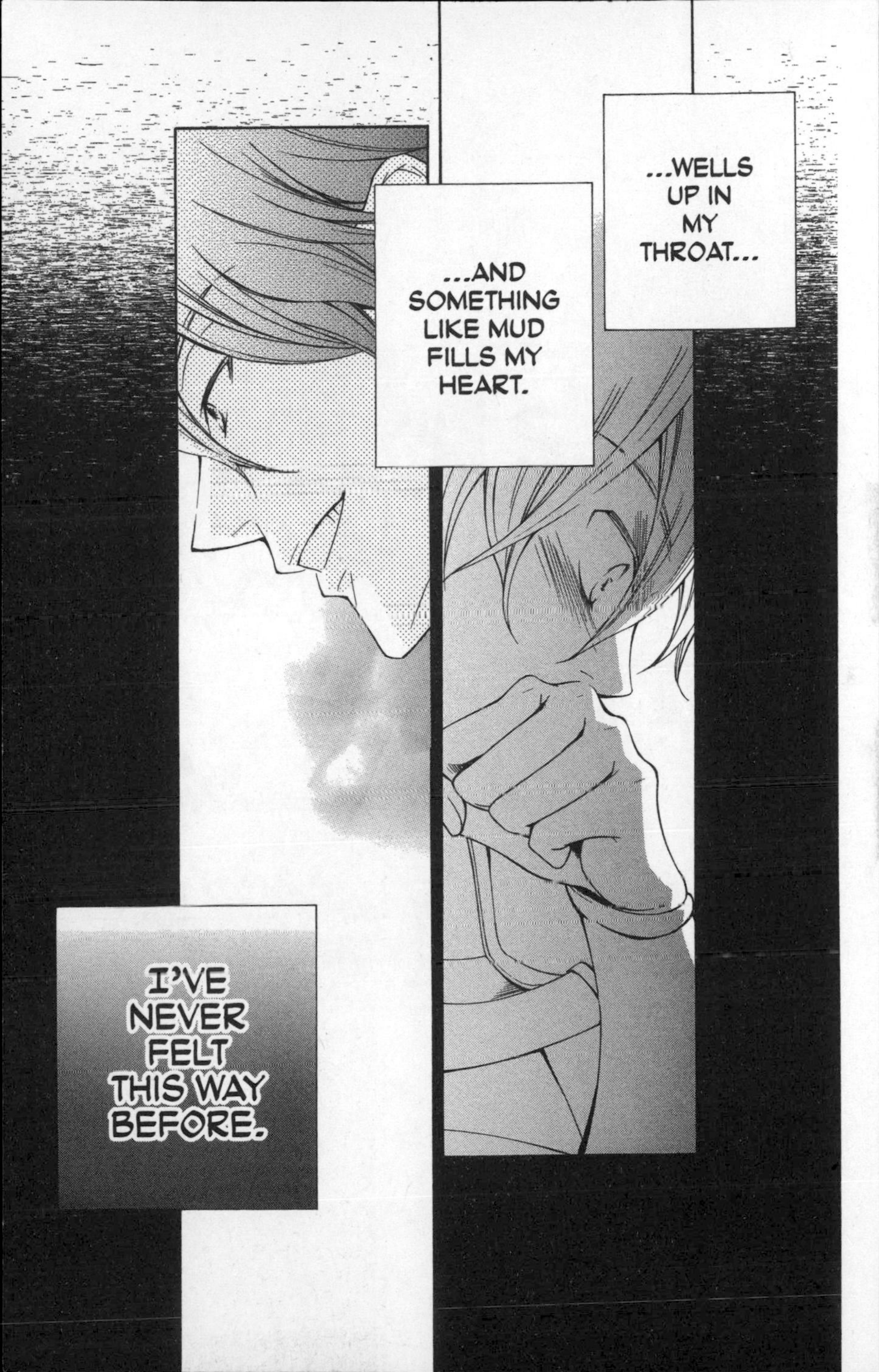
...WELLS UP IN MY THROAT...
...AND SOMETHING LIKE MUD FILLS MY HEART.
I'VE NEVER FELT THIS WAY BEFORE.

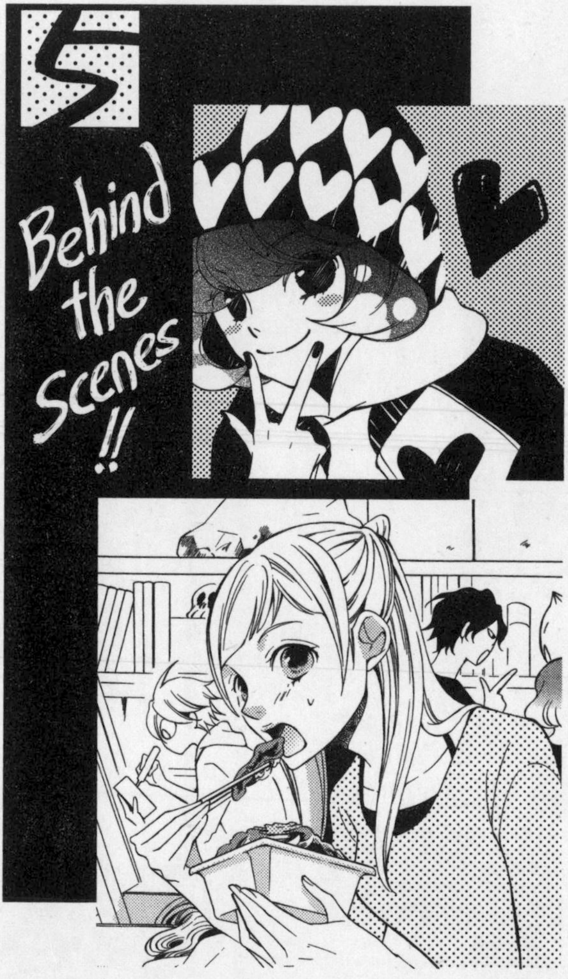
5
Behind the Scenes!!

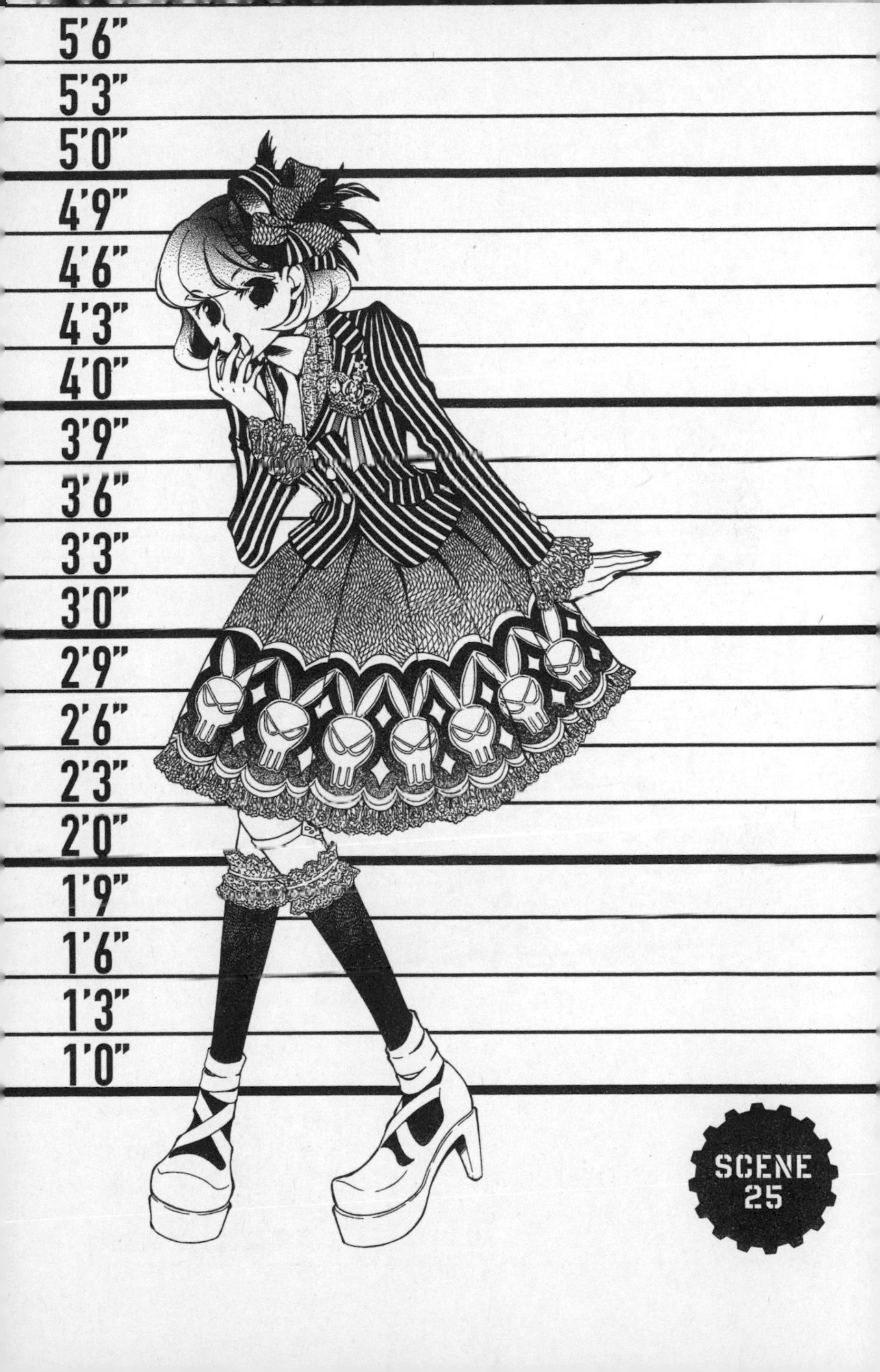
5'6"
5'3"
5'0"
4'9"
4'6"
4'3"
4'0"
3'9"
3'6"
3'3"
3'0"
2'9"
2'6"
2'3"
2'0"
1'9"
1'6"
1'3"
1'0"
SCENE
25

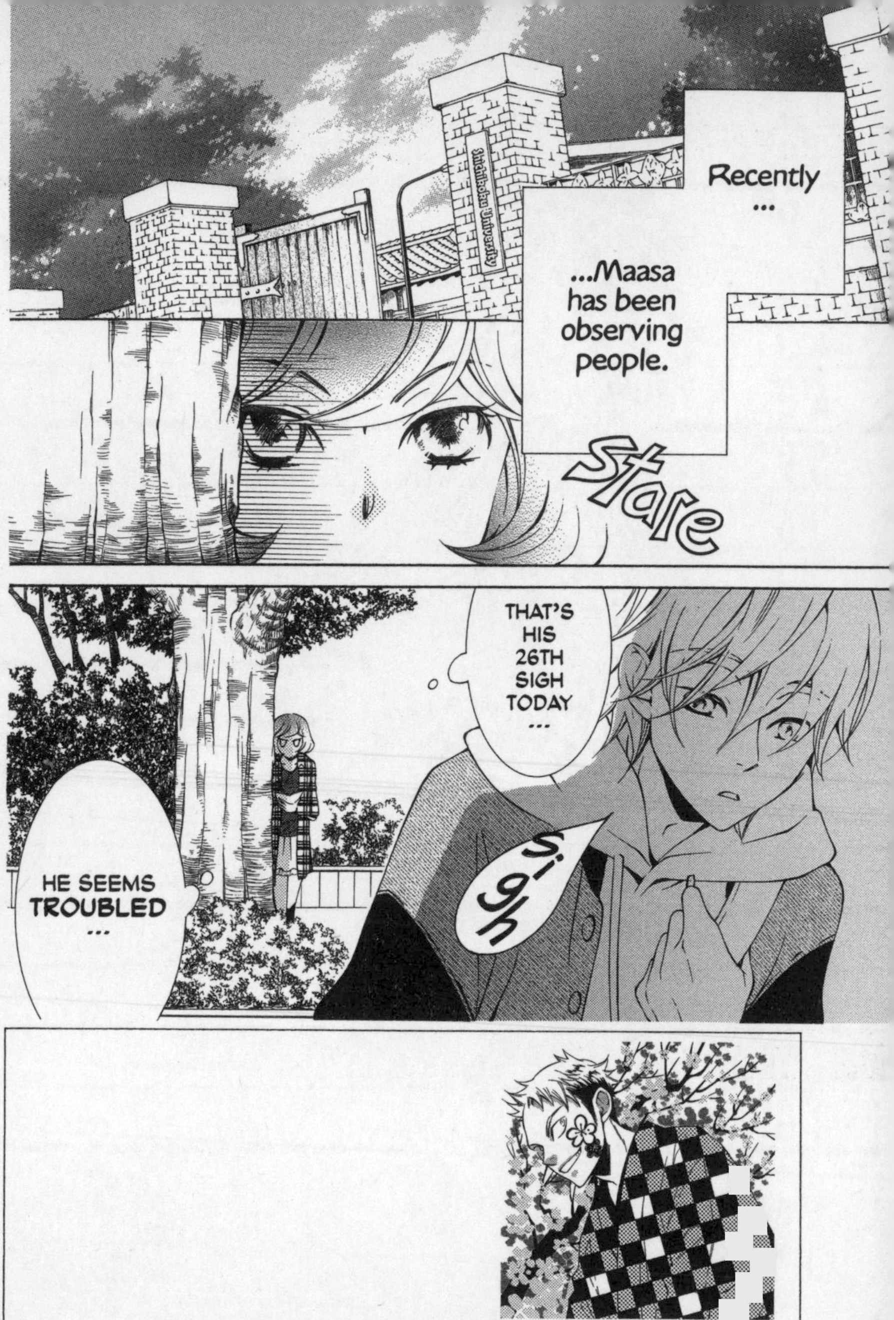
Recently ...
...Maasa has been observing people.
Shichikoku University
Stare
THAT'S HIS 26TH SIGH TODAY ...
Sigh
HE SEEMS TROUBLED ...

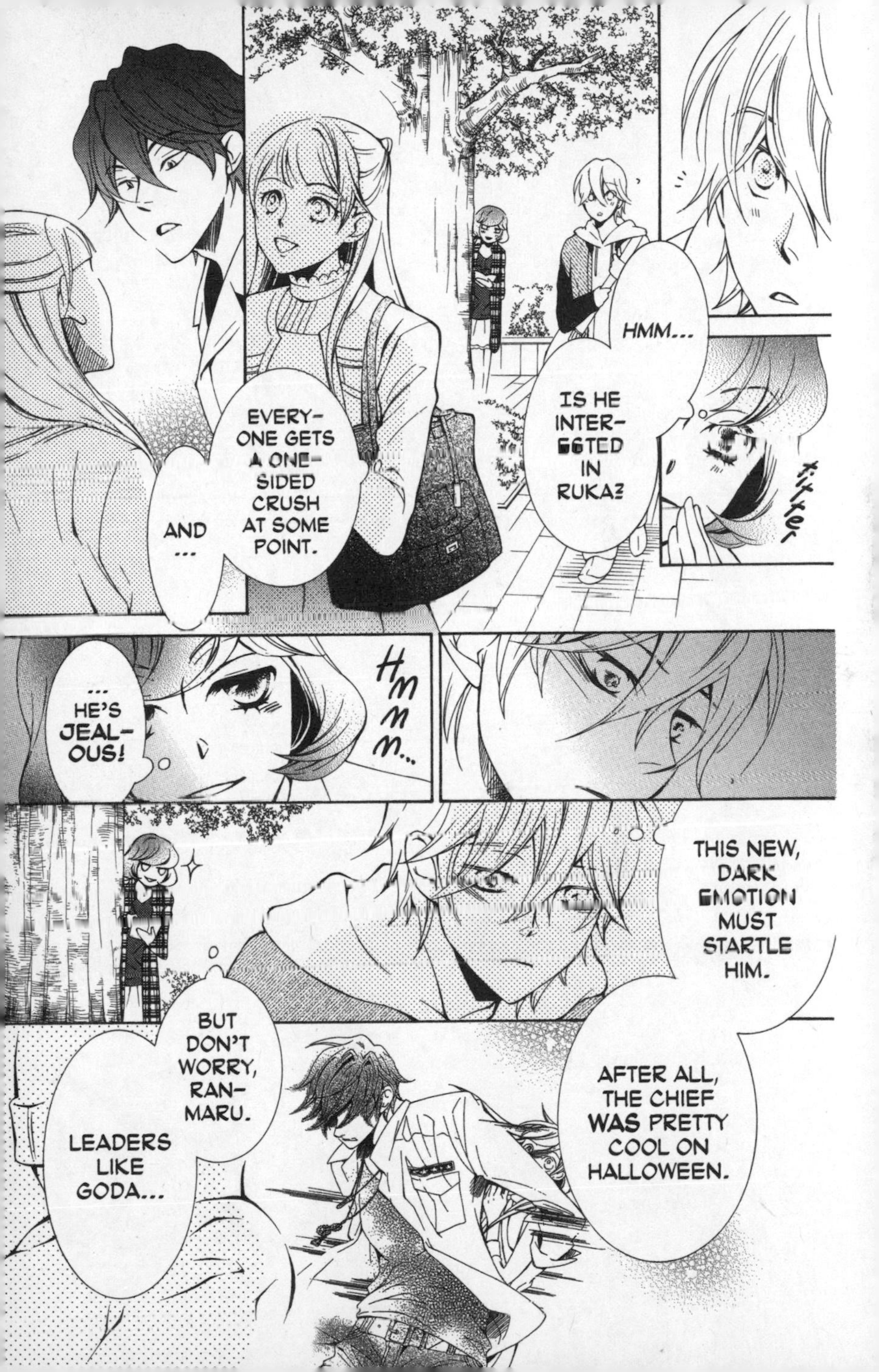
HMM...
IS HE INTER-ESTED IN RUKA?
titter
EVERY-ONE GETS A ONE-SIDED CRUSH AT SOME POINT.
AND ...
... HE'S JEAL-OUS!
Hmmmn...
THIS NEW, DARK EMOTION MUST STARTLE HIM.
AFTER ALL, THE CHIEF WAS PRETTY COOL ON HALLOWEEN.
BUT DON'T WORRY, RAN-MARU.
LEADERS LIKE GODA...

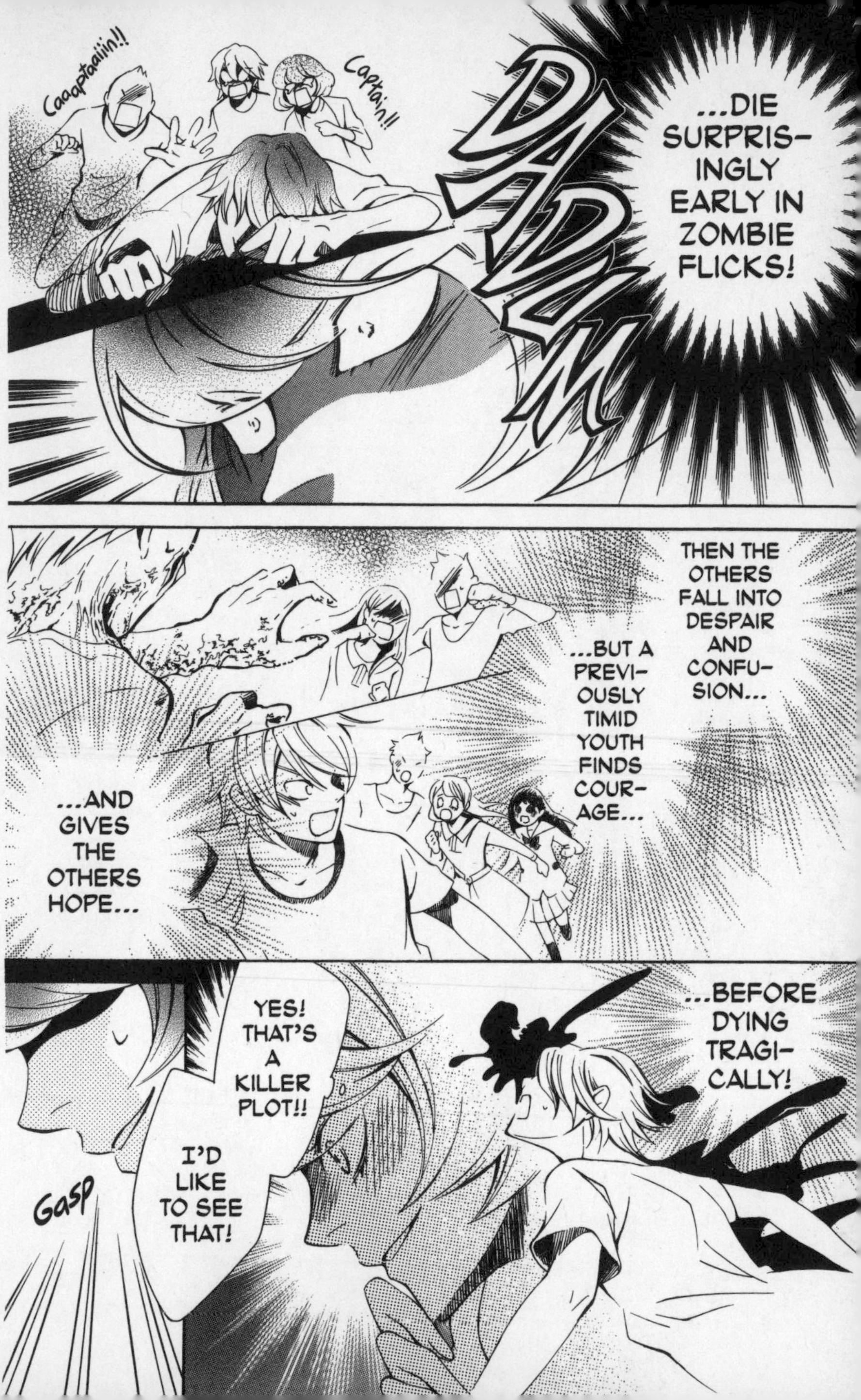
...DIE SURPRISINGLY EARLY IN ZOMBIE FLICKS!
DADUM
Captain!!
Caaaptaiiin!!
THEN THE OTHERS FALL INTO DESPAIR AND CONFUSION...
...BUT A PREVIOUSLY TIMID YOUTH FINDS COURAGE...
...AND GIVES THE OTHERS HOPE...
...BEFORE DYING TRAGICALLY!
YES! THAT'S A KILLER PLOT!!
I'D LIKE TO SEE THAT!
Gasp

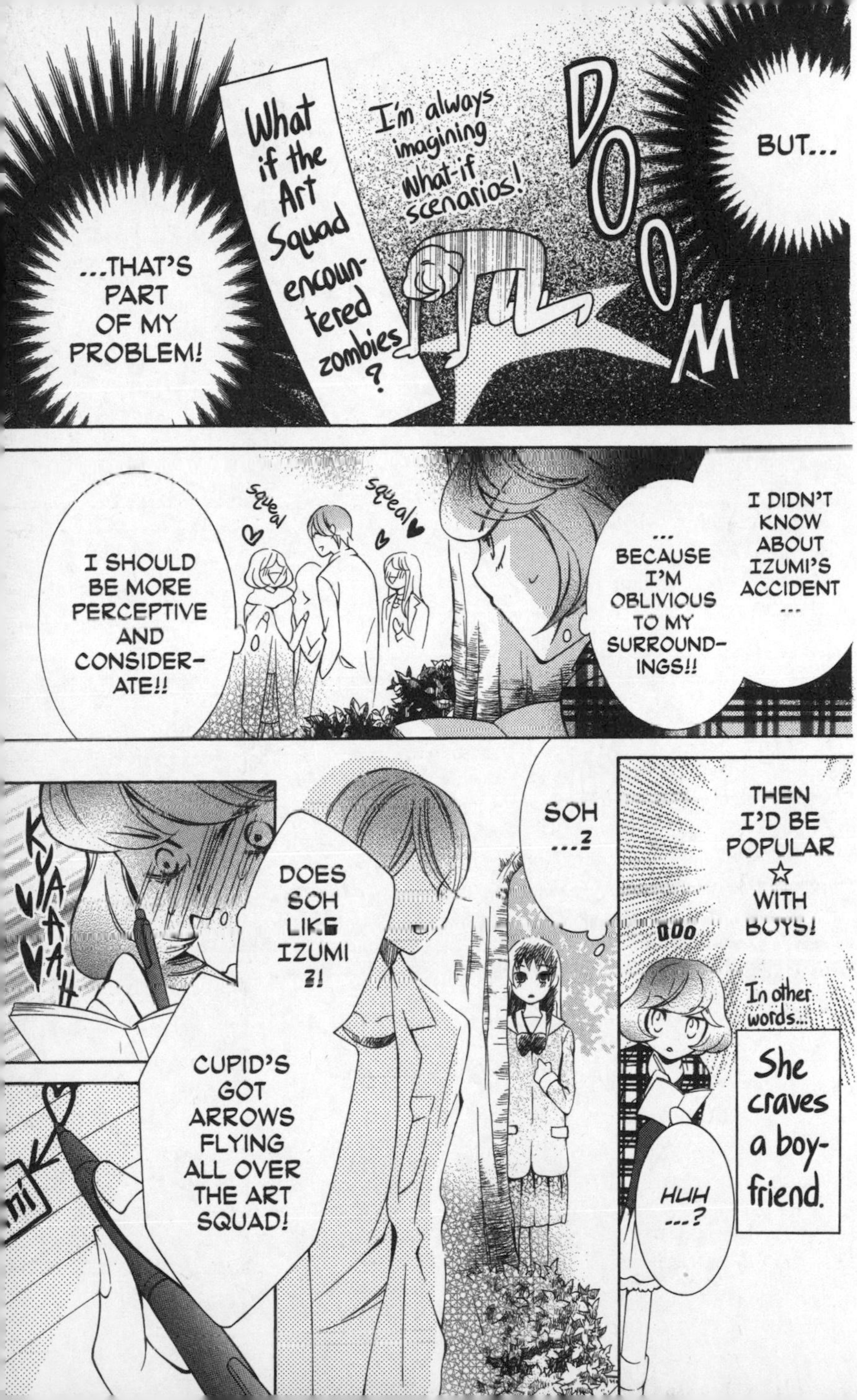
BUT...
DOOOM
I'm always imagining what-if scenarios!
What if the Art Squad encountered zombies?
...THAT'S PART OF MY PROBLEM!
I DIDN'T KNOW ABOUT IZUMI'S ACCIDENT...
...BECAUSE I'M OBLIVIOUS TO MY SURROUNDINGS!!
squeal
squeal
I SHOULD BE MORE PERCEPTIVE AND CONSIDER-ATE!!
THEN I'D BE POPULAR ☆ WITH BOYS!
In other words...
She craves a boy-friend.
HUH...?
SOH...?
DOES SOH LIKE IZUMI?!
KYAAAAH
CUPID'S GOT ARROWS FLYING ALL OVER THE ART SQUAD!

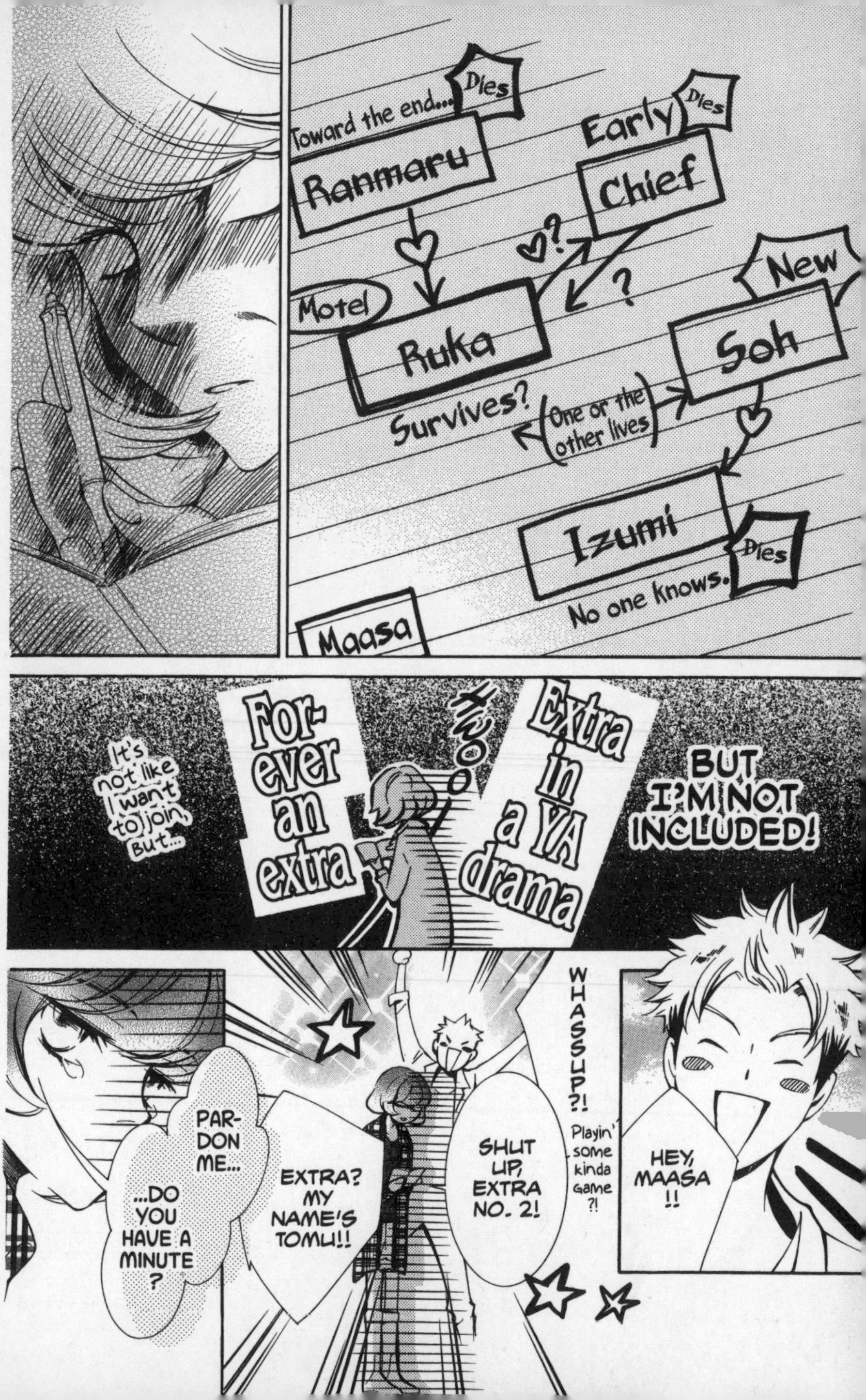
Toward the end...
Dies
Ranmaru
Early
Dies
Chief
Motel
Ruka
?
New
Soh
Survives?
One or the other lives
Izumi
Dies
No one knows.
Maasa
BUT I'M NOT INCLUDED!
Extra in a YA drama
Forever an extra
It's not like I want to join, but...
HEY, MAASA!!
Playin' some kinda game?!
WHASSUP?!
SHUT UP, EXTRA NO. 2!
EXTRA? MY NAME'S TOMU!!
PARDON ME...
...DO YOU HAVE A MINUTE?

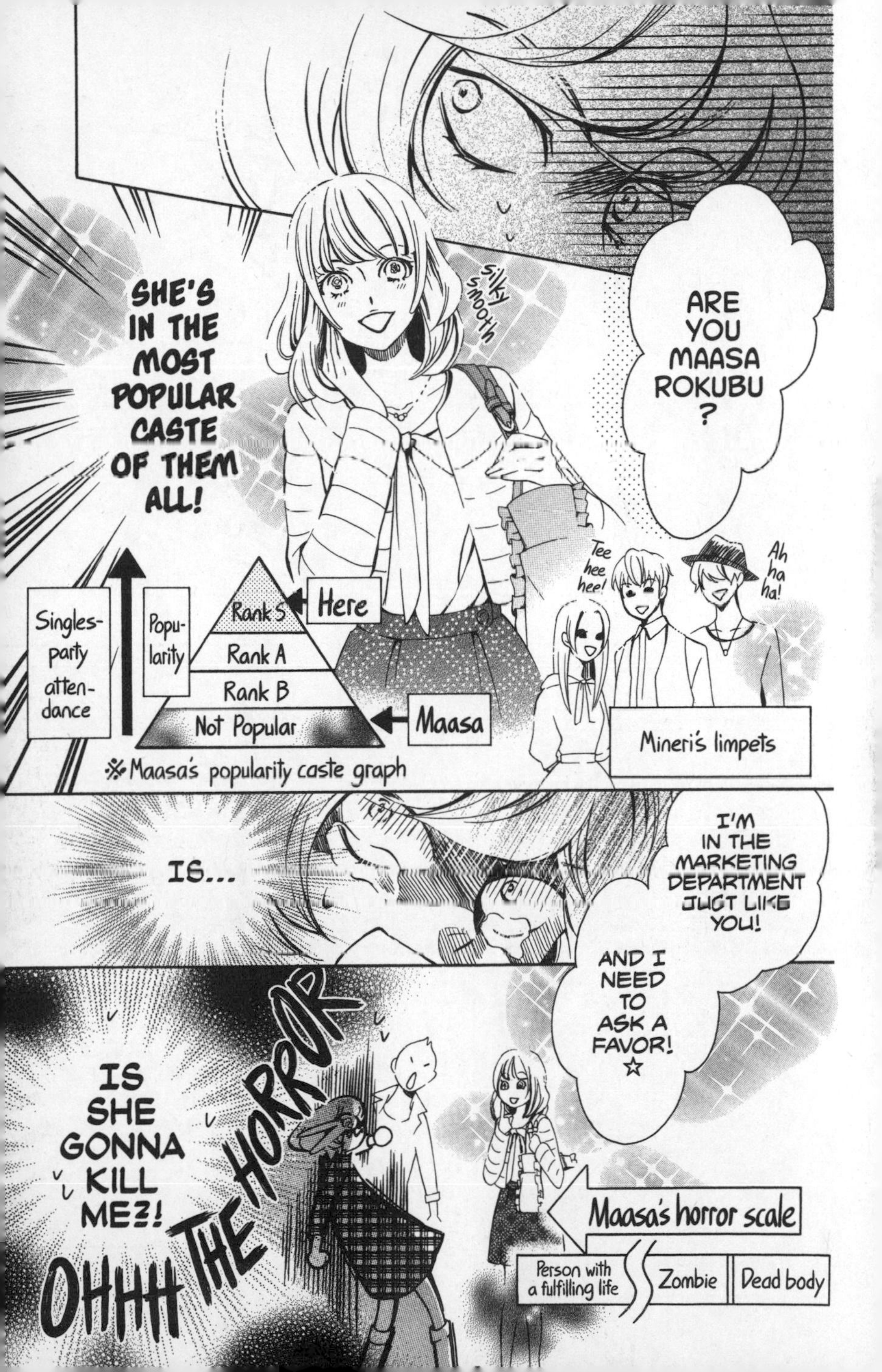
ARE YOU MAASA ROKUBU?
silky smooth
SHE'S IN THE MOST POPULAR CASTE OF THEM ALL!
Ah ha ha!
Tee hee hee!
Mineri's limpets
Here
Maasa
Rank S
Rank A
Rank B
Not Popular
Popularity
Singles-party attendance
※Maasa's popularity caste graph
I'M IN THE MARKETING DEPARTMENT JUST LIKE YOU!
IS...
AND I NEED TO ASK A FAVOR! ☆
Maasa's horror scale
Person with a fulfilling life
Zombie
Dead body
IS SHE GONNA KILL ME?!
OHHH THE HORROR

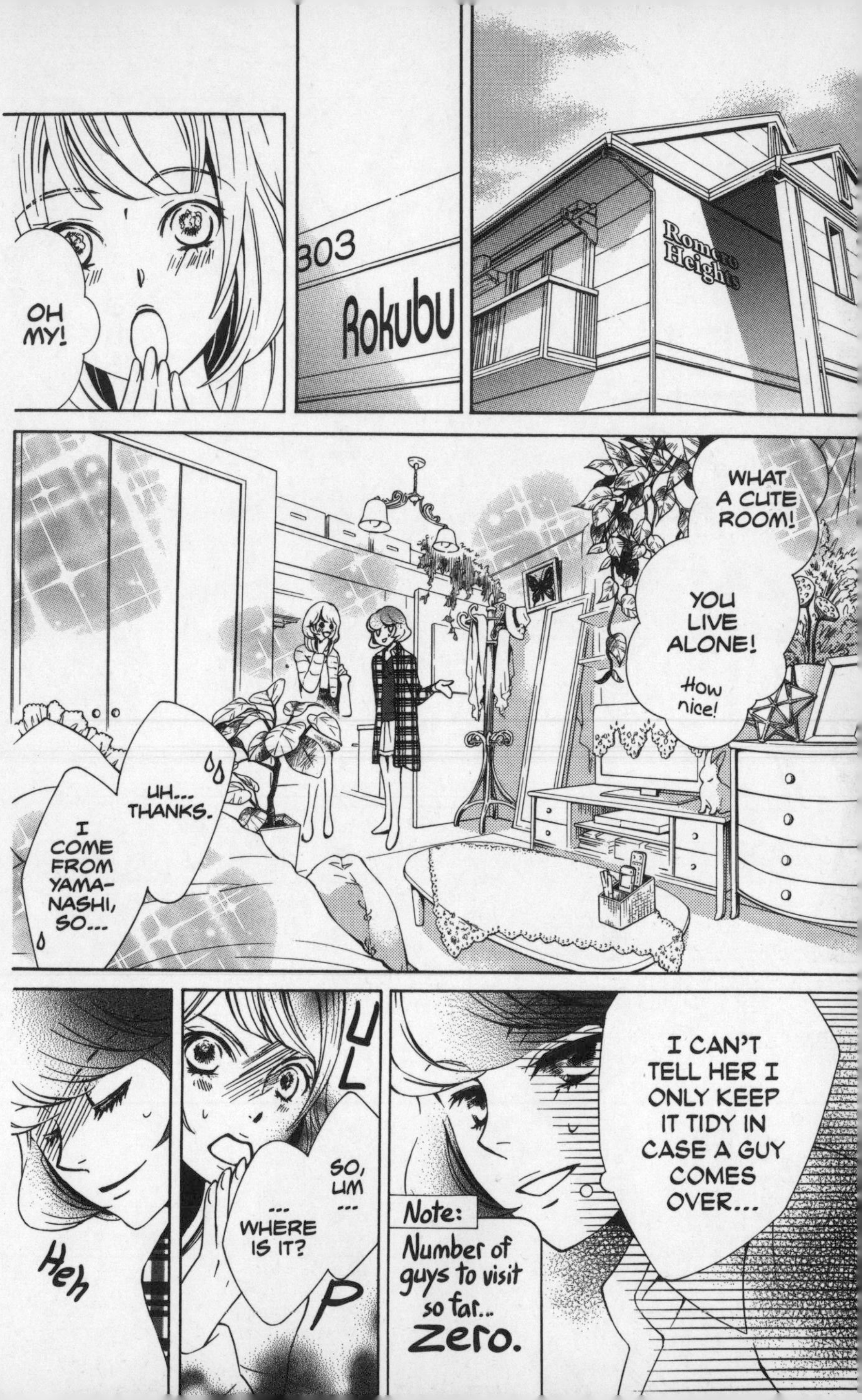
Romero Heights
303
Rokubu
OH MY!
WHAT A CUTE ROOM!
YOU LIVE ALONE! How nice!
UH... THANKS.
I COME FROM YAMANASHI, SO...
I CAN'T TELL HER I ONLY KEEP IT TIDY IN CASE A GUY COMES OVER...
Note:
Number of guys to visit so far... Zero.
ULP
SO, UM ...
... WHERE IS IT?
Heh

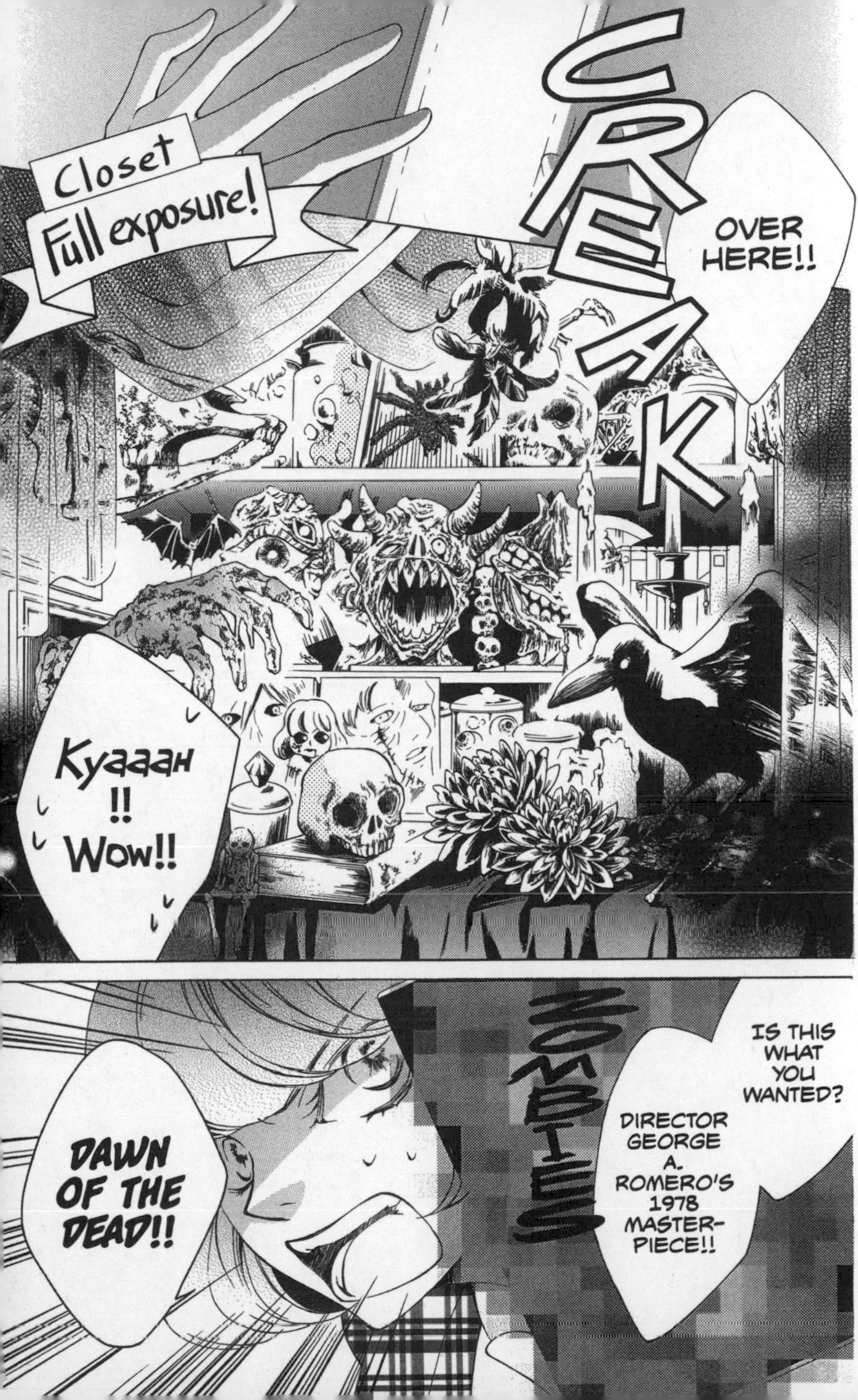
CREAK
OVER HERE!!
Closet Full exposure!
Kyaaah!! Wow!!
IS THIS WHAT YOU WANTED?
DIRECTOR GEORGE A. ROMERO'S 1978 MASTER-PIECE!!
ZOMBIES
DAWN OF THE DEAD!!

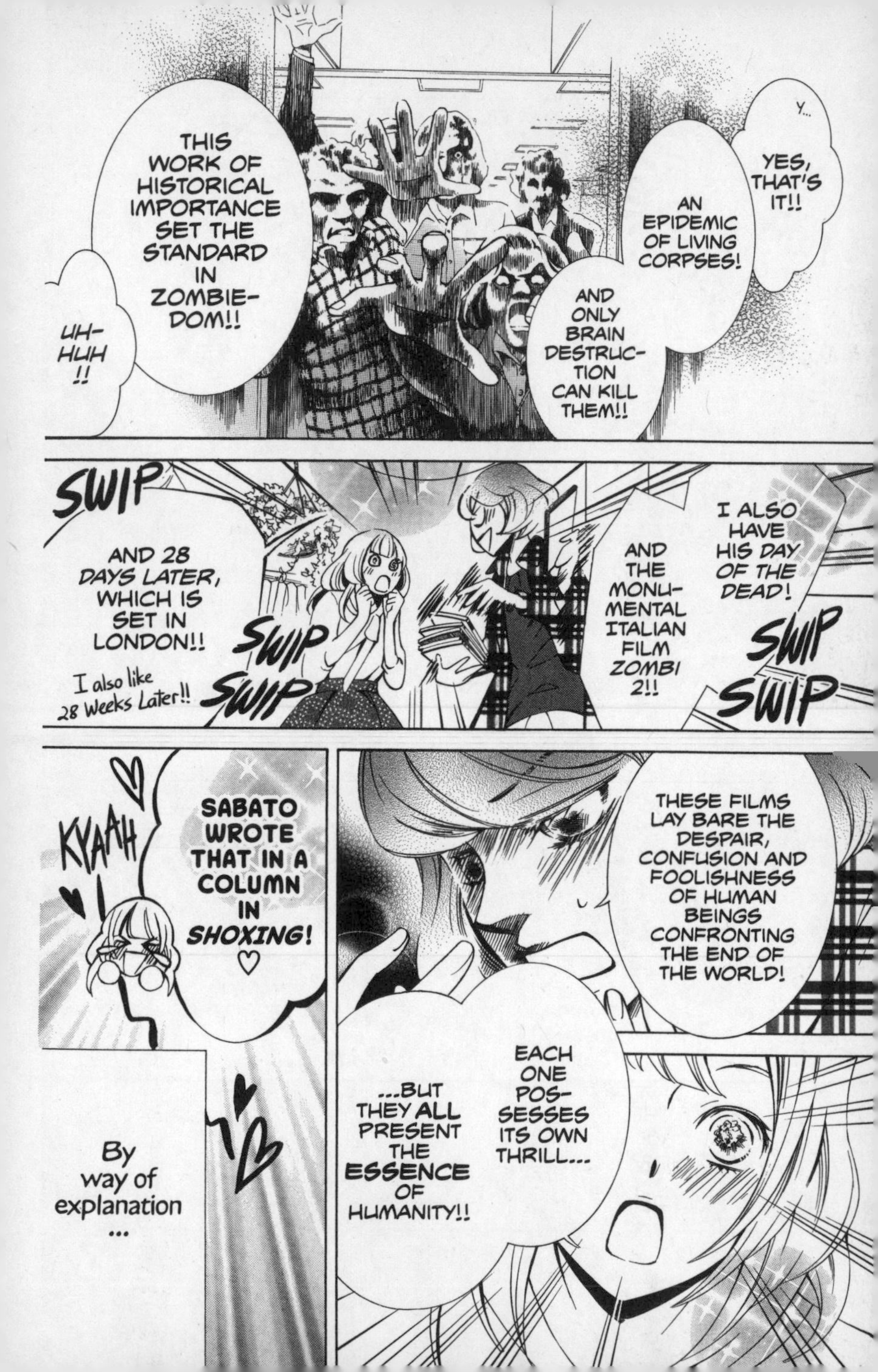
Y...
YES, THAT'S IT!!
AN EPIDEMIC OF LIVING CORPSES!
AND ONLY BRAIN DESTRUCTION CAN KILL THEM!!
THIS WORK OF HISTORICAL IMPORTANCE SET THE STANDARD IN ZOMBIE-DOM!!
UH-HUH!!
I ALSO HAVE HIS DAY OF THE DEAD!
SWIP
SWIP
AND THE MONUMENTAL ITALIAN FILM ZOMBI 2!!
SWIP
SWIP
AND 28 DAYS LATER, WHICH IS SET IN LONDON!!
I also like 28 Weeks Later!!
SWIP
THESE FILMS LAY BARE THE DESPAIR, CONFUSION AND FOOLISHNESS OF HUMAN BEINGS CONFRONTING THE END OF THE WORLD!
EACH ONE POSSESSES ITS OWN THRILL...
...BUT THEY ALL PRESENT THE ESSENCE OF HUMANITY!!
SABATO WROTE THAT IN A COLUMN IN SHOXING! ♡
KYAAH
By way of explanation...

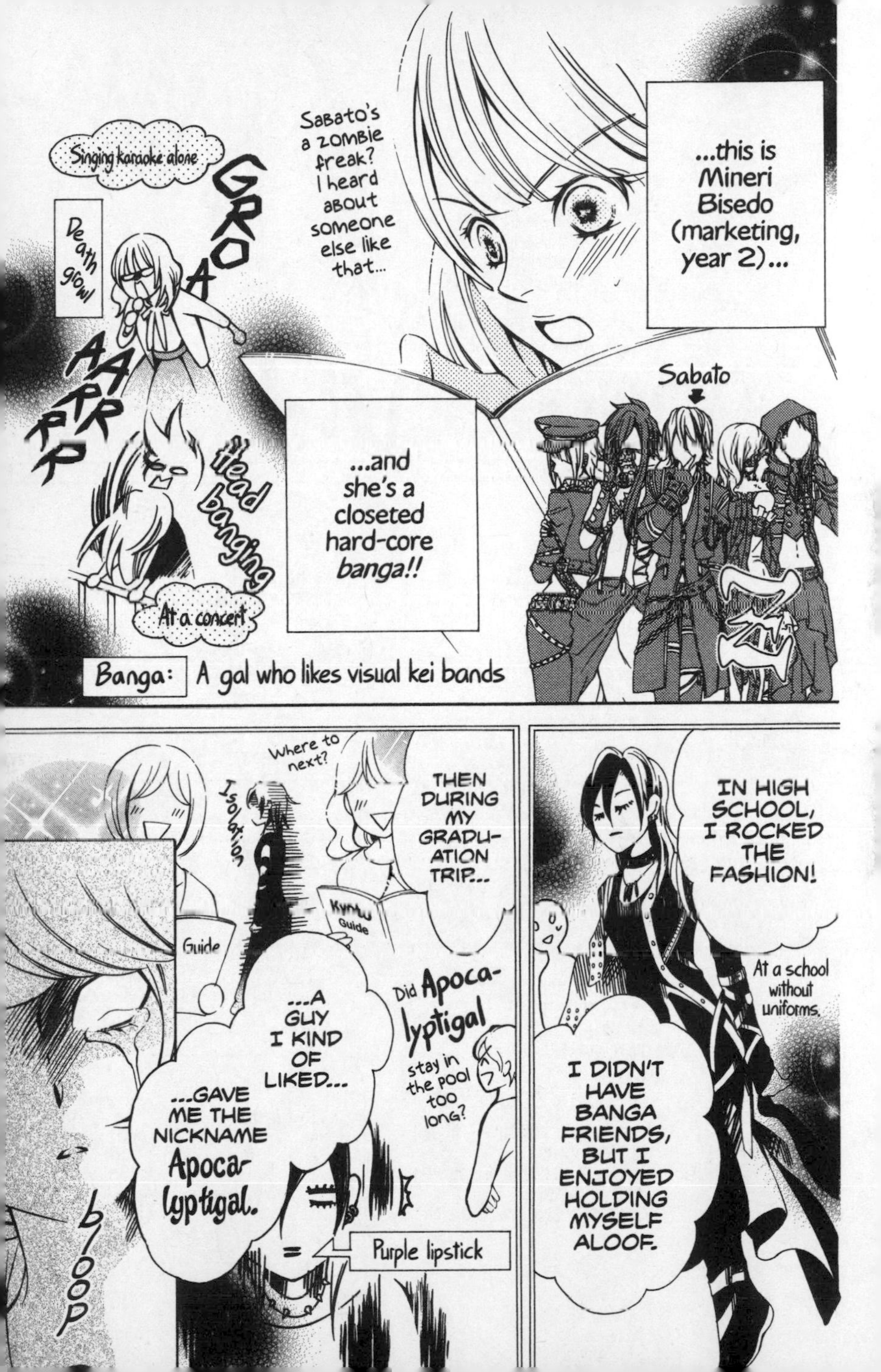
...this is Mineri Bisedo (marketing, year 2)...
Sabato's a zombie freak? I heard about someone else like that...
Singing karaoke alone
GROAARRR
Death growl
Sabato
...and she's a closeted hard-core banga!!
Head banging
At a concert
Banga: A gal who likes visual kei bands
IN HIGH SCHOOL, I ROCKED THE FASHION!
At a school without uniforms.
I DIDN'T HAVE BANGA FRIENDS, BUT I ENJOYED HOLDING MYSELF ALOOF.
THEN DURING MY GRADUATION TRIP...
Where to next?
Isolation
Guide
Guide
...A GUY I KIND OF LIKED...
Did Apoca-lyptigal stay in the pool too long?
...GAVE ME THE NICKNAME Apoca-lyptigal.
Purple lipstick
bloop

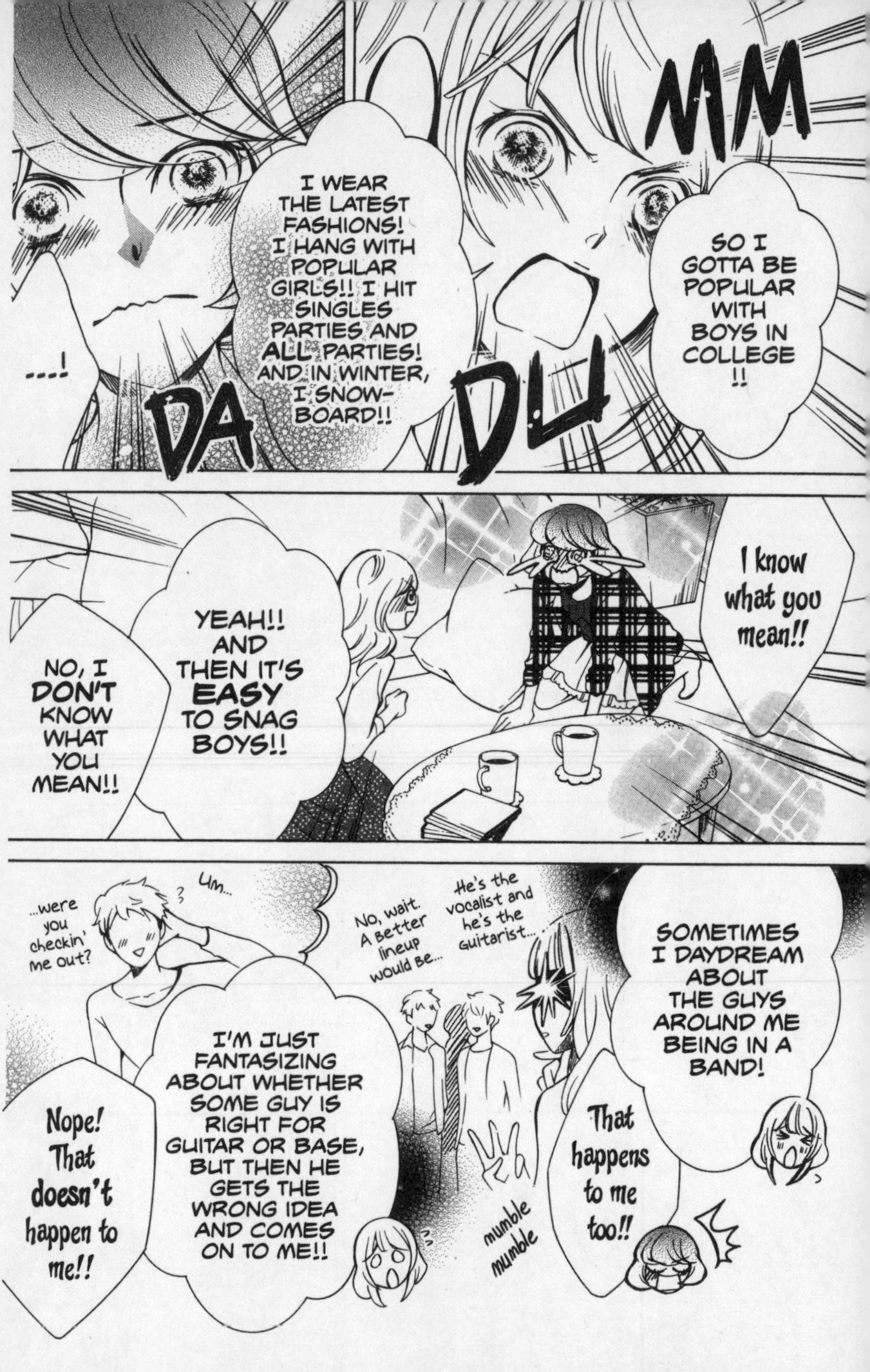
MM
SO I GOTTA BE POPULAR WITH BOYS IN COLLEGE!!
DU
I WEAR THE LATEST FASHIONS! I HANG WITH POPULAR GIRLS!! I HIT SINGLES PARTIES AND ALL PARTIES! AND IN WINTER, I SNOW-BOARD!!
DA
...!
I know what you mean!!
YEAH!! AND THEN IT'S EASY TO SNAG BOYS!!
NO, I DON'T KNOW WHAT YOU MEAN!!
SOMETIMES I DAYDREAM ABOUT THE GUYS AROUND ME BEING IN A BAND!
He's the vocalist and he's the guitarist...
No, wait. A better lineup would be...
That happens to me too!!
mumble mumble
I'M JUST FANTASIZING ABOUT WHETHER SOME GUY IS RIGHT FOR GUITAR OR BASE, BUT THEN HE GETS THE WRONG IDEA AND COMES ON TO ME!!
Um...
...were you checkin' me out?
Nope! That doesn't happen to me!!

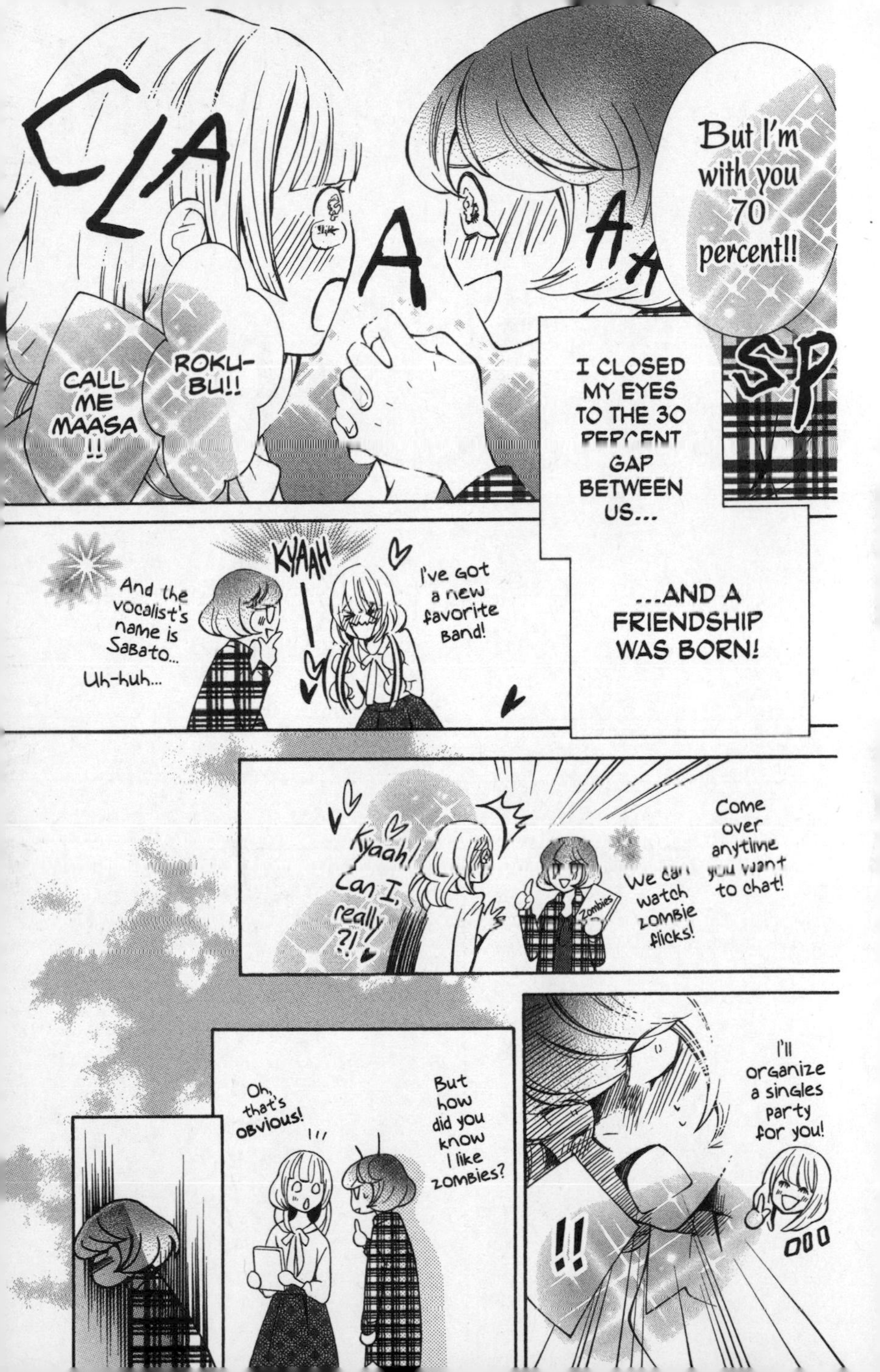
But I'm with you 70 percent!!
SP
CLA A A
ROKU-BU!!
CALL ME MAASA!!
I CLOSED MY EYES TO THE 30 PERCENT GAP BETWEEN US...
...AND A FRIENDSHIP WAS BORN!
I've got a new favorite band!
KYAAH
And the vocalist's name is Sabato...
Uh-huh...
Come over anytime you want to chat!
We can watch zombie flicks!
Zombies
Kyaah! Can I, really?!
I'll organize a singles party for you!
!!
But how did you know I like zombies?
Oh, that's obvious!

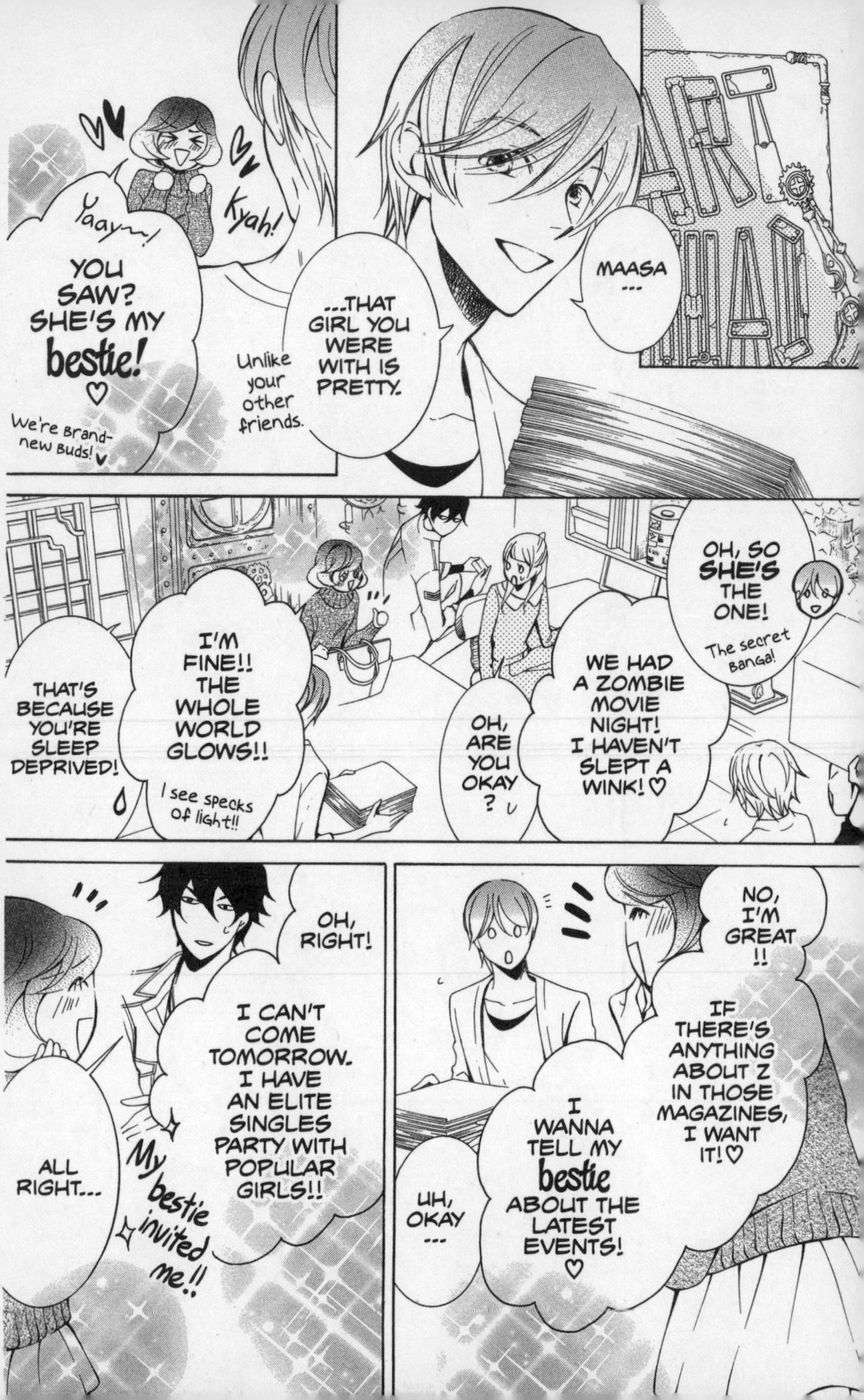
MAASA...
...THAT GIRL YOU WERE WITH IS PRETTY.
Unlike your other friends.
Kyah!
Yaay~!
YOU SAW? SHE'S MY bestie! ♡
We're brand-new buds! ♥
OH, SO SHE'S THE ONE!
The secret Banga!
WE HAD A ZOMBIE MOVIE NIGHT! I HAVEN'T SLEPT A WINK! ♡
OH, ARE YOU OKAY?
I'M FINE!! THE WHOLE WORLD GLOWS!!
I see specks of light!!
THAT'S BECAUSE YOU'RE SLEEP DEPRIVED!
NO, I'M GREAT!!
IF THERE'S ANYTHING ABOUT Z IN THOSE MAGAZINES, I WANT IT! ♡
I WANNA TELL MY bestie ABOUT THE LATEST EVENTS! ♡
UH, OKAY...
OH, RIGHT!
I CAN'T COME TOMORROW. I HAVE AN ELITE SINGLES PARTY WITH POPULAR GIRLS!!
My bestie invited me!!
ALL RIGHT...

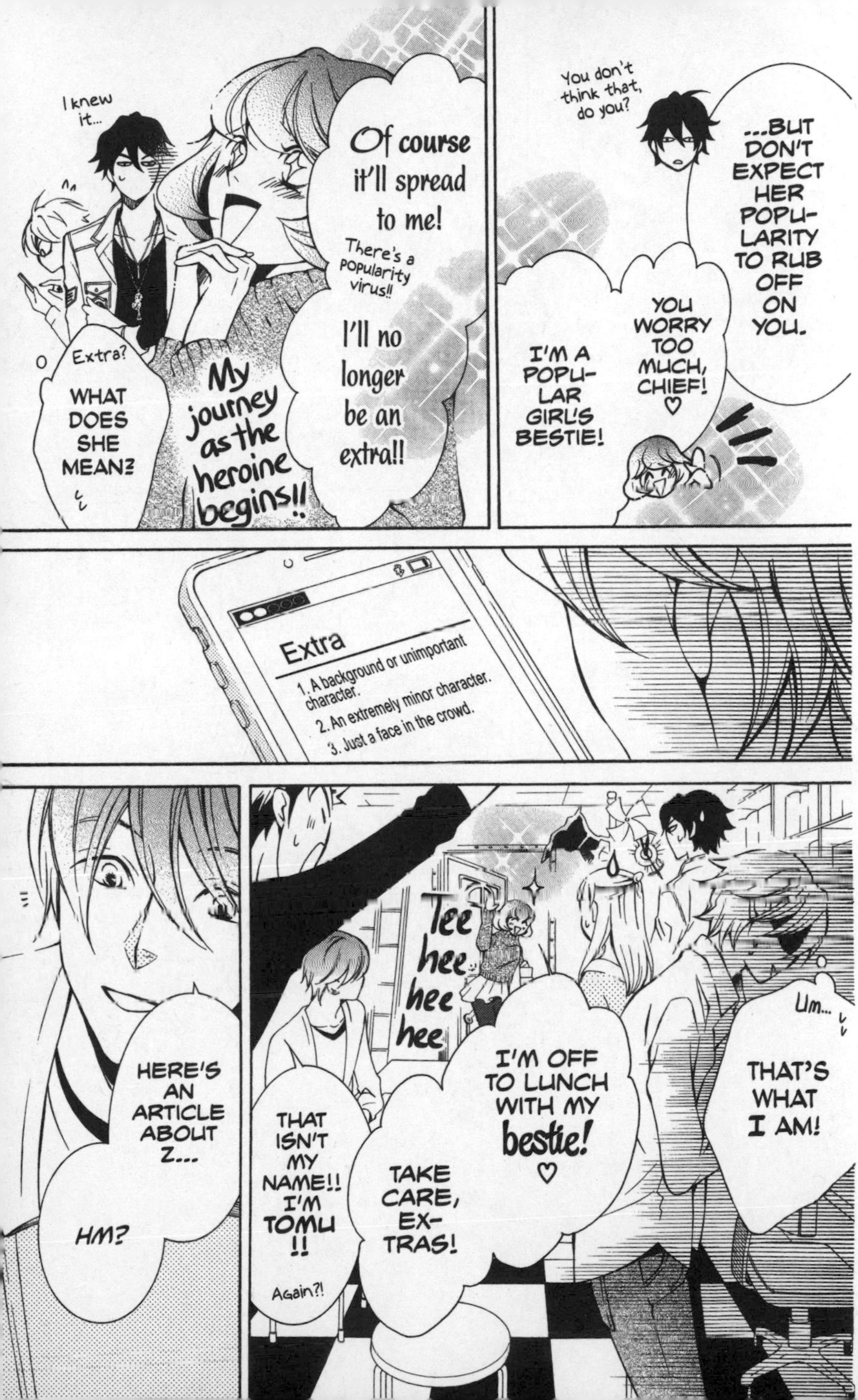
You don't think that, do you?
...BUT DON'T EXPECT HER POPULARITY TO RUB OFF ON YOU.
YOU WORRY TOO MUCH, CHIEF! ♡
I'M A POPULAR GIRL'S BESTIE!
Of course it'll spread to me!
There's a popularity virus!!
I'll no longer be an extra!!
My journey as the heroine begins!!
I knew it...
Extra?
WHAT DOES SHE MEAN?
Extra
1. A background or unimportant character.
2. An extremely minor character.
3. Just a face in the crowd.
Um...
THAT'S WHAT I AM!
I'M OFF TO LUNCH WITH MY bestie! ♡
Tee hee hee hee
TAKE CARE, EXTRAS!
THAT ISN'T MY NAME!! I'M TOMU!!
Again?!
HERE'S AN ARTICLE ABOUT Z...
HM?

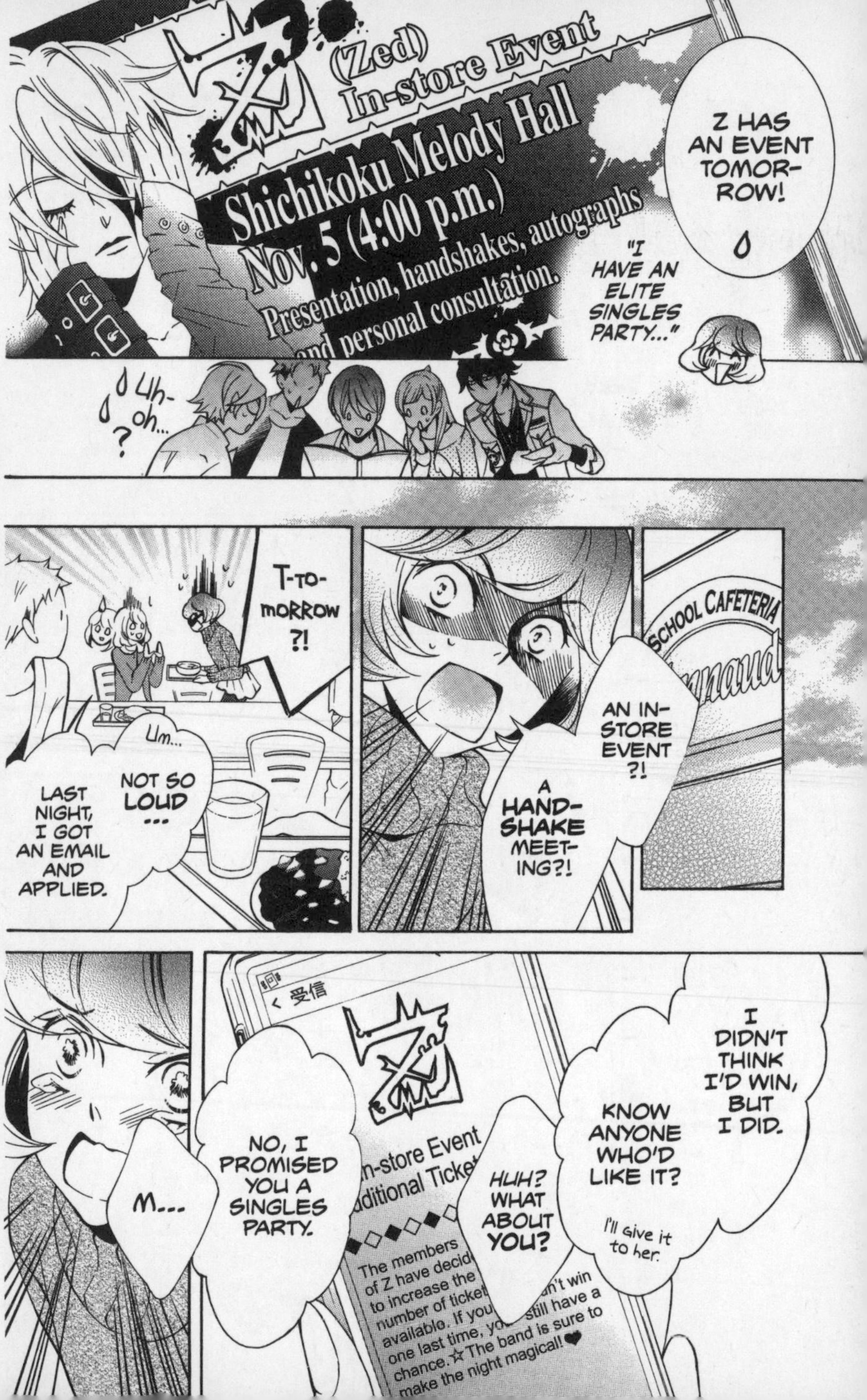
(Zed)
In-store Event
Shichikoku Melody Hall
Nov. 5 (4:00 p.m.)
Presentation, handshakes, autographs and personal consultation.
Z HAS AN EVENT TOMORROW!
"I HAVE AN ELITE SINGLES PARTY..."
Uh-oh...
SCHOOL CAFETERIA
AN IN-STORE EVENT?!
A HANDSHAKE MEETING?!
T-TO-MORROW?!
Um...
NOT SO LOUD...
LAST NIGHT, I GOT AN EMAIL AND APPLIED.
I DIDN'T THINK I'D WIN, BUT I DID.
KNOW ANYONE WHO'D LIKE IT?
I'll give it to her.
受信
HUH? WHAT ABOUT YOU?
NO, I PROMISED YOU A SINGLES PARTY.
M...

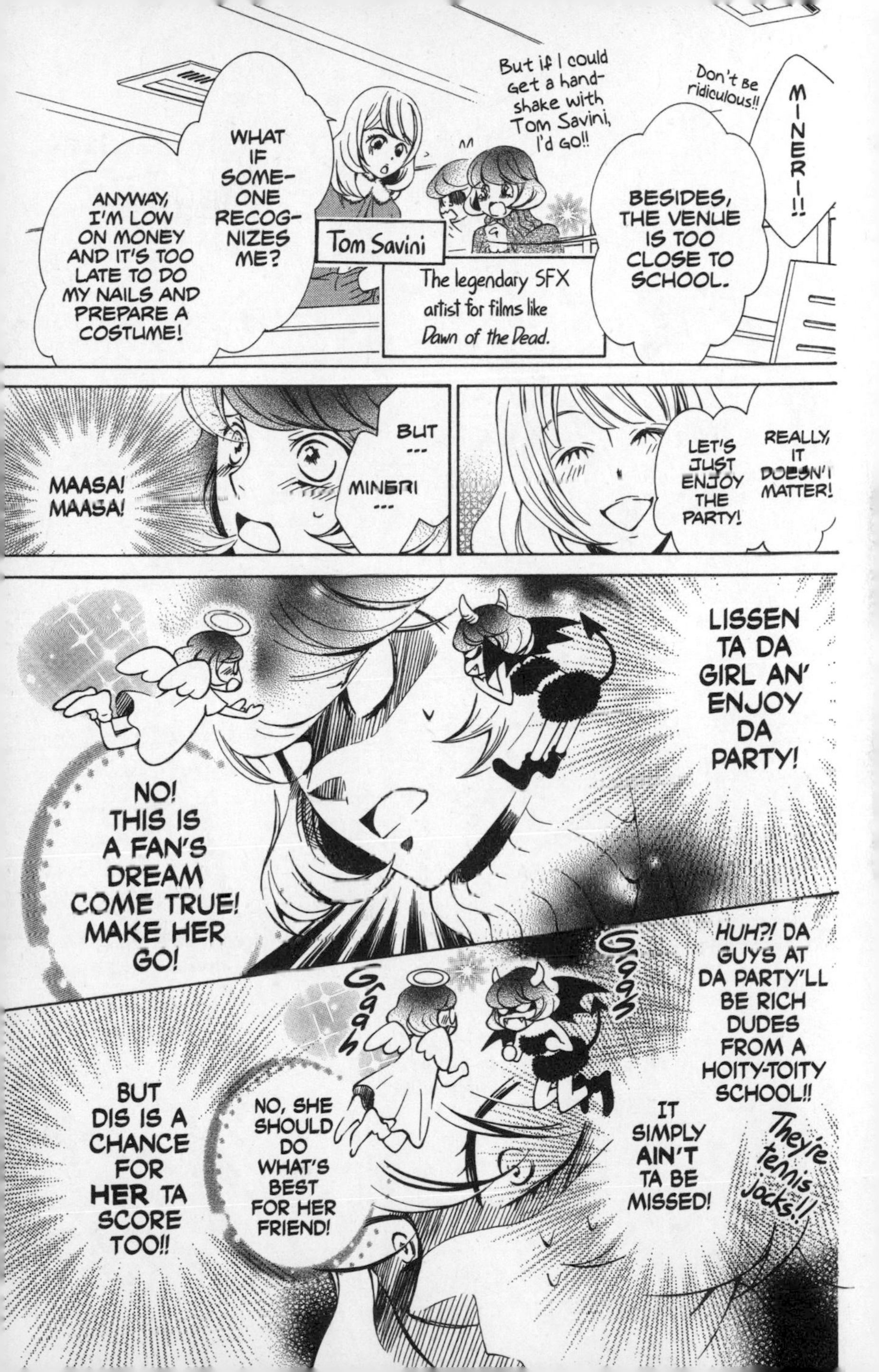
MINERI!!
Don't be ridiculous!!
BESIDES, THE VENUE IS TOO CLOSE TO SCHOOL.
But if I could get a handshake with Tom Savini, I'd go!!
Tom Savini
The legendary SFX artist for films like *Dawn of the Dead*.
WHAT IF SOMEONE RECOGNIZES ME?
ANYWAY, I'M LOW ON MONEY AND IT'S TOO LATE TO DO MY NAILS AND PREPARE A COSTUME!
REALLY, IT DOESN'T MATTER!
LET'S JUST ENJOY THE PARTY!
BUT... MINERI...
MAASA! MAASA!
LISSEN TA DA GIRL AN' ENJOY DA PARTY!
NO! THIS IS A FAN'S DREAM COME TRUE! MAKE HER GO!
Graah
HUH?! DA GUYS AT DA PARTY'LL BE RICH DUDES FROM A HOITY-TOITY SCHOOL!!
They're tennis jocks!!
IT SIMPLY AIN'T TA BE MISSED!
Graah
NO, SHE SHOULD DO WHAT'S BEST FOR HER FRIEND!
BUT DIS IS A CHANCE FOR HER TA SCORE TOO!!

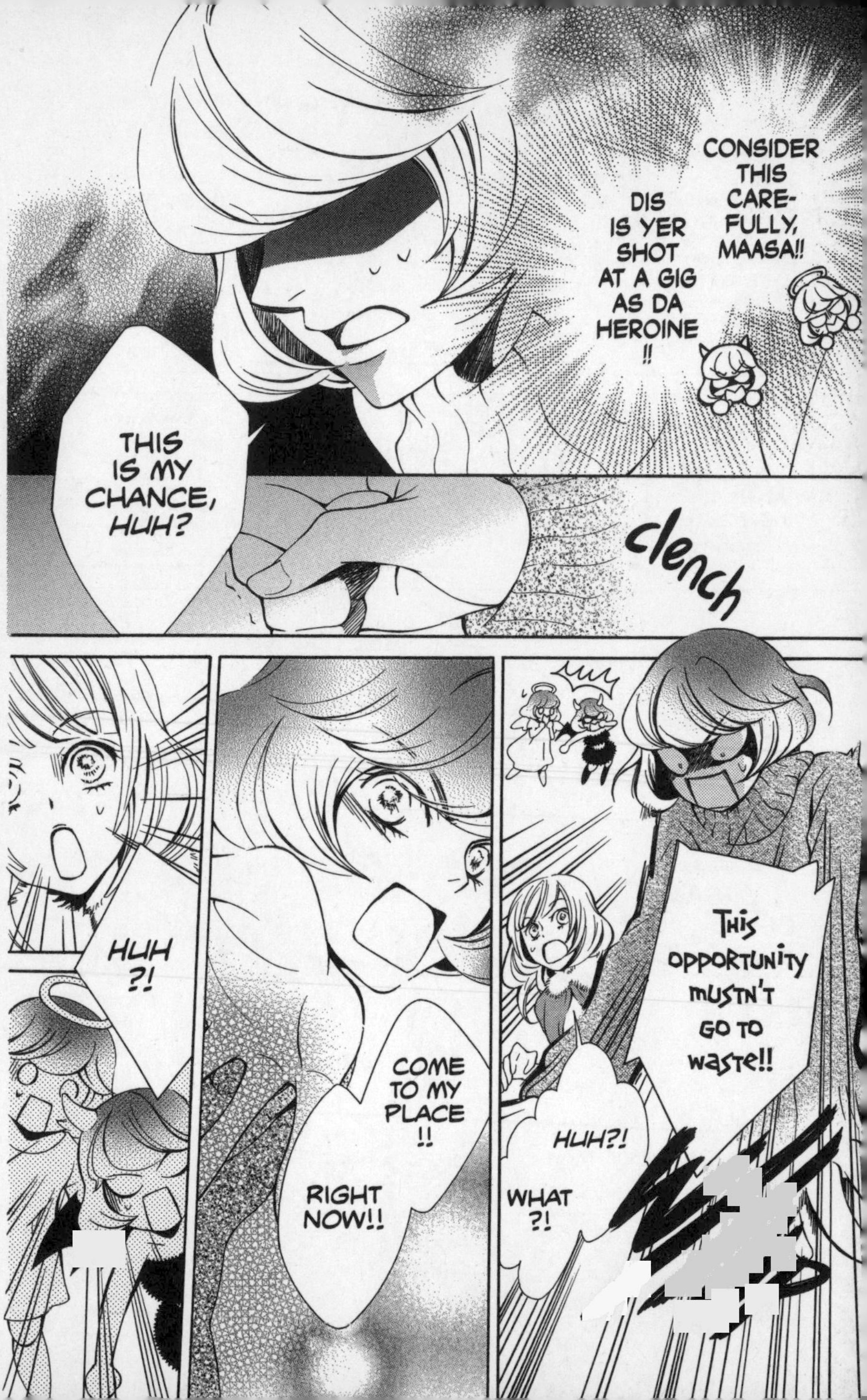
CONSIDER THIS CARE-FULLY, MAASA!!
DIS IS YER SHOT AT A GIG AS DA HEROINE!!
THIS IS MY CHANCE, HUH?
clench
THIS OPPORTUNITY MUSTN'T GO TO WASTE!!
HUH?!
WHAT?!
COME TO MY PLACE!!
RIGHT NOW!!
HUH?!

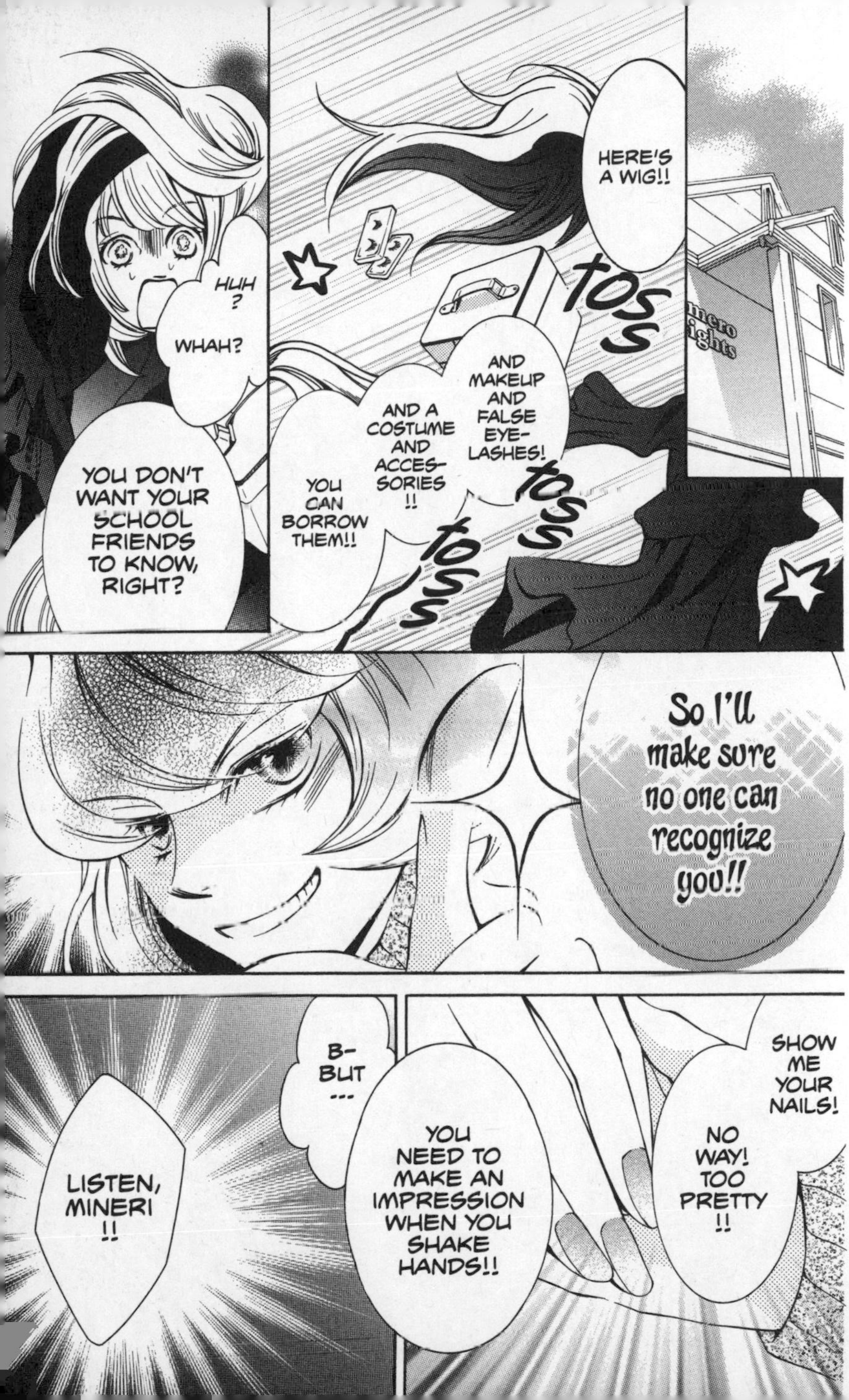
HERE'S A WIG!!
TOSS
AND MAKEUP AND FALSE EYE-LASHES!
TOSS
AND A COSTUME AND ACCES-SORIES!!
TOSS
YOU CAN BORROW THEM!!
HUH? WHAH?
YOU DON'T WANT YOUR SCHOOL FRIENDS TO KNOW, RIGHT?
So I'll make sure no one can recognize you!!
SHOW ME YOUR NAILS!
NO WAY! TOO PRETTY!!
B-BUT---
YOU NEED TO MAKE AN IMPRESSION WHEN YOU SHAKE HANDS!!
LISTEN, MINERI!!

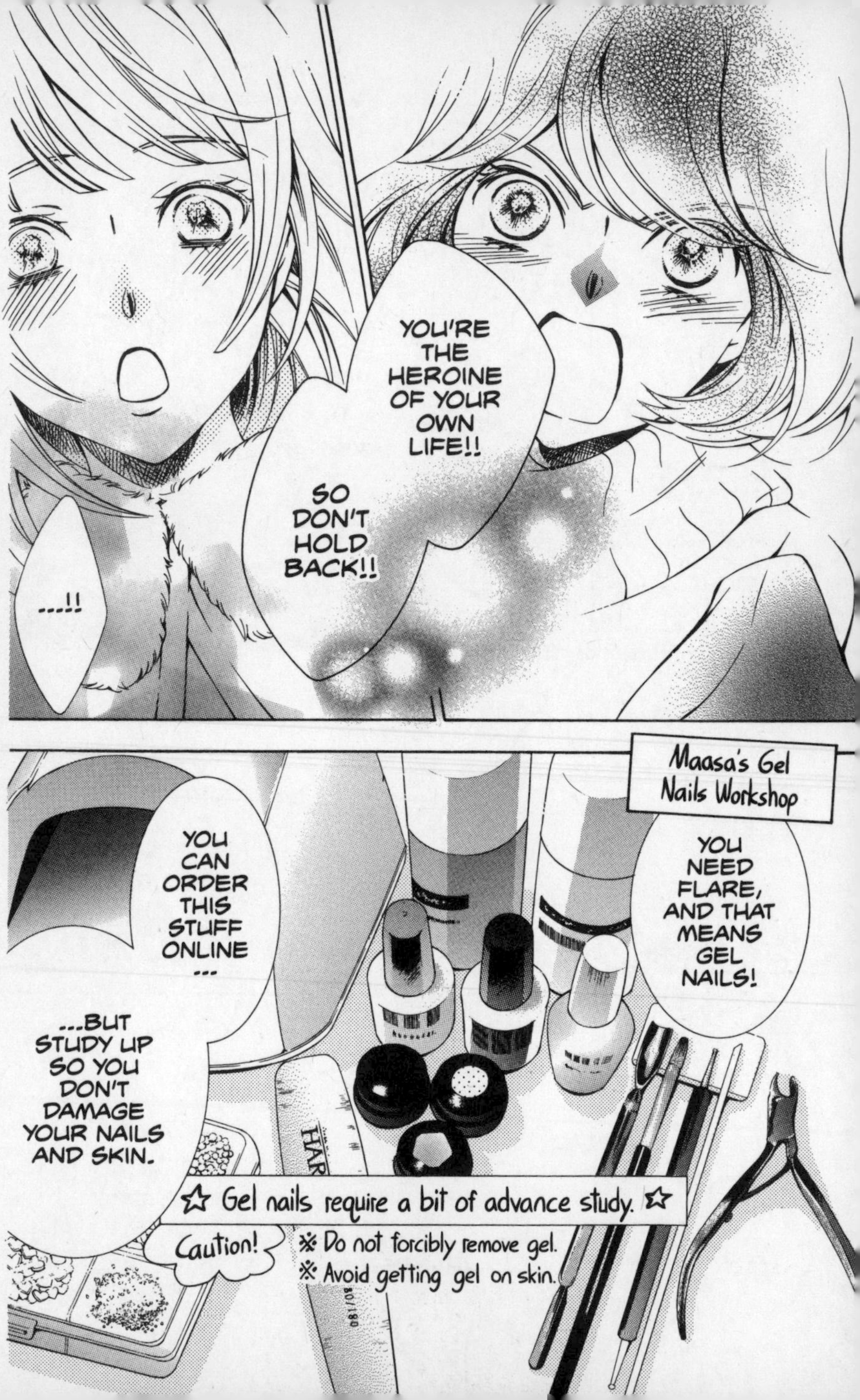
YOU'RE THE HEROINE OF YOUR OWN LIFE!!
SO DON'T HOLD BACK!!
...!!
Maasa's Gel Nails Workshop
YOU NEED FLARE, AND THAT MEANS GEL NAILS!
YOU CAN ORDER THIS STUFF ONLINE...
...BUT STUDY UP SO YOU DON'T DAMAGE YOUR NAILS AND SKIN.
☆ Gel nails require a bit of advance study. ☆
Caution!
※ Do not forcibly remove gel.
※ Avoid getting gel on skin.

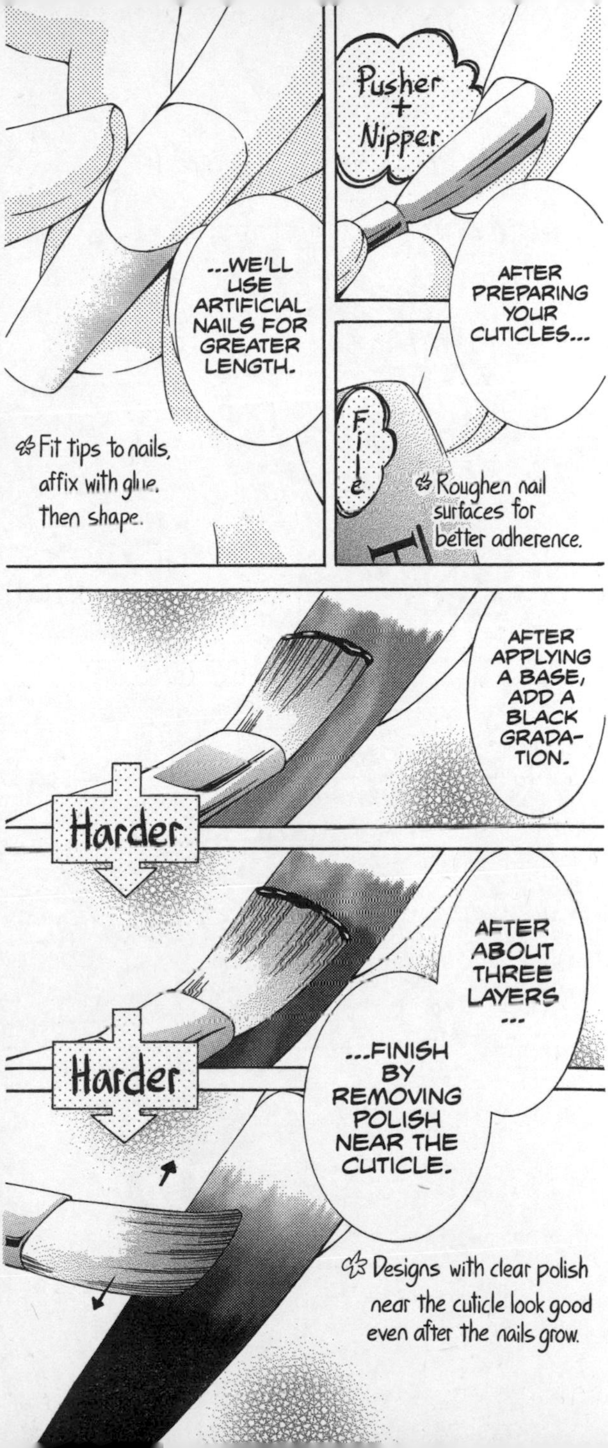

Pusher + Nipper
AFTER PREPARING YOUR CUTICLES...
File
Roughen nail surfaces for better adherence.
...WE'LL USE ARTIFICIAL NAILS FOR GREATER LENGTH.
Fit tips to nails, affix with glue, then shape.
AFTER APPLYING A BASE, ADD A BLACK GRADATION.
Harder
AFTER ABOUT THREE LAYERS...
...FINISH BY REMOVING POLISH NEAR THE CUTICLE.
Harder
Designs with clear polish near the cuticle look good even after the nails grow.

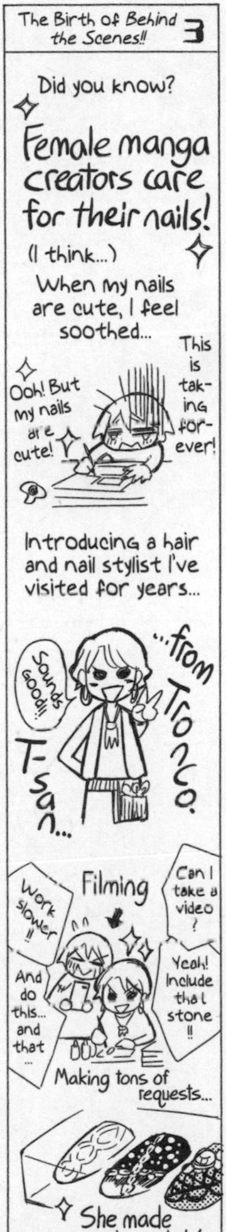

The Birth of Behind the Scenes!! 3
Did you know?
Female manga creators care for their nails!
(I think...)
When my nails are cute, I feel soothed...
This is tak-ing for-ever!
Ooh! But my nails are cute!
Introducing a hair and nail stylist I've visited for years...
...from Tronco.
T-san...
Sounds good!!
Filming
Can I take a video?
Work slower!!
Yeah! Include that stone!!
And do this... and that...
Making tons of requests...
She made sample nails!
Thanks a million!!

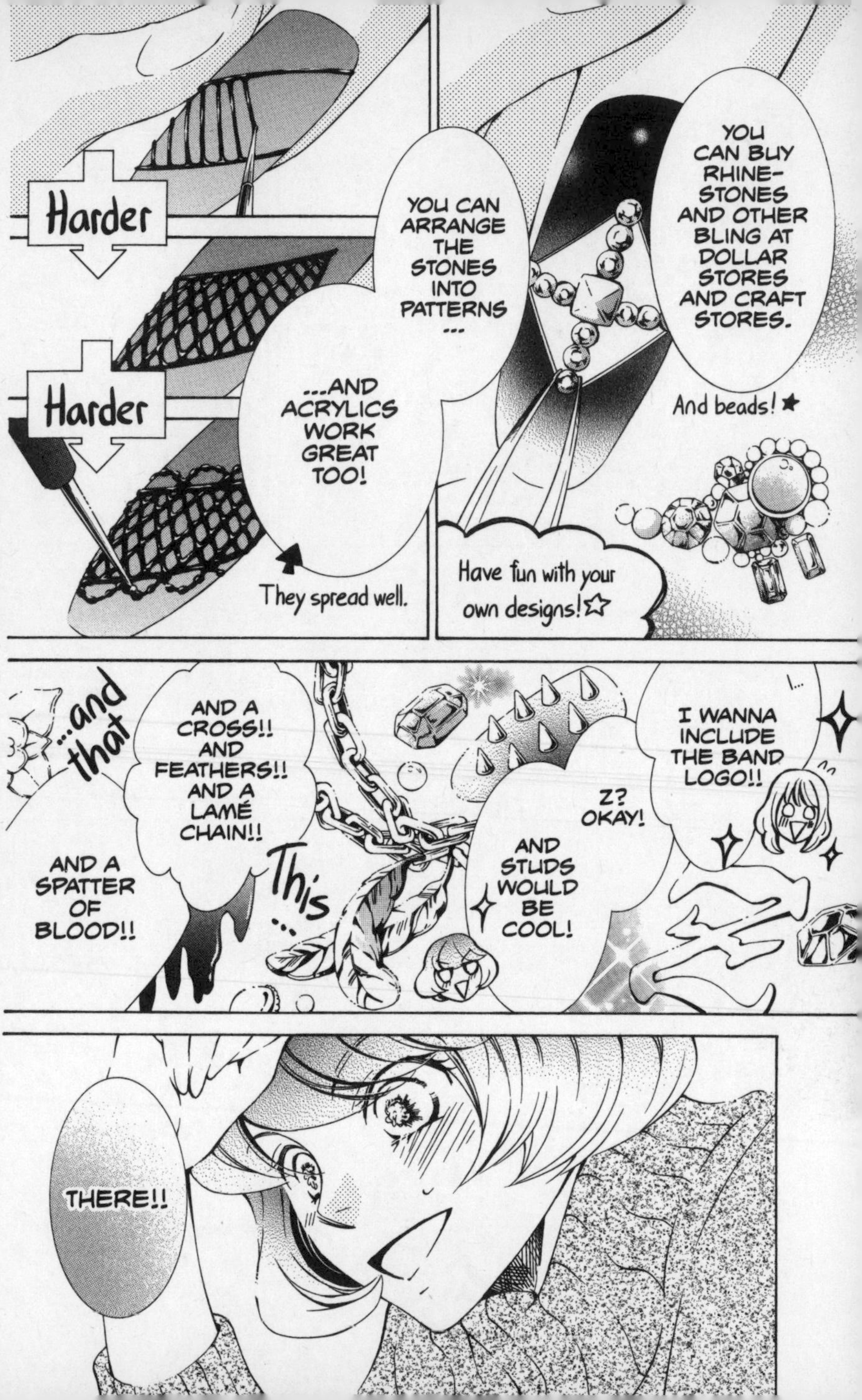
YOU CAN BUY RHINE-STONES AND OTHER BLING AT DOLLAR STORES AND CRAFT STORES.
And beads! ★
YOU CAN ARRANGE THE STONES INTO PATTERNS...
Have fun with your own designs! ☆
...AND ACRYLICS WORK GREAT TOO!
They spread well.
Harder
Harder
I...
I WANNA INCLUDE THE BAND LOGO!!
Z? OKAY!
AND STUDS WOULD BE COOL!
This...
AND A CROSS!! AND FEATHERS!! AND A LAMÉ CHAIN!!
...and that
AND A SPATTER OF BLOOD!!
THERE!!

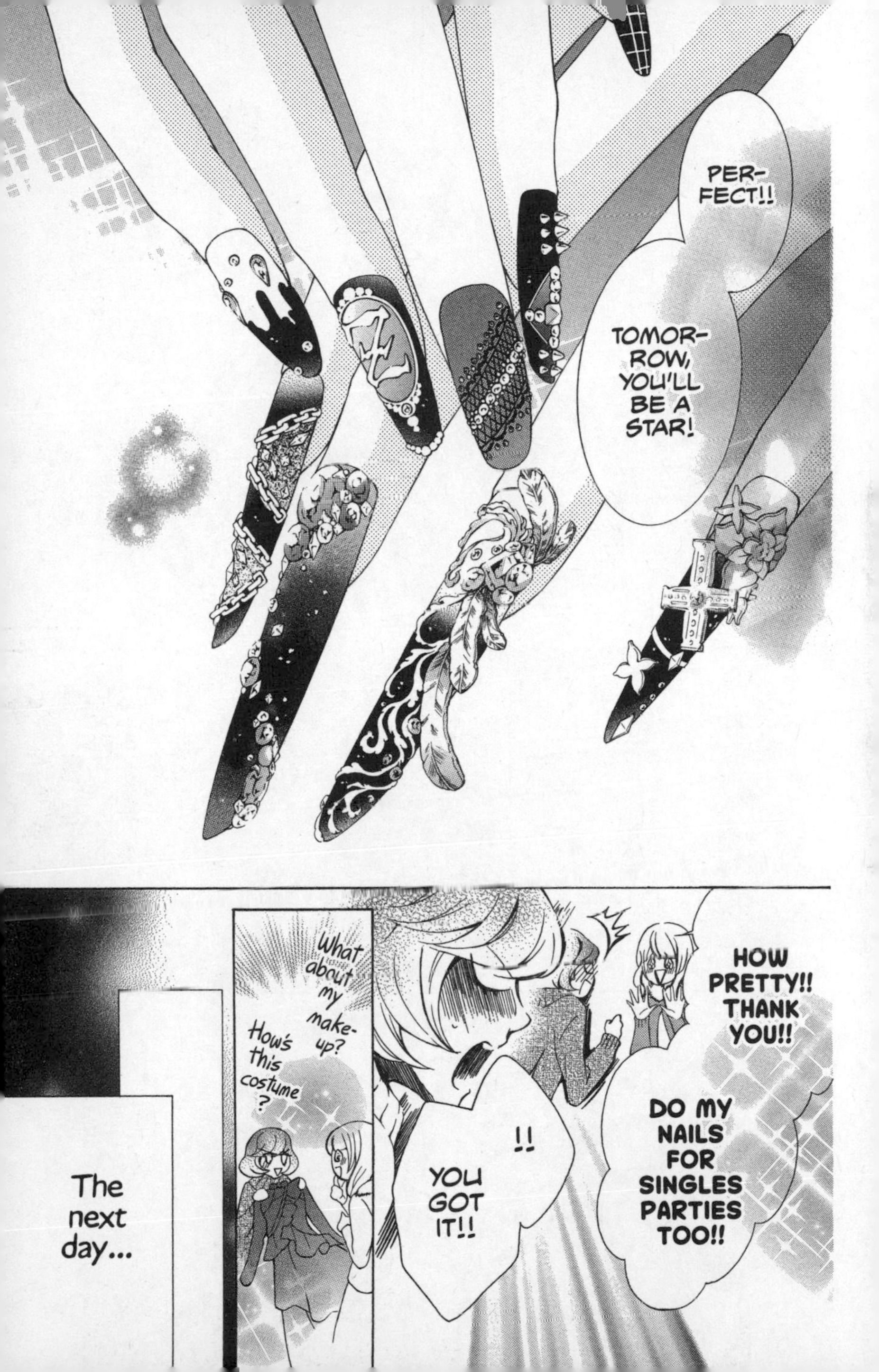
PER-FECT!!
TOMORROW, YOU'LL BE A STAR!
HOW PRETTY!! THANK YOU!!
DO MY NAILS FOR SINGLES PARTIES TOO!!
!!
YOU GOT IT!!
What about my make-up?
How's this costume?
The next day...

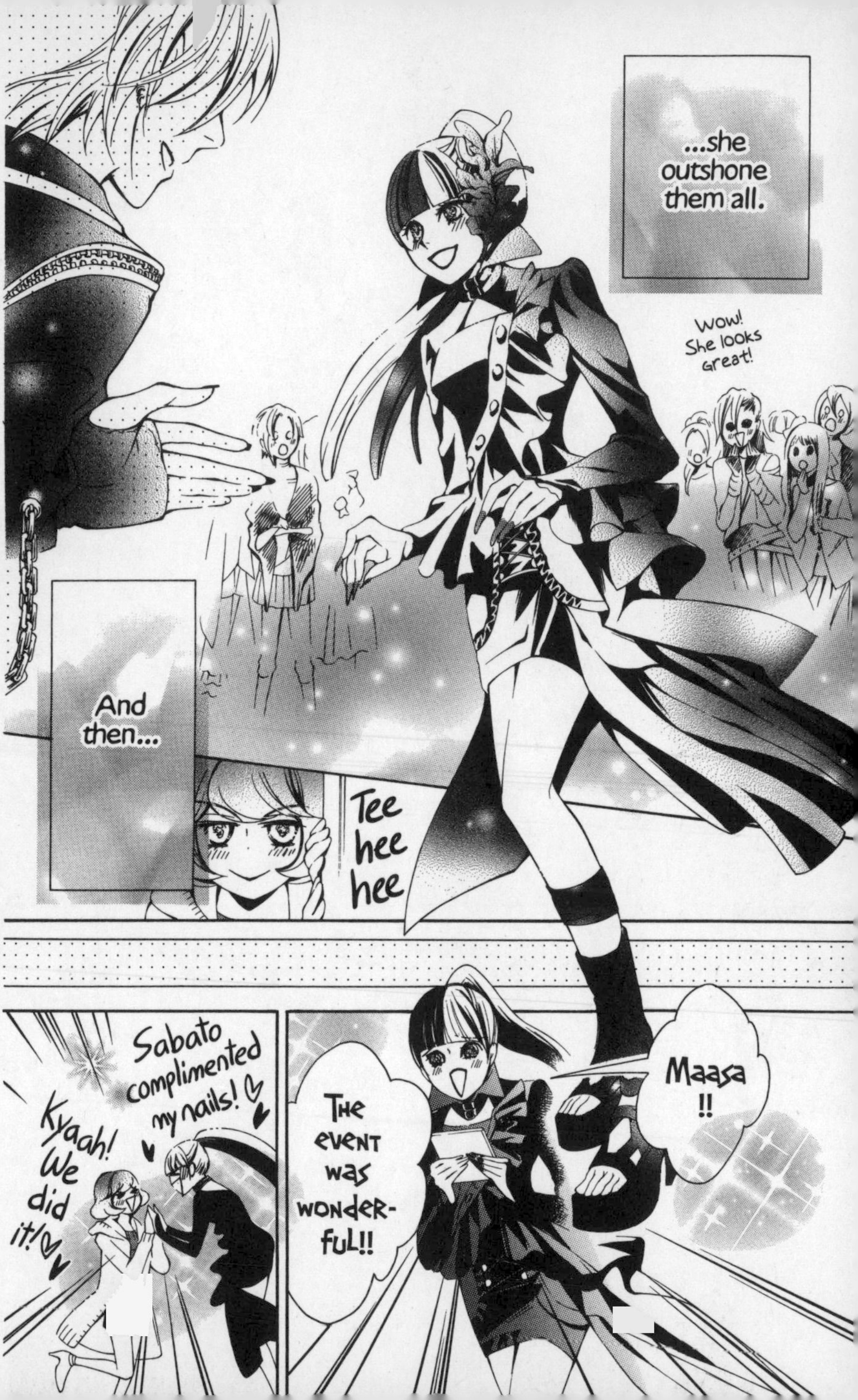
...she outshone them all.
Wow! She looks Great!
And then...
Tee hee hee
Maasa!!
The event was wonder-ful!!
Sabato complimented my nails!
Kyaah! We did it!

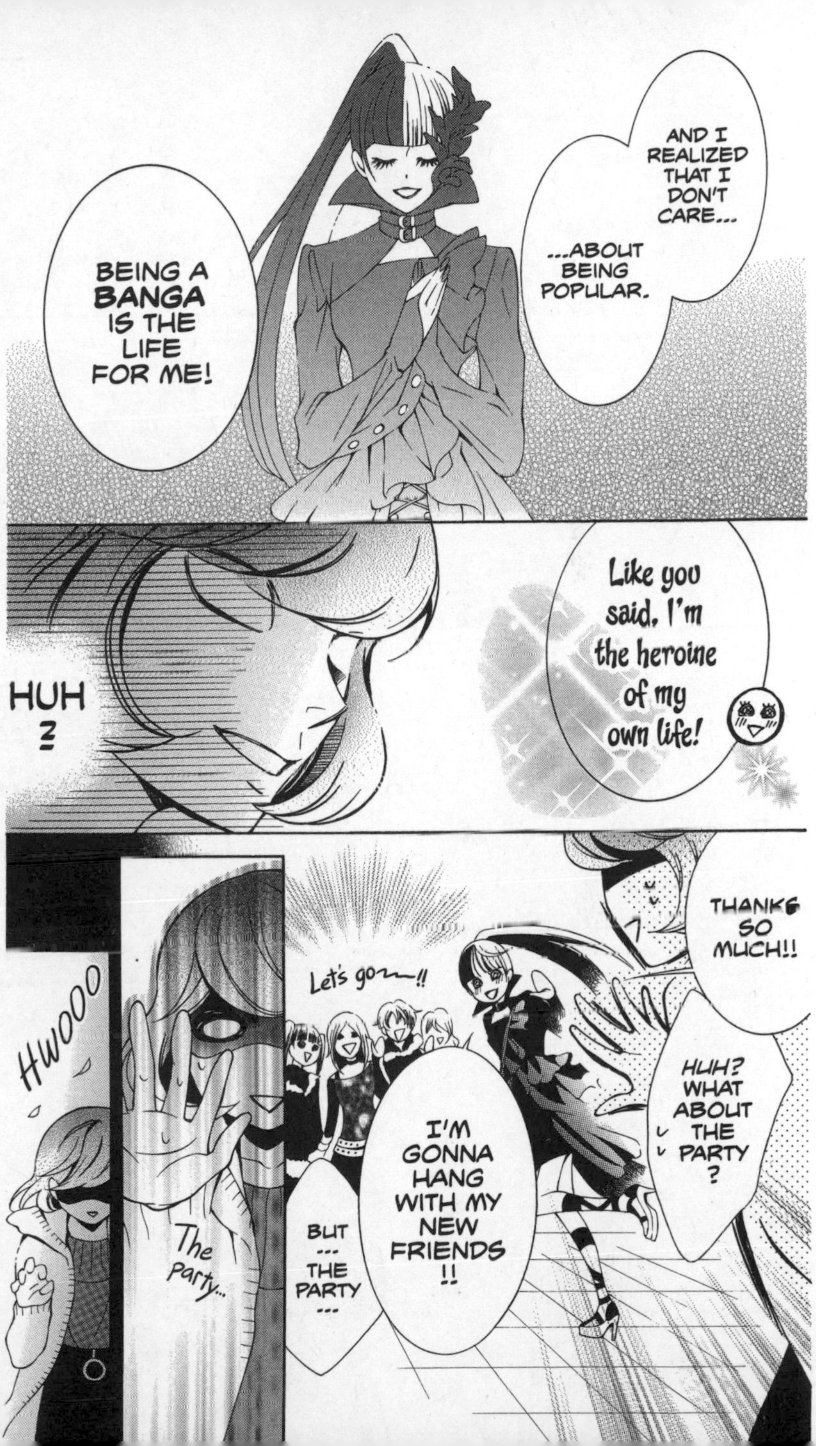
AND I REALIZED THAT I DON'T CARE...
...ABOUT BEING POPULAR.
BEING A BANGA IS THE LIFE FOR ME!
Like you said, I'm the heroine of my own life!
HUH?
THANKS SO MUCH!!
HUH? WHAT ABOUT THE PARTY?
Let's go~!!
I'M GONNA HANG WITH MY NEW FRIENDS!!
BUT... THE PARTY...
HWOOO
The party...

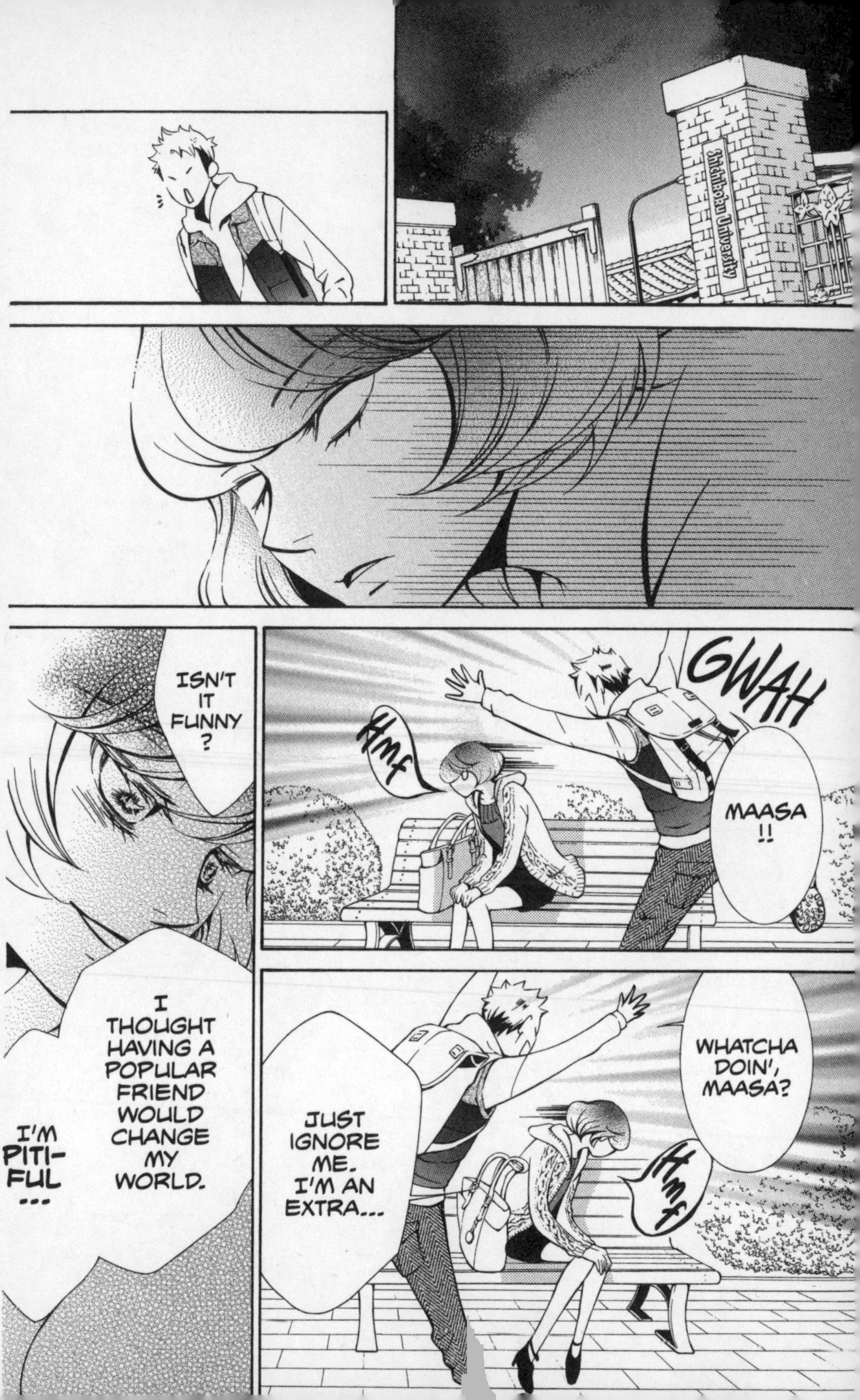
GWAH
MAASA!!
Hmf
WHATCHA DOIN', MAASA?
Hmf
JUST IGNORE ME. I'M AN EXTRA...
ISN'T IT FUNNY?
I THOUGHT HAVING A POPULAR FRIEND WOULD CHANGE MY WORLD.
I'M PITI-FUL...

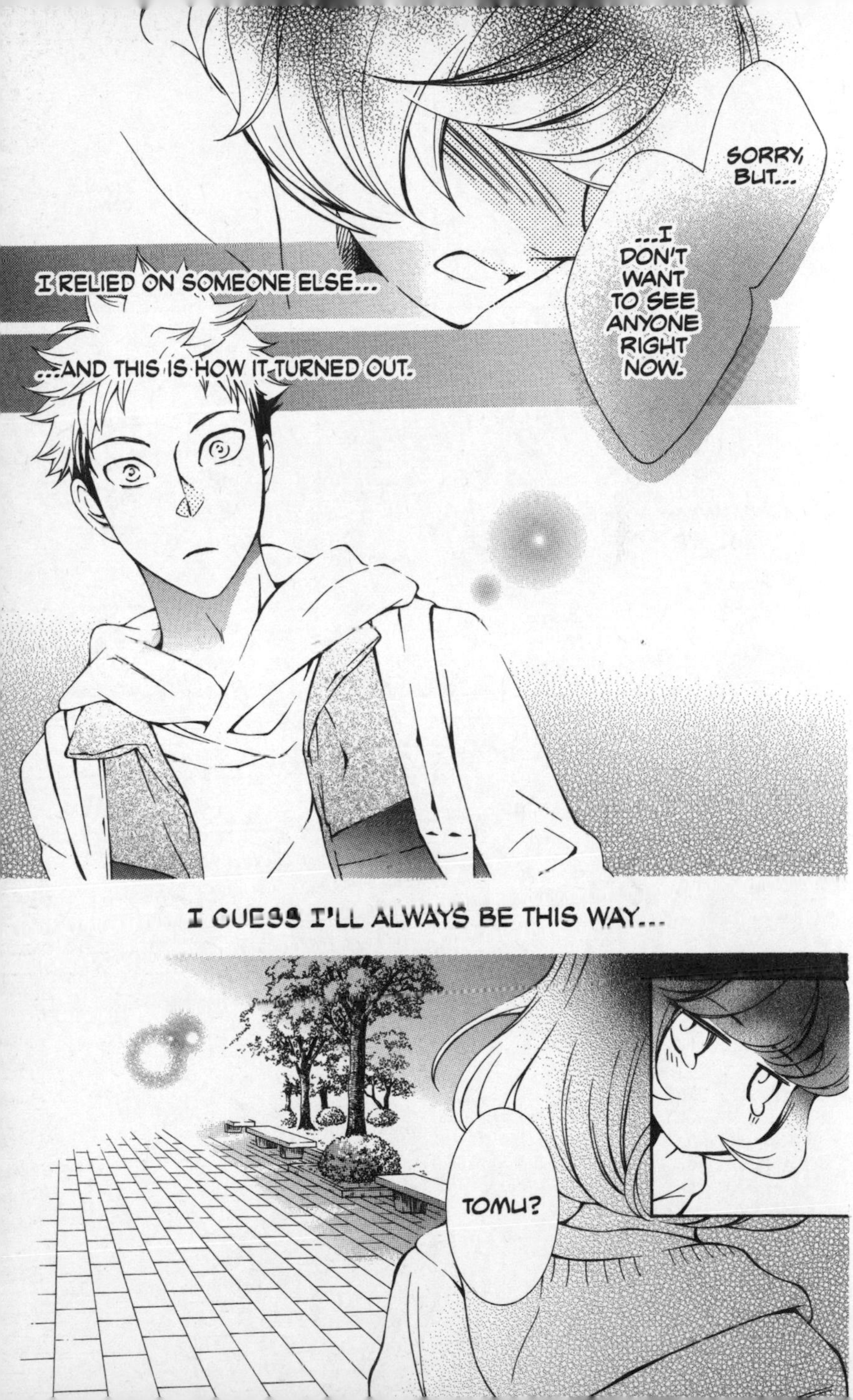
SORRY, BUT...
...I DON'T WANT TO SEE ANYONE RIGHT NOW.
I RELIED ON SOMEONE ELSE...
...AND THIS IS HOW IT TURNED OUT.
I GUESS I'LL ALWAYS BE THIS WAY...
TOMU?

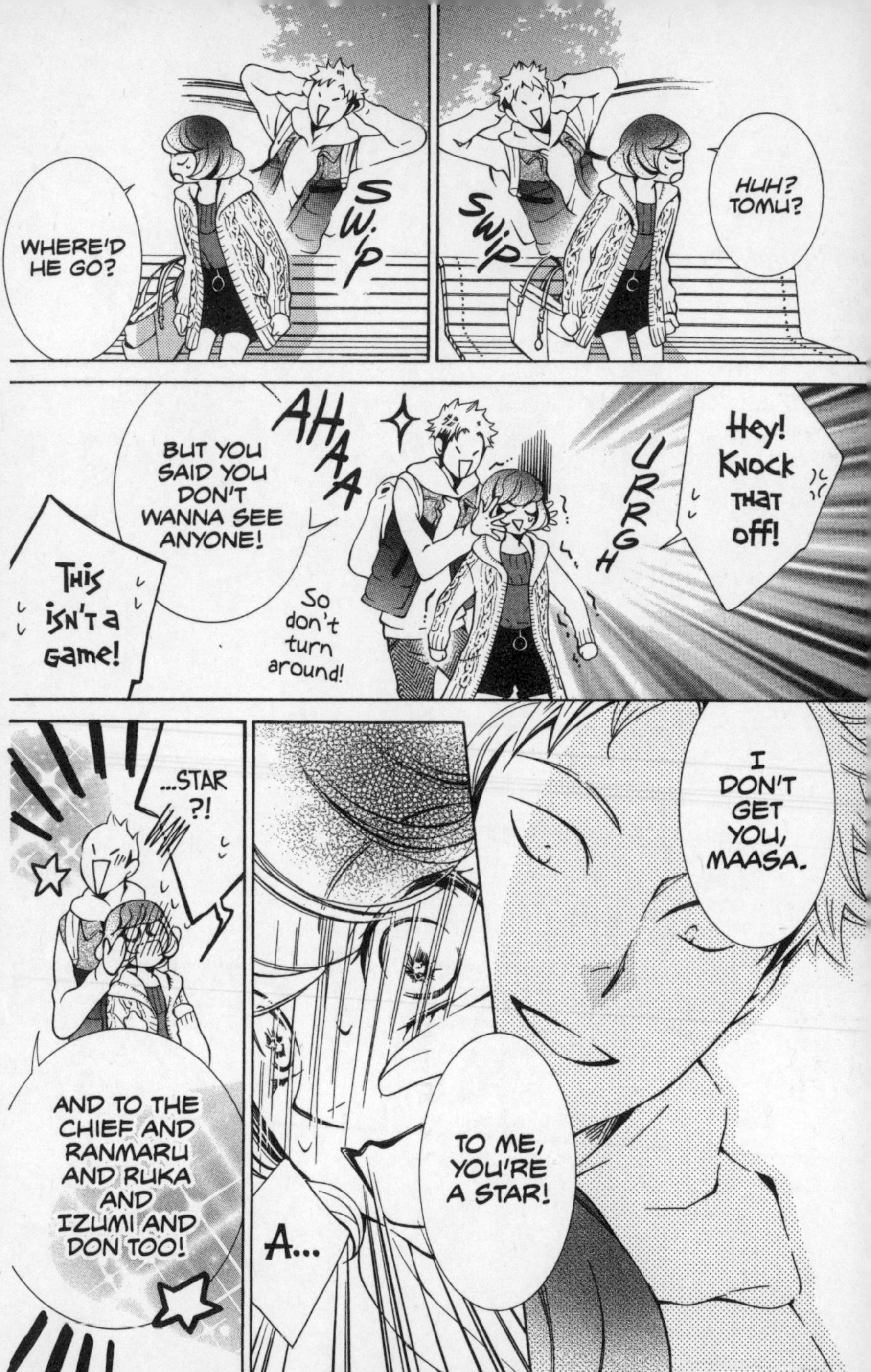
HUH? TOMU?
SWIP
SWIP
WHERE'D HE GO?
Hey! Knock that off!
URRGH
AHAAA
BUT YOU SAID YOU DON'T WANNA SEE ANYONE!
So don't turn around!
This isn't a game!
I DON'T GET YOU, MAASA.
TO ME, YOU'RE A STAR!
A...
...STAR ?!
AND TO THE CHIEF AND RANMARU AND RUKA AND IZUMI AND DON TOO!

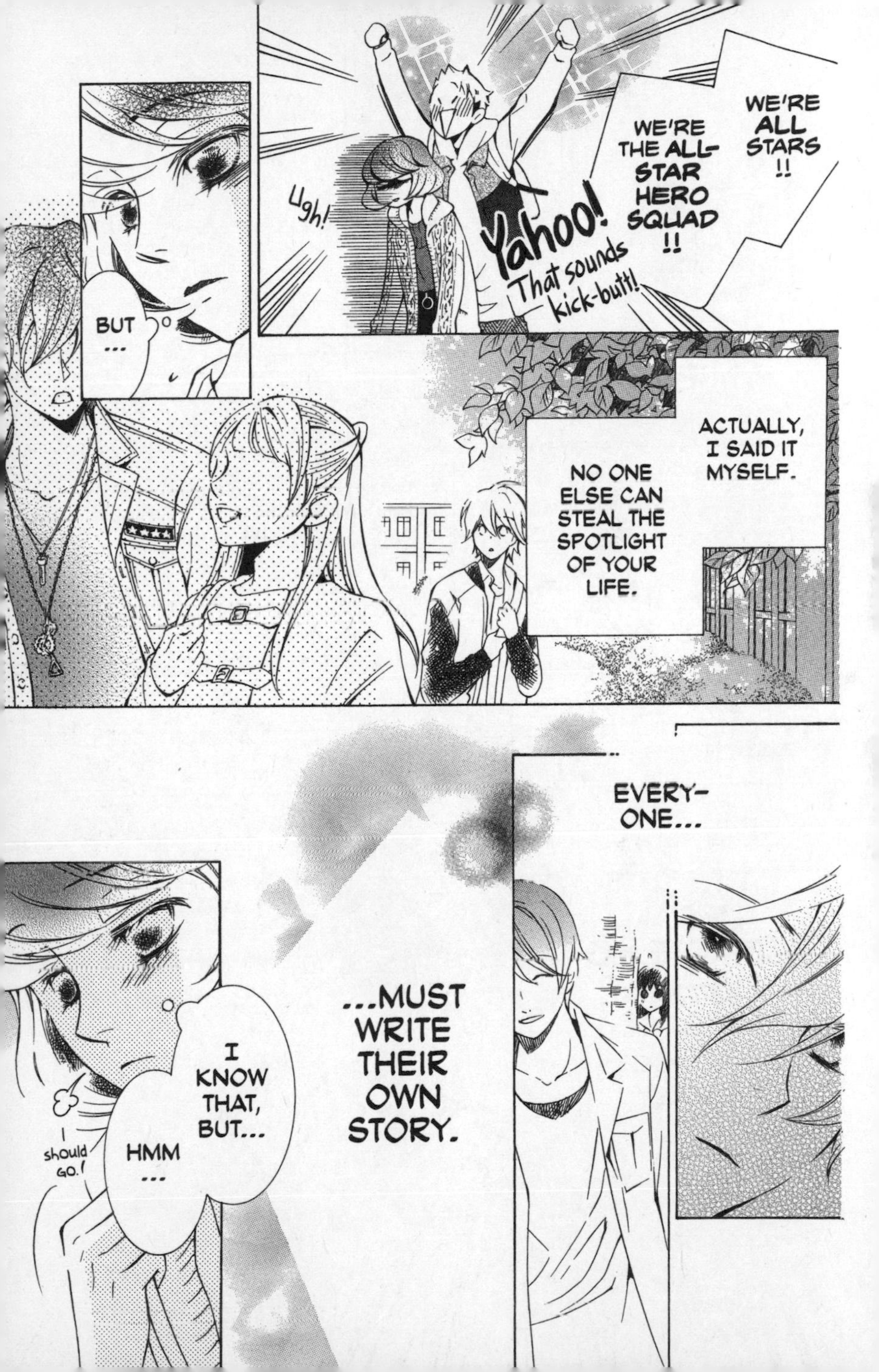
WE'RE ALL STARS !!
WE'RE THE ALL-STAR HERO SQUAD !!
Yahoo! That sounds kick-butt!
Ugh!
BUT ...
ACTUALLY, I SAID IT MYSELF.
NO ONE ELSE CAN STEAL THE SPOTLIGHT OF YOUR LIFE.
EVERY-ONE...
...MUST WRITE THEIR OWN STORY.
I KNOW THAT, BUT...
HMM ...
I should GO.!

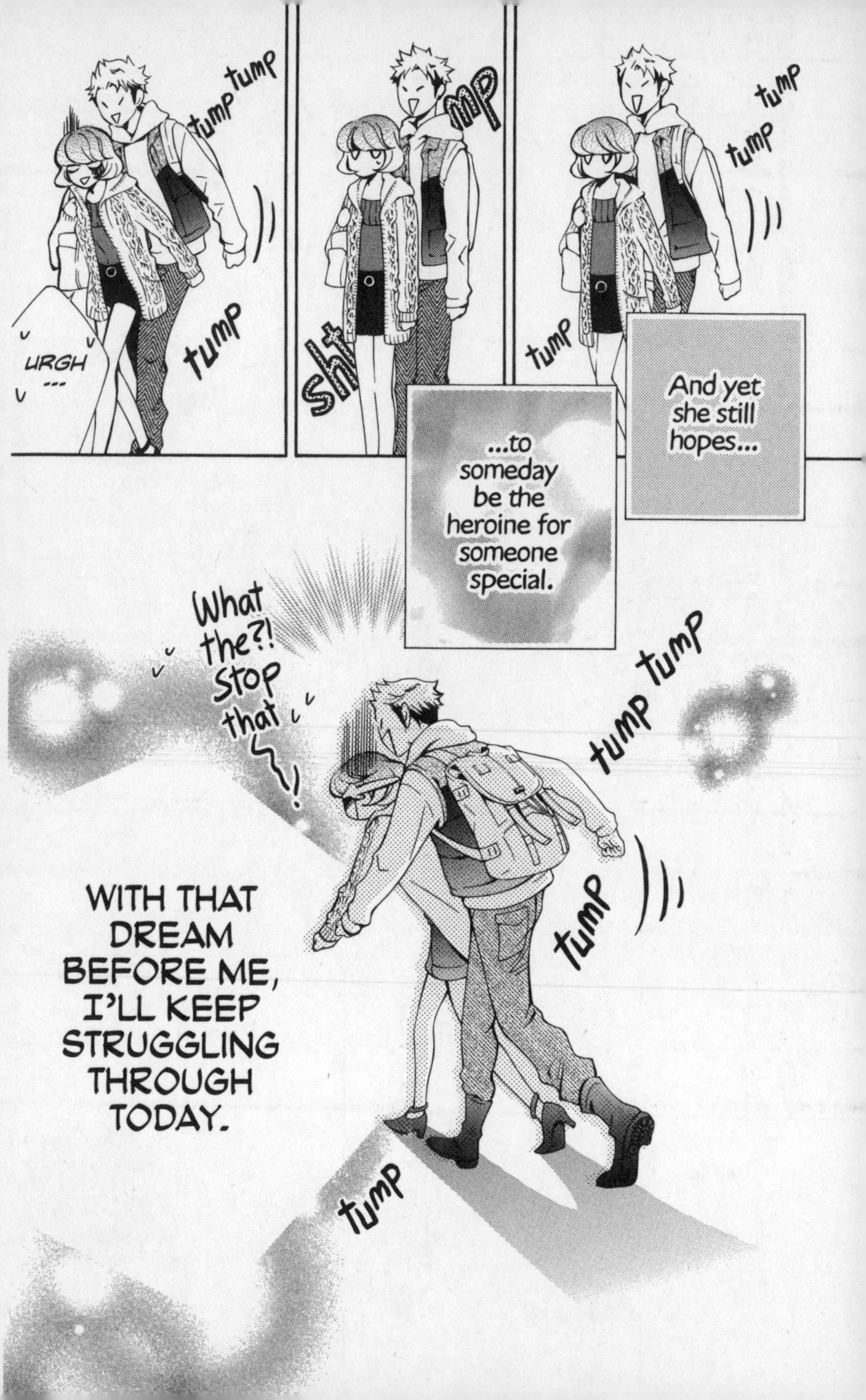
tump
tump
tump
MP
Sht
tump
tump
tump
URGH ...
And yet she still hopes...
...to someday be the heroine for someone special.
What the?! Stop that~!
tump tump
tump
tump
WITH THAT DREAM BEFORE ME, I'LL KEEP STRUGGLING THROUGH TODAY.

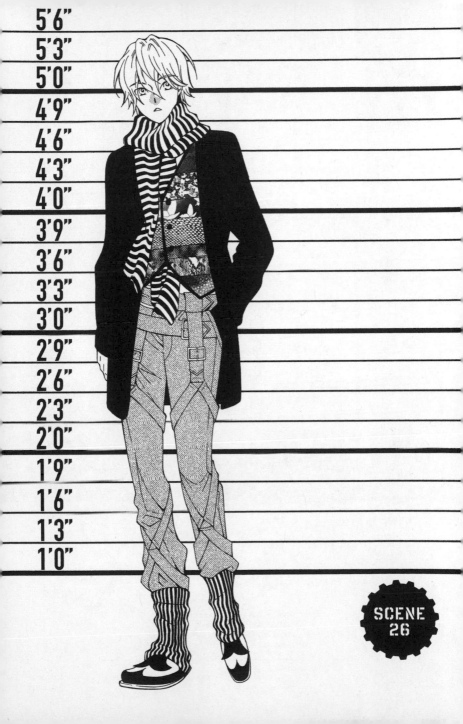

5'6"
5'3"
5'0"
4'9"
4'6"
4'3"
4'0"
3'9"
3'6"
3'3"
3'0"
2'9"
2'6"
2'3"
2'0"
1'9"
1'6"
1'3"
1'0"

SCENE
26

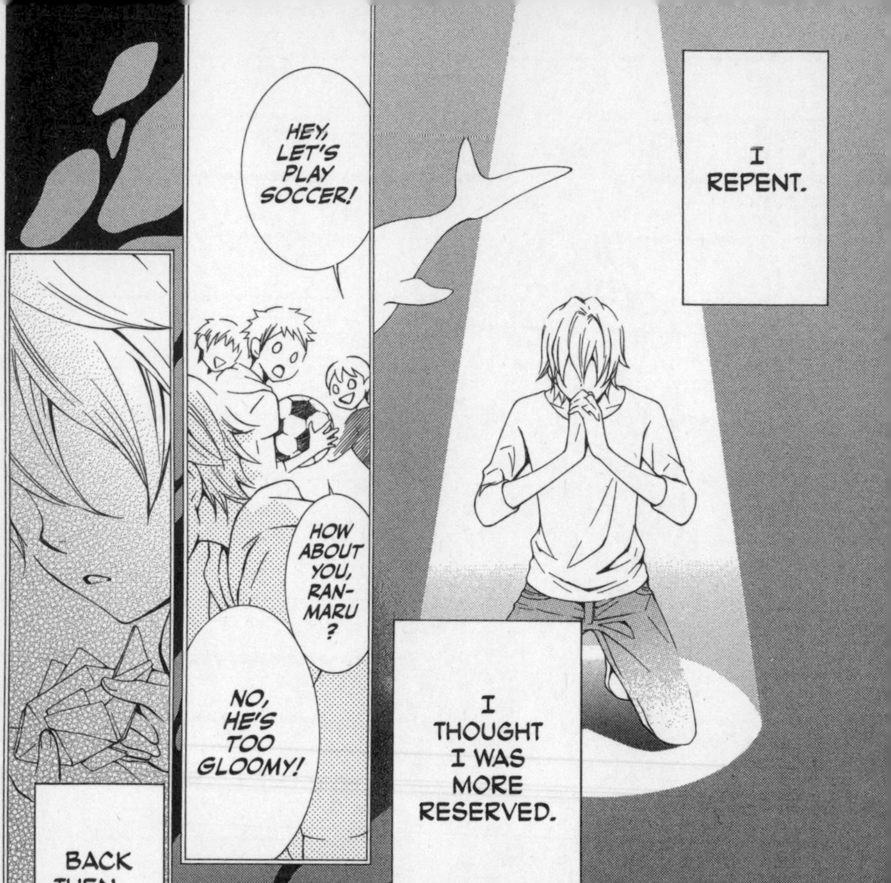
I REPENT.
I THOUGHT I WAS MORE RESERVED.
HEY, LET'S PLAY SOCCER!
HOW ABOUT YOU, RAN-MARU?
NO, HE'S TOO GLOOMY!
BACK THEN...

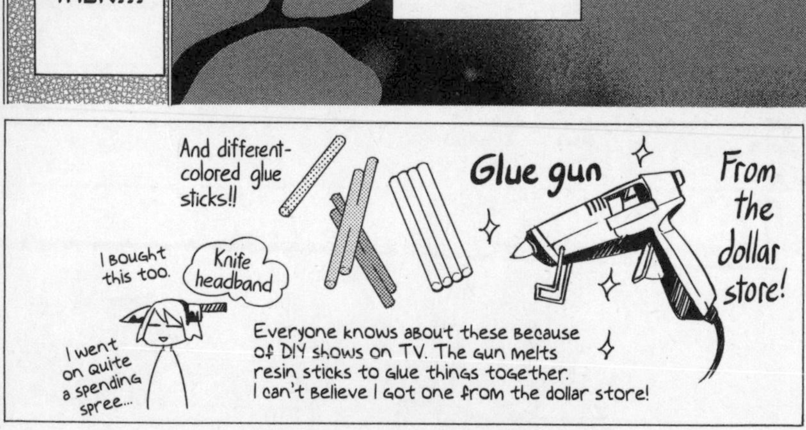
From the dollar store!
Glue gun
And different-colored glue sticks!!
Everyone knows about these because of DIY shows on TV. The gun melts resin sticks to glue things together. I can't believe I got one from the dollar store!
Knife headband
I bought this too.
I went on quite a spending spree...

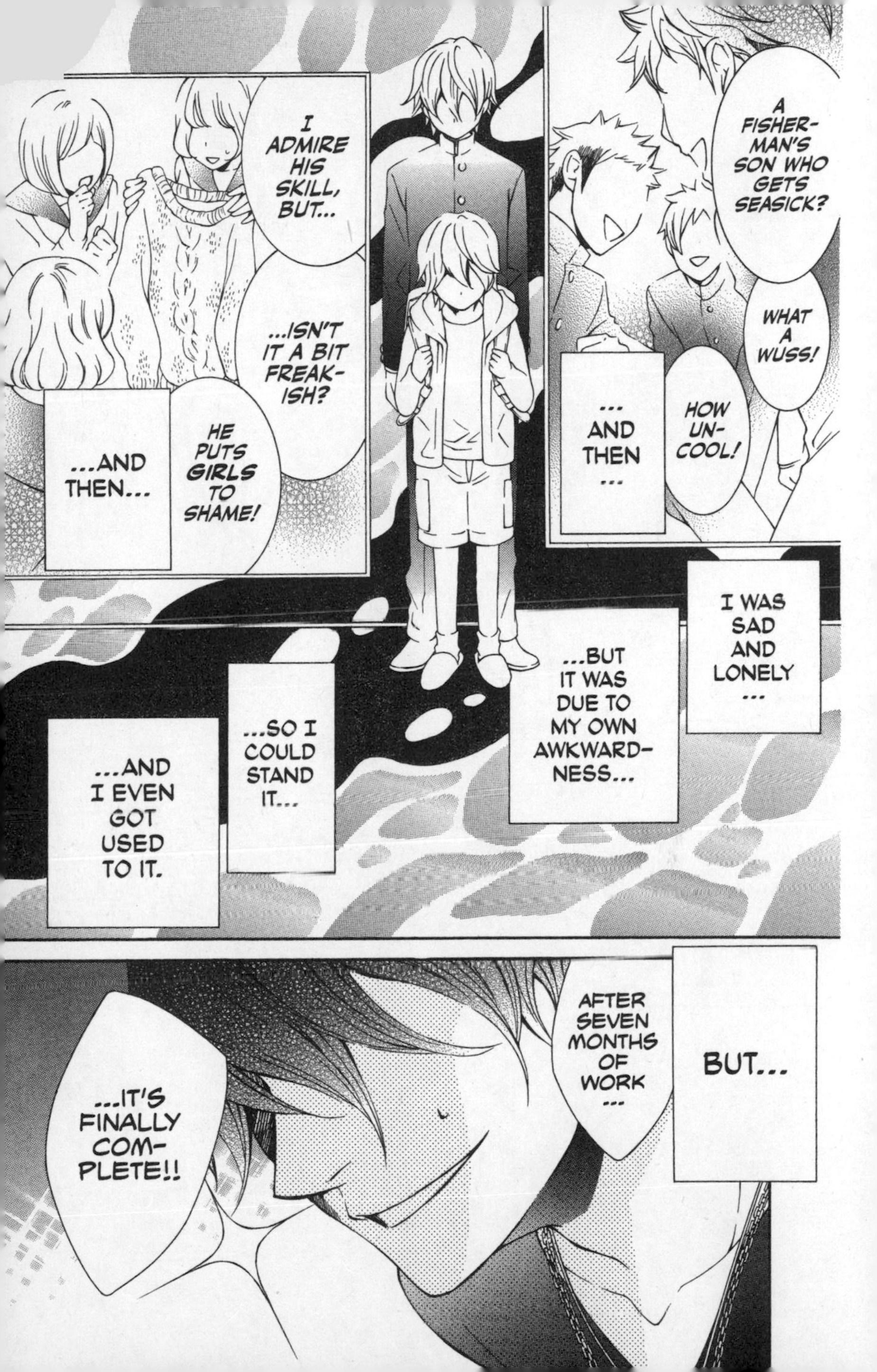
A FISHERMAN'S SON WHO GETS SEASICK?
WHAT A WUSS!
HOW UNCOOL!
...AND THEN...
I ADMIRE HIS SKILL, BUT...
...ISN'T IT A BIT FREAKISH?
HE PUTS GIRLS TO SHAME!
...AND THEN...
I WAS SAD AND LONELY...
...BUT IT WAS DUE TO MY OWN AWKWARDNESS...
...SO I COULD STAND IT...
...AND I EVEN GOT USED TO IT.
BUT...
AFTER SEVEN MONTHS OF WORK...
...IT'S FINALLY COMPLETE!!

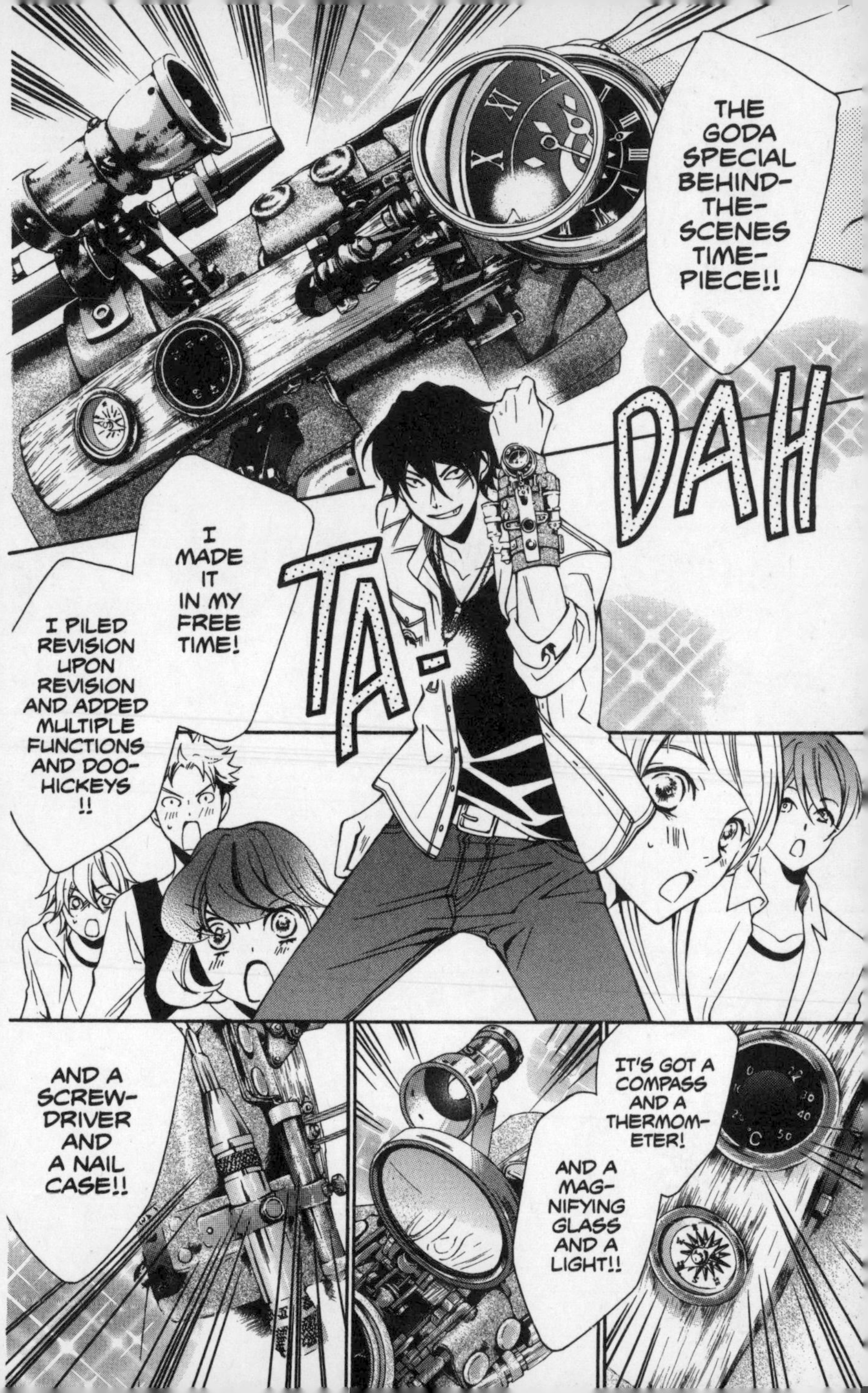
THE GODA SPECIAL BEHIND-THE-SCENES TIME-PIECE!!
TA-DAH
I MADE IT IN MY FREE TIME!
I PILED REVISION UPON REVISION AND ADDED MULTIPLE FUNCTIONS AND DOO-HICKEYS!!
IT'S GOT A COMPASS AND A THERMOM-ETER!
AND A MAG-NIFYING GLASS AND A LIGHT!!
AND A SCREW-DRIVER AND A NAIL CASE!!

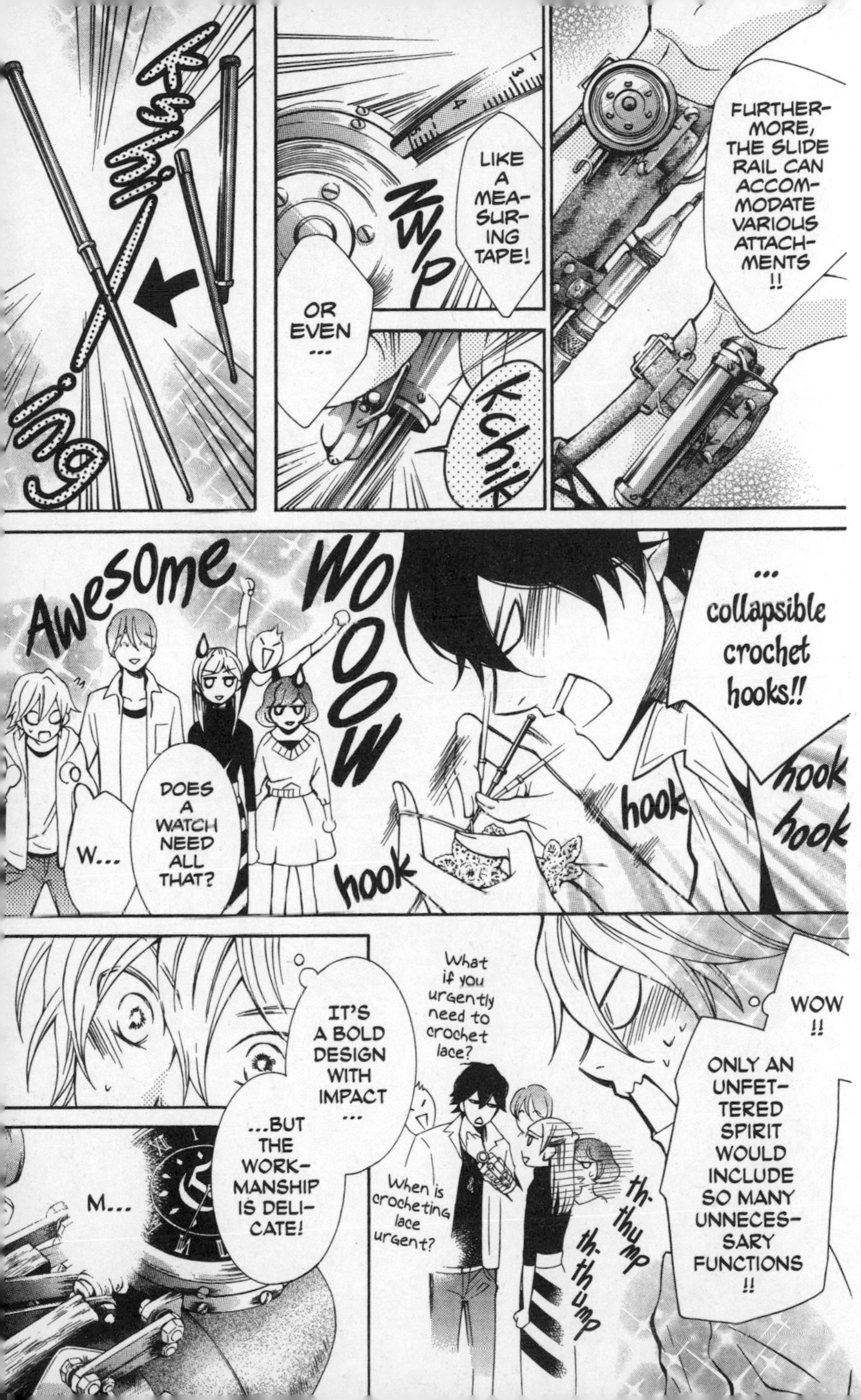
FURTHER-MORE, THE SLIDE RAIL CAN ACCOM-MODATE VARIOUS ATTACH-MENTS!!
LIKE A MEA-SUR-ING TAPE!
NWIP
OR EVEN...
kchik
Kshiiing
...collapsible crochet hooks!!
hook hook
hook
hook
hook
WOOOOW
Awesome
DOES A WATCH NEED ALL THAT?
W...
WOW!!
ONLY AN UNFET-TERED SPIRIT WOULD INCLUDE SO MANY UNNECES-SARY FUNCTIONS!!
th-thump
th-thump
What if you urgently need to crochet lace?
When is crocheting lace urgent?
IT'S A BOLD DESIGN WITH IMPACT...
...BUT THE WORK-MANSHIP IS DELI-CATE!
M...

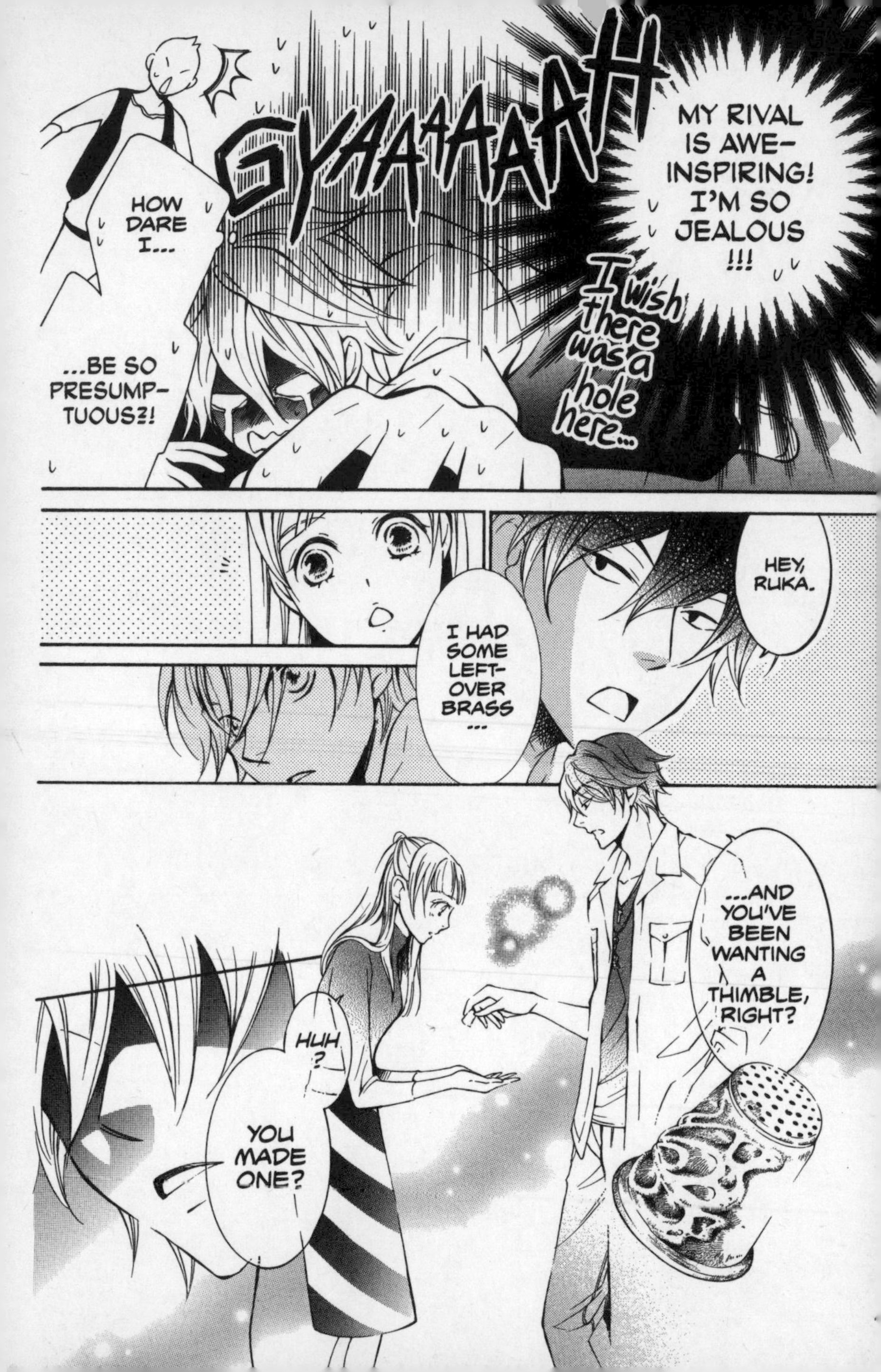
GYAAAAAAH
MY RIVAL IS AWE-INSPIRING! I'M SO JEALOUS!!!
I wish there was a hole here...
HOW DARE I...
...BE SO PRESUMPTUOUS?!
HEY, RUKA.
I HAD SOME LEFT-OVER BRASS...
...AND YOU'VE BEEN WANTING A THIMBLE, RIGHT?
HUH?
YOU MADE ONE?

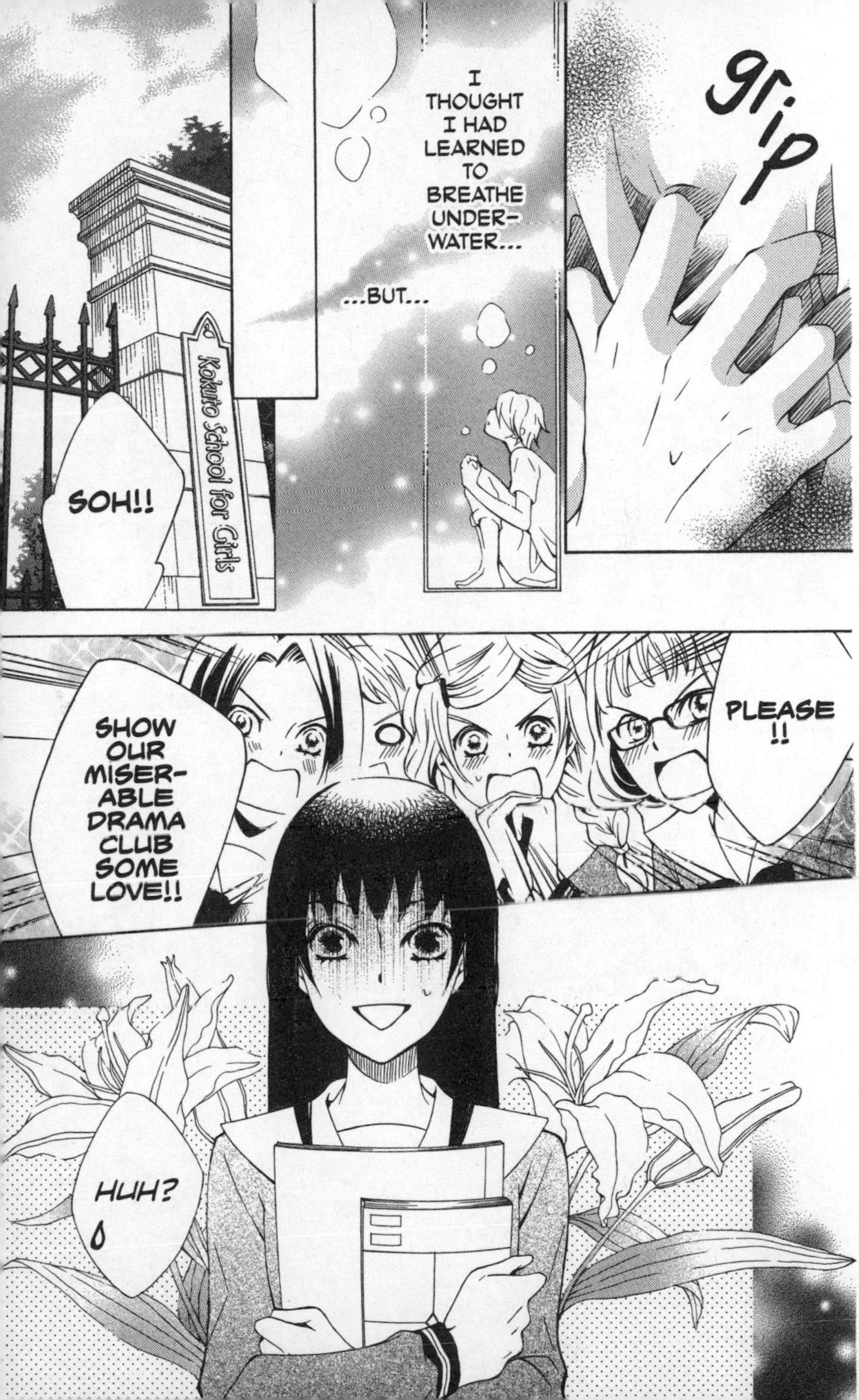
grip
I THOUGHT I HAD LEARNED TO BREATHE UNDER-WATER...
...BUT...
Kokuto School for Girls
SOH!!
PLEASE !!
SHOW OUR MISER-ABLE DRAMA CLUB SOME LOVE!!
HUH?

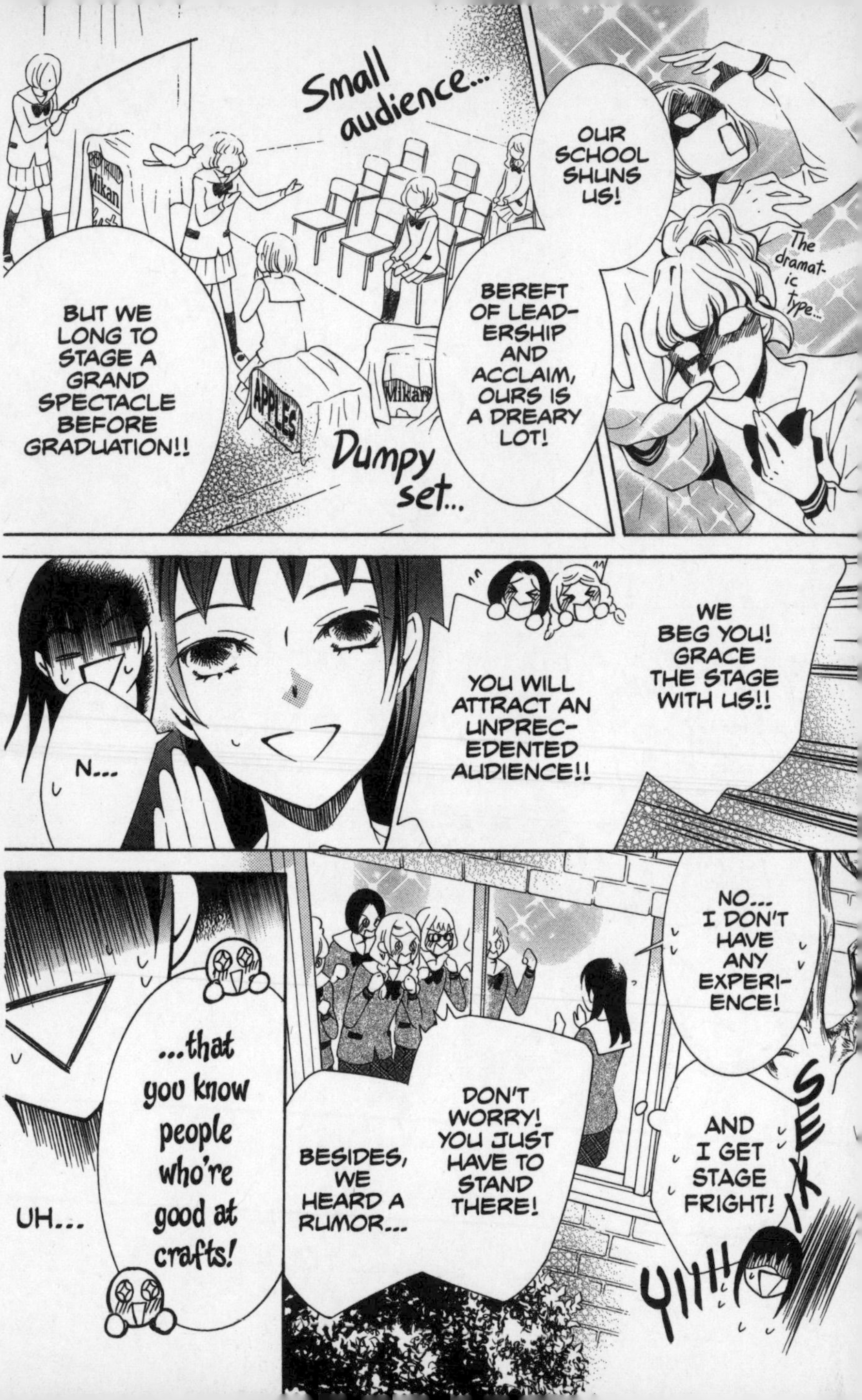
OUR SCHOOL SHUNS US!
The dramatic type...
BEREFT OF LEADERSHIP AND ACCLAIM, OURS IS A DREARY LOT!
Small audience...
Dumpy set...
BUT WE LONG TO STAGE A GRAND SPECTACLE BEFORE GRADUATION!!
WE BEG YOU! GRACE THE STAGE WITH US!!
YOU WILL ATTRACT AN UNPRECEDENTED AUDIENCE!!
N...
NO... I DON'T HAVE ANY EXPERIENCE!
AND I GET STAGE FRIGHT!
EEK
YIII!
DON'T WORRY! YOU JUST HAVE TO STAND THERE!
BESIDES, WE HEARD A RUMOR...
...that you know people who're good at crafts!
UH...

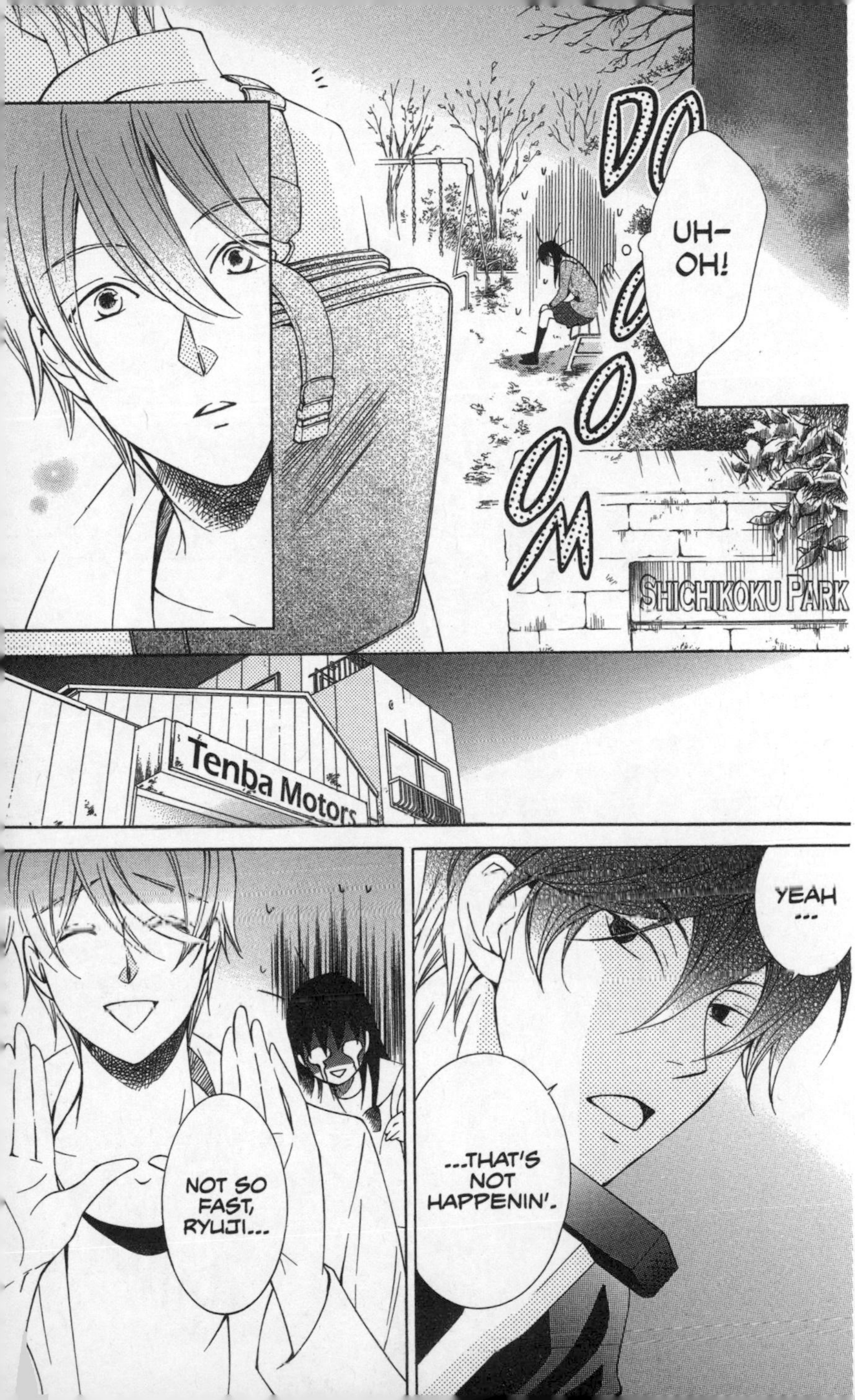
UH-OH!
DOOOOOM
SHICHIKOKU PARK
Tenba Motors
YEAH...
...THAT'S NOT HAPPENIN'.
NOT SO FAST, RYUJI...

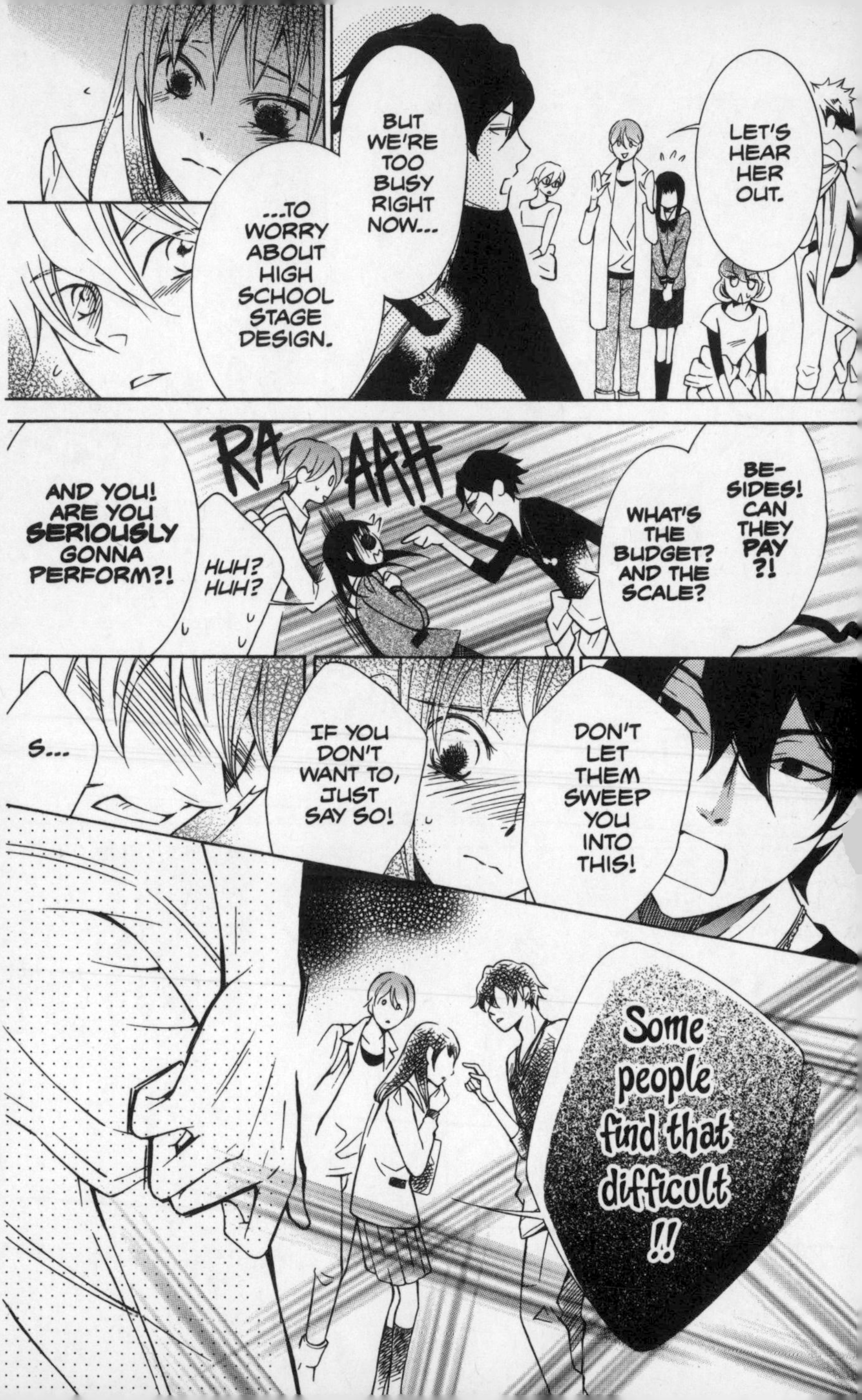
LET'S HEAR HER OUT.
BUT WE'RE TOO BUSY RIGHT NOW...
...TO WORRY ABOUT HIGH SCHOOL STAGE DESIGN.
BE-SIDES! CAN THEY PAY?!
WHAT'S THE BUDGET? AND THE SCALE?
RAAAH
HUH? HUH?
AND YOU! ARE YOU SERIOUSLY GONNA PERFORM?!
DON'T LET THEM SWEEP YOU INTO THIS!
IF YOU DON'T WANT TO, JUST SAY SO!
S...
Some people find that difficult!!

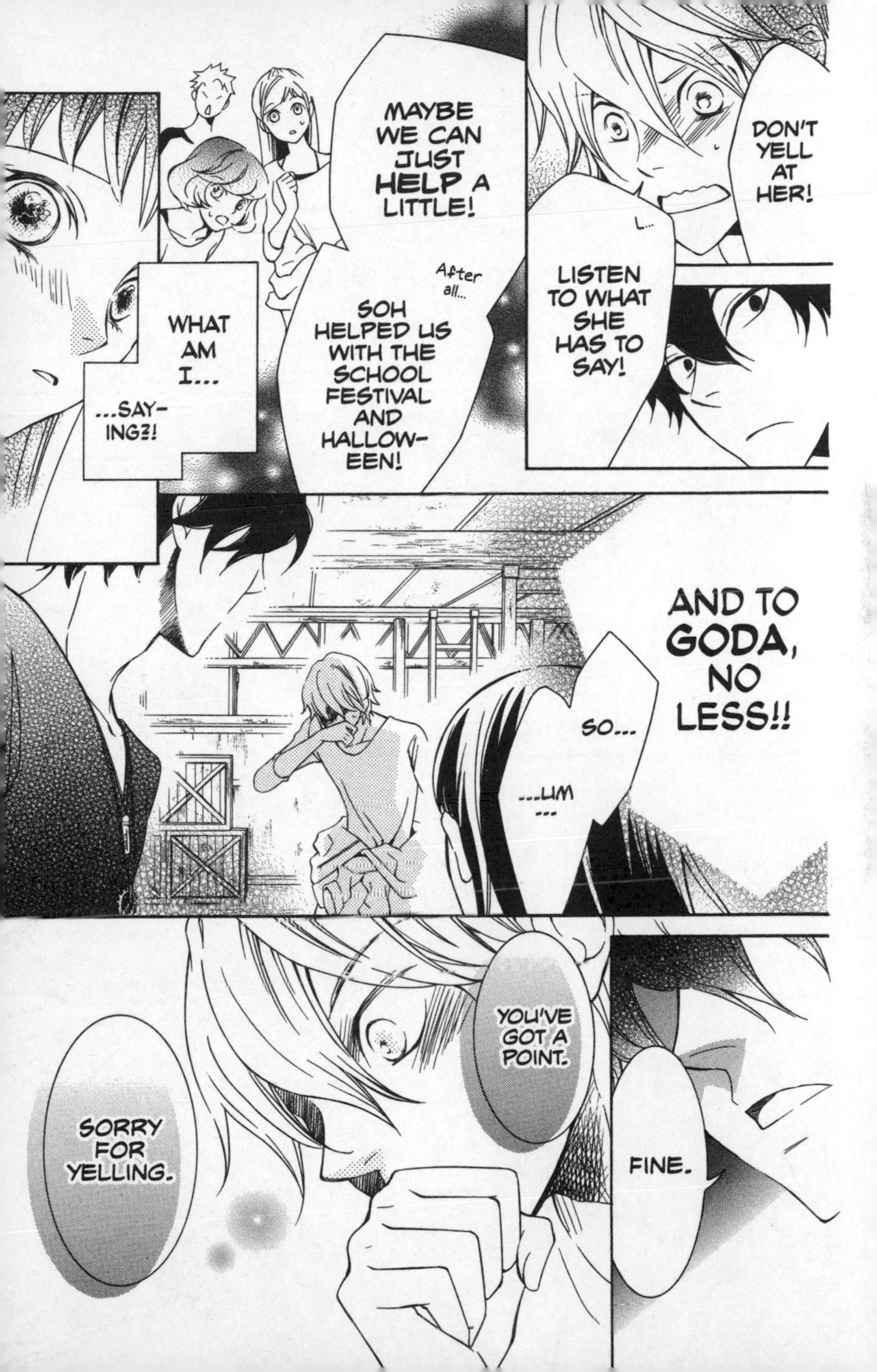
DON'T YELL AT HER!
I...
LISTEN TO WHAT SHE HAS TO SAY!
MAYBE WE CAN JUST HELP A LITTLE!
After all...
SOH HELPED US WITH THE SCHOOL FESTIVAL AND HALLOW-EEN!
WHAT AM I...
...SAY-ING?!
AND TO GODA, NO LESS!!
SO...
...UM...
FINE.
YOU'VE GOT A POINT.
SORRY FOR YELLING.

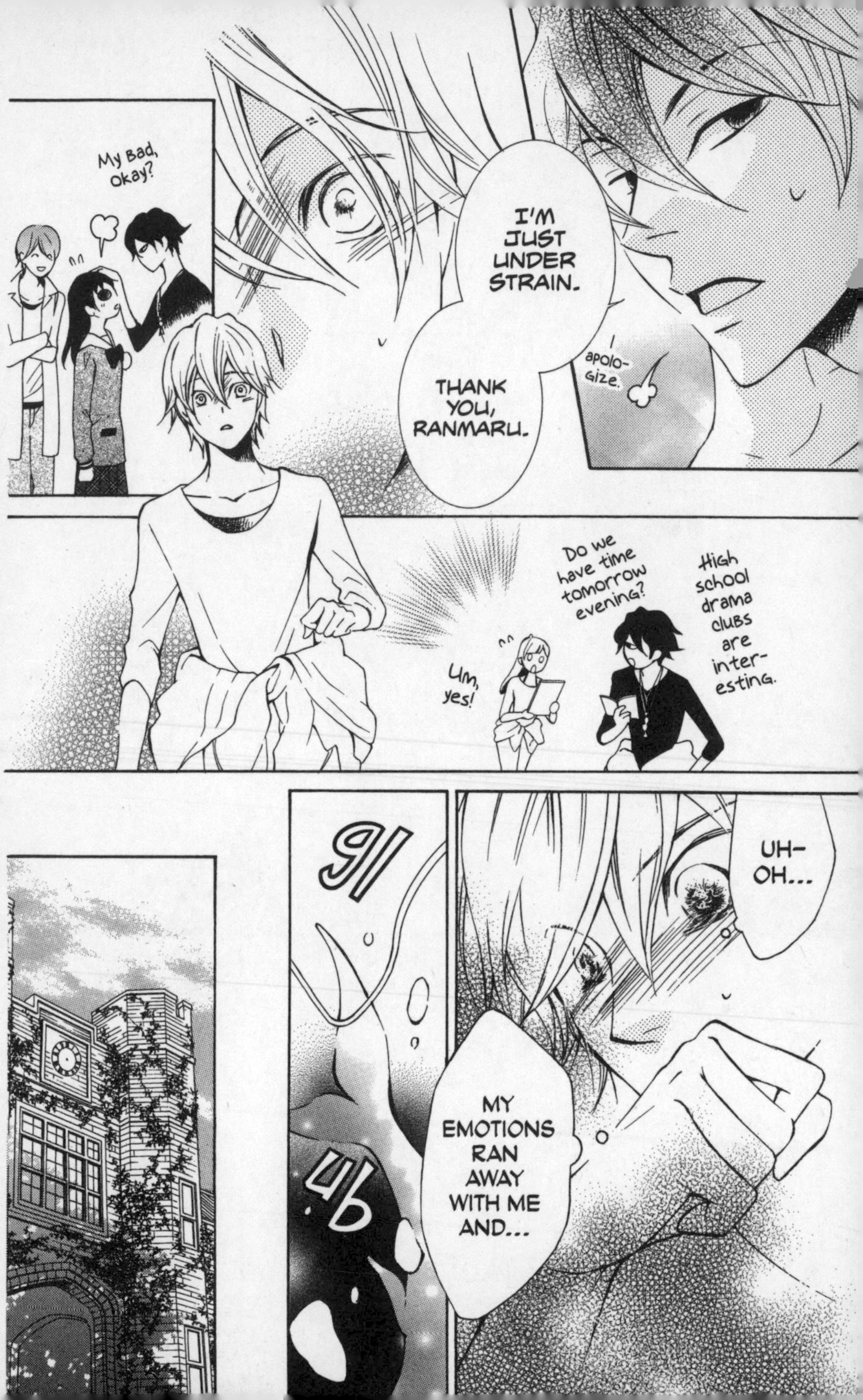
I'M JUST UNDER STRAIN.
I apologize.
THANK YOU, RANMARU.
My Bad, Okay?
High school drama clubs are interesting.
Do we have time tomorrow evening?
Um, yes!
UH-OH...
MY EMOTIONS RAN AWAY WITH ME AND...

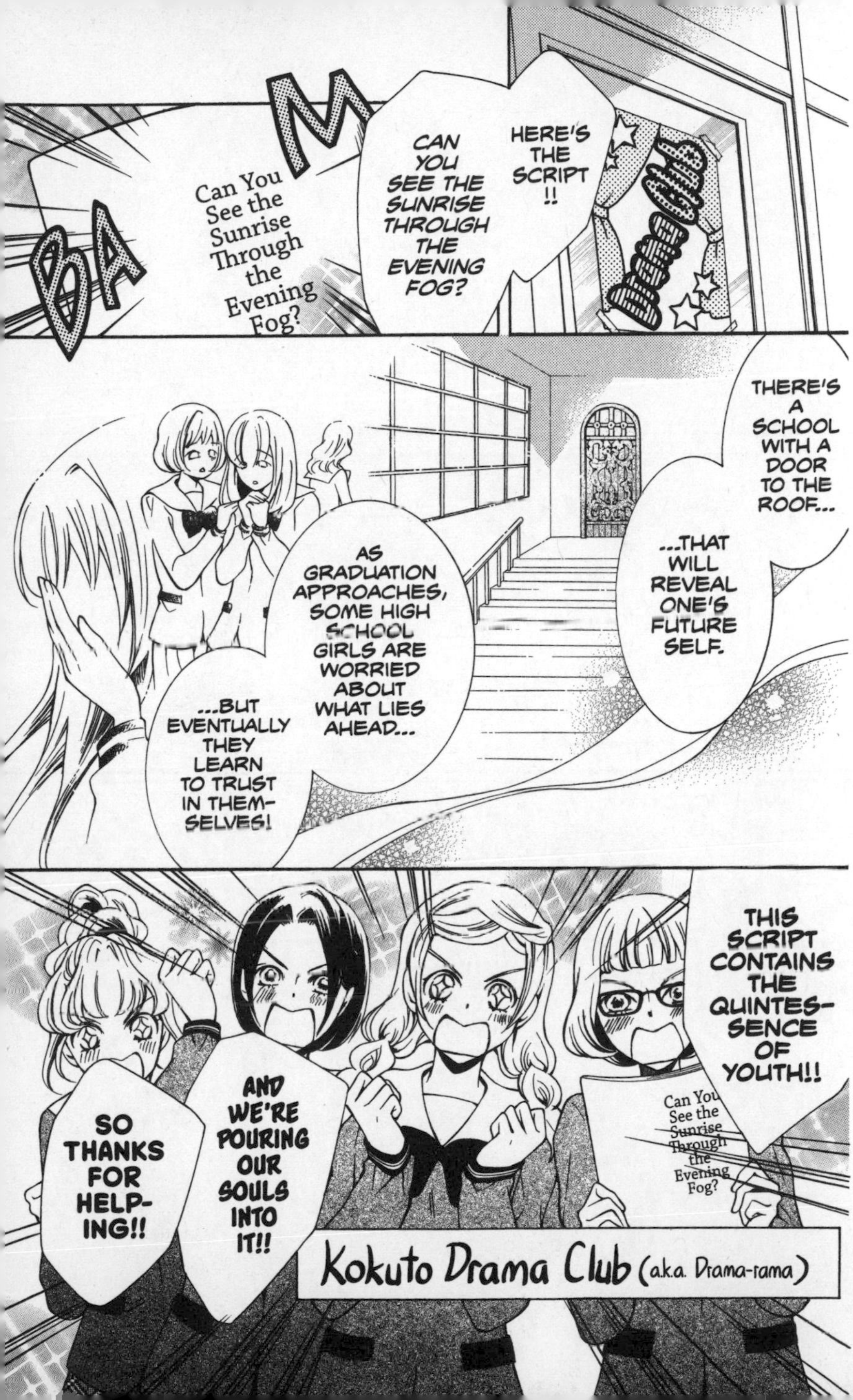
HERE'S THE SCRIPT!!
CAN YOU SEE THE SUNRISE THROUGH THE EVENING FOG?
Can You See the Sunrise Through the Evening Fog?
BAM
THERE'S A SCHOOL WITH A DOOR TO THE ROOF...
...THAT WILL REVEAL ONE'S FUTURE SELF.
AS GRADUATION APPROACHES, SOME HIGH SCHOOL GIRLS ARE WORRIED ABOUT WHAT LIES AHEAD...
...BUT EVENTUALLY THEY LEARN TO TRUST IN THEM-SELVES!
THIS SCRIPT CONTAINS THE QUINTES-SENCE OF YOUTH!!
Can You See the Sunrise Through the Evening Fog?
AND WE'RE POURING OUR SOULS INTO IT!!
SO THANKS FOR HELP-ING!!
Kokuto Drama Club (a.k.a. Drama-rama)

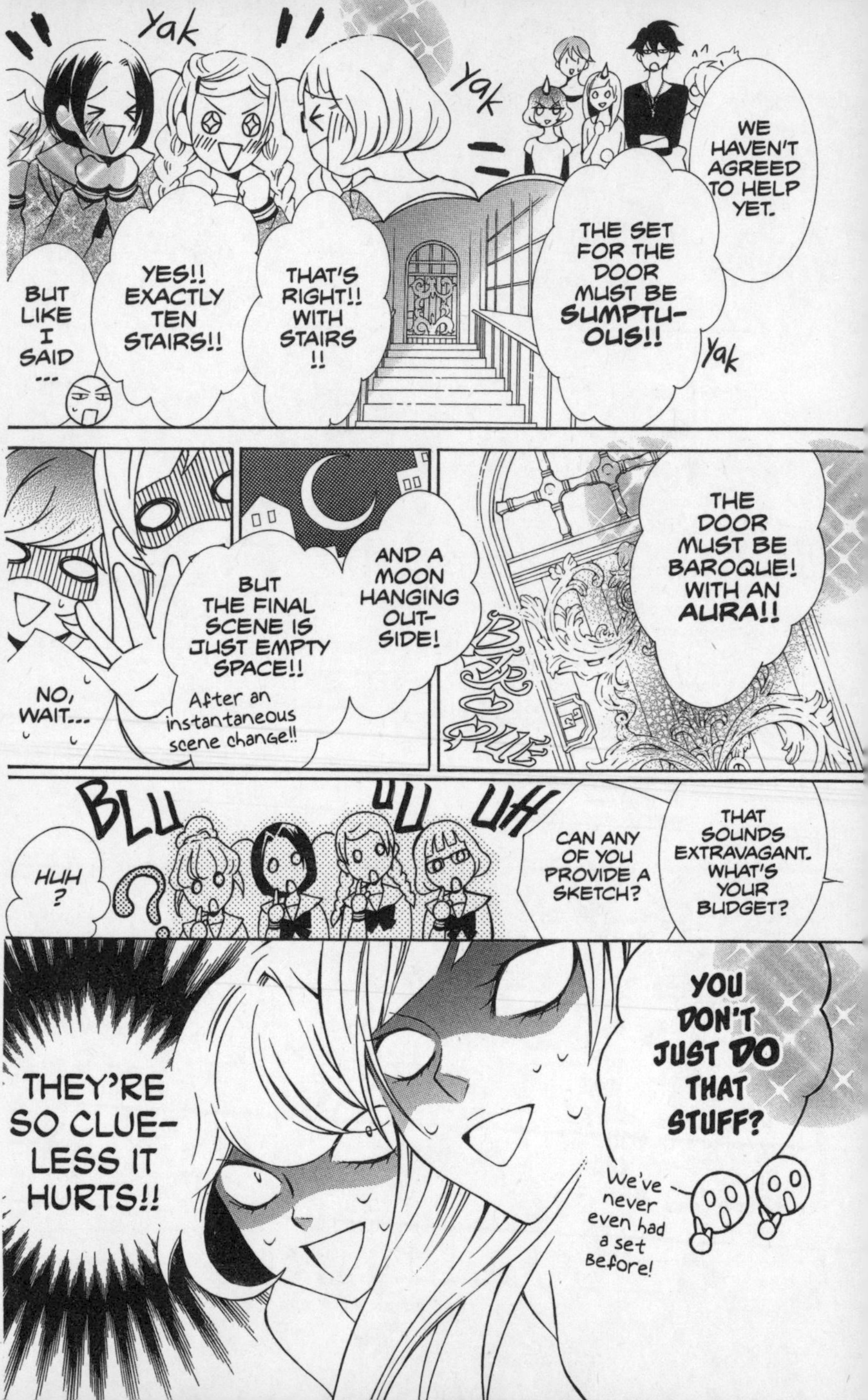
Yak
Yak
Yak
WE HAVEN'T AGREED TO HELP YET.
THE SET FOR THE DOOR MUST BE SUMPTUOUS!!
THAT'S RIGHT!! WITH STAIRS!!
YES!! EXACTLY TEN STAIRS!!
BUT LIKE I SAID...
THE DOOR MUST BE BAROQUE! WITH AN AURA!!
BAROQUE
AND A MOON HANGING OUTSIDE!
BUT THE FINAL SCENE IS JUST EMPTY SPACE!!
After an instantaneous scene change!!
NO, WAIT...
THAT SOUNDS EXTRAVAGANT. WHAT'S YOUR BUDGET?
CAN ANY OF YOU PROVIDE A SKETCH?
BLUUUH
HUH?
YOU DON'T JUST DO THAT STUFF?
We've never even had a set before!
THEY'RE SO CLUELESS IT HURTS!!

The Birth of Behind the Scenes!! 4

Revealed at last!!

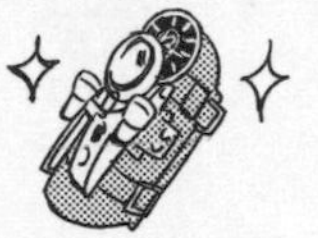

The Goda Special Behind-the-Scenes Timepiece!!

by Forêt-sama!!

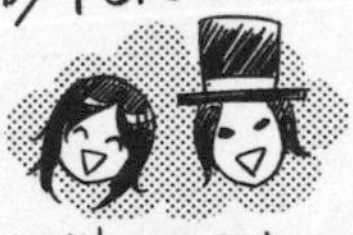

Michiko-san Joh-san

Check out a photo of the real thing on my author bio page!! It's incredibly cool!!!

They're really busy, but they gave me lots of ideas.

Crochet hooks, tape measure, light...

I like it when Goda crochets lace!

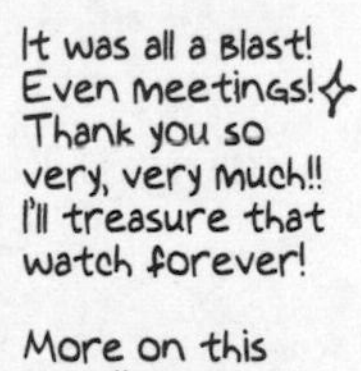

It was all a blast! Even meetings! Thank you so very, very much!! I'll treasure that watch forever!

More on this later!!

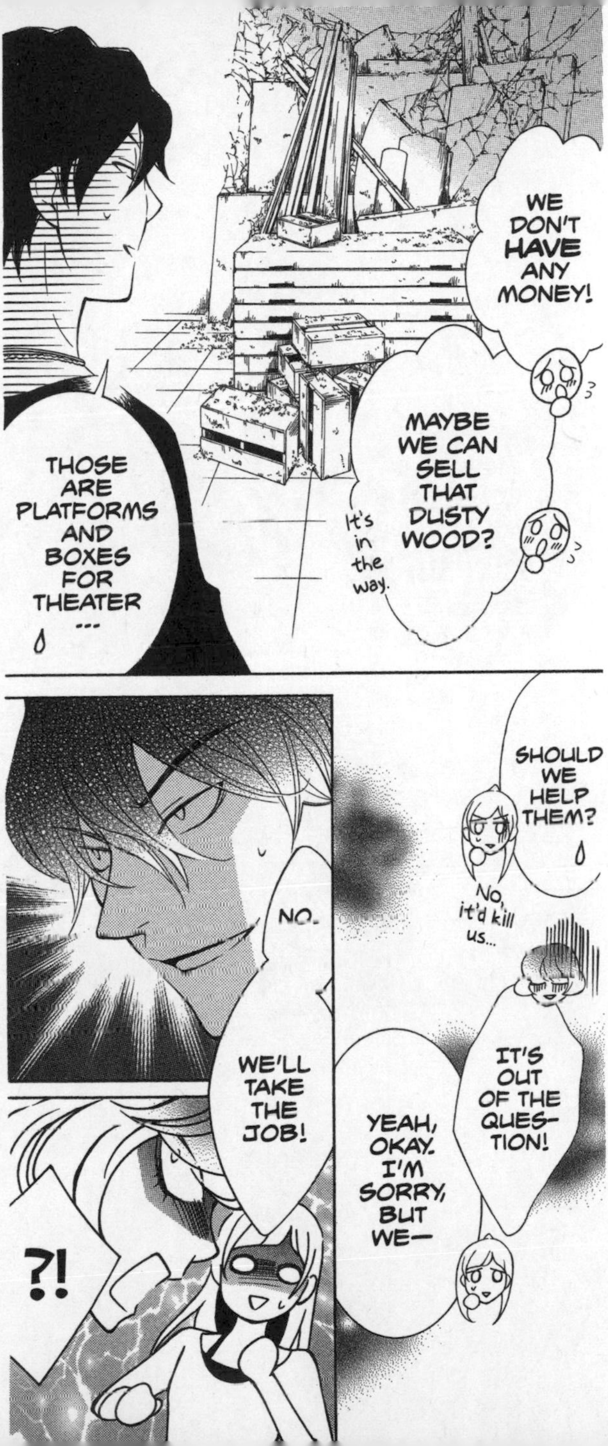
WE DON'T HAVE ANY MONEY!
MAYBE WE CAN SELL THAT DUSTY WOOD?
It's in the way.
THOSE ARE PLATFORMS AND BOXES FOR THEATER ...
SHOULD WE HELP THEM?
No, it'd kill us...
NO.
IT'S OUT OF THE QUESTION!
YEAH, OKAY. I'M SORRY, BUT WE—
WE'LL TAKE THE JOB!
?!

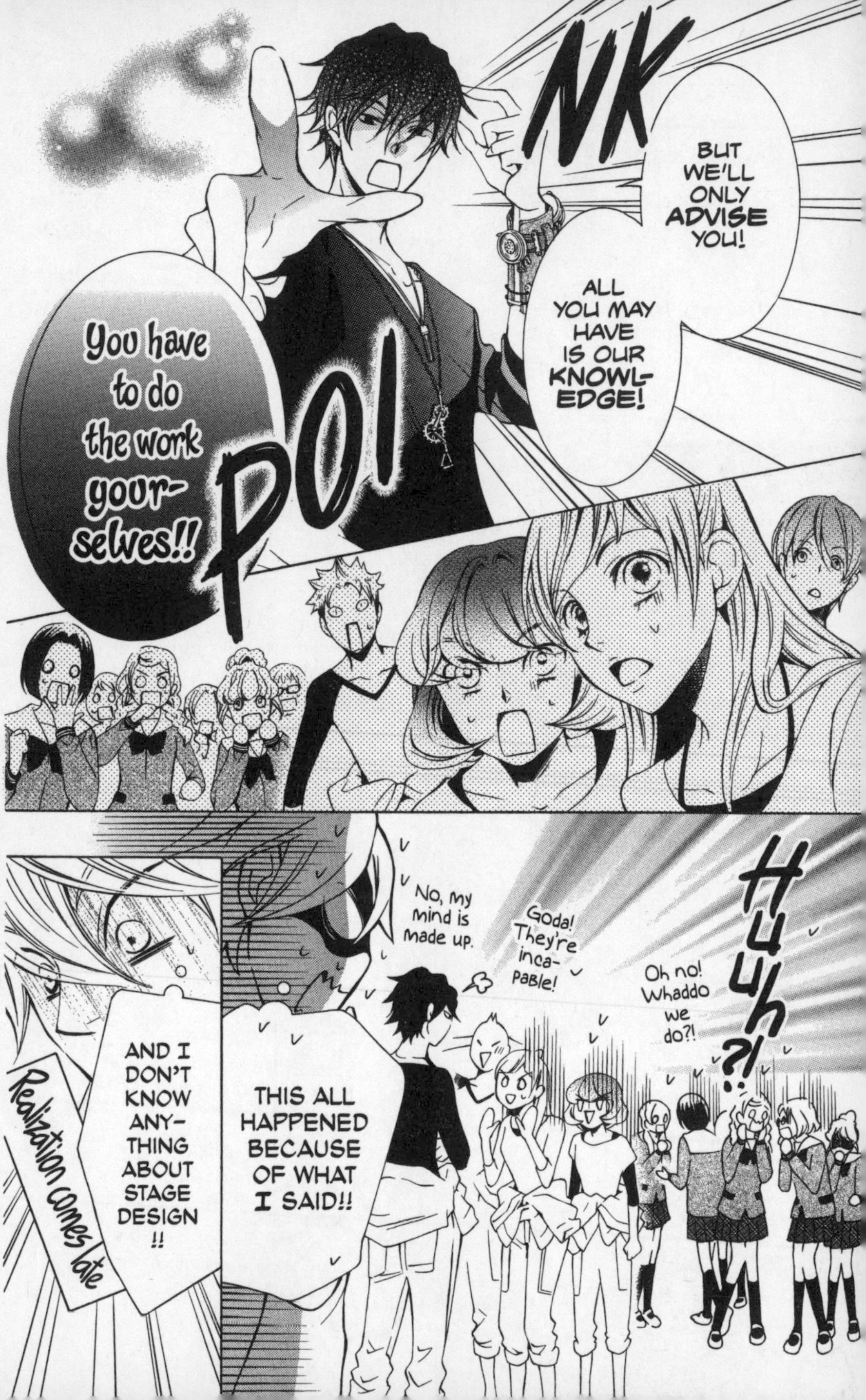
NK
BUT WE'LL ONLY ADVISE YOU!
ALL YOU MAY HAVE IS OUR KNOWL-EDGE!
POI
You have to do the work your-selves!!
HUUH?!
Oh no! Whaddo we do?!
Goda! They're inca-pable!
No, my mind is made up.
THIS ALL HAPPENED BECAUSE OF WHAT I SAID!!
AND I DON'T KNOW ANY-THING ABOUT STAGE DESIGN!!
Realization comes late

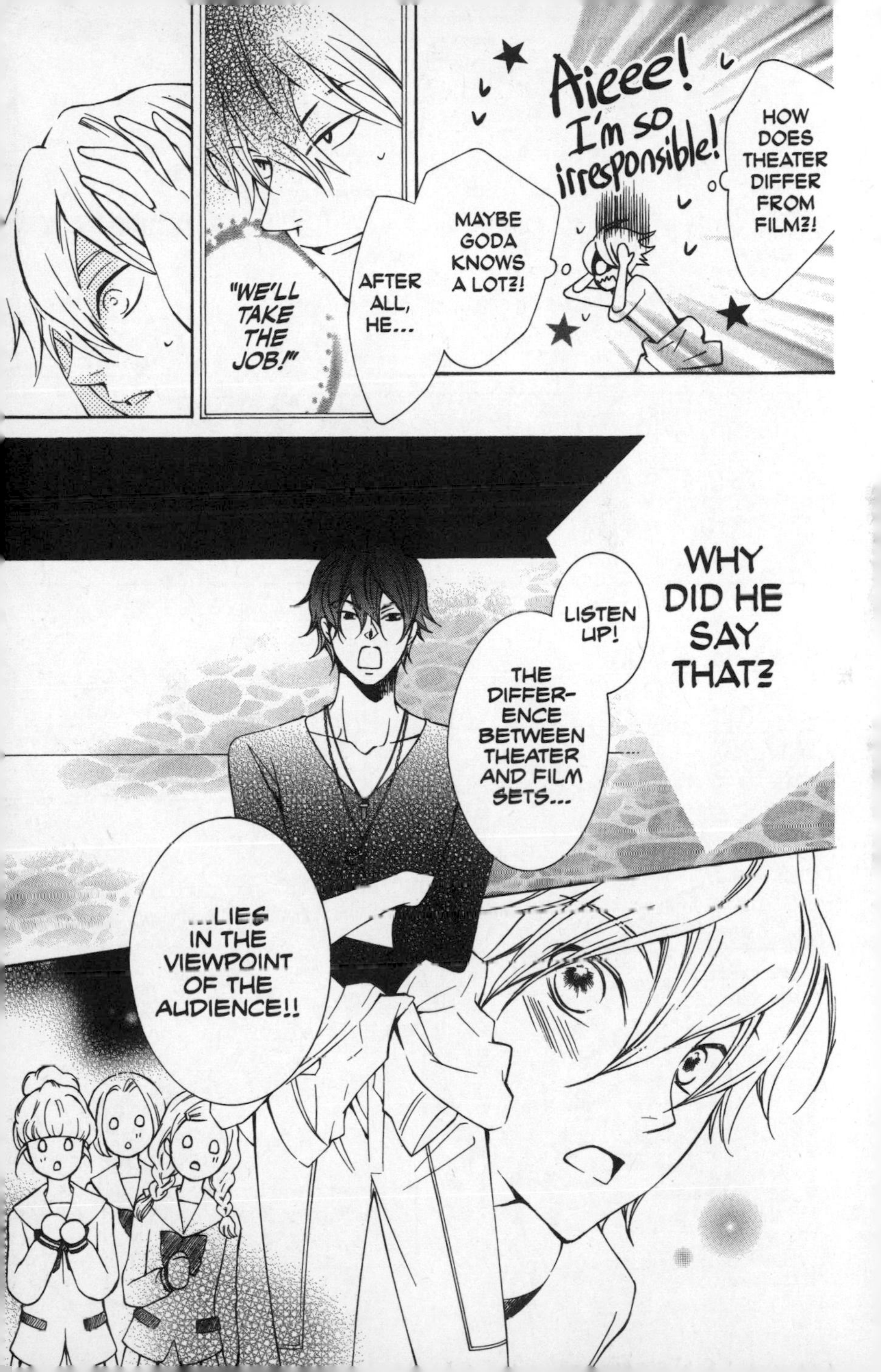
HOW DOES THEATER DIFFER FROM FILM?!
Aieee! I'm so irresponsible!
MAYBE GODA KNOWS A LOT?!
AFTER ALL, HE...
"WE'LL TAKE THE JOB!"
WHY DID HE SAY THAT?
LISTEN UP!
THE DIFFERENCE BETWEEN THEATER AND FILM SETS...
...LIES IN THE VIEWPOINT OF THE AUDIENCE!!

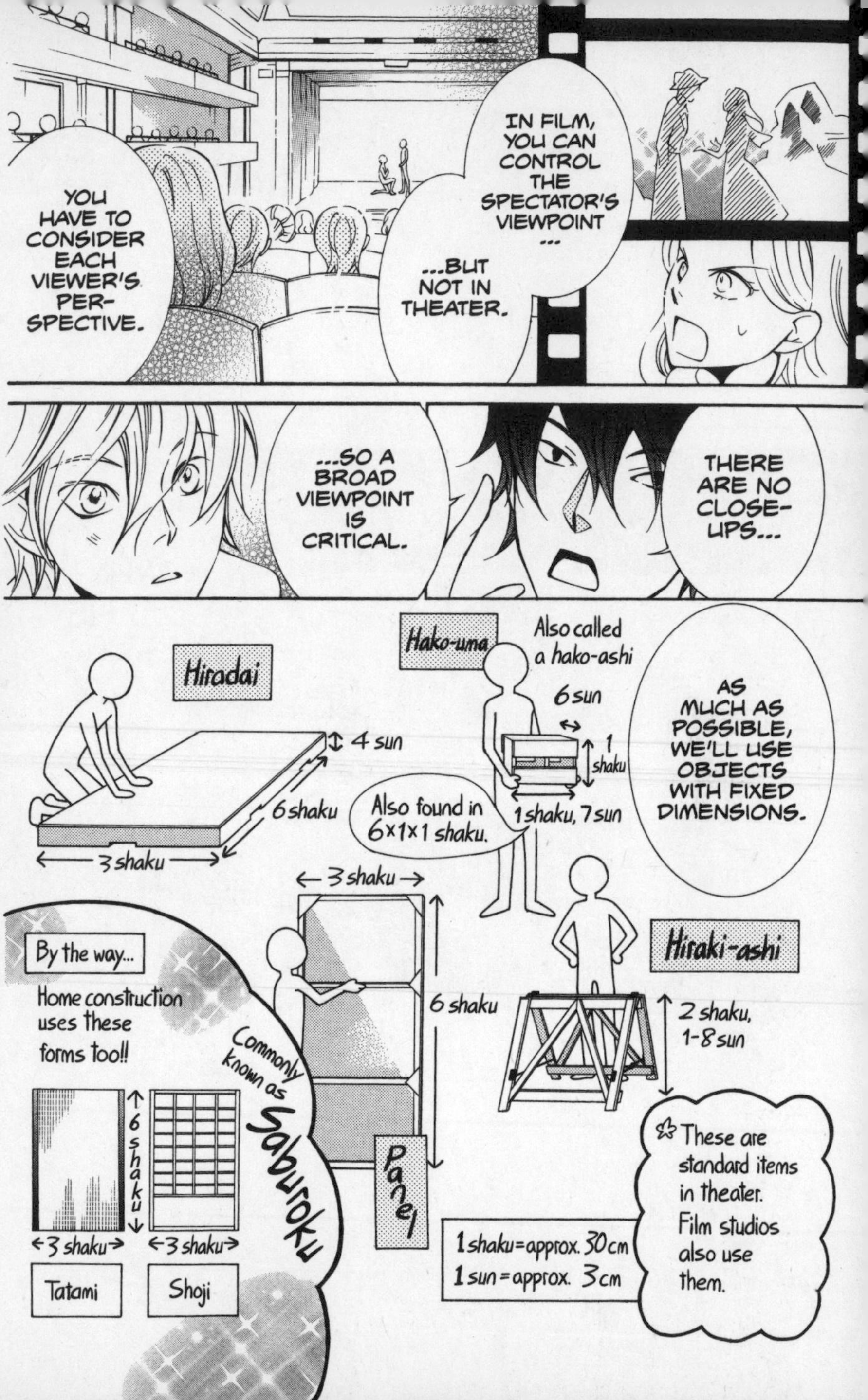
IN FILM, YOU CAN CONTROL THE SPECTATOR'S VIEWPOINT...
...BUT NOT IN THEATER.
YOU HAVE TO CONSIDER EACH VIEWER'S PER-SPECTIVE.
THERE ARE NO CLOSE-UPS...
...SO A BROAD VIEWPOINT IS CRITICAL.
AS MUCH AS POSSIBLE, WE'LL USE OBJECTS WITH FIXED DIMENSIONS.
Hako-uma
Also called a hako-ashi
6 sun
1 shaku
1 shaku, 7 sun
Also found in 6×1×1 shaku.
Hiradai
4 sun
6 shaku
3 shaku
Hiraki-ashi
2 shaku, 1-8 sun
These are standard items in theater. Film studios also use them.
1 shaku=approx. 30cm
1 sun=approx. 3cm
3 shaku
6 shaku
Panel
Commonly known as Saburoku
By the way...
Home construction uses these forms too!!
6 shaku
3 shaku
3 shaku
Tatami
Shoji

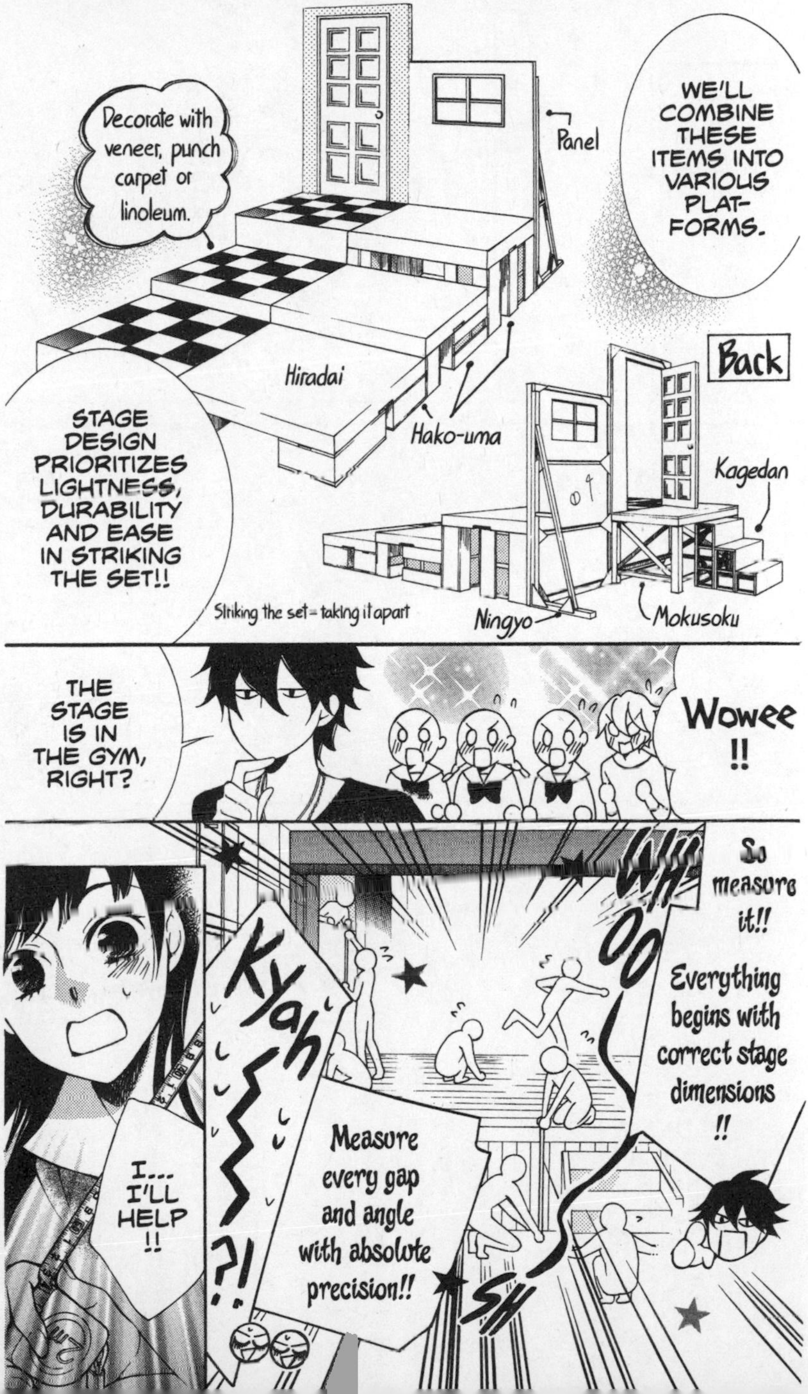
WE'LL COMBINE THESE ITEMS INTO VARIOUS PLAT-FORMS.
Panel
Decorate with veneer, punch carpet or linoleum.
Back
Hiradai
Hako-uma
Kagedan
STAGE DESIGN PRIORITIZES LIGHTNESS, DURABILITY AND EASE IN STRIKING THE SET!!
Mokusoku
Ningyo
Striking the set = taking it apart
Wowee!!
THE STAGE IS IN THE GYM, RIGHT?
So measure it!!
Everything begins with correct stage dimensions!!
WHOOSH
Kyah?!
Measure every gap and angle with absolute precision!!
I... I'LL HELP!!

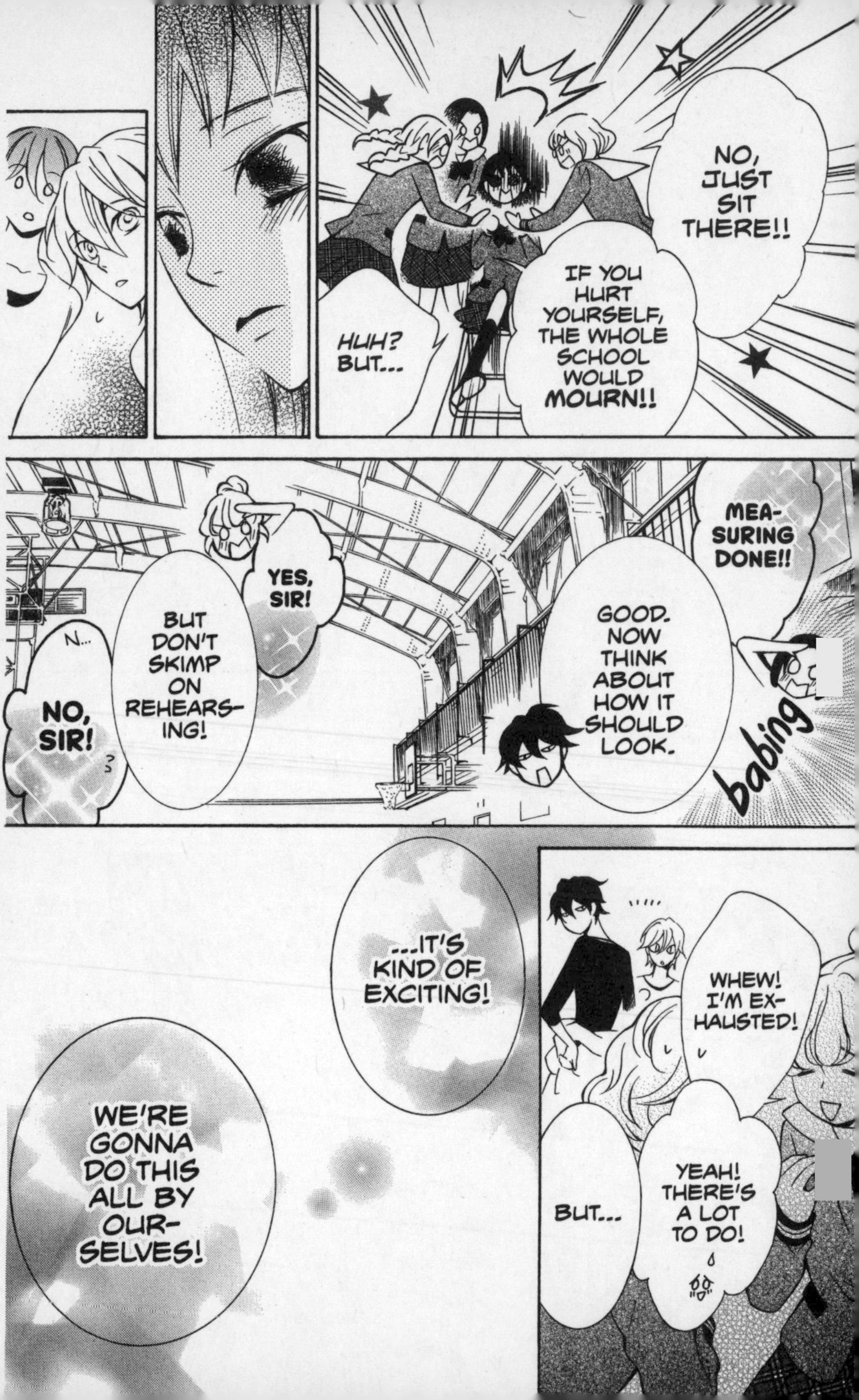
NO, JUST SIT THERE!!
IF YOU HURT YOURSELF, THE WHOLE SCHOOL WOULD MOURN!!
HUH? BUT...
MEA-SURING DONE!!
babing
GOOD. NOW THINK ABOUT HOW IT SHOULD LOOK.
YES, SIR!
BUT DON'T SKIMP ON REHEARS-ING!
N...
NO, SIR!
WHEW! I'M EX-HAUSTED!
YEAH! THERE'S A LOT TO DO!
BUT...
...IT'S KIND OF EXCITING!
WE'RE GONNA DO THIS ALL BY OUR-SELVES!

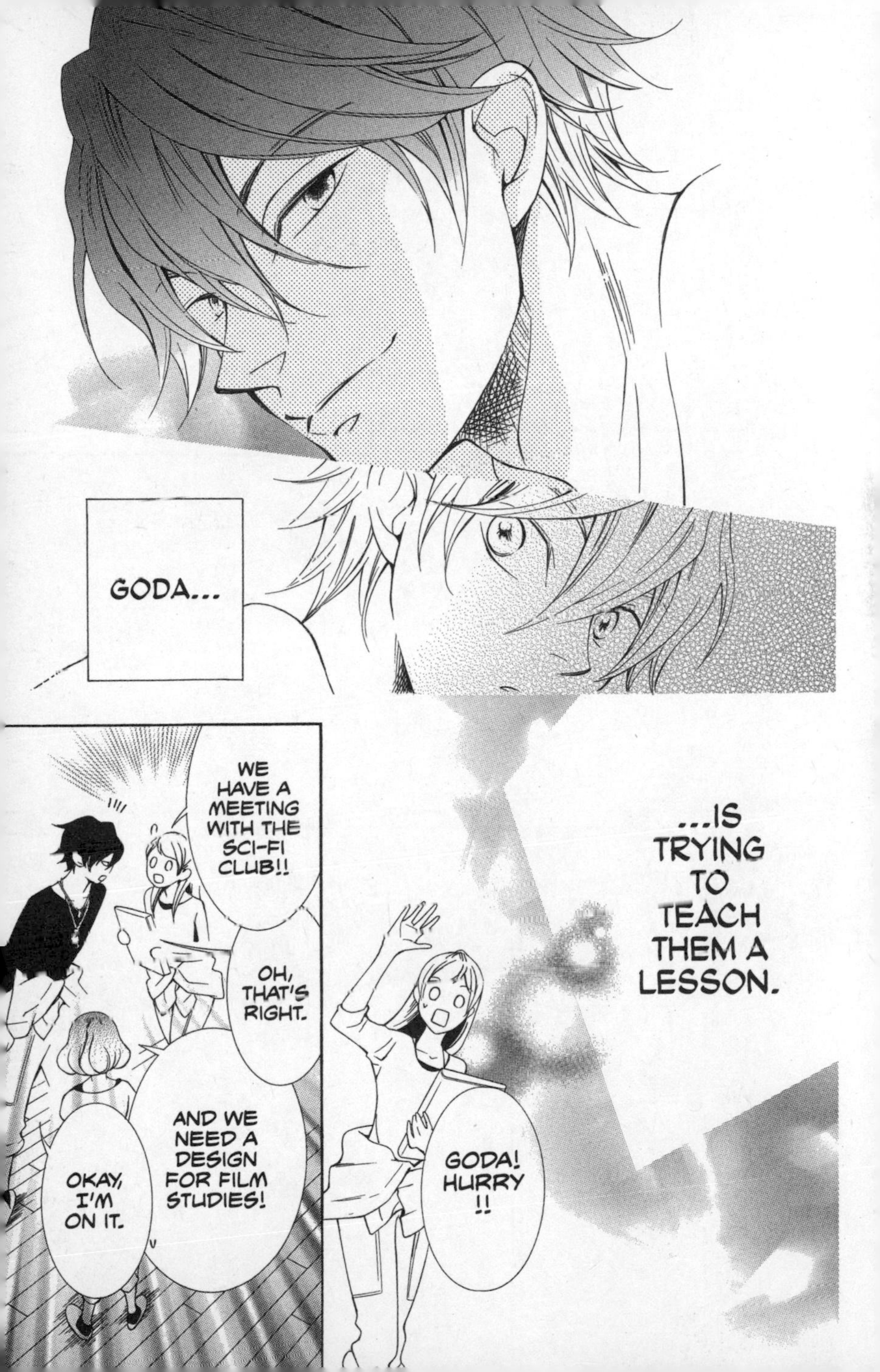
GODA...
...IS TRYING TO TEACH THEM A LESSON.
GODA! HURRY!!
WE HAVE A MEETING WITH THE SCI-FI CLUB!!
OH, THAT'S RIGHT.
AND WE NEED A DESIGN FOR FILM STUDIES!
OKAY, I'M ON IT.

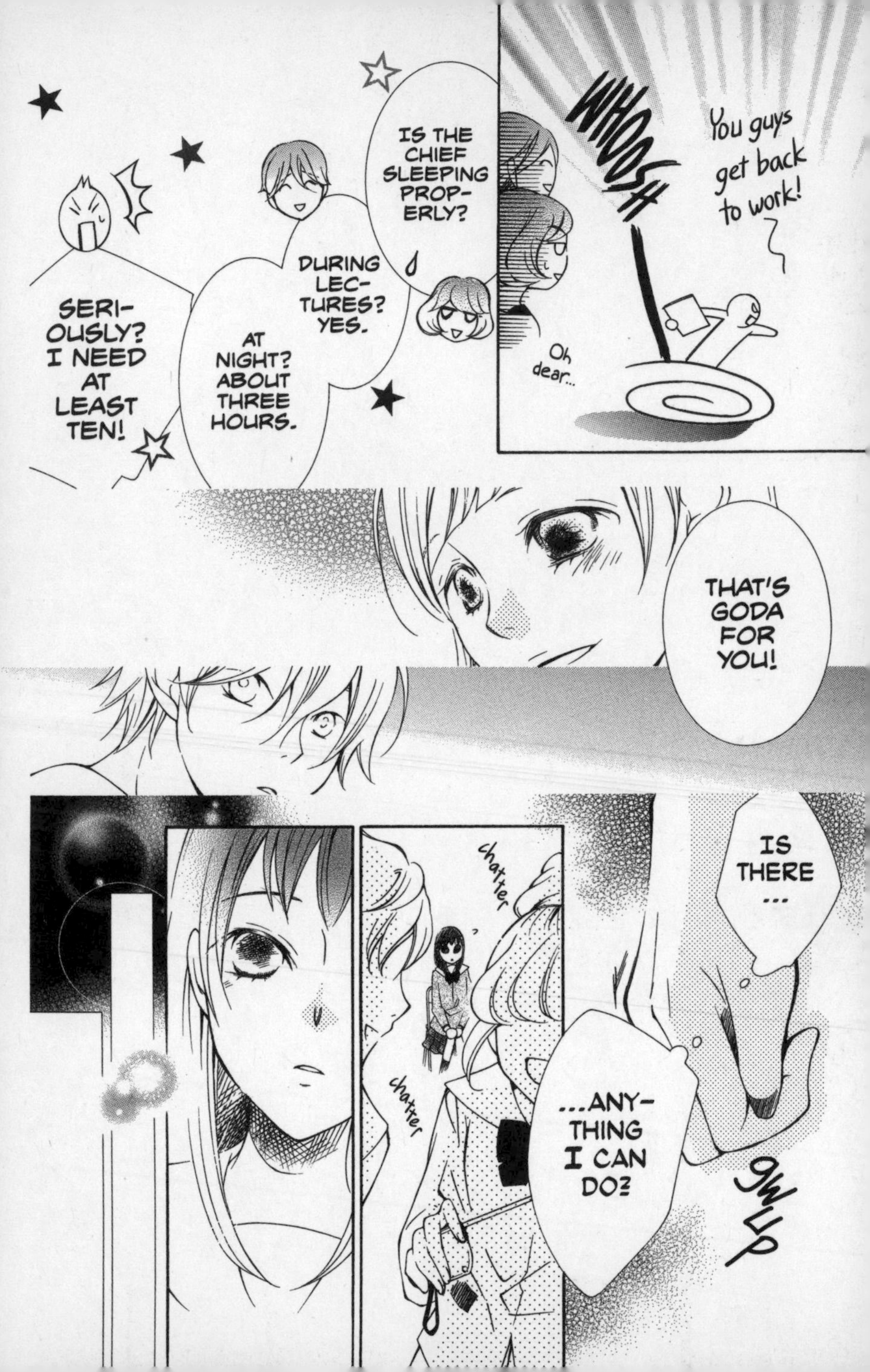
You guys get back to work!
WHOOSH
Oh dear...
IS THE CHIEF SLEEPING PROPERLY?
DURING LECTURES? YES.
AT NIGHT? ABOUT THREE HOURS.
SERIOUSLY? I NEED AT LEAST TEN!
THAT'S GODA FOR YOU!
IS THERE...
...ANYTHING I CAN DO?
GULP
chatter
chatter

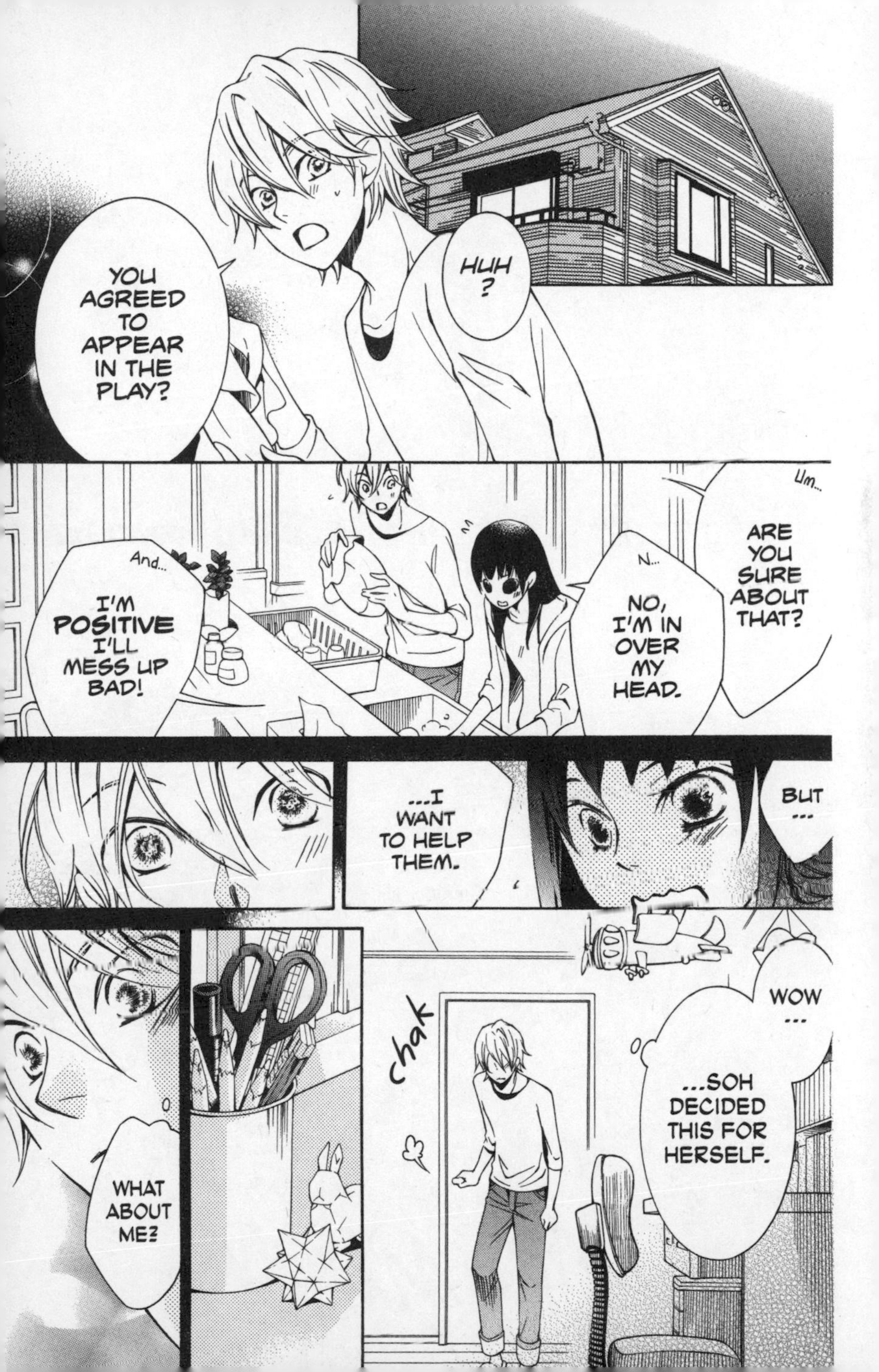
HUH?
YOU AGREED TO APPEAR IN THE PLAY?
Um... ARE YOU SURE ABOUT THAT?
N... NO, I'M IN OVER MY HEAD.
And... I'M **POSITIVE** I'LL MESS UP BAD!
BUT...
...I WANT TO HELP THEM.
WOW...
...SOH DECIDED THIS FOR HERSELF.
chak
WHAT ABOUT ME?

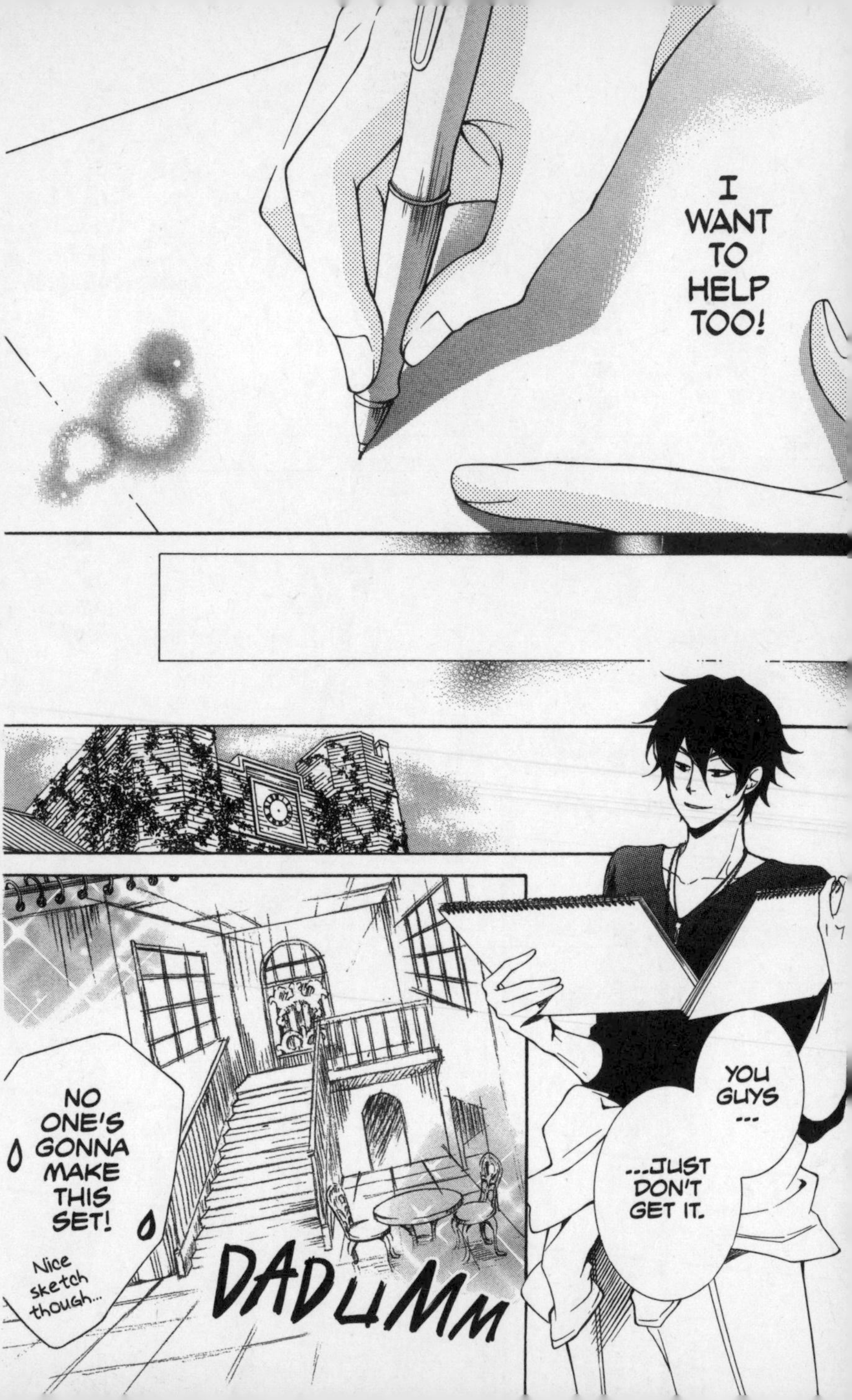
I WANT TO HELP TOO!
YOU GUYS...
...JUST DON'T GET IT.
NO ONE'S GONNA MAKE THIS SET!
DADUMM
Nice sketch though...

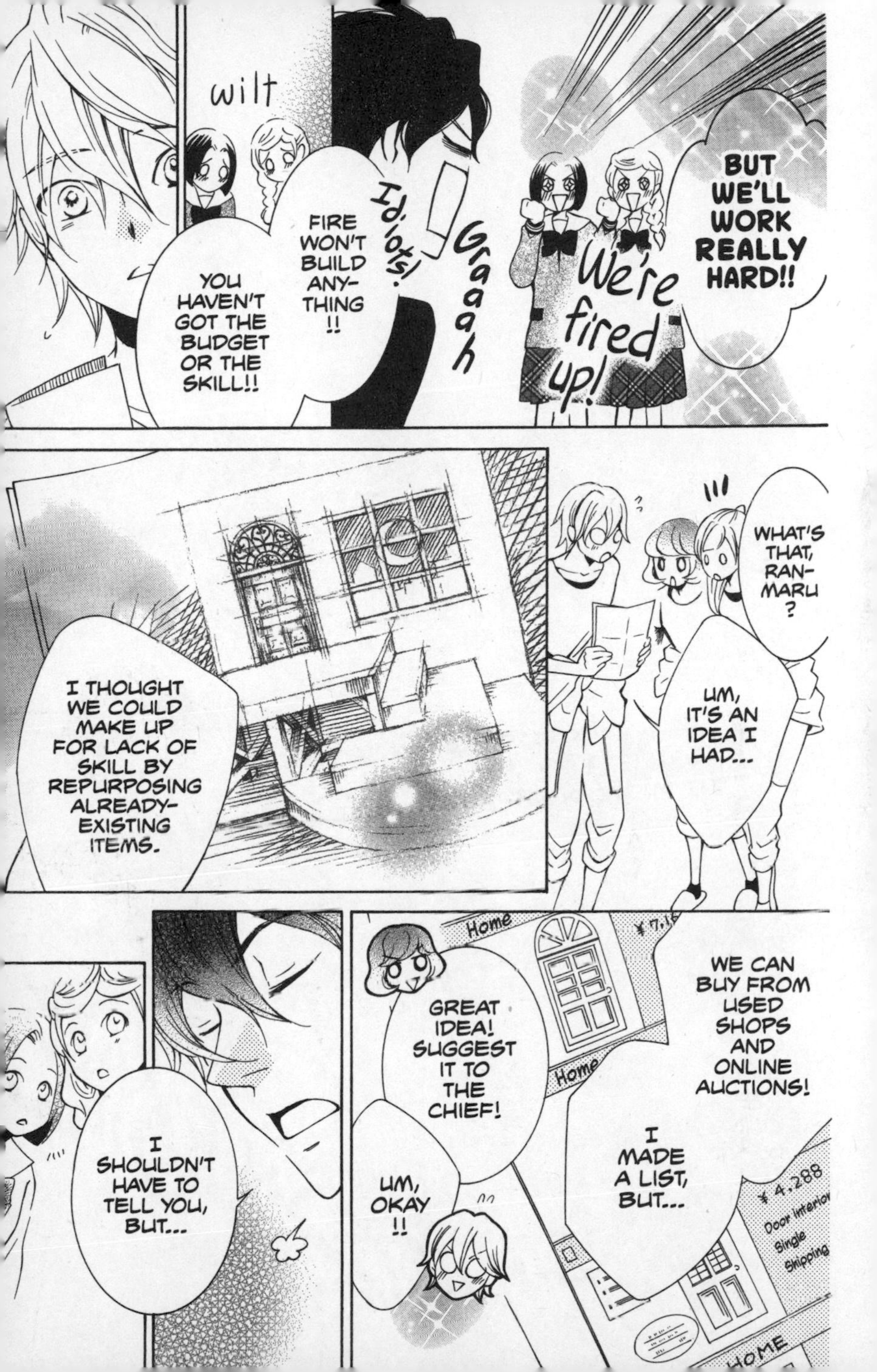
BUT WE'LL WORK REALLY HARD!!
We're fired up!
Graaaah
Idiots!
FIRE WON'T BUILD ANY-THING!!
YOU HAVEN'T GOT THE BUDGET OR THE SKILL!!
wilt
WHAT'S THAT, RAN-MARU?
UM, IT'S AN IDEA I HAD...
I THOUGHT WE COULD MAKE UP FOR LACK OF SKILL BY REPURPOSING ALREADY-EXISTING ITEMS.
Home
Home
WE CAN BUY FROM USED SHOPS AND ONLINE AUCTIONS!
I MADE A LIST, BUT...
¥4,288
Door Interior
Single
Shipping
HOME
GREAT IDEA! SUGGEST IT TO THE CHIEF!
UM, OKAY!!
I SHOULDN'T HAVE TO TELL YOU, BUT...

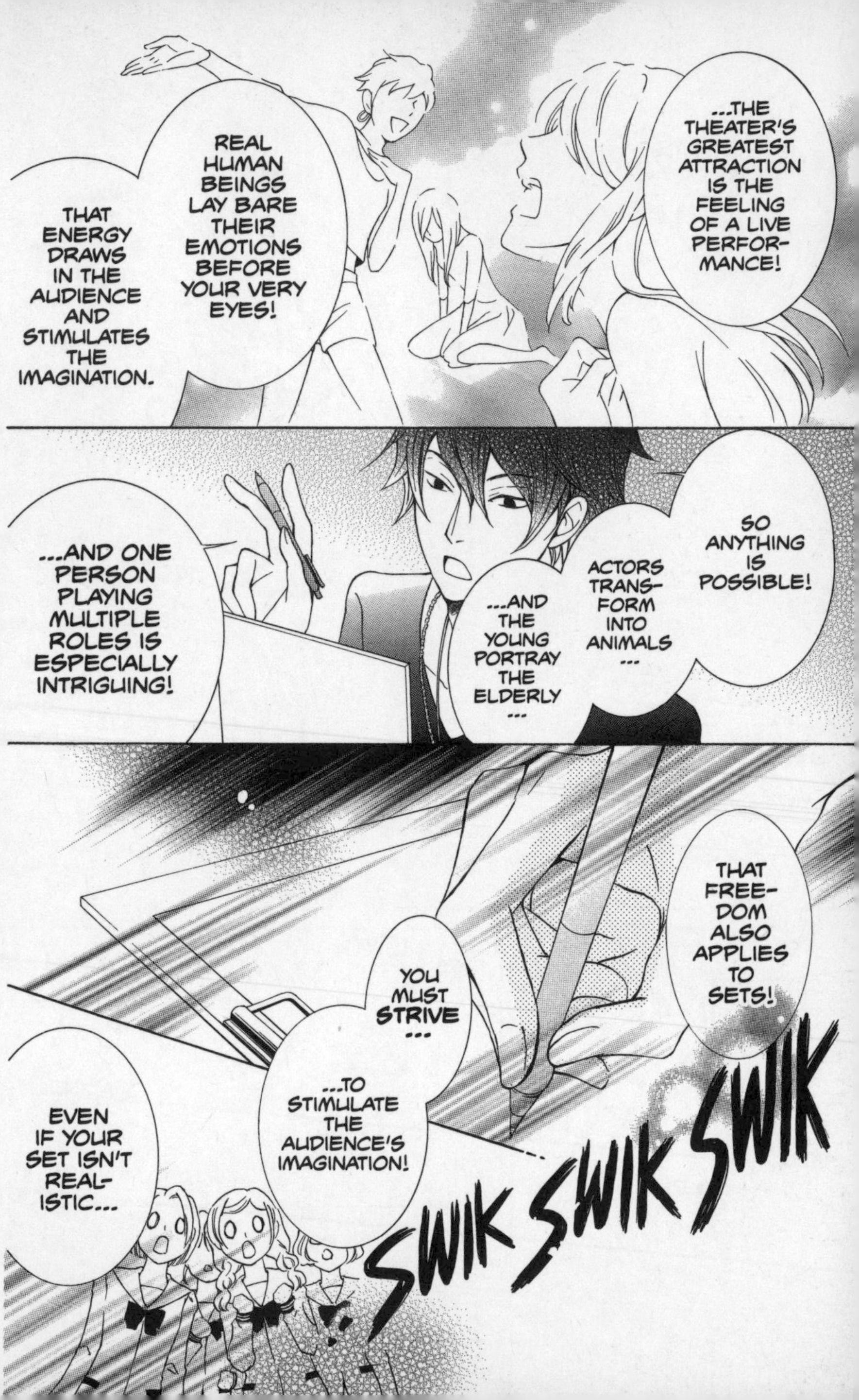
...THE THEATER'S GREATEST ATTRACTION IS THE FEELING OF A LIVE PERFOR-MANCE!
REAL HUMAN BEINGS LAY BARE THEIR EMOTIONS BEFORE YOUR VERY EYES!
THAT ENERGY DRAWS IN THE AUDIENCE AND STIMULATES THE IMAGINATION.
SO ANYTHING IS POSSIBLE!
ACTORS TRANS-FORM INTO ANIMALS...
...AND THE YOUNG PORTRAY THE ELDERLY...
...AND ONE PERSON PLAYING MULTIPLE ROLES IS ESPECIALLY INTRIGUING!
THAT FREE-DOM ALSO APPLIES TO SETS!
SWIK SWIK SWIK
YOU MUST STRIVE...
...TO STIMULATE THE AUDIENCE'S IMAGINATION!
EVEN IF YOUR SET ISN'T REAL-ISTIC...

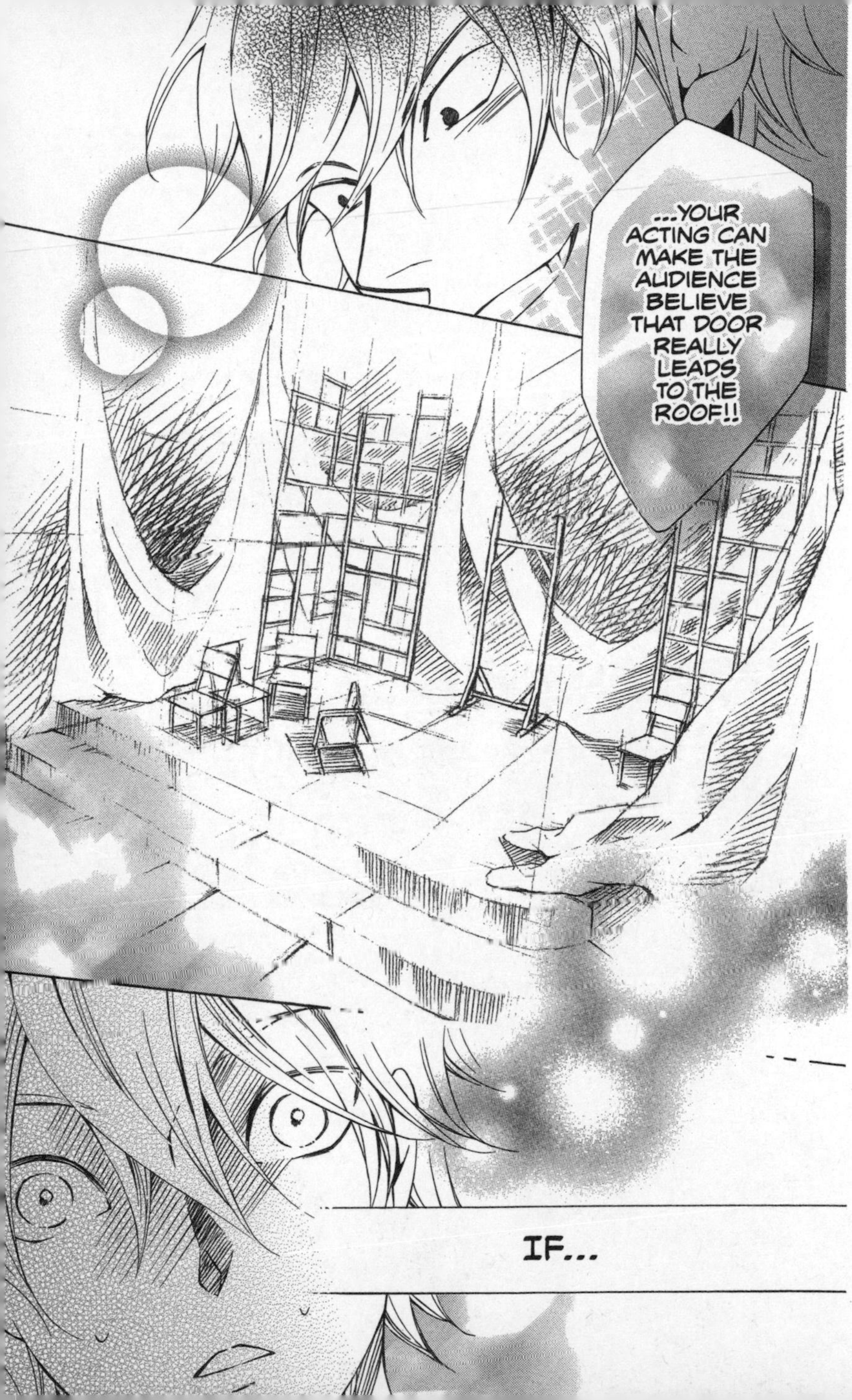
...YOUR ACTING CAN MAKE THE AUDIENCE BELIEVE THAT DOOR REALLY LEADS TO THE ROOF!!
IF...

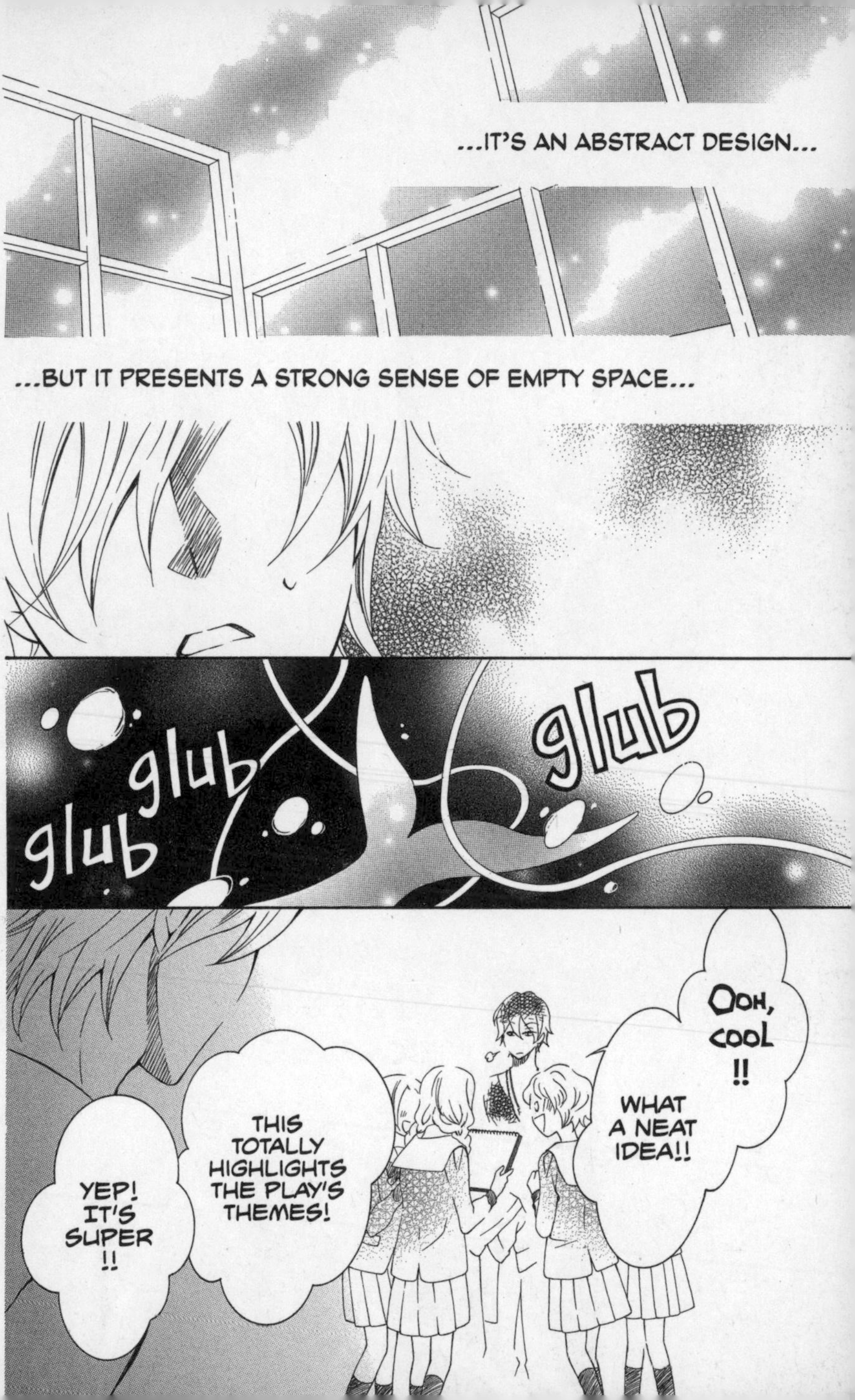
...IT'S AN ABSTRACT DESIGN...
...BUT IT PRESENTS A STRONG SENSE OF EMPTY SPACE...
glub
glub
glub
OOH, COOL !!
WHAT A NEAT IDEA!!
THIS TOTALLY HIGHLIGHTS THE PLAY'S THEMES!
YEP! IT'S SUPER !!

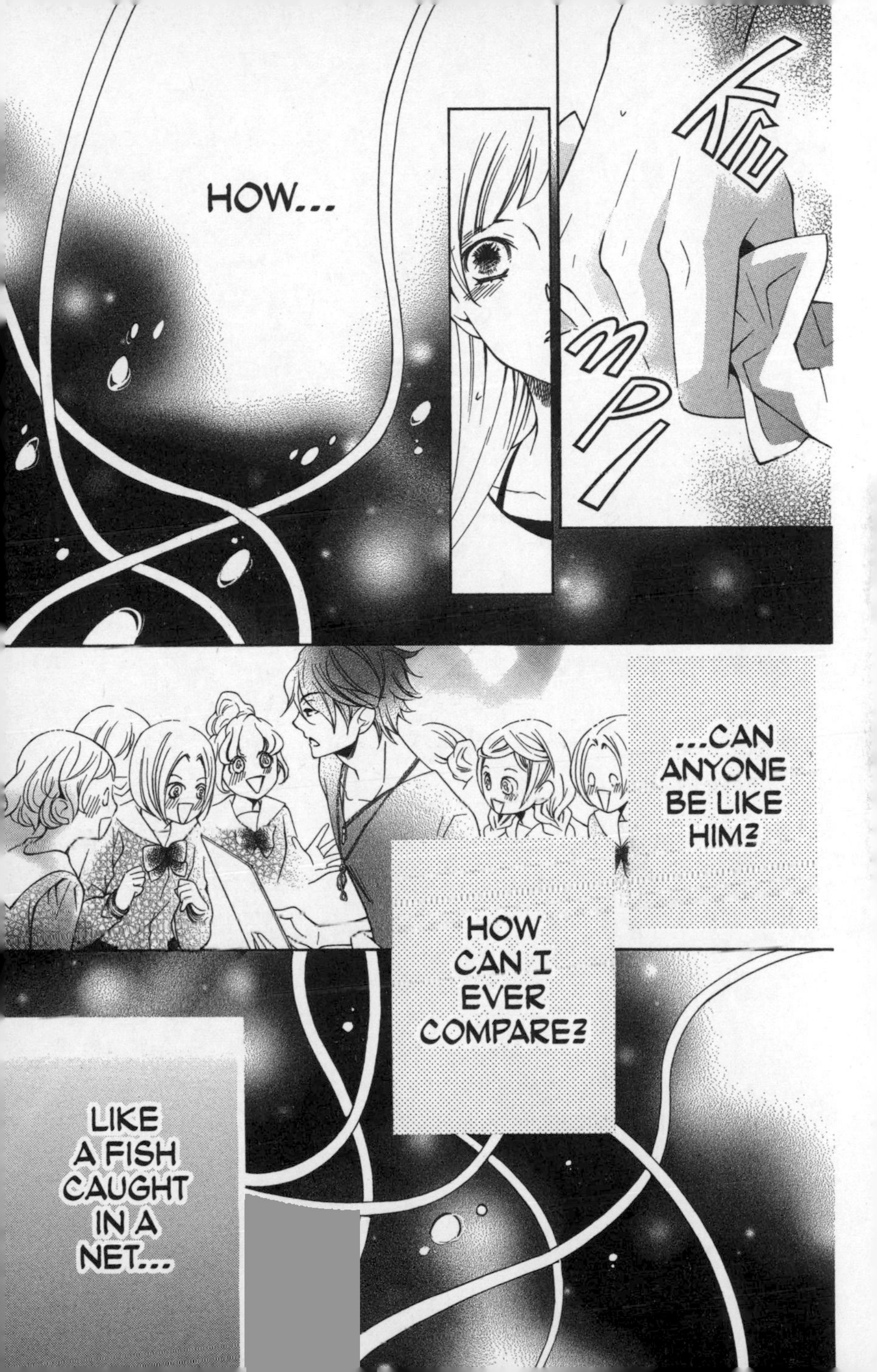
KYUMPI
HOW...
...CAN ANYONE BE LIKE HIM?
HOW CAN I EVER COMPARE?
LIKE A FISH CAUGHT IN A NET...

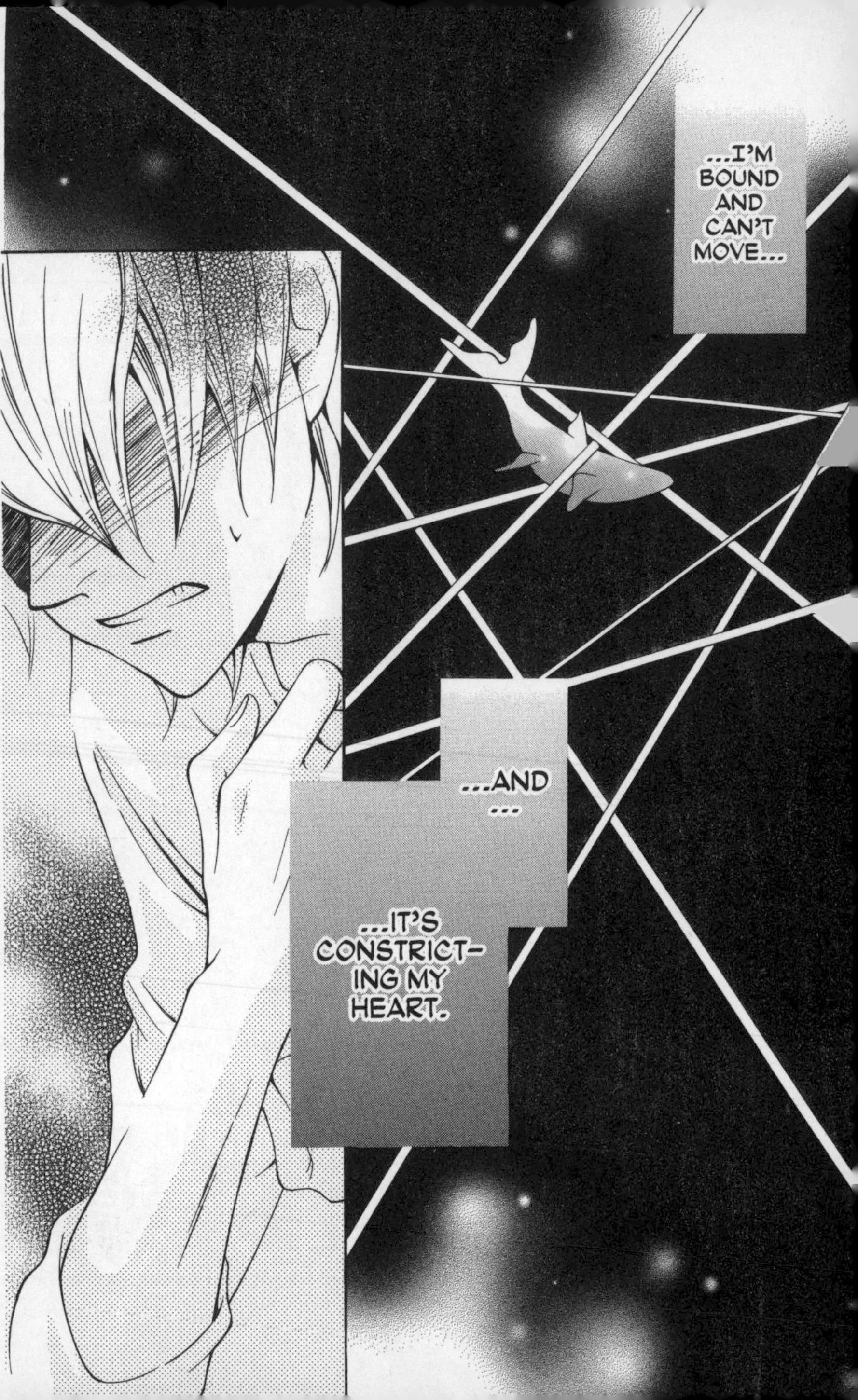
...I'M BOUND AND CAN'T MOVE...
...AND ...
...IT'S CONSTRICT-ING MY HEART.

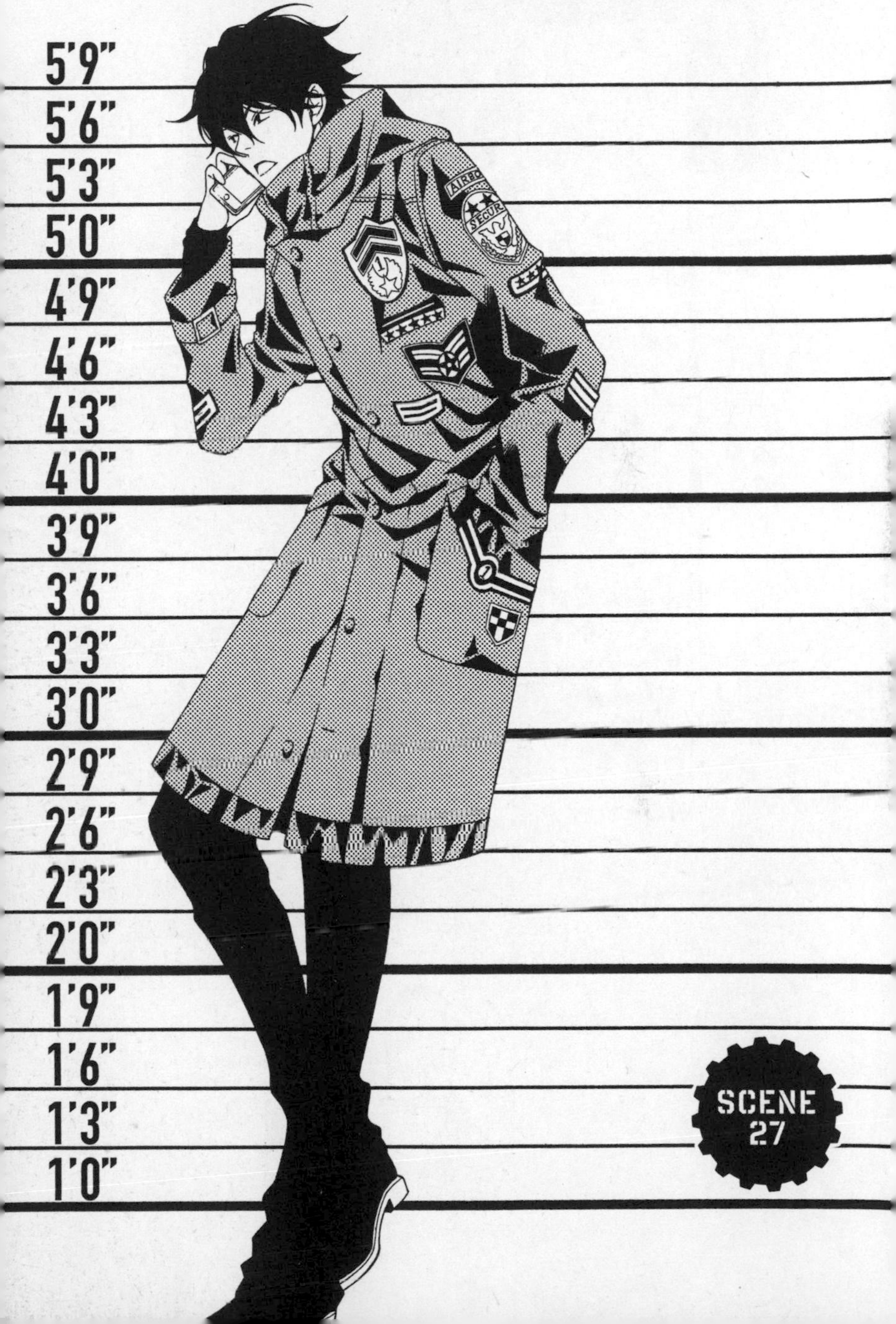
5'9"
5'6"
5'3"
5'0"
4'9"
4'6"
4'3"
4'0"
3'9"
3'6"
3'3"
3'0"
2'9"
2'6"
2'3"
2'0"
1'9"
1'6"
1'3"
1'0"
SCENE
27

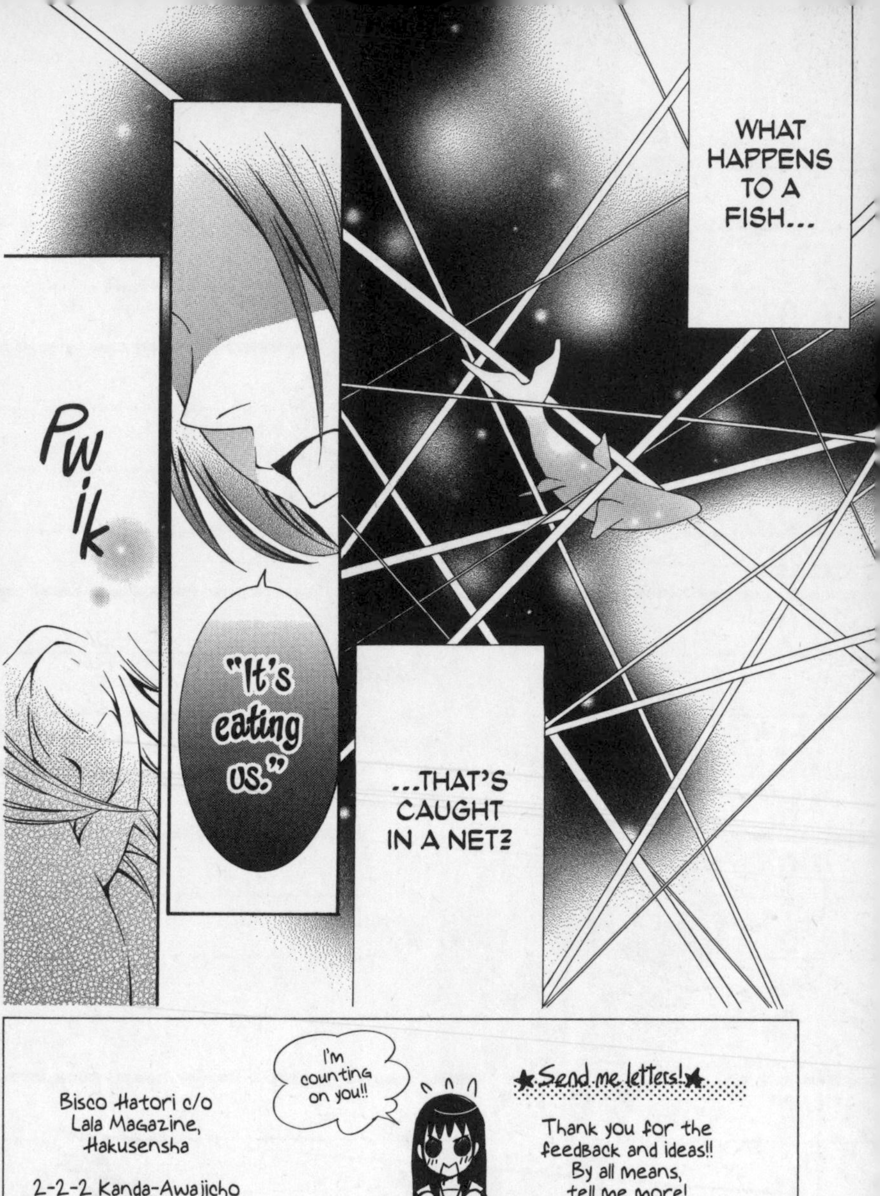
WHAT HAPPENS TO A FISH...
...THAT'S CAUGHT IN A NET?
"It's eating us."
Pwik

★Send me letters!★

Thank you for the feedback and ideas!! By all means, tell me more!

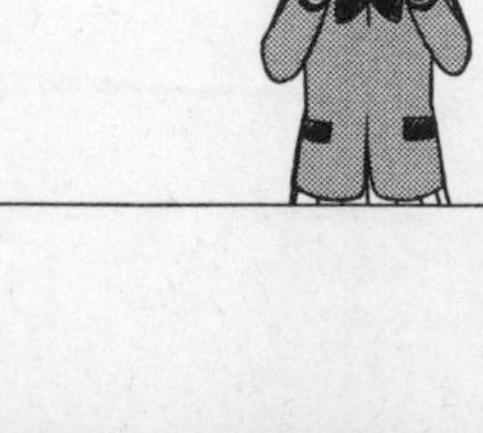
I'm counting on you!!

Bisco Hatori c/o
Lala Magazine,
Hakusensha

2-2-2 Kanda-Awajicho
Chyodia-ku
Tokyo, Japan
101-0063

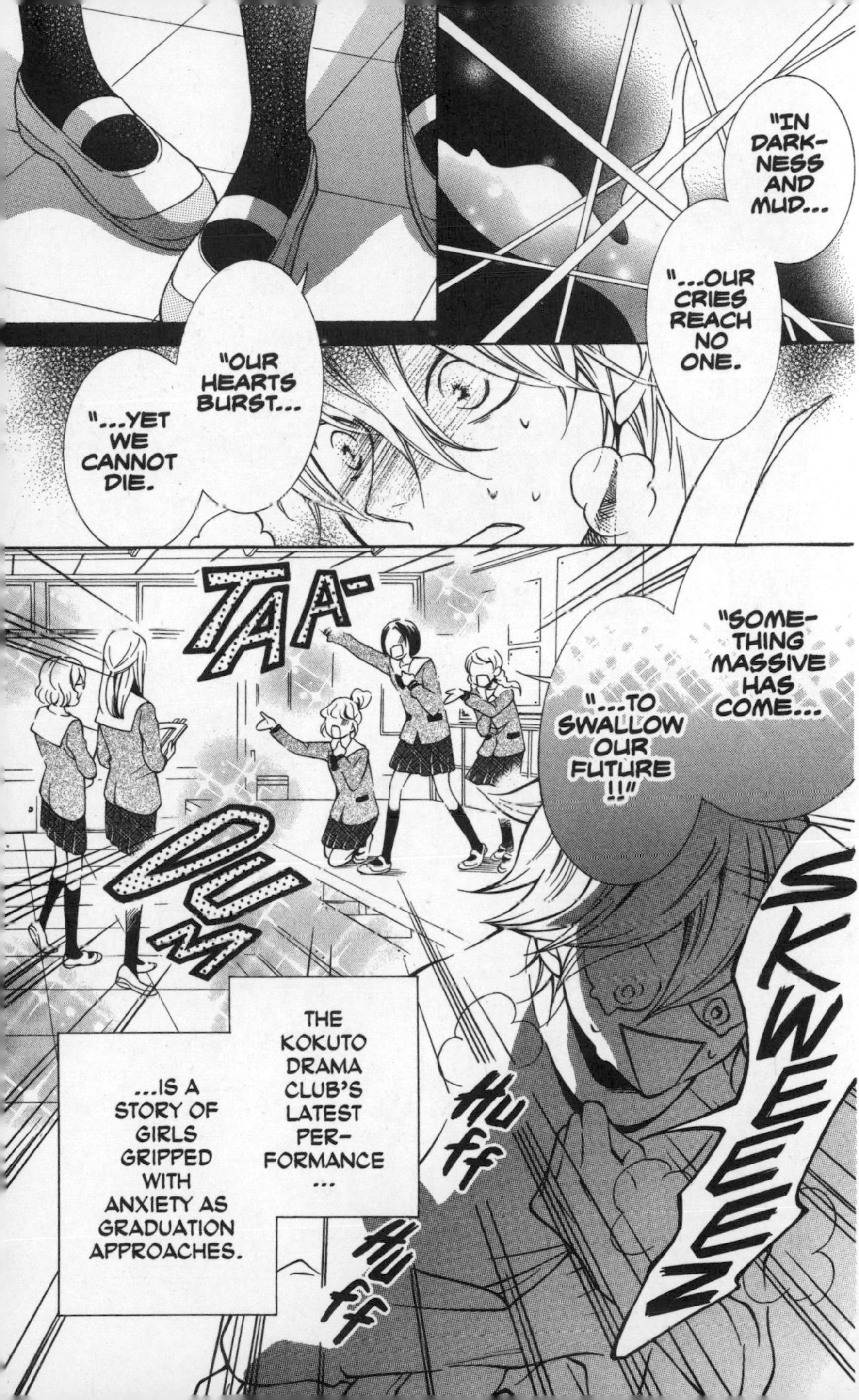
"IN DARKNESS AND MUD...
"...OUR CRIES REACH NO ONE.
"OUR HEARTS BURST...
"...YET WE CANNOT DIE.
"SOMETHING MASSIVE HAS COME...
"...TO SWALLOW OUR FUTURE!!"
SKWEEEEEN
HUFF HUFF
TAA-DUM
THE KOKUTO DRAMA CLUB'S LATEST PERFORMANCE...
...IS A STORY OF GIRLS GRIPPED WITH ANXIETY AS GRADUATION APPROACHES.

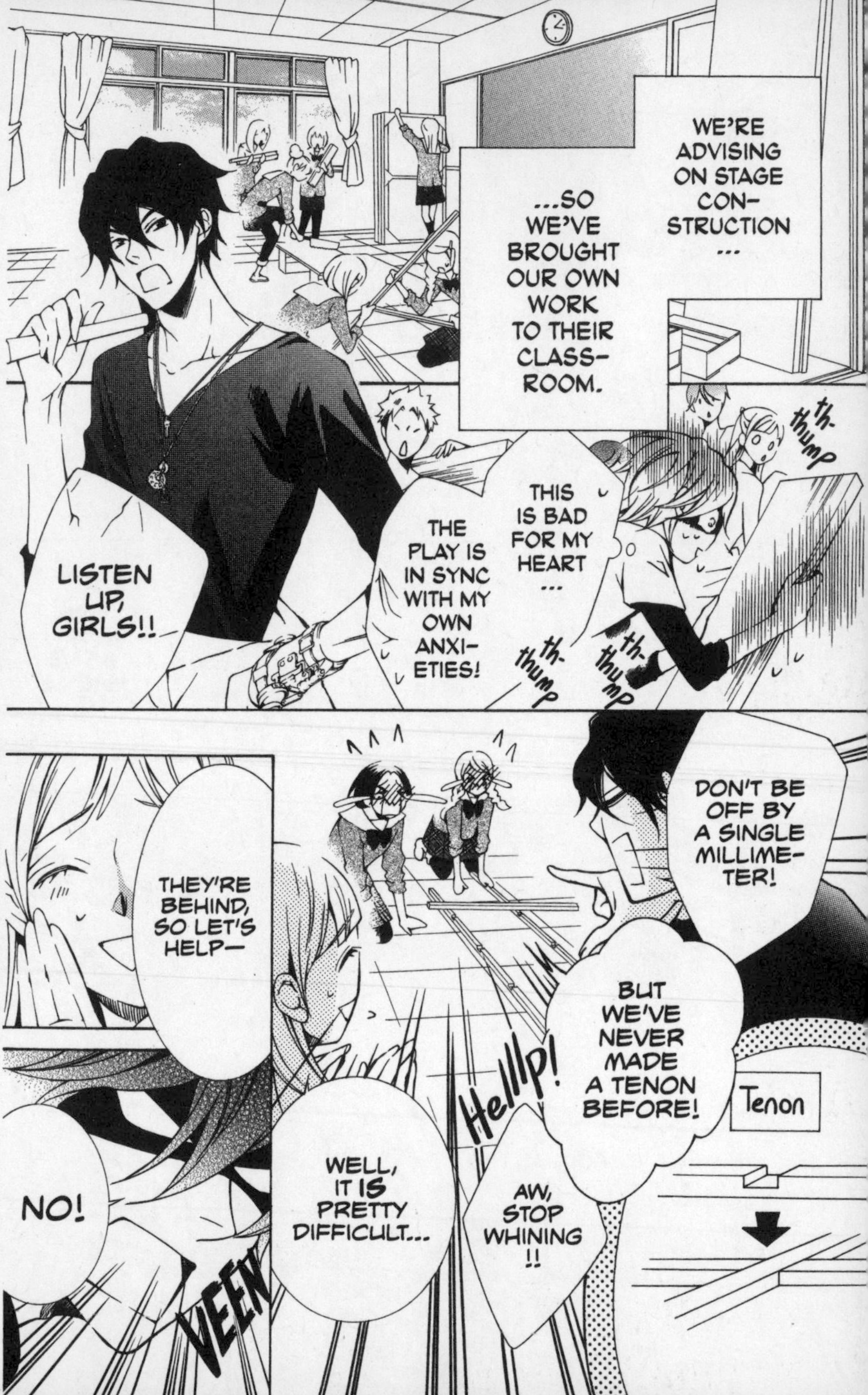
WE'RE ADVISING ON STAGE CON-STRUCTION...
...SO WE'VE BROUGHT OUR OWN WORK TO THEIR CLASS-ROOM.
th-thump
THIS IS BAD FOR MY HEART...
THE PLAY IS IN SYNC WITH MY OWN ANXI-ETIES!
th-thump
th-thump
LISTEN UP, GIRLS!!
DON'T BE OFF BY A SINGLE MILLIME-TER!
BUT WE'VE NEVER MADE A TENON BEFORE!
Tenon
AW, STOP WHINING!!
Helllp!
WELL, IT IS PRETTY DIFFICULT...
THEY'RE BEHIND, SO LET'S HELP—
NO!
VEEN

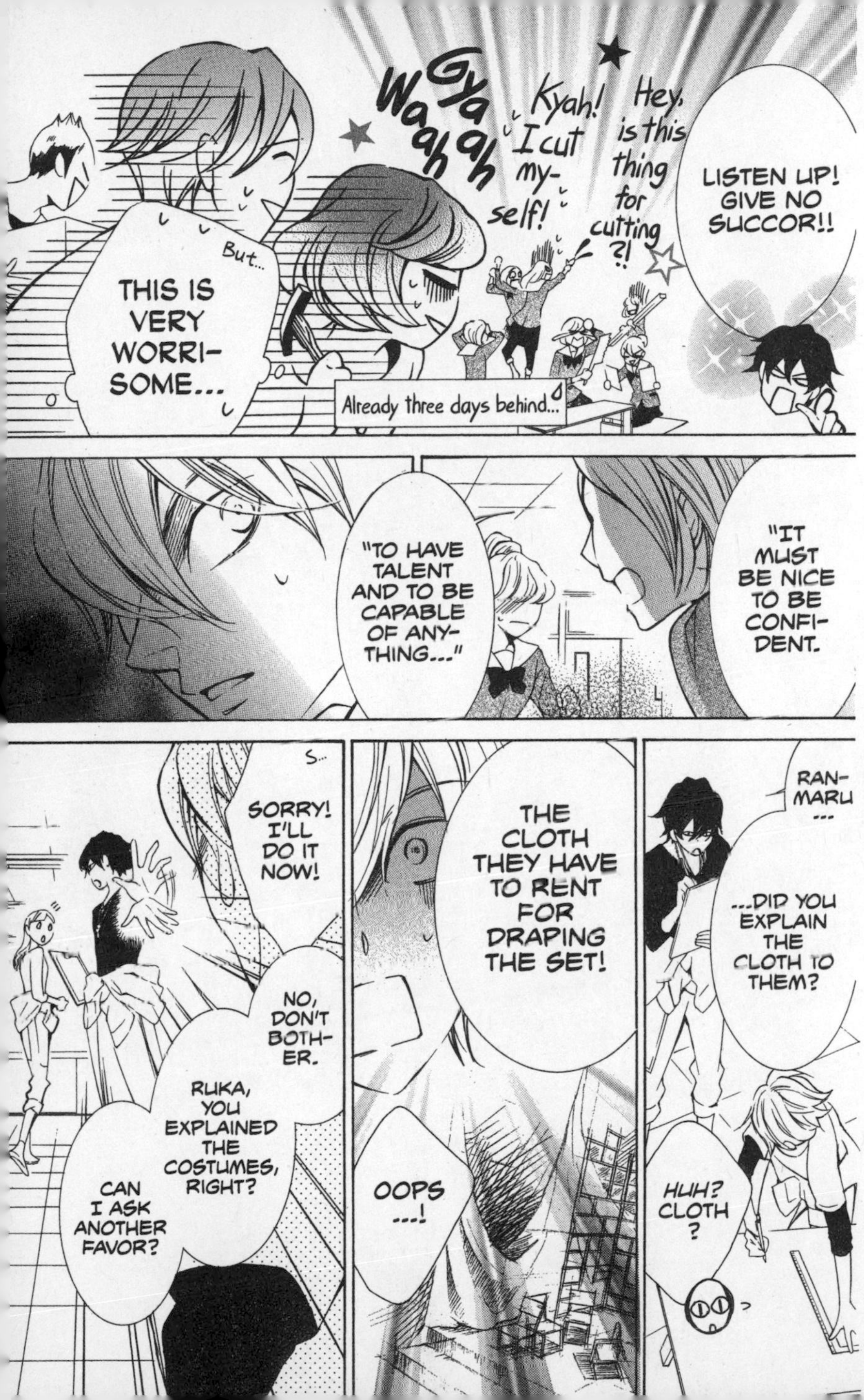
LISTEN UP! GIVE NO SUCCOR!!
Hey, is this thing for cutting?!
Kyah! I cut my-self!
Gyaa Waaahah
Already three days behind...
But...
THIS IS VERY WORRI-SOME...
"IT MUST BE NICE TO BE CONFI-DENT.
"TO HAVE TALENT AND TO BE CAPABLE OF ANY-THING..."
RAN-MARU...
...DID YOU EXPLAIN THE CLOTH TO THEM?
HUH? CLOTH?
THE CLOTH THEY HAVE TO RENT FOR DRAPING THE SET!
OOPS...!
S...
SORRY! I'LL DO IT NOW!
NO, DON'T BOTHER.
RUKA, YOU EXPLAINED THE COSTUMES, RIGHT?
CAN I ASK ANOTHER FAVOR?

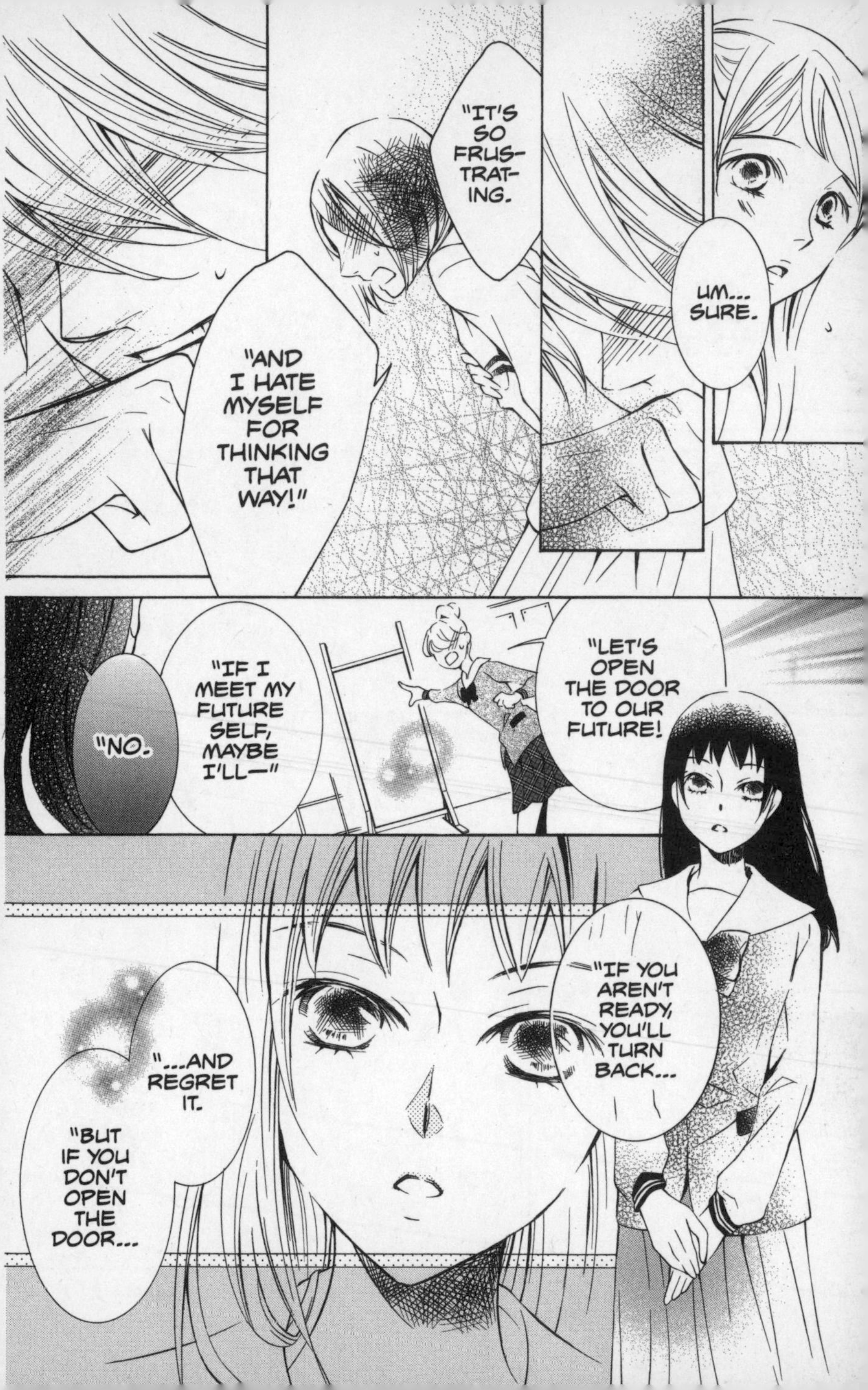
"IT'S SO FRUS-TRAT-ING.
"AND I HATE MYSELF FOR THINKING THAT WAY!"
UM... SURE.
"LET'S OPEN THE DOOR TO OUR FUTURE!
"IF I MEET MY FUTURE SELF, MAYBE I'LL—"
"NO.
"IF YOU AREN'T READY, YOU'LL TURN BACK...
"...AND REGRET IT.
"BUT IF YOU DON'T OPEN THE DOOR...

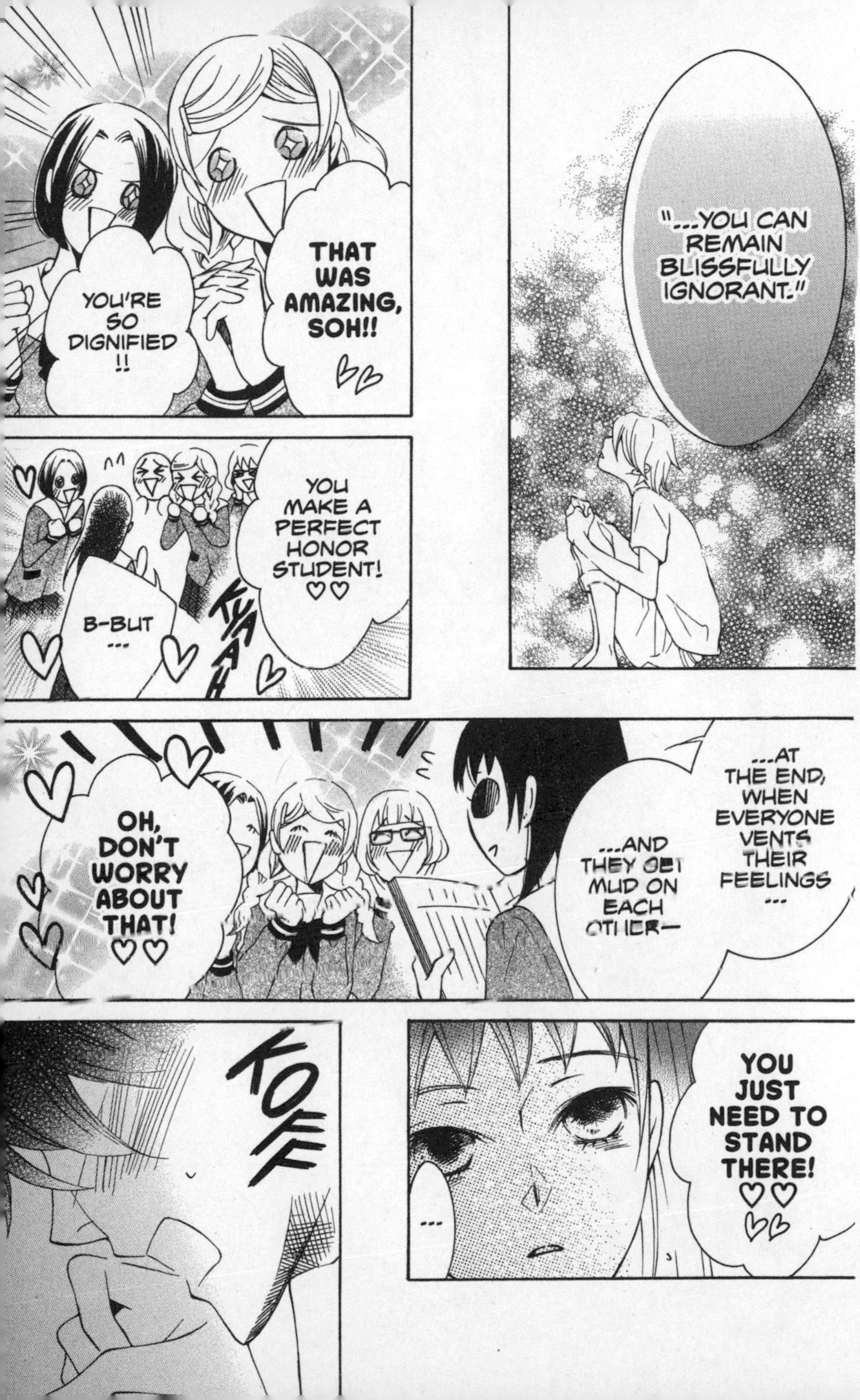
"...YOU CAN REMAIN BLISSFULLY IGNORANT."
THAT WAS AMAZING, SOH!!
YOU'RE SO DIGNIFIED!!
YOU MAKE A PERFECT HONOR STUDENT!
KYAAAH
B-BUT...
...AT THE END, WHEN EVERYONE VENTS THEIR FEELINGS...
...AND THEY GET MUD ON EACH OTHER—
OH, DON'T WORRY ABOUT THAT!
YOU JUST NEED TO STAND THERE!
...
KOFF

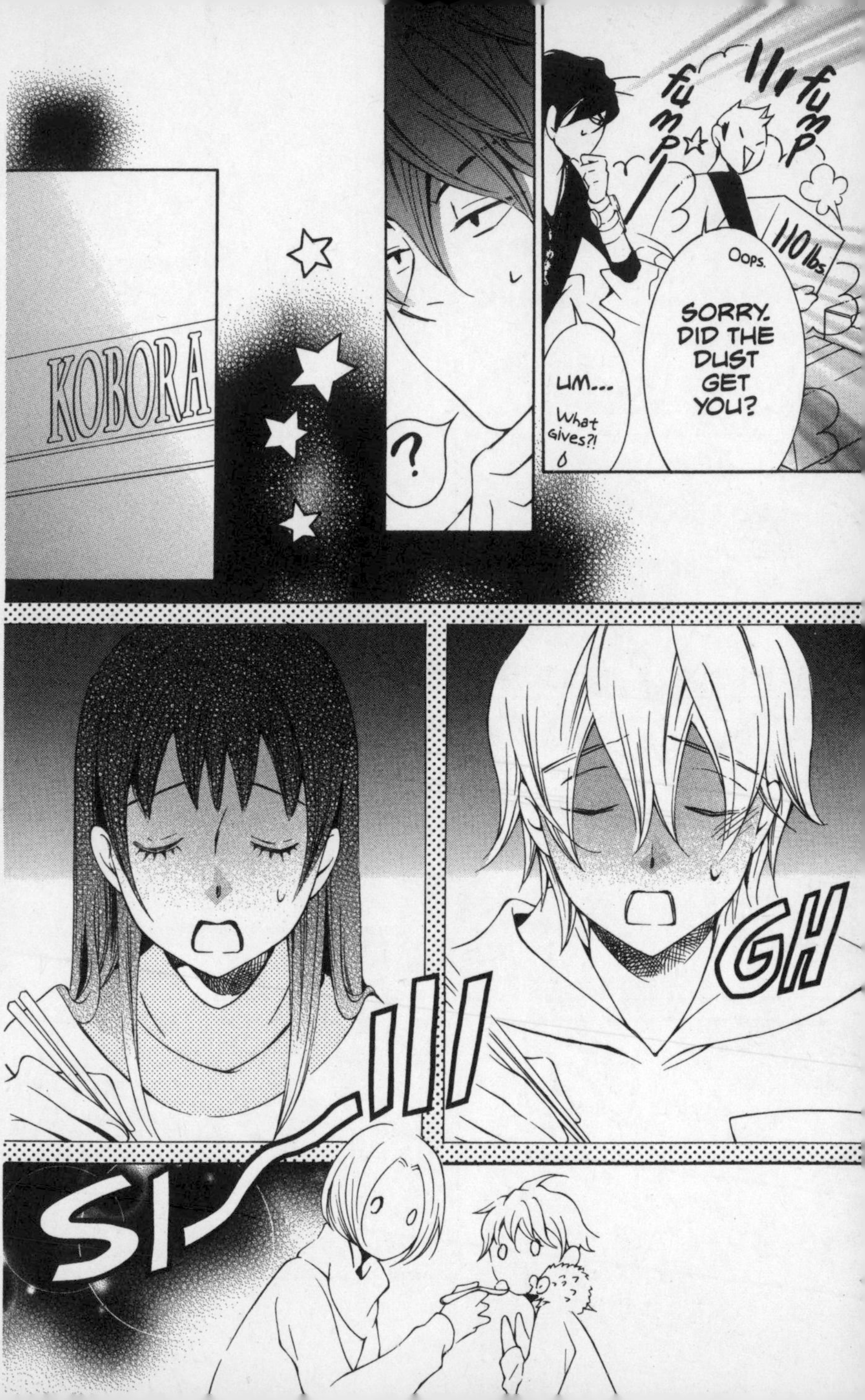
fump
fump
110 lbs
Oops.
SORRY. DID THE DUST GET YOU?
UM...
What gives?!
?
KOBORA
GH
SI
III

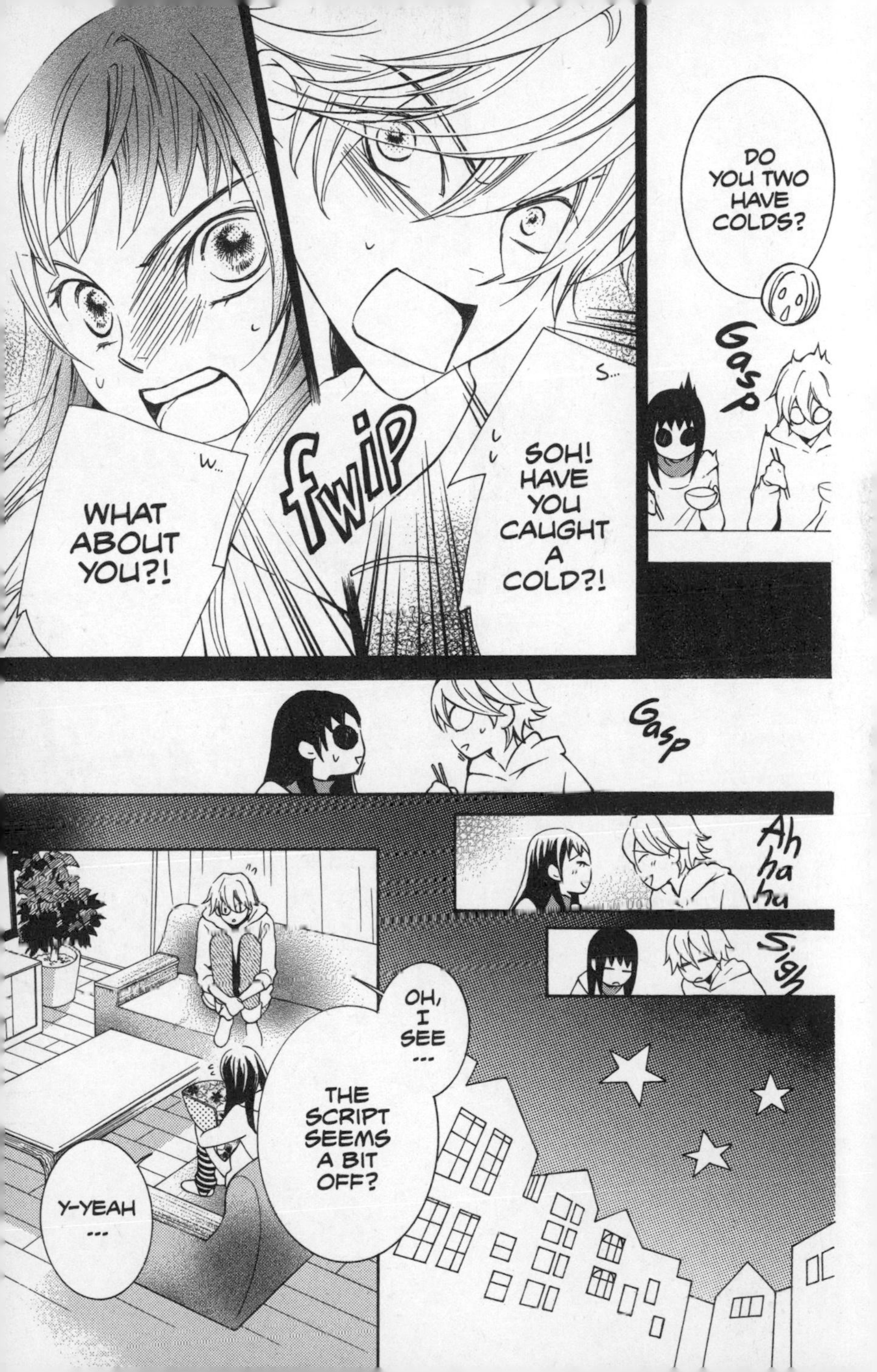
DO YOU TWO HAVE COLDS?
Gasp
S...
SOH! HAVE YOU CAUGHT A COLD?!
fwip
W...
WHAT ABOUT YOU?!
Gasp
Ah ha hu
Sigh
OH, I SEE ...
THE SCRIPT SEEMS A BIT OFF?
Y-YEAH ...

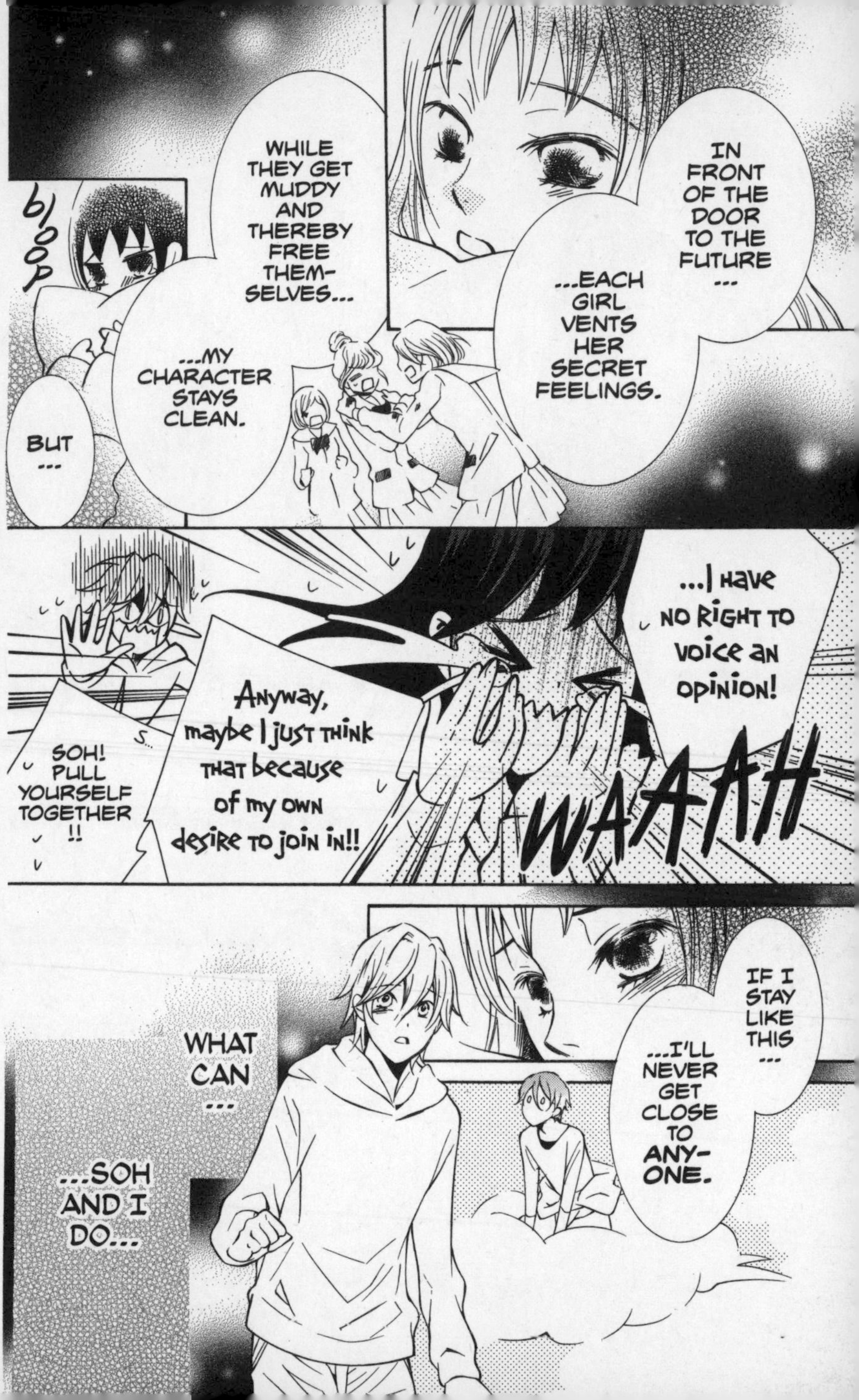
IN FRONT OF THE DOOR TO THE FUTURE ...
...EACH GIRL VENTS HER SECRET FEELINGS.
WHILE THEY GET MUDDY AND THEREBY FREE THEM-SELVES...
...MY CHARACTER STAYS CLEAN.
BLOOP
BUT ...
...I HAVE NO RIGHT TO VOICE AN OPINION!
WAAAH
Anyway, maybe I just think that because of my own desire to join in!!
SOH! PULL YOURSELF TOGETHER !!
IF I STAY LIKE THIS ...
...I'LL NEVER GET CLOSE TO ANY-ONE.
WHAT CAN ...
...SOH AND I DO...

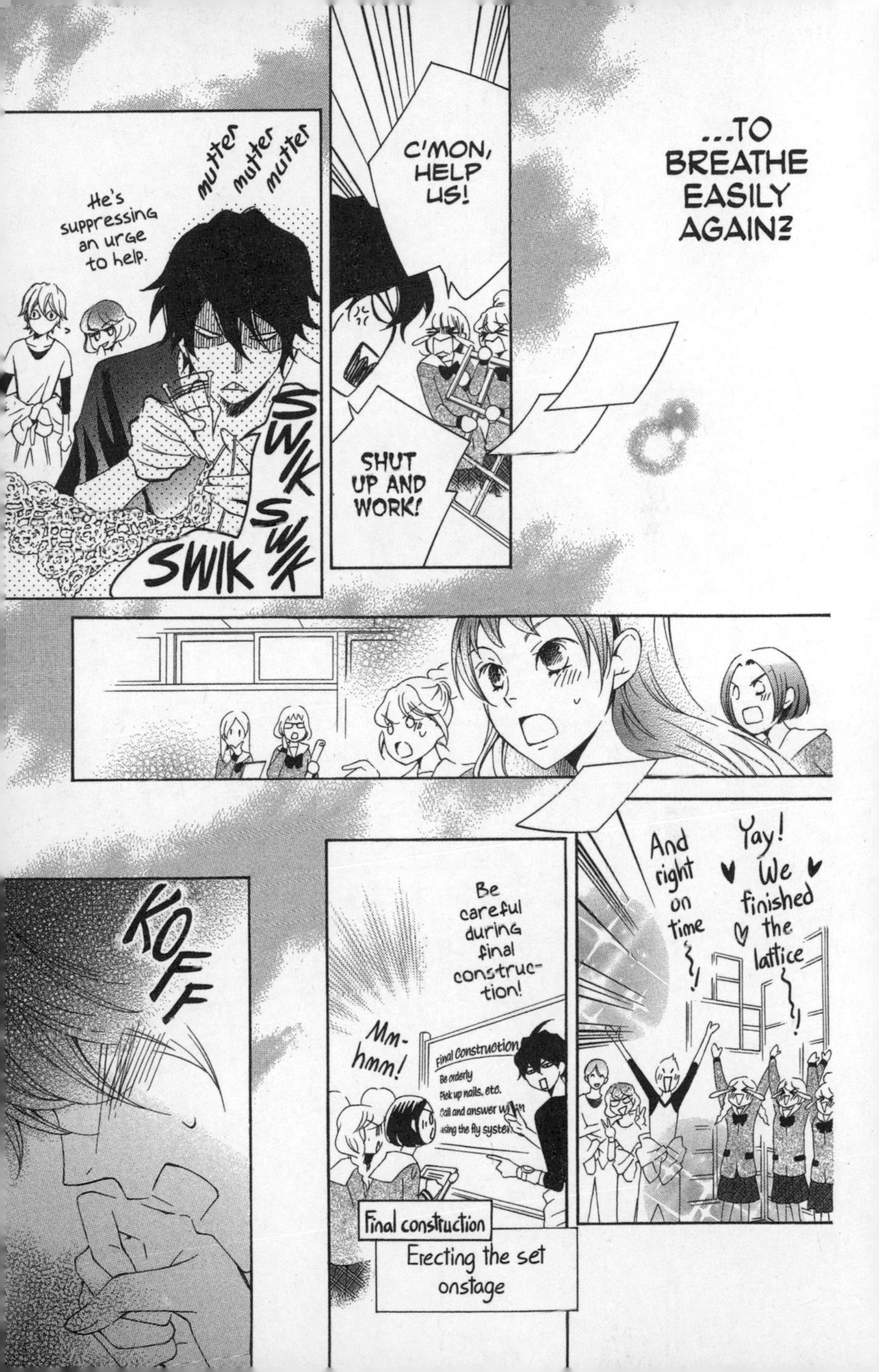
...TO BREATHE EASILY AGAIN?
C'MON, HELP US!
SHUT UP AND WORK!
mutter mutter mutter
He's suppressing an urge to help.
SWIK SWIK SWIK
Yay! We finished the lattice~!
And right on time~!
Be careful during final construction!
Mm-hmm!
Final Construction
Be orderly
Pick up nails, etc.
Final construction
Erecting the set onstage
KOFF

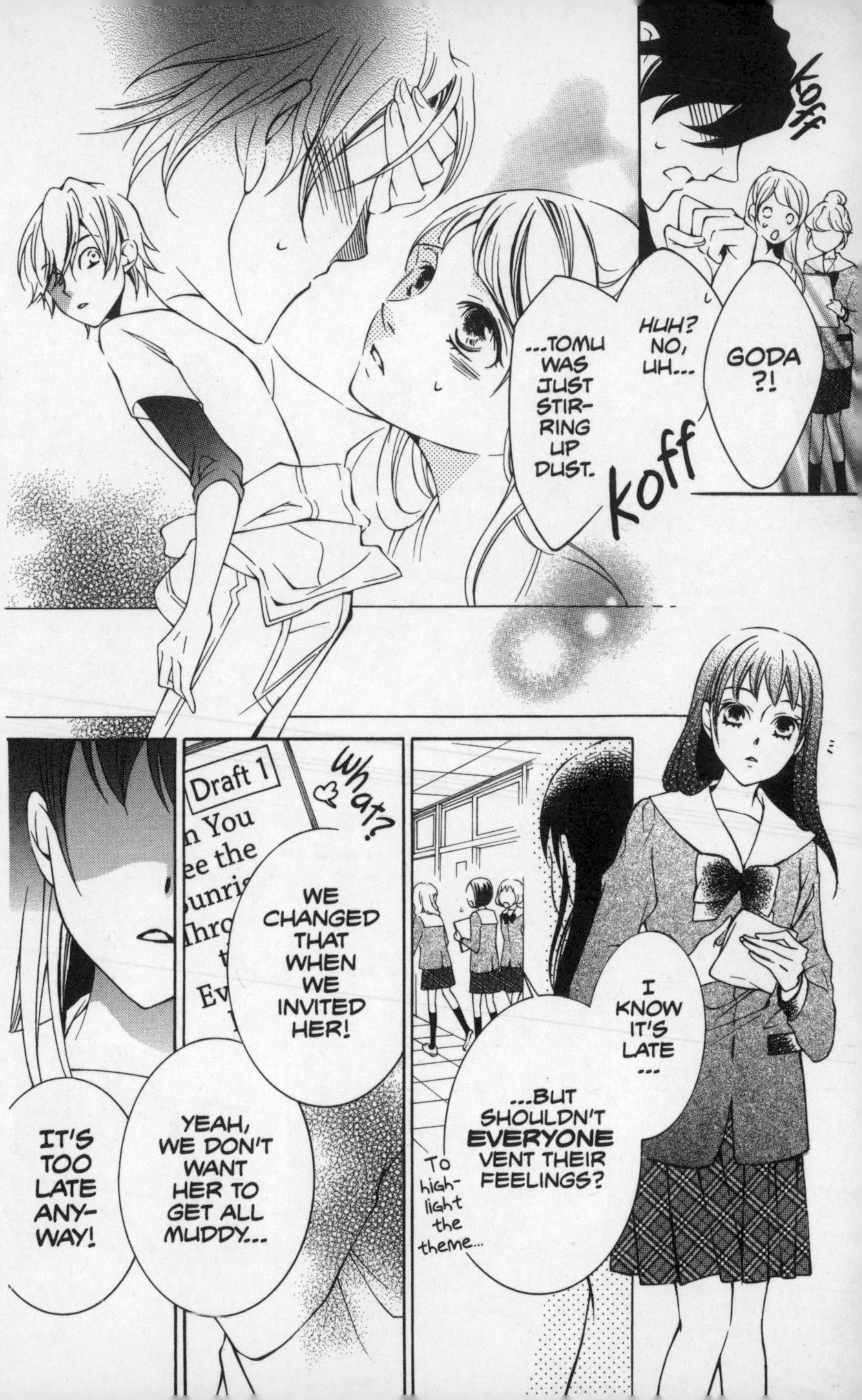
koff
GODA ?!
HUH? NO, UH...
...TOMU WAS JUST STIRRING UP DUST.
koff
I KNOW IT'S LATE...
...BUT SHOULDN'T **EVERYONE** VENT THEIR FEELINGS?
To highlight the theme...
Draft 1
What?
WE CHANGED THAT WHEN WE INVITED HER!
YEAH, WE DON'T WANT HER TO GET ALL MUDDY...
IT'S TOO LATE ANYWAY!

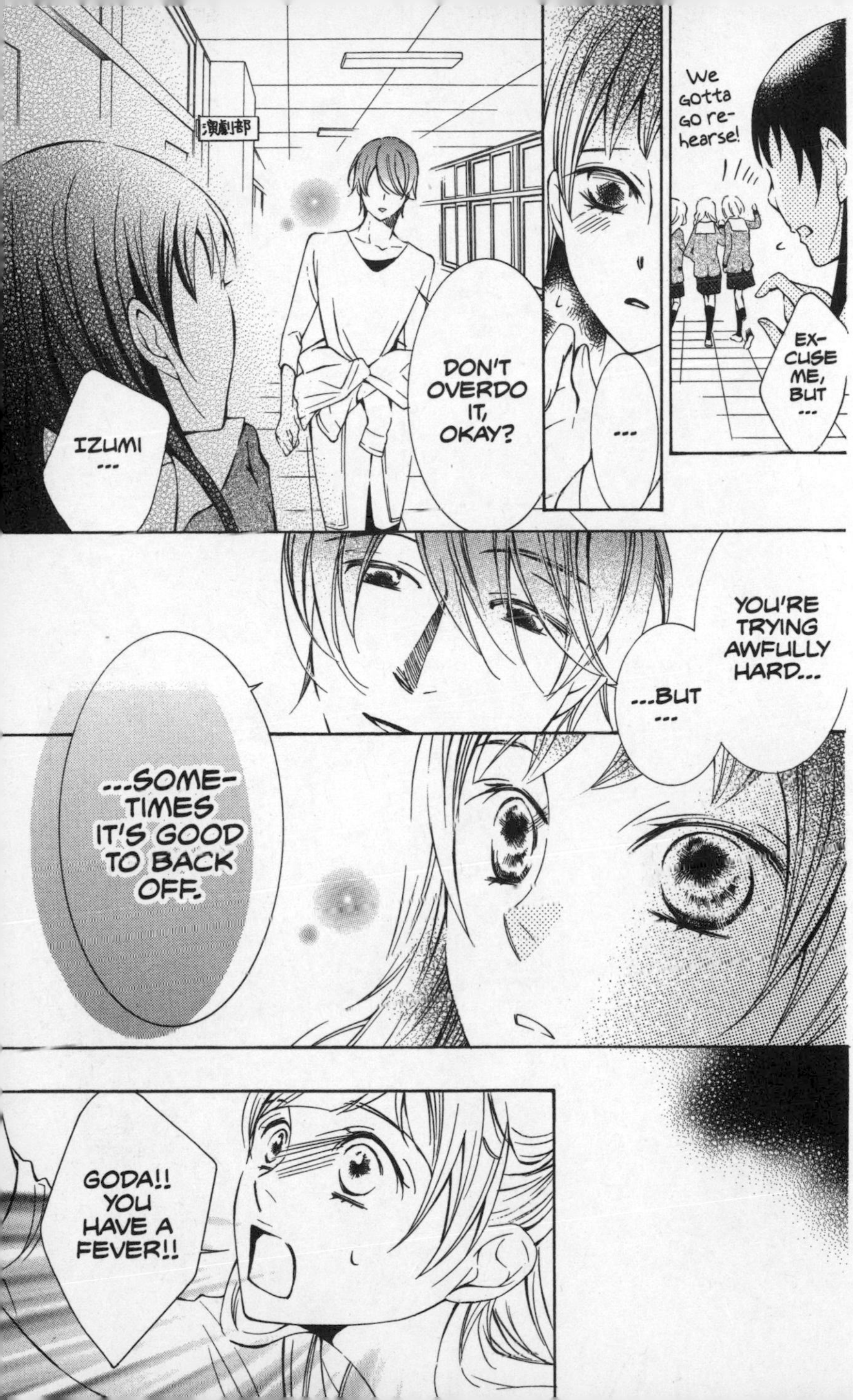
We gotta go re-hearse!
EXCUSE ME, BUT...
...
演劇部
DON'T OVERDO IT, OKAY?
IZUMI...
YOU'RE TRYING AWFULLY HARD...
...BUT...
...SOME-TIMES IT'S GOOD TO BACK OFF.
GODA!! YOU HAVE A FEVER!!

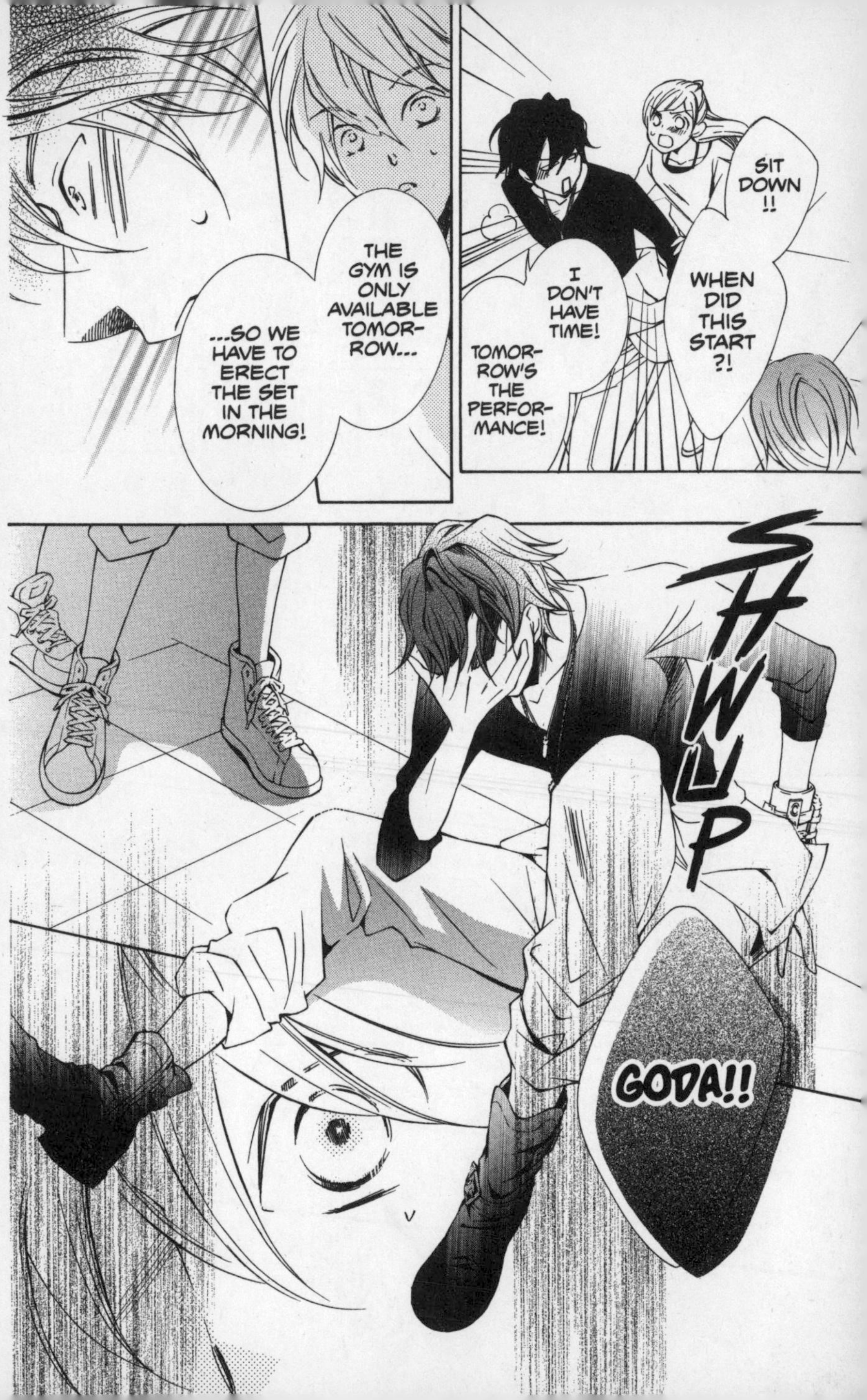
SIT DOWN!!
WHEN DID THIS START?!
I DON'T HAVE TIME!
TOMORROW'S THE PERFORMANCE!
THE GYM IS ONLY AVAILABLE TOMORROW...
...SO WE HAVE TO ERECT THE SET IN THE MORNING!
SHWUP
GODA!!

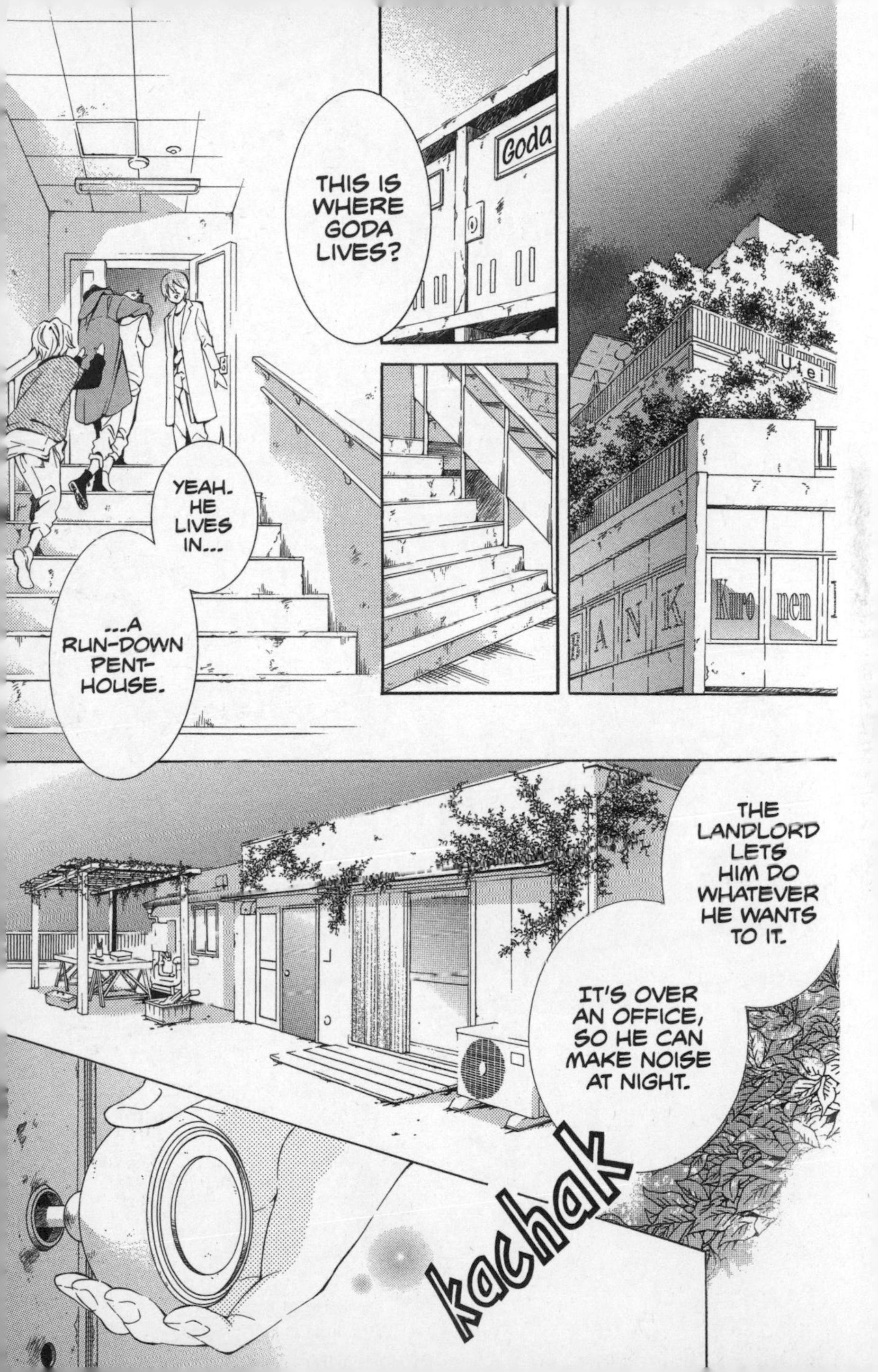
Utei
BANK
Kuro
nen
Goda
THIS IS WHERE GODA LIVES?
YEAH. HE LIVES IN...
...A RUN-DOWN PENT-HOUSE.
THE LANDLORD LETS HIM DO WHATEVER HE WANTS TO IT.
IT'S OVER AN OFFICE, SO HE CAN MAKE NOISE AT NIGHT.
kachak

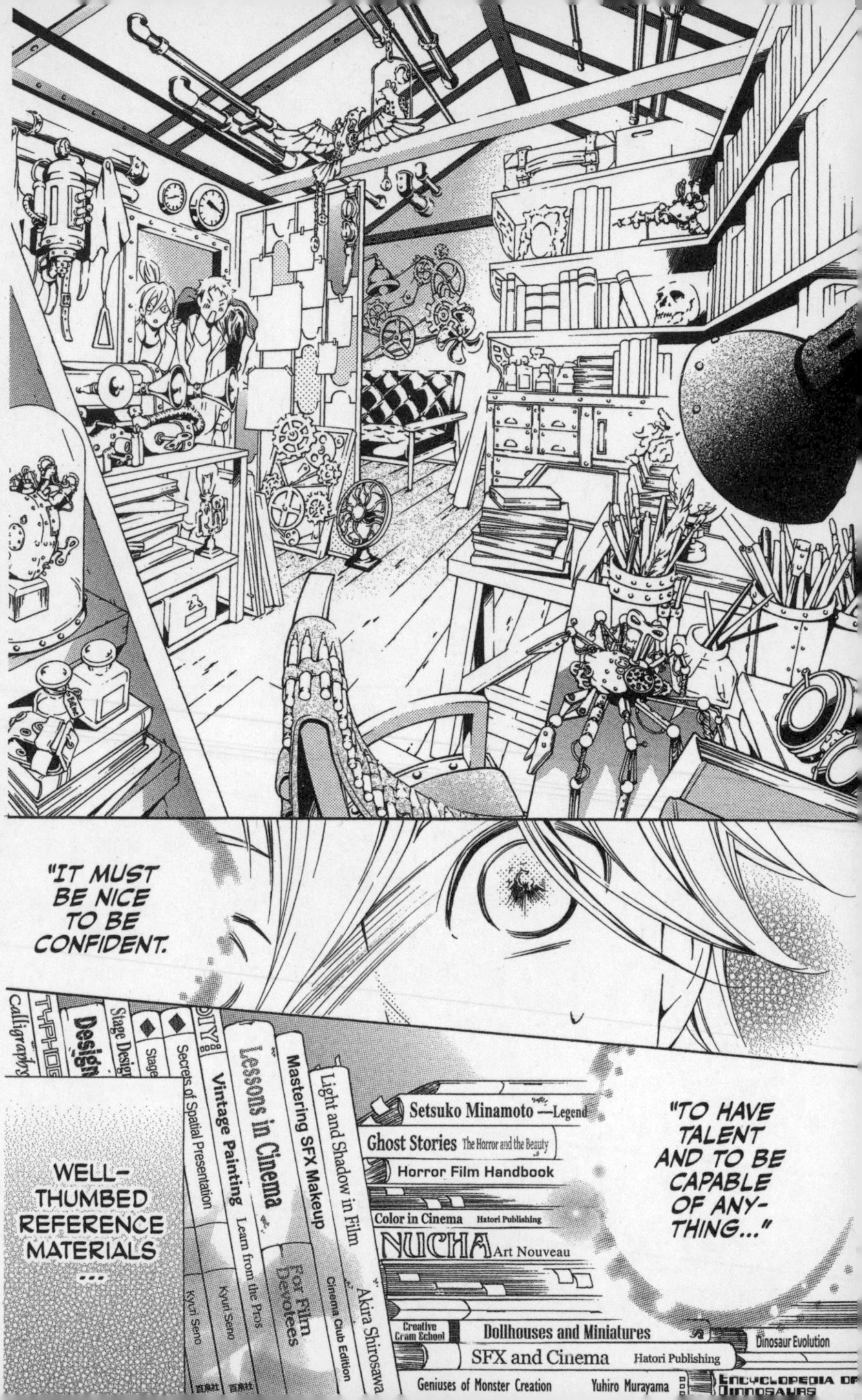
"IT MUST BE NICE TO BE CONFIDENT.
"TO HAVE TALENT AND TO BE CAPABLE OF ANYTHING..."
Setsuko Minamoto —Legend
Ghost Stories The Horror and the Beauty
Horror Film Handbook
Color in Cinema Hatori Publishing
NUCHA Art Nouveau
Creative Cram School
Dollhouses and Miniatures
Dinosaur Evolution
SFX and Cinema Hatori Publishing
Geniuses of Monster Creation Yuhiro Murayama
Encyclopedia of Dinosaurs
Light and Shadow in Film Akira Shirosawa
Mastering SFX Makeup Cinema Club Edition
Lessons in Cinema For Film Devotees
Vintage Painting Learn from the Pros Kyuri Seno
Secrets of Spatial Presentation Kyuri Seno
DIY
Stage
Stage Design
Design
Calligraphy
WELL-THUMBED REFERENCE MATERIALS ...

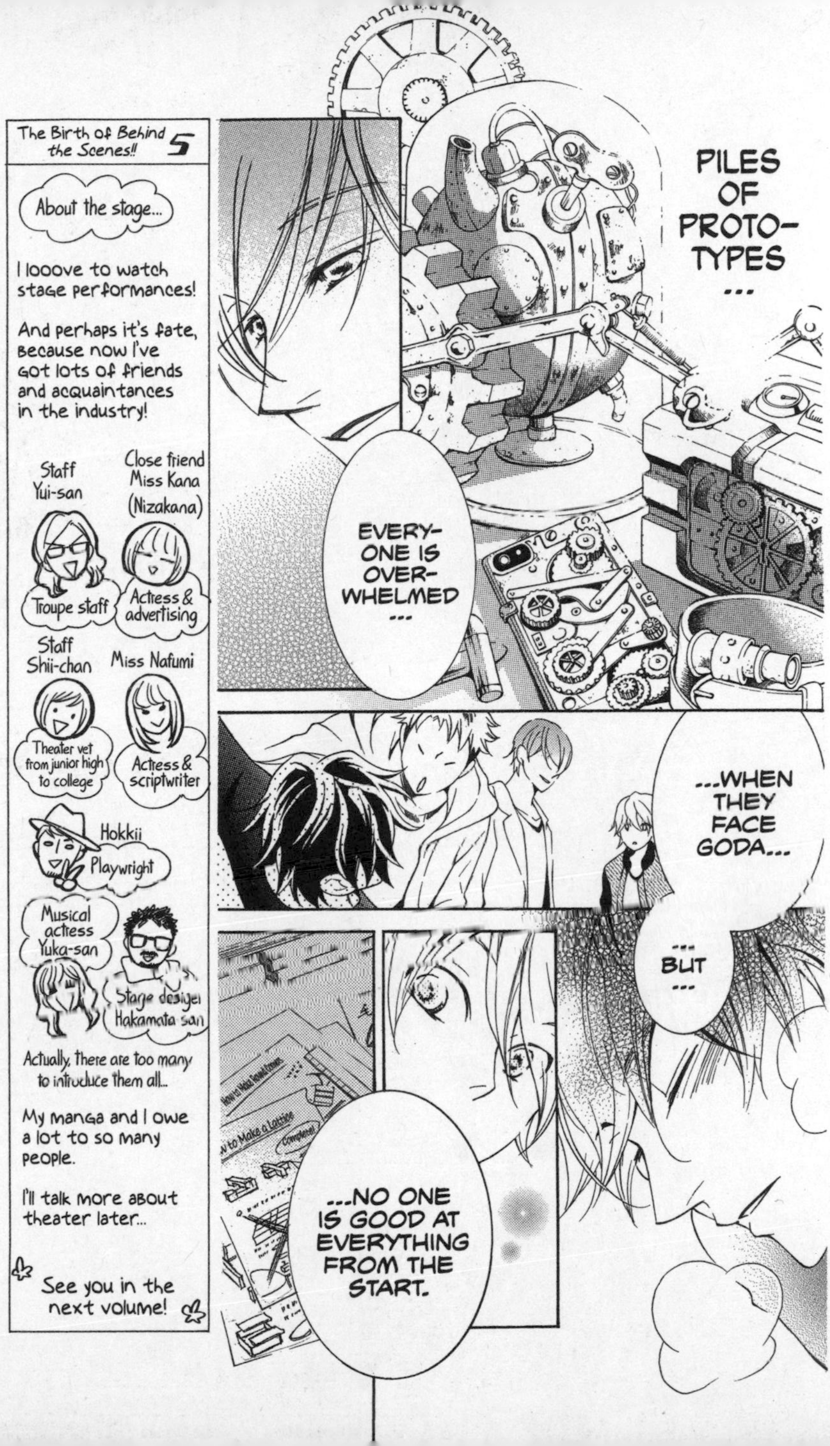
PILES OF PROTO-TYPES...
EVERY-ONE IS OVER-WHELMED...
...WHEN THEY FACE GODA...
...BUT...
Complete!
...NO ONE IS GOOD AT EVERYTHING FROM THE START.

The Birth of Behind the Scenes!! 5

About the stage...

I looove to watch stage performances!

And perhaps it's fate, because now I've got lots of friends and acquaintances in the industry!

Staff Yui-san — Troupe staff

Close friend Miss Kana (Nizakana) — Actress & advertising

Staff Shii-chan — Theater vet from junior high to college

Miss Nafumi — Actress & scriptwriter

Hokkii — Playwright

Musical actress Yuka-san

Stage designer Hakamata-san

Actually, there are too many to introduce them all...

My manga and I owe a lot to so many people.

I'll talk more about theater later...

See you in the next volume!

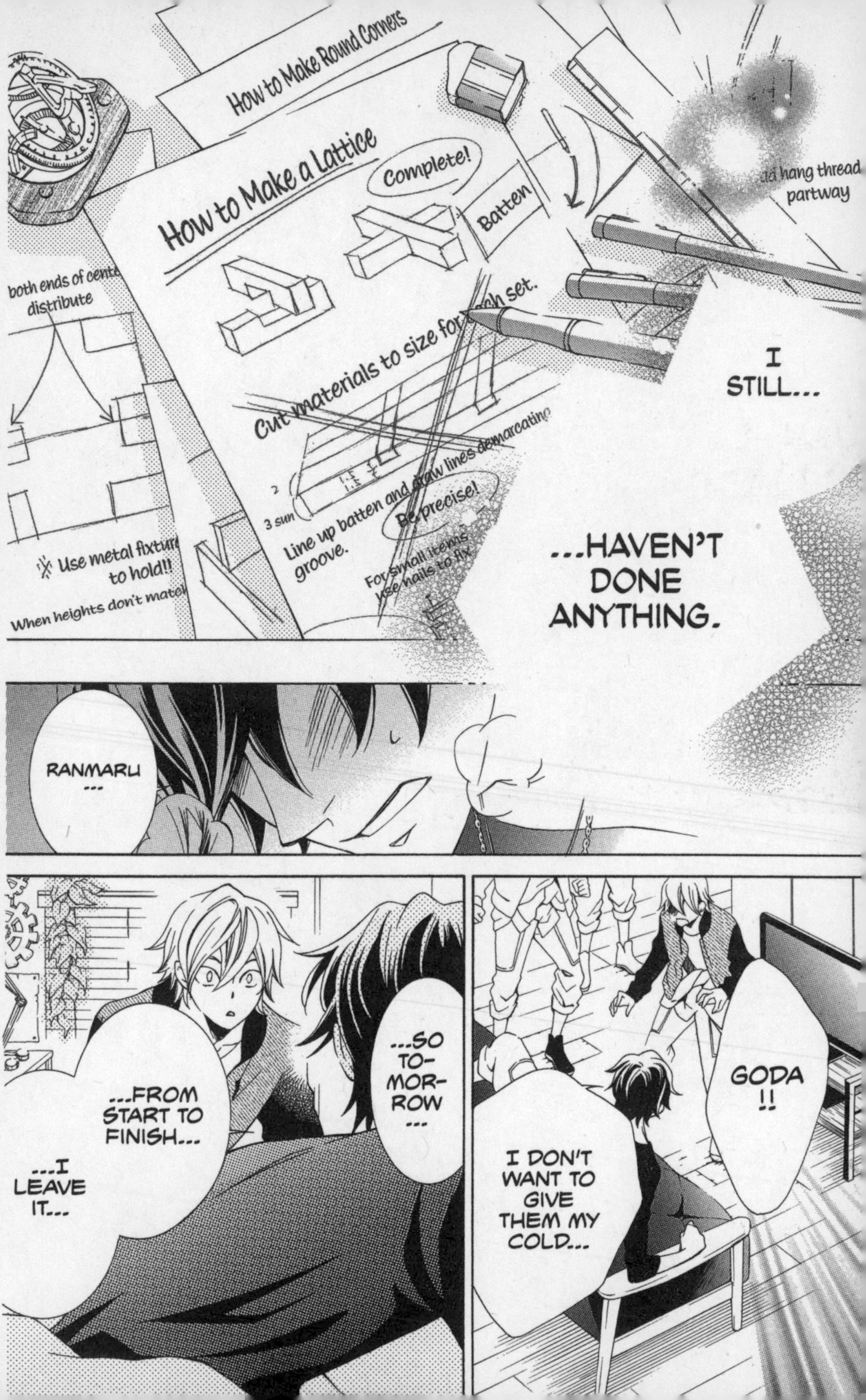

I STILL...
...HAVEN'T DONE ANYTHING.
hang thread partway
How to Make Round Corners
How to Make a Lattice
Complete!
Batten
Cut materials to size for each set.
Line up batten and draw lines demarcating groove.
Be precise!
For small items use nails to fix.
3 sun
both ends of cente
distribute
※ Use metal fixtur to hold!!
When heights don't matc
RANMARU...
GODA!!
I DON'T WANT TO GIVE THEM MY COLD...
...SO TOMORROW...
...FROM START TO FINISH...
...I LEAVE IT...

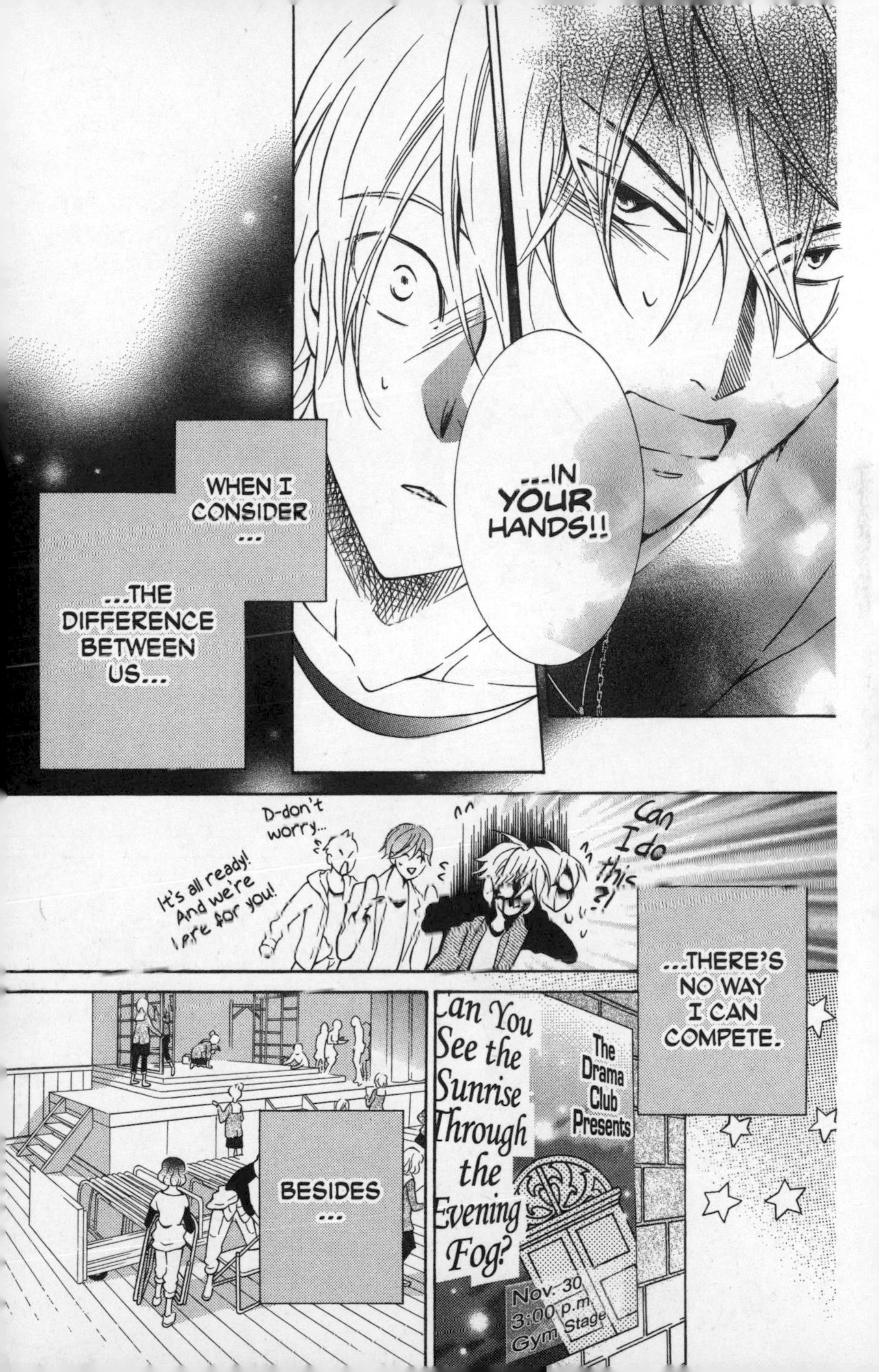
...IN YOUR HANDS!!
WHEN I CONSIDER ...
...THE DIFFERENCE BETWEEN US...
Can I do this?!
D-don't worry...
It's all ready! And we're here for you!
...THERE'S NO WAY I CAN COMPETE.
The Drama Club Presents
Can You See the Sunrise Through the Evening Fog?
Nov. 30 3:00 p.m. Gym Stage
BESIDES ...

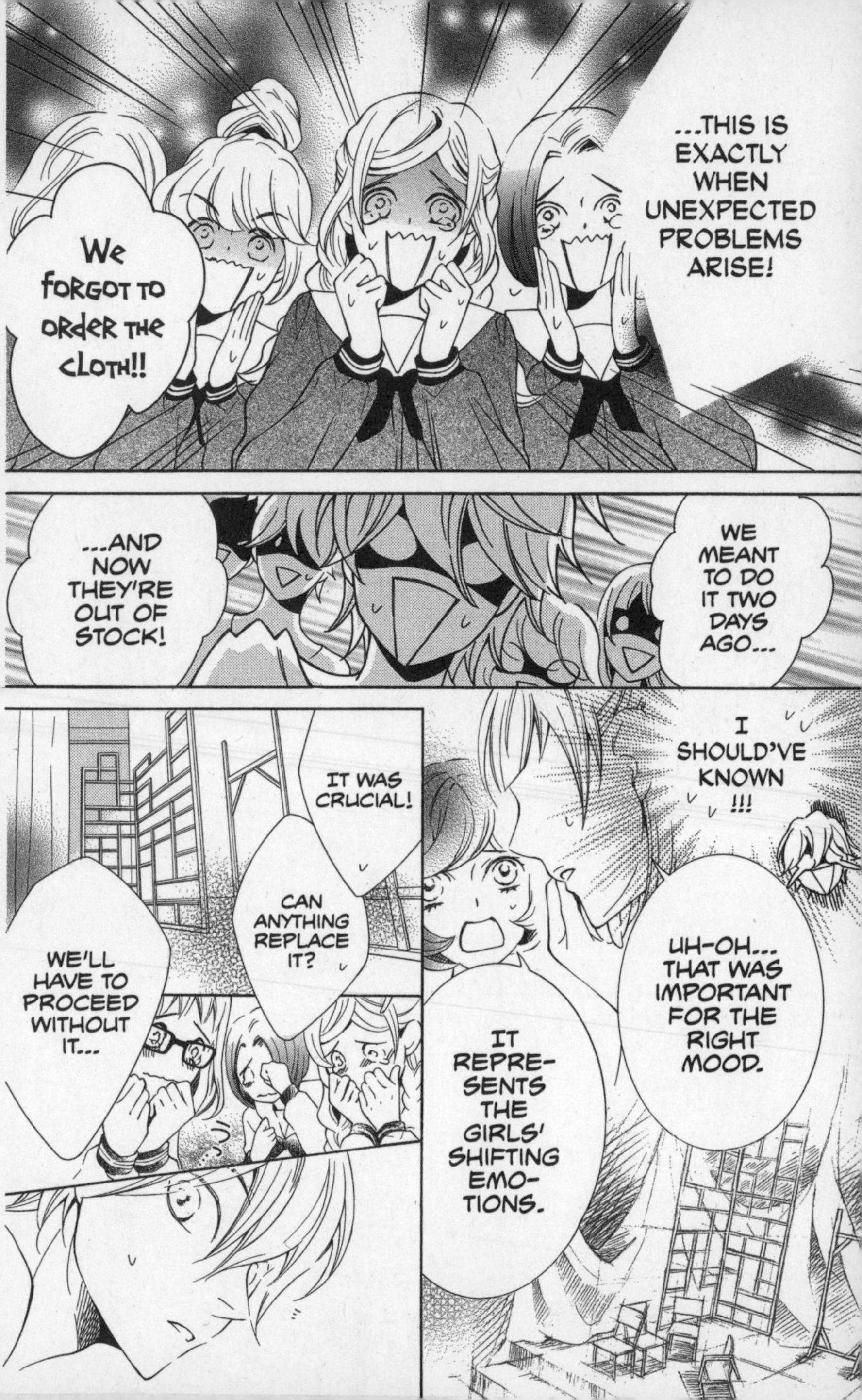
...THIS IS EXACTLY WHEN UNEXPECTED PROBLEMS ARISE!
We forgot to order the cloth!!
WE MEANT TO DO IT TWO DAYS AGO...
...AND NOW THEY'RE OUT OF STOCK!
I SHOULD'VE KNOWN !!!
UH-OH... THAT WAS IMPORTANT FOR THE RIGHT MOOD.
IT REPRE-SENTS THE GIRLS' SHIFTING EMO-TIONS.
IT WAS CRUCIAL!
CAN ANYTHING REPLACE IT?
WE'LL HAVE TO PROCEED WITHOUT IT...

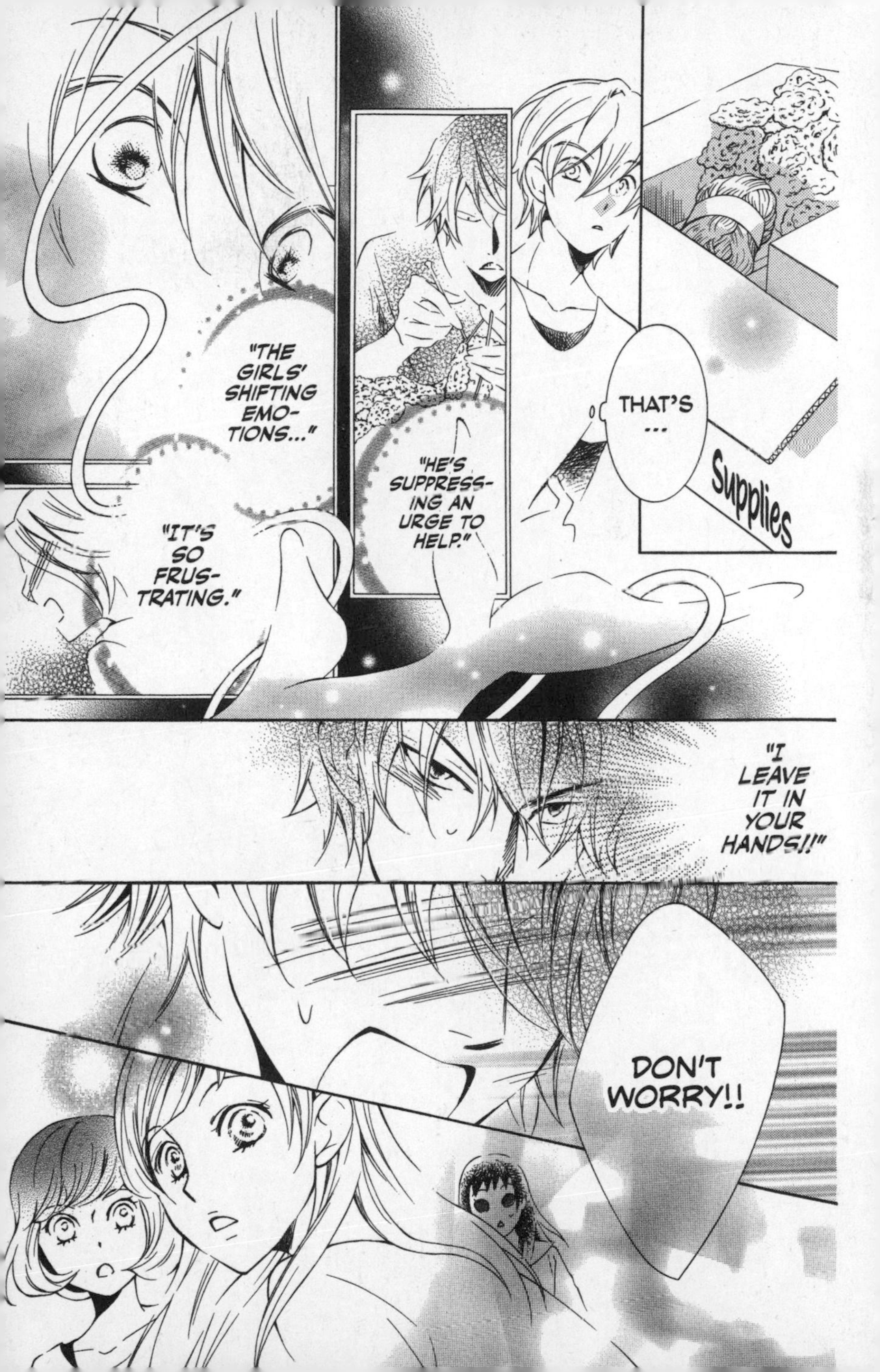
THAT'S ...
Supplies
"HE'S SUPPRESSING AN URGE TO HELP."
"THE GIRLS' SHIFTING EMOTIONS..."
"IT'S SO FRUSTRATING."
"I LEAVE IT IN YOUR HANDS!!"
DON'T WORRY!!

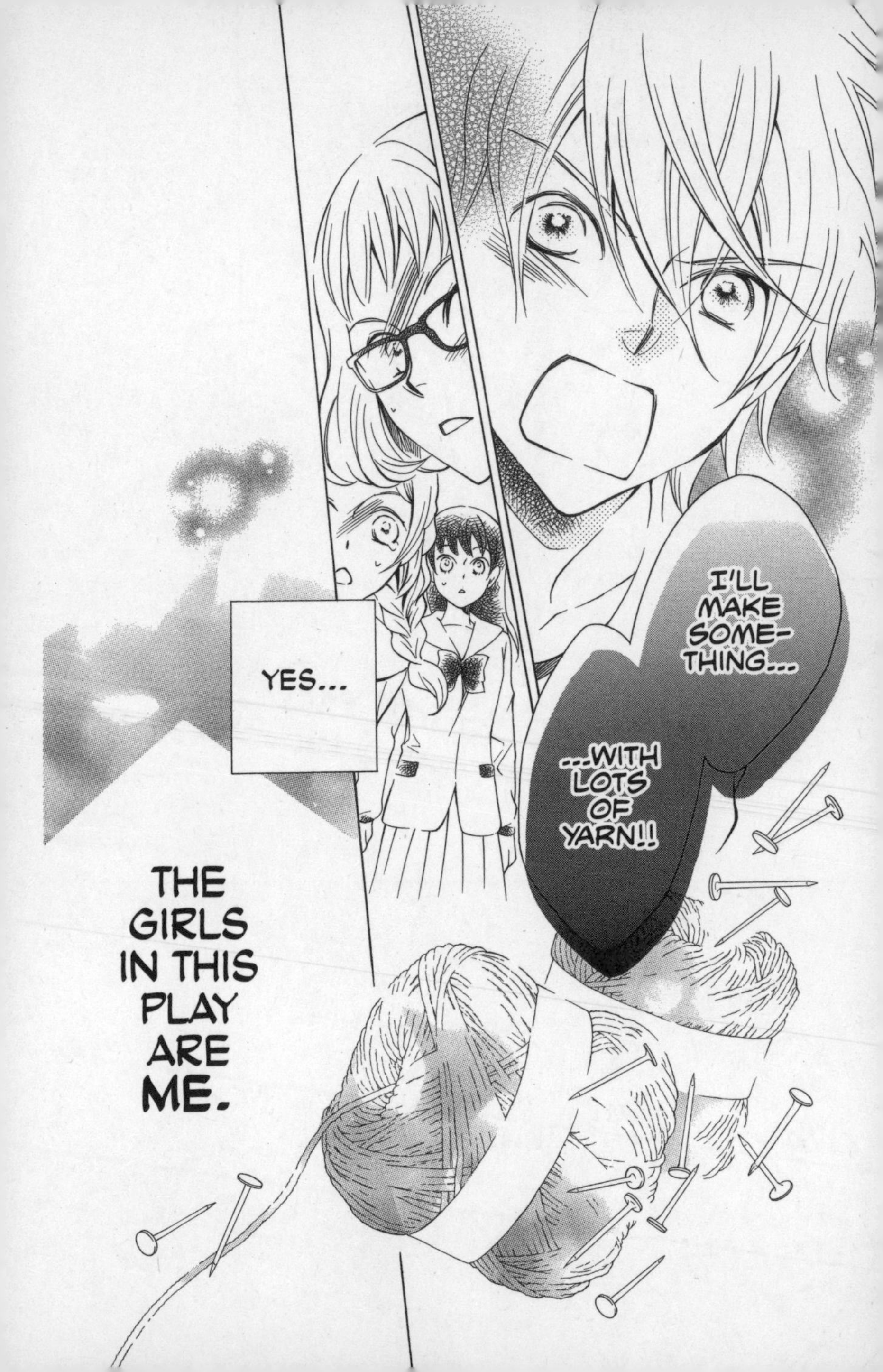
I'LL MAKE SOME-THING...
...WITH LOTS OF YARN!!
YES...
THE GIRLS IN THIS PLAY ARE ME.

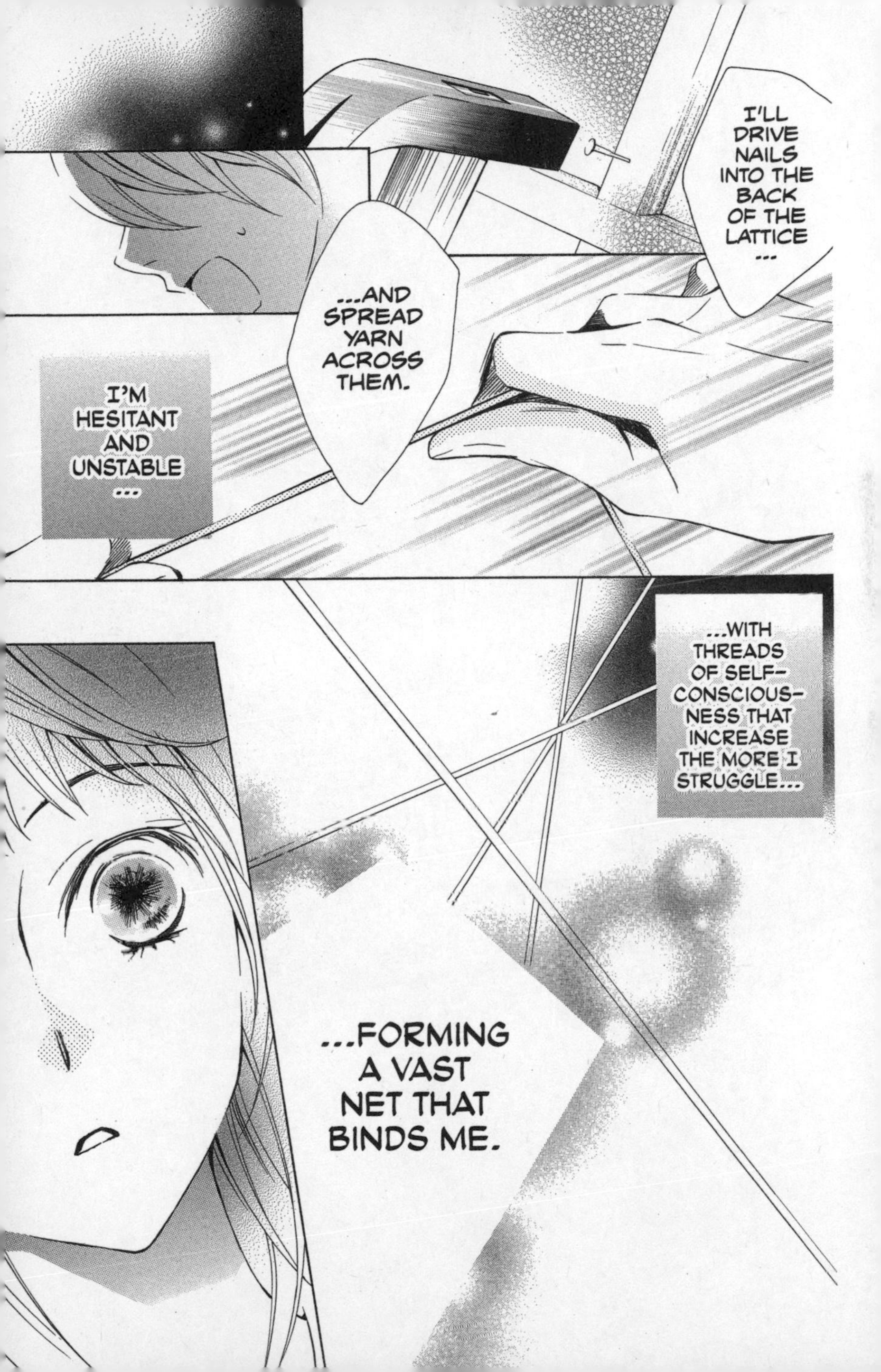
I'LL DRIVE NAILS INTO THE BACK OF THE LATTICE...
...AND SPREAD YARN ACROSS THEM.
I'M HESITANT AND UNSTABLE...
...WITH THREADS OF SELF-CONSCIOUSNESS THAT INCREASE THE MORE I STRUGGLE...
...FORMING A VAST NET THAT BINDS ME.

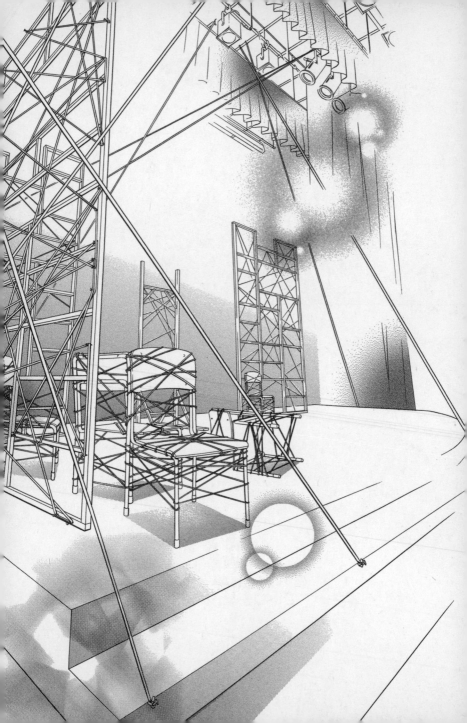

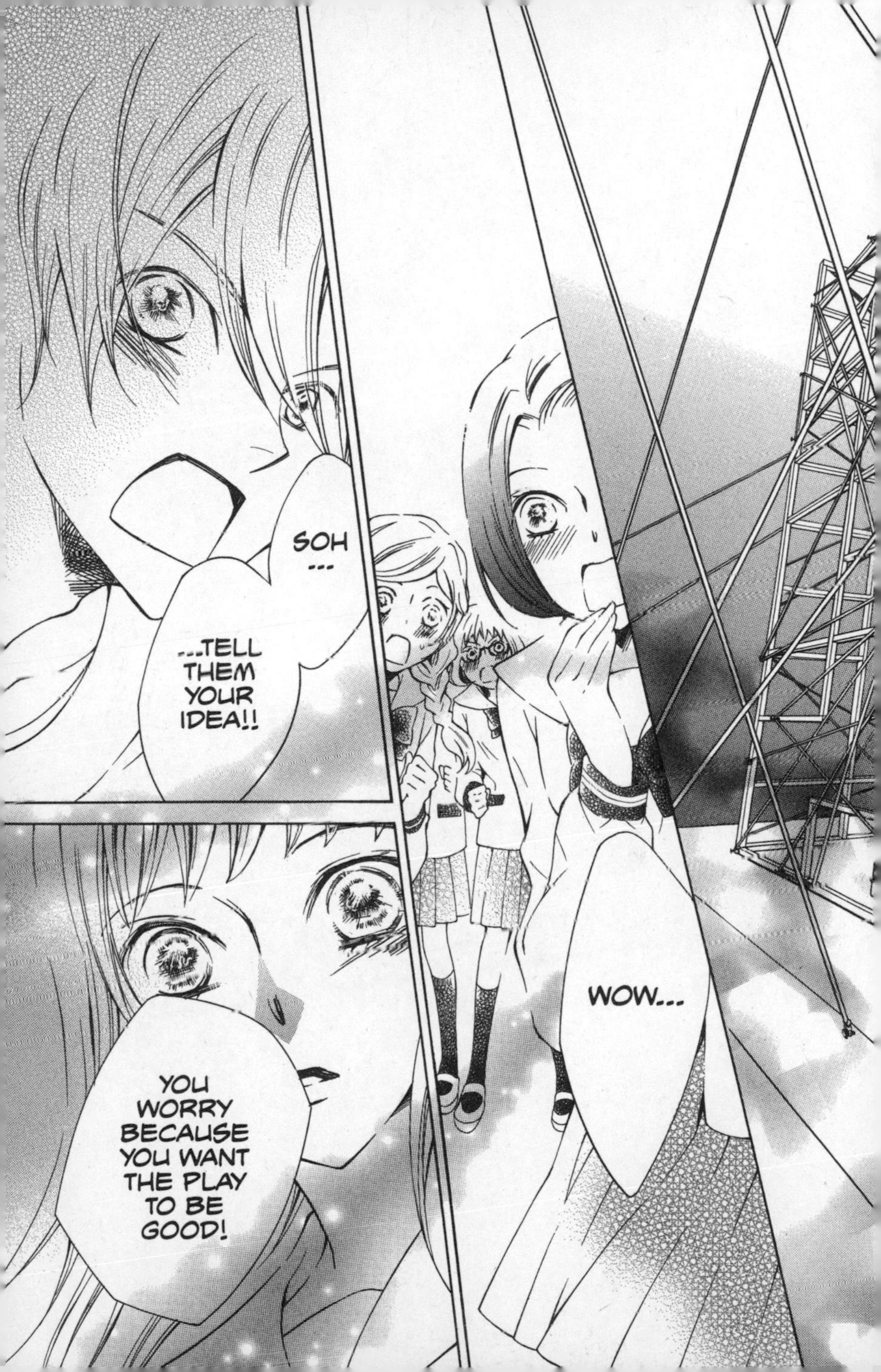
WOW...
SOH...
...TELL THEM YOUR IDEA!!
YOU WORRY BECAUSE YOU WANT THE PLAY TO BE GOOD!

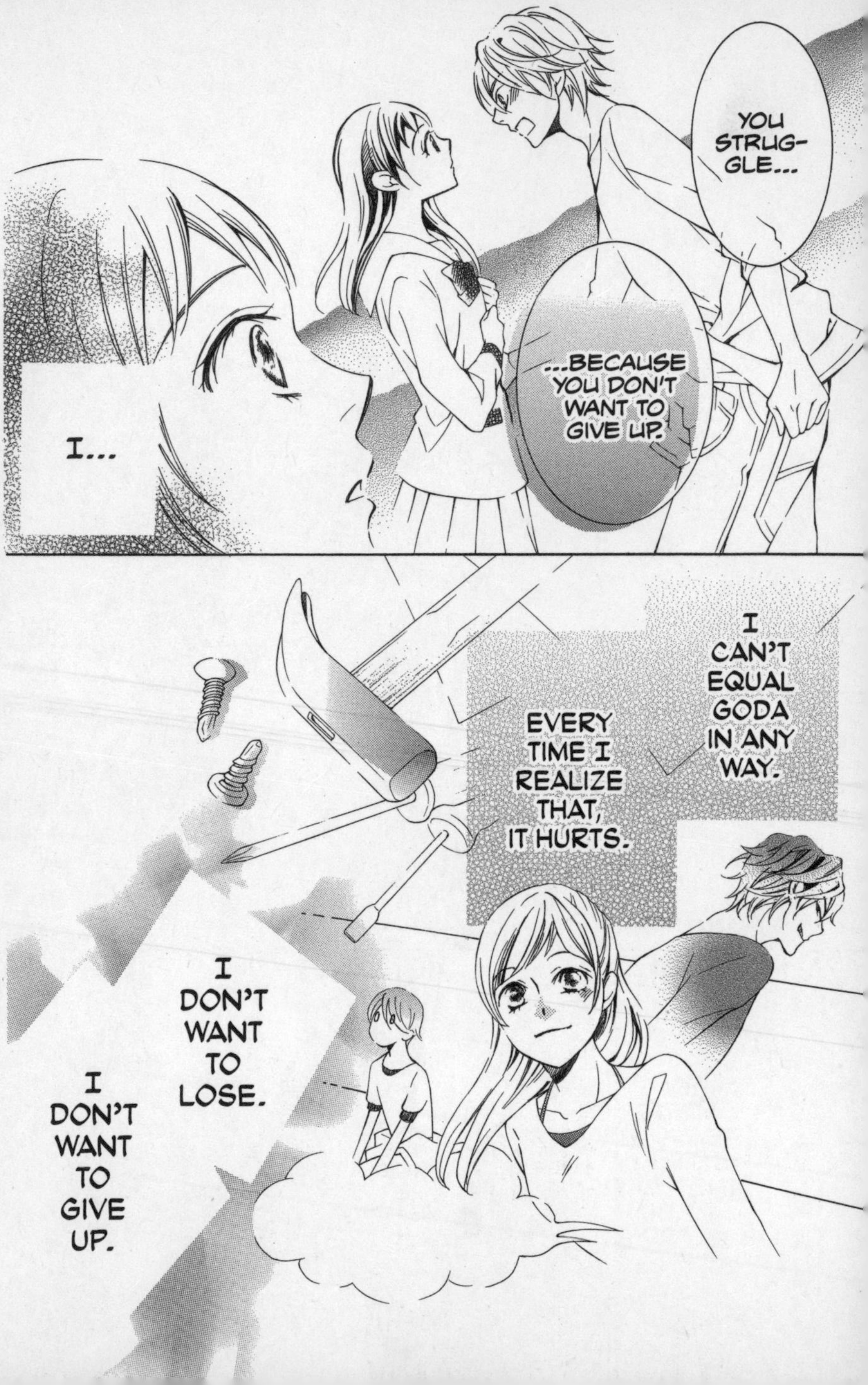
YOU STRUG-GLE...
...BECAUSE YOU DON'T WANT TO GIVE UP.
I...
I CAN'T EQUAL GODA IN ANY WAY.
EVERY TIME I REALIZE THAT, IT HURTS.
I DON'T WANT TO LOSE.
I DON'T WANT TO GIVE UP.

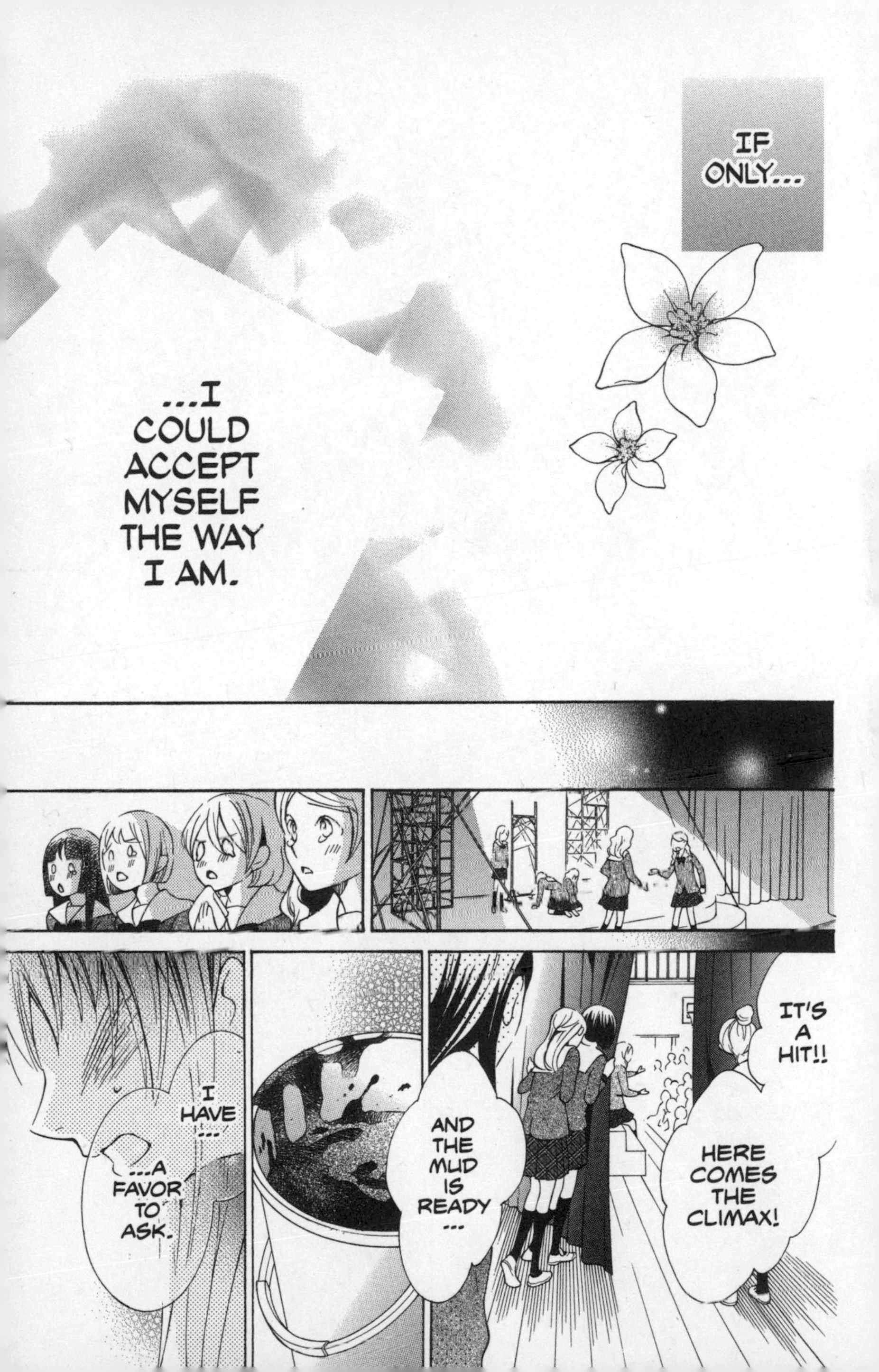
IF ONLY...
...I COULD ACCEPT MYSELF THE WAY I AM.
IT'S A HIT!!
HERE COMES THE CLIMAX!
AND THE MUD IS READY...
I HAVE...
...A FAVOR TO ASK.

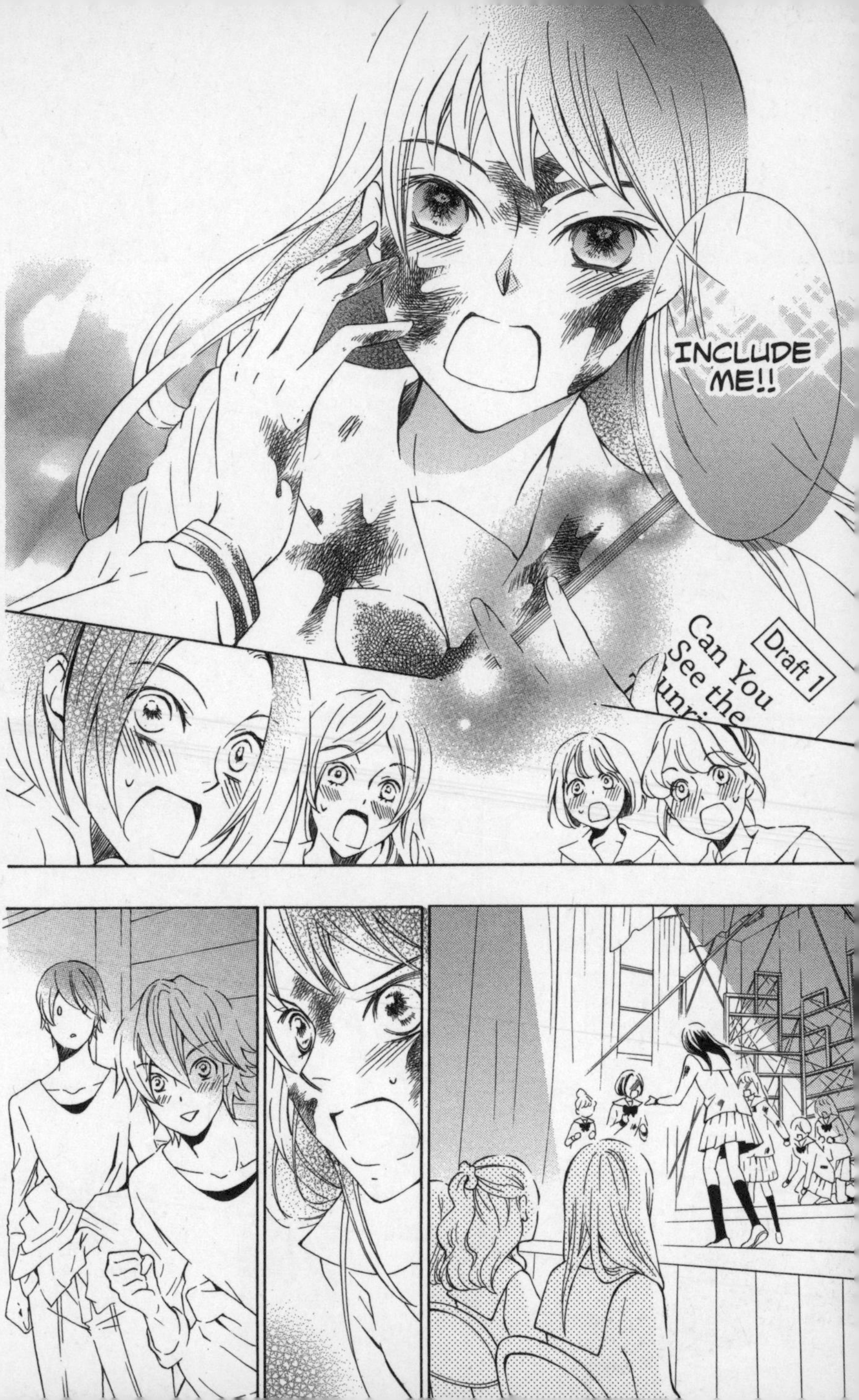
INCLUDE ME!!
Draft 1
Can You See the

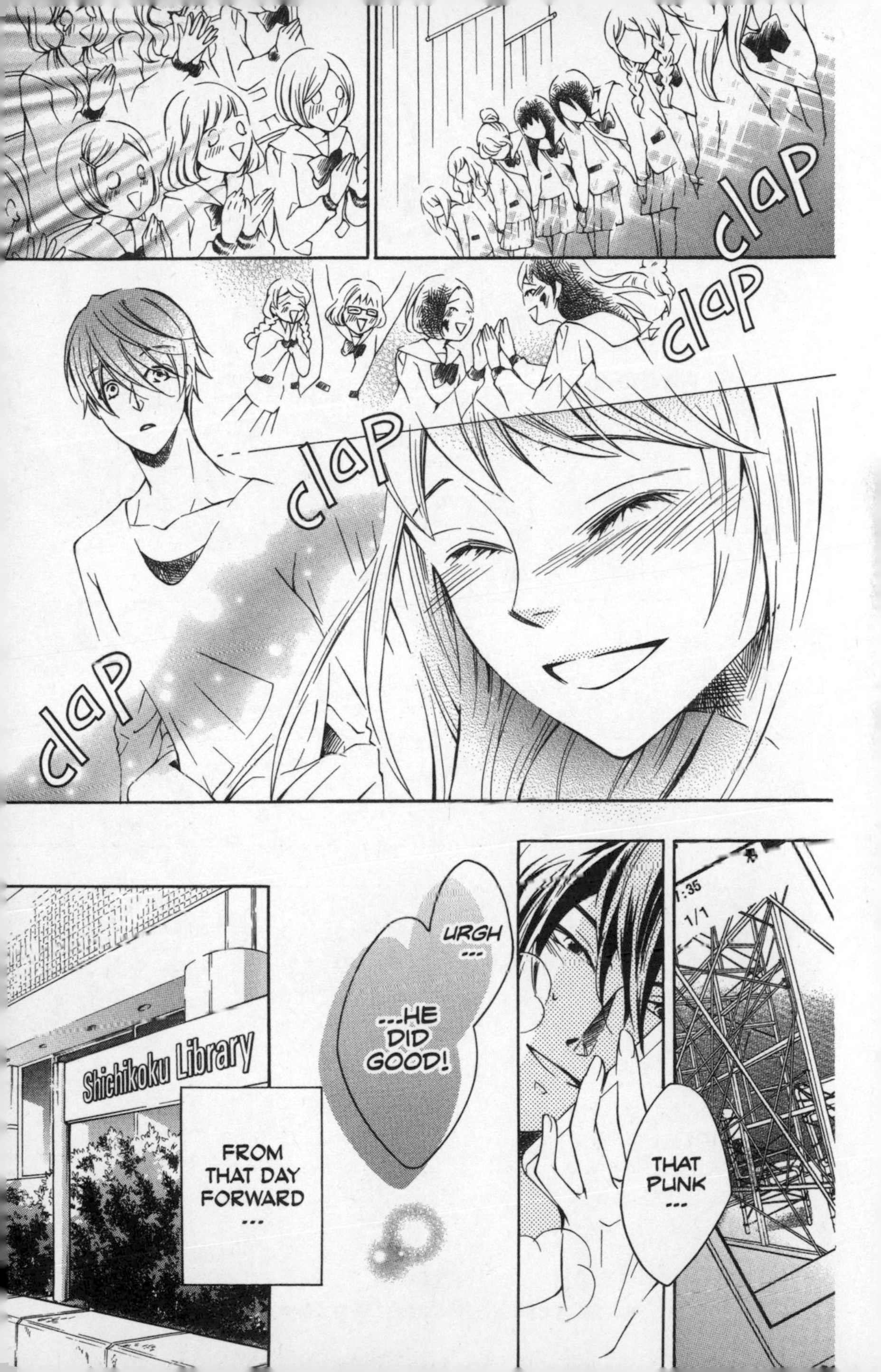
clap
clap
clap
clap
1:35
1/1
THAT PUNK ...
URGH ...
...HE DID GOOD!
Shichikoku Library
FROM THAT DAY FORWARD ...

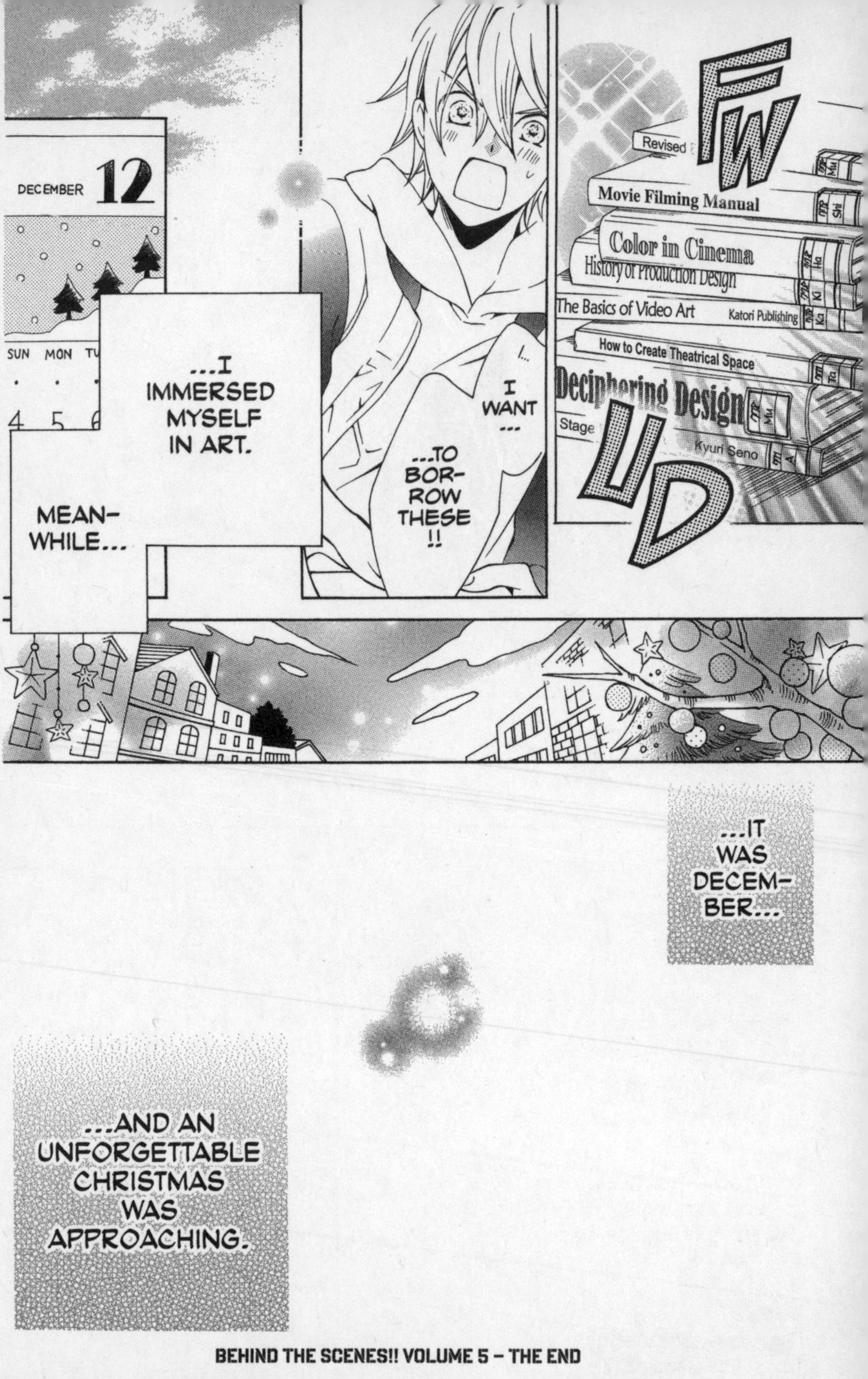
Revised
Movie Filming Manual
Color in Cinema
History of Production Design
The Basics of Video Art
Katori Publishing
How to Create Theatrical Space
Deciphering Design
Stage
Kyuri Seno
FW
UD
I WANT...
...TO BORROW THESE!!
DECEMBER 12
SUN MON TU
...I IMMERSED MYSELF IN ART.
MEANWHILE...
...IT WAS DECEMBER...
...AND AN UNFORGETTABLE CHRISTMAS WAS APPROACHING.

BEHIND THE SCENES!! VOLUME 5 – THE END

Special Thanks!!

Ms. O
Everyone on the
editorial staff

Everyone involved in
publishing this book

Rodemu-sama
Forêt-sama
Osamu Hakamata, Hakamadan
Shigetora Hirakawa-sama
Kamaty Moon-sama
Yajima-sama

Narumi Sasaki-sama
Kana (by NIZAKANA)-sama
K-sama

And everyone
who reads
this book!!

Bisco

2017. Mar.

Staff:
Yui Natsuki, Aya Aomura, Umeko,
Shizuru Onda, Keiko, Miki Namiki,
Shii Tsunokawa

Helpers:
Meiji-sama, Shida-sama,
Terashima-sama

GLOSSARY

Page 18, panel 5: Fermented soybeans
Natto is a type of fermented soybean considered to be an acquired taste due to its strong smell and slimy texture.

Page 19, panel 1: Pickled plum
umeboshi is an unripe ume (similar to a plum or an apricot) pickled in salt.

Page 22, panel 2: Yakiniku
Grilled meat, usually beef, cooked over griddles.

Page 61, panel 3: Futon beaters
Called *futon tataki* in Japanese, they are used to beat dust out of futons while they are being aired, similar to carpet beaters.

Page 69, panel 4: Takoyaki
Fried octopus balls, a popular festival food.

Page 73, panel 2: From *Nansō Satomi Hakkenden*
A Japanese series of 106 novels, written from 1818 to 1842 by Kyokutei Bakin. Sometimes translated as *The Tale of Eight Dogs*, it is about eight samurai half brothers who are descended from a dog.

Page 107, panel 1: Visual kei
A Japanese musical aesthetic similar to glam rock with elaborate costumes, hair and makeup.

AUTHOR BIO

I always have FM NACK5 on the radio when I work on my manga, and the other day they said a program I've listened to since it began has been on the air for 14 years. I was like, "?!!??" I simply cannot keep up with time...

-Bisco Hatori

Bisco Hatori made her manga debut with *Isshun kan no Romance* (A Moment of Romance) in *LaLa DX* magazine. The comedy *Ouran High School Host Club* was her breakout hit and was published in English by VIZ Media. Her other works include *Detarame Mousouryoku Opera* (Sloppy Vaporous Opera), *Petite Pêche!* and the vampire romance *Millennium Snow*, which was also published in English by VIZ Media.

Behind the Scenes!!

VOLUME 5

Shojo Beat Edition

STORY AND ART BY Bisco Hatori

English Translation & Adaptation/John Werry
Touch-Up Art & Lettering/Sabrina Heep
Design/ Izumi Evers
Editor/Pancha Diaz

Urakata!! by Bisco Hatori
© Bisco Hatori 2017
All rights reserved.
First published in Japan in 2017 by HAKUSENSHA, Inc., Tokyo.
English language translation rights arranged with HAKUSENSHA, Inc.,
Tokyo.

Printed in the U.S.A.

Published by VIZ Media, LLC
P.O. Box 77010
San Francisco, CA 94107

10 9 8 7 6 5 4 3 2 1
First printing, February 2018

www.viz.com

www.shojobeat.com

YOU MAY BE READING THE WRONG WAY!

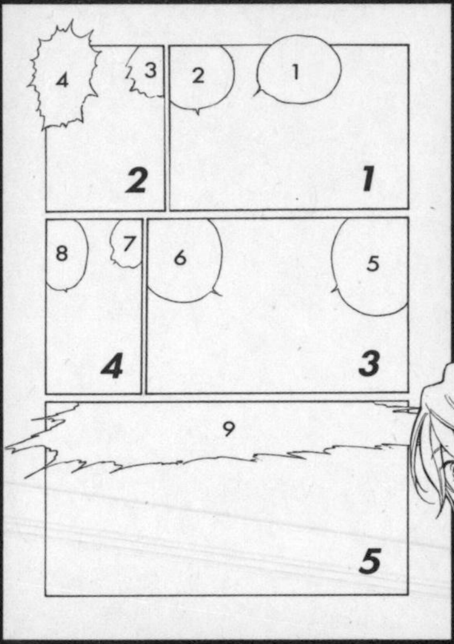
1
2
1
3
4
2
5
6
3
7
8
4
9
5

This book reads from right to left to maintain the original presentation and art of the Japanese edition, so action, sound effects and word balloons are reversed. This diagram shows how to follow the panels.
Turn to the other side of the book to begin.

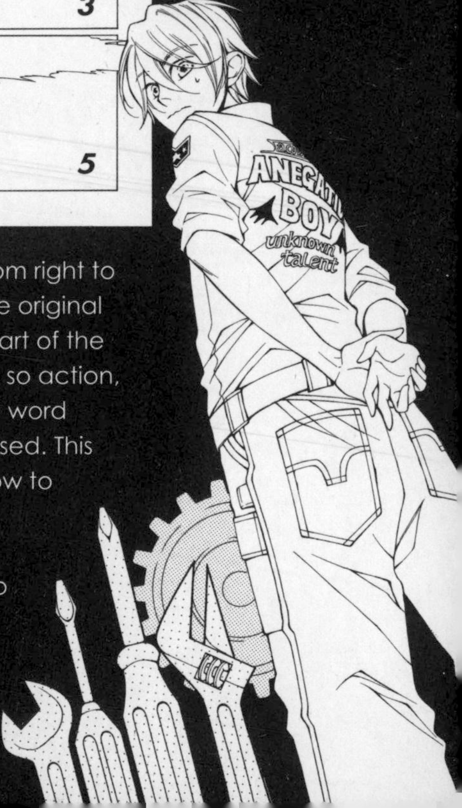
BOY
unknown talent